BROOKLANDS
BOOKS

# ASTON MARTIN

## 1972-1985

Compiled by
R.M.Clarke

ISBN 0 948207 590

BROOKLANDS BOOKS LTD.
P.O. BOX 146, COBHAM,
SURREY, KT11 1LG. UK

Printed in Hong Kong

BROOKLANDS BOOKS

## BROOKLANDS ROAD TEST SERIES

Abarth Gold Portfolio 1950-1971
AC Ace & Aceca 1953-1983
Alfa Romeo Giulietta Gold Portfolio 1954-1965
Alfa Romeo Giulia Berlinas 1962-1976
Alfa Romeo Giulia Coupés 1963-1976
Alfa Romeo Giulia Coupés Gold P. 1963-1976
Alfa Romeo Spider 1966-1990
Alfa Romeo Spider Gold Portfolio 1966-1991
Alfa Romeo Alfasud 1972-1984
Alfa Romeo Alfetta Gold Portfolio 1972-1987
Alfa Romeo Alfetta GTV6 1980-1987
Allard Gold Portfolio 1937-1959
Alvis Gold Portfolio 1919-1967
AMX & Javelin Muscle Portfolio1968-1974
Armstrong Siddeley Gold Portfolio 1945-1960
Austin A30 & A35 1951-1962
Austin Healey 100 & 100/6 Gold P. 1952-1959
Austin Healey 3000 Gold Portfolio 1959-1967
Austin Healey Sprite 1958-1971
Barracuda Muscle Portfolio 1964-1974
BMW Six Cyl. Coupés 1969-1975
BMW 1600 Collection No.1 1966-1981
BMW 2002 Gold Portfolio1968-1976
BMW 316, 318, 320 (4 cyl.) Gold P. 1975-1990
BMW 320, 323, 325 (6 cyl.) Gold P .1977-1990
BMW M Series Performance Portfolio1976-1993
BMW 5 Series Gold Portfolio1981-1987
Bristol Cars Gold Portfolio 1946-1992
Buick Automobiles 1947-1960
Buick Muscle Cars 1965-1970
Cadillac Automobiles 1949-1959
Cadillac Automobiles 1960-1969
Charger Muscle Portfolio1966-1974
Chevrolet 1955-1957
Chevrolet Impala & SS 1958-1971
Chevrolet Corvair 1959-1969
Chevy II & Nova SS Muscle Portfolio 1962-1974
Chevy El Camino & SS 1959-1987
Chevelle & SS Muscle Portfolio 1964-1972
Chevrolet Muscle Cars 1966-1971
Chevy Blazer 1969-1981
Chevrolet Corvette Gold Portfolio 1953-1962
Chevrolet Corvette Sting Ray Gold P. 1963-1967
Chevrolet Corvette Gold Portfolio 1968-1977
High Performance Corvettes 1983-1989
Camaro Muscle Portfolio 1967-1973
Chevrolet Camaro Z28 & SS 1966-1973
Chevrolet Camaro & Z28 1973-1981
High Performance Camaros 1982-1988
Chrysler 300 Gold Portfolio 1955-1970
Chrysler Valiant 1960-1962
Citroen Traction Avant Gold Portfolio 1934-1957
Citroen 2CV Gold Portfolio 1948-1989
Citroen DS & ID 1955-1975
Citroen DS & ID Gold Portfolio 1955-1975
Citroen SM 1970-1975
Cobras & Replicas 1962-1983
Shelby Cobra Gold Portfolio 1962-1969
Cobras & Cobra Replicas Gold P. 1962-1989
Cunningham Automobiles 1951-1955
Daimler SP250 Sports & V-8 250 Saloon Gold Portfolio 1959-1969
Datsun Roadsters 1962-1971
Datsun 240Z 1970-1973
Datsun 280Z & ZX 1975-1983
The De Lorean 1977-1993
De Tomaso Collection No. 1 1962-1981
Dodge Muscle Cars 1967-1970
Dodge Viper on the Road
Excalibur Collection No. 1 1952-1981
Facel Vega 1954-1964
Ferrari Dino 1965-1974
Ferrari Dino 308 1974-1979
Ferrari 308 & Mondial 1980-1984
Fiat 500 Gold Portfolio 1936-1972
Fiat 600 & 850 Gold Portfolio 1955-1972
Fiat Pininfarina 124 & 2000 Spider 1968-1985
Fiat-Bertone X1/9 1973-1988
Ford Consul, Zephyr, Zodiac Mk.I & II 1950-1962
Ford Zephyr, Zodiac, Executive, Mk.III & Mk.IV 1962-1971
Ford Cortina 1600E & GT 1967-1970
High Performance Capris Gold P. 1969-1987
Capri Muscle Portfolio 1974-1987
High Performance Fiestas 1979-1991
High Performance Escorts Mk.I 1968-1974
High Performance Escorts Mk.II 1975-1980
High Performance Escorts 1980-1985
High Performance Escorts 1985-1990
High Performance Sierras & Merkurs Gold Portfolio 1983-1990
Ford Automobiles 1949-1959
Ford Fairlane 1955-1970
Ford Ranchero 1957-1959
Ford Thunderbird 1955-1957
Ford Thunderbird 1958-1963
Ford Thunderbird 1964-1976
Ford GT40 Gold Portfolio 1964-1987
Ford Bronco 1966-1977
Ford Bronco 1978-1988
Holden 1948-1962
Honda CRX 1983-1987
Isetta 1953-1964
ISO & Bizzarrini Gold Portfolio 1962-1974
Jaguar and SS Gold Portfolio 1931-1951
Jaguar XK120, 140, 150 Gold P. 1948-1960
Jaguar Mk.VII, VIII, IX, X, 420 Gold P.1950-1970
Jaguar Mk.1 & Mk.2 Gold Portfolio 1959-1969
Jaguar E-Type Gold Portfolio 1961-1971
Jaguar E-Type V-12 1971-1975
Jaguar XJ12, XJ5.3, V12 Gold P. 1972-1990
Jaguar XJ6 Series II 1973-1979
Jaguar XJ6 Series III 1979-1986
Jaguar XJS Gold Portfolio 1975-1990
Jeep CJ5 & CJ6 1960-1976
Jeep CJ5 & CJ7 1976-1986
Jensen Cars 1946-1967
Jensen Cars 1967-1979
Jensen Interceptor Gold Portfolio 1966-1986
Jensen Healey 1972-1976
Lagonda Gold Portfolio 1919-1964
Lamborghini Cars 1964-1970
Lamborghini Countach & Urraco 1974-1980
Lamborghini Countach & Jalpa 1980-1985
Lancia Fulvia Gold Portfolio 1963-1976
Lancia Beta Gold Portfolio 1972-1984
Lancia Stratos 1972-1985
Land Rover Series I 1948-1958
Land Rover Series II & IIa 1958-1971
Land Rover Series III 1971-1985
Land Rover 90 & 110 Defender Gold Portfolio 1983-1994
Land Rover Discovery 1989-1994
Lincoln Gold Portfolio 1949-1960
Lincoln Continental 1961-1969
Lincoln Continental 1969-1976
Lotus Sports Racers Gold Portfolio 1953-1965
Lotus & Caterham Seven Gold P. 1957-1989
Lotus Elite 1957-1964
Lotus Elite & Eclat 1974-1982
Lotus Elan Gold Portfolio 1962-1974
Lotus Elan Collection No. 2 1963-1972
Lotus Elan & SE 1989-1992
Lotus Cortina Gold Portfolio 1963-1970
Lotus Europa Gold Portfolio 1966-1975
Lotus Elite & Eclat 1974-1982
Lotus Turbo Esprit 1980-1986
Marcos Cars 1960-1988
Maserati 1965-1970
Maserati 1970-1975
Mercedes 190 & 300 SL 1954-1963
Mercedes 230/250/280SL 1963-1971
Mercedes Benz SLs & SLCs Gold P. 1971-1989
Mercedes S & 600 1965-1972
Mercedes S Class 1972-1979
Mercury Muscle Cars 1966-1971
Messerschmitt Gold Portfolio1954-1964
Metropolitan 1954-1962
MG Gold Portfolio 1929-1939
MG TC 1945-1949
MG TD 1949-1953
MG TF 1953-1955
MGA & Twin Cam Gold Portfolio 1955-1962
MG Midget Gold Portfolio1961-1979
MGB Roadsters 1962-1980
MGB MGC & V8 Gold Portfolio 1962-1980
MGB GT 1965-1980
Mini Cooper Gold Portfolio 1961-1971
Mini Muscle Cars 1961-1979
Mini Moke Gold Portfolio1964-1994
Mopar Muscle Cars 1964-1967
Morgan Three-Wheeler Gold Portfolio 1910-1952
Morgan Plus 4 & Four 4 Gold P. 1936-1967
Morgan Cars 1960-1970
Morgan Cars Gold Portfolio 1968-1989
Morris Minor Collection No. 1 1948-1980
Shelby Mustang Muscle Portfolio 1965-1970
High Performance Mustang IIs 1974-1978
High Performance Mustangs 1982-1988
Oldsmobile Automobiles 1955-1963
Oldsmobile Muscle Cars 1964-1971
Oldsmobile Toronado 1966-1978
Opel GT 1968-1973
Packard Gold Portfolio 1946-1958
Pantera Gold Portfolio 1970-1989
Panther Gold Portfolio 1972-1990
Plymouth Muscle Cars 1966-1971
Pontiac Tempest & GTO 1961-1965
Pontiac Muscle Cars 1966-1972
Pontiac Firebird & Trans-Am 1973-1981
High Performance Firebirds 1982-1988
Pontiac Fiero 1984-1988
Porsche 356 Gold Portfolio1953-1965
Porsche 911 1965-1969
Porsche 911 1970-1972
Porsche 911 1973-1977
Porsche 911 Carrera 1973-1977
Porsche 911 Turbo 1975-1984
Porsche 911 SC 1978-1983
Porsche 914 Collection No. 1 1969-1983
Porsche 914 Gold Portfolio 1969-1976
Porsche 924 Gold Portfolio 1975-1988
Porsche 928 1977-1989
Porsche 944 Gold Portfolio1981-1991
Range Rover Gold Portfolio 1970-1992
Reliant Scimitar 1964-1986
Riley Gold Portfolio 1924-1939
Riley 1.5 & 2.5 Litre Gold Portfolio 1945-1955
Rolls Royce Silver Cloud & Bentley 'S' Series Gold Portfolio 1955-1965
Rolls Royce Silver Shadow Gold P. 1965-1980
Rover P4 1949-1959
Rover P4 1955-1964
Rover 3 & 3.5 Litre Gold Portfolio 1958-1973
Rover 2000 & 2200 1963-1977
Rover 3500 1968-1977
Rover 3500 & Vitesse 1976-1986
Saab Sonett Collection No.1 1966-1974
Saab Turbo 1976-1983
Studebaker Gold Portfolio 1947-1966
Studebaker Hawks & Larks 1956-1963
Avanti 1962-1990
Sunbeam Tiger & Alpine Gold P. 1959-1967
Toyota MR2 1984-1988
Toyota Land Cruiser 1956-1984
Triumph TR2 & TR3 Gold Portfolio 1952-1961
Triumph TR4, TR5, TR250 1961-1968
Triumph TR6 Gold Portfolio 1969-1976
Triumph TR7 & TR8 Gold Portfolio 1975-1982
Triumph Herald 1959-1971
Triumph Vitesse 1962-1971
Triumph Spitfire Gold Portfolio 1962-1980
Triumph 2000, 2.5, 2500 1963-1977
Triumph GT6 Gold Portfolio 1966-1974
Triumph Stag 1970-1980
TVR Gold Portfolio 1959-1986
VW Beetle Gold Portfolio1935-1967
VW Beetle Gold Portfolio1968-1991
VW Beetle Collection No.1 1970-1982
VW Karmann Ghia 1955-1982
VW Bus, Camper, Van 1954-1967
VW Bus, Camper, Van 1968-1979
VW Bus, Camper, Van 1979-1989
VW Scirocco 1974-1981
VW Golf GTI 1976-1986
Volvo PV444 & PV544 1945-1965
Volvo Amazon-120 Gold Portfolio 1956-1970
Volvo 1800 Gold Portfolio 1960-1973

## BROOKLANDS ROAD & TRACK SERIES

Road & Track on Alfa Romeo 1949-1963
Road & Track on Alfa Romeo 1964-1970
Road & Track on Alfa Romeo 1971-1976
Road & Track on Alfa Romeo 1977-1989
Road & Track on Aston Martin 1962-1990
R & T on Auburn Cord and Duesenburg 1952-84
Road & Track on Audi & Auto Union 1952-1980
Road & Track on Audi & Auto Union 1980-1986
Road & Track on Austin Healey 1953-1970
Road & Track on BMW Cars 1966-1974
Road & Track on BMW Cars 1975-1978
Road & Track on BMW Cars 1979-1983
R & T on Cobra, Shelby & Ford GT40 1962-1992
Road & Track on Corvette 1953-1967
Road & Track on Corvette 1968-1982
Road & Track on Corvette 1982-1986
Road & Track on Corvette 1986-1990
Road & Track on Datsun Z 1970-1983
Road & Track on Ferrari 1975-1981
Road & Track on Ferrari 1981-1984
Road & Track on Ferrari 1984-1988
Road & Track on Fiat Sports Cars 1968-1987
Road & Track on Jaguar 1950-1960
Road & Track on Jaguar 1961-1968
Road & Track on Jaguar 1968-1974
Road & Track on Jaguar 1974-1982
Road & Track on Jaguar 1983-1989
Road & Track on Lamborghini 1964-1985
Road & Track on Lotus 1972-1981
Road & Track on Maserati 1952-1974
Road & Track on Maserati 1975-1983
R & T on Mazda RX7 & MX5 Miata 1986-1991
Road & Track on Mercedes 1952-1962
Road & Track on Mercedes 1963-1970
Road & Track on Mercedes 1971-1979
Road & Track on Mercedes 1980-1987
Road & Track on MG Sports Cars 1949-1961
Road & Track on MG Sports Cars 1962-1980
Road & Track on Mustang 1964-1977
R & T on Nissan 300-ZX & Turbo 1984-1989
Road & Track on Peugeot 1955-1986
Road & Track on Pontiac 1960-1983
Road & Track on Porsche 1951-1967
Road & Track on Porsche 1968-1971
Road & Track on Porsche 1972-1975
Road & Track on Porsche 1975-1978
Road & Track on Porsche 1979-1982
Road & Track on Porsche 1982-1985
Road & Track on Porsche 1985-1988
R & T on Rolls Royce & Bentley 1950-1965
R & T on Rolls Royce & Bentley 1966-1984
Road & Track on Saab 1972-1992
R & T on Toyota Sports & GT Cars 1966-1984
R & T on Triumph Sports Cars 1953-1967
R & T on Triumph Sports Cars 1967-1974
R & T on Triumph Sports Cars 1974-1982
Road & Track on Volkswagen 1951-1968
Road & Track on Volkswagen 1968-1978
Road & Track on Volkswagen 1978-1985
Road & Track on Volvo 1957-1974
Road & Track on Volvo 1977-1994
R&T - Henry Manney at Large & Abroad
R&T - Peter Egan's "Side Glances"

## BROOKLANDS CAR AND DRIVER SERIES

Car and Driver on BMW 1955-1977
Car and Driver on BMW 1977-1985
C and D on Cobra, Shelby & Ford GT40 1963-84
Car and Driver on Corvette 1956-1967
Car and Driver on Corvette 1968-1977
Car and Driver on Corvette 1978-1982
Car and Driver on Corvette 1983-1988
C and D on Datsun Z 1600 & 2000 1966-1984
Car and Driver on Ferrari 1955-1962
Car and Driver on Ferrari 1963-1975
Car and Driver on Ferrari 1976-1983
Car and Driver on Mopar 1956-1967
Car and Driver on Mopar 1968-1975
Car and Driver on Mustang 1964-1972
Car and Driver on Pontiac 1961-1975
Car and Driver on Porsche 1955-1962
Car and Driver on Porsche 1963-1970
Car and Driver on Porsche 1970-1976
Car and Driver on Porsche 1977-1981
Car and Driver on Porsche 1982-1986
Car and Driver on Saab 1956-1985
Car and Driver on Volvo 1955-1986

## BROOKLANDS PRACTICAL CLASSICS SERIES

PC on Austin A40 Restoration
PC on Land Rover Restoration
PC on Metalworking in Restoration
PC on Midget/Sprite Restoration
PC on Mini Cooper Restoration
PC on MGB Restoration
PC on Morris Minor Restoration
PC on Sunbeam Rapier Restoration
PC on Triumph Herald/Vitesse
PC on Spitfire Restoration
PC on Beetle Restoration
PC on 1930s Car Restoration

## BROOKLANDS HOT ROD 'MUSCLECAR & HI-PO ENGINES' SERIES

Chevy 265 & 283
Chevy 302 & 327
Chevy 348 & 409
Chevy 350 & 400
Chevy 396 & 427
Chevy 454 thru 512
Chrysler Hemi
Chrysler 273, 318, 340 & 360
Chrysler 361, 383, 400, 413, 426, 440
Ford 289, 302, Boss 302 & 351W
Ford 351C & Boss 351
Ford Big Block

## BROOKLANDS RESTORATION SERIES

Auto Restoration Tips & Techniques
Basic Bodywork Tips & Techniques
Basic Painting Tips & Techniques
Camaro Restoration Tips & Techniques
Chevrolet High Performance Tips & Techniques
Chevy Engine Swapping Tips & Techniques
Chevy-GMC Pickup Repair
Chrysler Engine Swapping Tips & Techniques
Custom Painting Tips & Techniques
Engine Swapping Tips & Techniques
Ford Pickup Repair
How to Build a Street Rod
Land Rover Restoration Tips & Techniques
MG 'T' Series Restoration Guide
Mustang Restoration Tips & Techniques
Performance Tuning - Chevrolets of the '60's
Performance Tuning - Pontiacs of the '60's

## BROOKLANDS MILITARY VEHICLES SERIES

Allied Military Vehicles No.1 1942-1945
Allied Military Vehicles No.2 1941-1946
Complete WW2 Military Jeep Manual
Dodge Military Vehicles No.1 1940-1945
Hail To The Jeep
Land Rovers in Military Service
Mil. & Civ Amphibians 1940-1990
Off Road Jeeps: Civ. & Mil. 1944-1971
US Military Vehicles 1941-1945
US Army Military Vehicles WW2-TM9-2800
VW Kubelwagen Military Portfolio1940-1990
WW2 Jeep Military Portfolio 1941-1945

1654

**BROOKLANDS BOOKS**

CONTENTS

**BROOKLANDS BOOKS**

*ACKNOWLEDGEMENTS*

This is the first Aston Martin book in the Brooklands series. For many years, Adrian Feather has skilfully recorded the history of the earlier models of this prestigious marque and his books are still available from good bookstores. He did not venture into the V-8 era however, and our correspondence shows that enthusiasts are now impatient for information on the most recent products from Newport Pagnell.

This book is a double first for Brooklands as it opens a new range of titles to be known as Gold Portfolios. This is our way of identifying books which contain almost twice as many articles as those in our standard range. We hope this will satisfy the needs of historians and other enthusiasts who demand more exhaustive coverage of a particular subject.

All the road tests and other stories reprinted in our series are copyright and it is only with the help and cooperation of the original publishers that we can make them available once again. We are sure that Aston Martin owners and others who follow the hobby will wish to join with us in thanking the management of Autocar, Autosport, Car and Car Conversions, Car and Driver, Modern Motor, Motor, Motor Sport, Motor Trend, Road & Track, Thoroughbred and Classic Cars, Sporting Cars, Sports Car Graphic, Sports Car World, What Car? and Wheels for their understanding, generosity and on-going support.

R.M. Clarke

The Aston Martin V8 with re-styled frontal treatment.

# Aston Martin and their latest models

In the high-performance car field, no name means more in Great Britain than Aston Martin. Originally formed by Lionel Martin, one of the greatest enthusiasts I have ever known, the company soon gained a reputation for superb quality, in spite of a chronic shortage of funds. Even then there was a racing background, largely due to the backing of Count Lou Zborowski, but when Lou was killed the situation became impossible. Eventually A. C. Bertelli took over and produced some excellent small sports cars in the late 1920s and early '30s. Racing was still in the blood, the cars covering themselves with glory in long-distance events, such as Le Mans and the Double-Twelve.

Following various vicissitudes, David Brown took over Aston Martin after the war. He had already acquired Lagonda and things really began to happen when the W. O. Bentley-designed six-cylinder engine of the latter car was dropped into the Aston Martin chassis. The great racing days of Aston Martin followed, culminating in outright victory at Le Mans.

Of recent years, the *marque* has rested on its laurels, but though the name has remained great, the company has failed to make ends meet, proving a heavy financial burden to the David Brown industrial empire. Various expedients were tried, but eventually it became known that the firm would no longer be carried by the parent group. A few months ago, it was taken over by Company Developments Ltd, a consortium of financial experts rather than motoring enthusiasts.

I was thus very glad to be invited to attend a meeting of this body and to hear a statement by S. W. Willson, the chairman. The latest models, incorporating a number of improvements, were on view and I took the opportunity to go round the factory and see the new cars being built.

Mr Willson explained that the previous troubles had been brought on by too much enthusiasm and not enough finance. Connections with the David Brown organisation have been completely severed, so the DBS designation must not be used, but Sir David still has a seat on the board. There has been a complete reorganisation in the interest of curbing unnecessary expenditure, but only 16

men have been made redundant out of a work force of just under 500.

The production of six or seven cars per week will be stepped up to 10 cars per week, and there it will stop. This is both for commercial considerations and also for a strong conviction that ownership of an Aston Martin should be like belonging to a very exclusive club. The company is catering for a very special class of motorist who requires a British hand-built car. Aston Martins will be 4-seater GT cars, not 2-seater sports cars, and will be designed to appeal to the connoisseur.

Such cars must be very costly, because a small-production specialist GT machine cannot be priced on the basis of mass production, in which vast savings are possible. In addition, the buyers of today are contributing to the development costs, ultimately running into millions of pounds, of the cars of the future. It is Mr Willson's view that many cars of this calibre have been under-priced for a number of years and, for the above reasons, he makes no apology for putting up Aston

Martin prices.

The current production run is of cars developed from the former DBS model, but there will be completely new models later on. There will be greater concentration on quality than ever before and quality control of a very high order will be applied. The new management are conscious of the success previously enjoyed in racing and consider that the time gap is now far too long. However, if you can't afford something you can't have it, though the intention is to make a comeback when that is possible, always on a financially controlled basis and without imperilling the company by over-spending on racing.

It is considered important, for the image and integrity of the car, to manufacture everything possible, especially the engine, in the Aston Martin factory. There is a vague possibility that an American engine might be used for the USA market, but only because of the special pollution requirements.

Two models are now built, the V8 and the Vantage, the latter having the traditional

*The bodies get plenty of hand-finishing by craftsmen.*

5

6-cylinder engine, the chassis and body being the same in both cases. Refrigerated air conditioning and a stereo cartridge player and radio, among other things, are standard in the V8 and extra for the Vantage. The body has been restyled, with a frontal treatment reminiscent of the traditional radiator, and two large 7 in quartz-halogen headlamps give an improved dipped beam. Repositioning the spare wheel gives greater luggage space and better bulkhead insulation reduces heat and noise transfer. The V8 costs £8949.27, including tax, and the Vantage £6949.48.

I watched Aston Martins being built at Newport Pagnell. The actual steel chassis pan consists of many pressings welded together and this is the only part still made by David Brown, though now on a basis of Aston Martin being the paying customer. Instead of the multiple tubes of the former Superleggera body structure, the frame, boxed at strategic points, is now made by Aston Martin and welded to the chassis pan on a jig. The aluminium panels are clinched and riveted, making no contribution to strength. The air conditioning ducts, which are built in at this stage, now have enormous capacity. Elaborate rust-proofing protects the body-chassis structure.

The front suspension is by wishbones and coil springs; a de Dion axle is at the rear on twin pairs of trailing arms and coil springs, with lateral location by a Watt's linkage. The Salisbury limited-slip differential unit carries the inboard brakes which, like those in front, have ventilated discs. The rack and pinion steering has power assistance as standard. There is a choice of the ZF 5-speed gearbox or the Chrysler Torqueflite automatic transmission.

Foundry work, such as the casting of the aluminium cylinder blocks and heads and the forging of the connecting rods, is done outside, but the machining is carried out in the Aston Martin factory. The crankshafts are forged, machined, and nitrided by Laystall, the steel-backed bearings being by Glacier Metal Co. The Hepworth and Grandage pistons each have two compression and one scraper ring, with T-slotted skirts. Each engine is built by one man, who has complete responsibility for it.

The V8 is a most impressive sight with its four overhead-camshafts. All eight cylinders have separate ramming pipes of equal length, each with its own throttle. The fuel-injection is by Bosch, a mechanical system having been chosen in this case. To cope with the fuel consumption of this potent power unit, a 21 gallon petrol tank is installed. Like another British manufacturer with a double-barrelled name, Aston Martin are reticent about the power of their engines.

Having seen Aston Martins being built, I can say that, unlike many high-performance cars, they really are largely the product of a single factory. In addition to the engines, the bodies are completely built on the premises, including the interior trim, and even the famous Italian manufacturers cannot claim to be so self-contained.

**JOHN BOLSTER**

### SPECIFICATION AND PERFORMANCE DATA

**Cars described:** Aston Martin V8 2-door 4-seater coupé, price £8949.27, and Vantage, price £6949.48, both including tax.

**Engine:** V8 100 mm x 85 mm (5340 cc). Compression ratio 9 to 1. Four overhead camshafts. Bosch fuel-injection. Vantage 6-cylinders 96 mm x 92 mm (3995 cc). Compression ratio 9.4 to 1. Twin overhead camshafts, 3 twin-choke Weber carburetters.

**Transmission:** Single dry-plate clutch and 5-speed all-synchromesh gearbox with central remote control, ratios 0.845, 1.0, 1.22, 1.78 and 2.90 to 1; or Torqueflite automatic transmission, ratios 1.0, 1.45, and 2.45 to 1, torque converter (stalled) ratio 2.1 to 1. Salisbury hypoid final drive with limited slip differential, ratio, V8 automatic 2.88 to 1, V8 manual 3.31 to 1, Vantage automatic 3.54 to 1, Vantage manual 3.73 to 1.

**Chassis:** Steel platform chassis with integral body framework and aluminium panels. Independent front suspension by wishbones, coil springs, and anti-roll bar. Power-assisted rack and pinion steering. De Dion rear axle on coil springs, twin pairs of trailing arms, with lateral Watt's linkage and roller-spline driveshafts. Telescopic front and piston-type rear dampers. Servo-assisted ventilated disc brakes, inboard at rear, with separate front and rear circuits. Light alloy bolt-on wheels fitted GR70 VR15 radial ply tyres.

**Equipment:** 12-volt lighting and starting. Speedometer. Rev counter. Ammeter. Oil pressure, oil temperature, water temperature, and fuel gauges. Clock. Heating, demisting, and ventilation system with heated rear window. Refrigerated air conditioning on V8. Windscreen wipers and washers. Flashing direction indicators. Reversing lights. Cigar lighters. Radio and cartridge stereo on V8.

**Dimensions:** Wheelbase 8 ft 6¾ in. Track 4 ft 11 in. Overall length 15 ft 3 in. Width 6 ft. Weight 3800 lb.

**Performance:** (Maker's figures) Maximum speed 160 mph. Acceleration: 0-60 mph 5.9 s, 0-100 mph 13.8 s, 0-120 mph 21.8 s (V8 and five-speed gearbox).

*New Aston Martins nearing completion at Newport Pagnell (above). Aston Martin V8 engines, three with Torqueflite and one with ZF five-speed transmission (below).*

*The Aston Martin now has more luggage space in the boot.*

# ...ston Martin will pull through

## ... provided that two plus two equals six

...e equation is that of someone ...'s good at figures, a success-...financier. Mr William ...lson, whose Company De-...opments Ltd bought Aston ...rtin last February for an un-...closed sum, goes farther: two ...s two should never equal ...ee or four, and preferably not ...e. By making it equal six, ...Willson, the new chairman of ...on Martin, hopes to have the ...andering AM concern out of ...red by the end of the year. ...may not know much about ...tor cars but I am good at ...ns."

...Have no fear. Aston Martin, ...shaky pillar of Britain's ...cialist establishment, is ...about to succumb to the ...ountants' chopper and be ...ned into a meat pie factory. ...r are its wares going to be re-...mped as anything less ex-...sive and desirable than they ...now. The new company in-...ds not only to continue mak-...cars, but also to make some ...ney as well. At a recent Press ...eption, held inauspiciously ...the works canteen (reflecting ...economy drive that's sweep-...through the premises), I ...the impression that AM is ...sound hands and that its ...ure is looking up, if not ...assured.

...There are no immediate plans ...expand production beyond ...out 10 cars a week from the ...sent seven or eight. In fact ...re will soon be no room for ...ansion because the manage-...nt intend to sell the seven acres ...land behind the existing east-...e factory. "I'd sooner look at ...ousing estate than a rubbish ...mp," said Mr Wilson. In other ...rds realizing one of the ...tory's most valuable assets ...kes sound commercial sense ...this time of need. Could the ...mped existing factory cope ...h any increase in production? ...ll, it seems it could because ...A will be using more bought-...t components in future, there-...releasing space hitherto ...lized for making some of ...eir own bits.

At the moment, the new pruned yet strengthened management team is concentrating on getting the company's found-ations right. There's a new pay and productivity scheme in the pipeline for the 500 employees (only 16 people have been made redundant since the take-over) as well as an intensive quality control programme designed to improve existing cars: like certain other complicated thoroughbreds, Aston Martins have not been noted for trouble-free service in the past. And talking of service, Mr Willson also spoke of a new we'll-come-to-you servicing scheme, which will release customers from the chore of getting their car to Newport Pagnell or an AM agent.

The nameplates on the face-lifted models we pictured last week (with two seven-inch QH lamps flanking a revised grille that reverts to classic AM shape) still read Aston Martin DBS V8, but once present stocks have been used (that economy drive again) the DB bit will be "dropped for marketing reasons" — even though David Brown, the former owner, re-mains the company's president and a board member. The two models will in future be known simply as the Aston Martin Vantage (six cylinder) and V8.

Mr Willson believes that many specialist car manufacturers have floundered in the past because they under-priced their products. Small production runs mean very high production costs (500 workers to make 10 cars a week is a distressing ratio for accountants), and people who want to enjoy the exclusivism of AM ownership must pay for the privilege — not just the cost of their own car but a proportion of its high development costs and that of future models as well.

All this was perhaps by way of a softener to the news that the V8's price was to be increased forthwith by £500 to £8949, and the Vantage's by £700 to £6949, increases determined after a realistic evaluation of the costs, said Mr Willson.

The weakness of the old Aston Martin set-up, it seems, was too much enthusiasm for cars, not enough for commercial matters. Even though that situation has now been reversed, the new company intends to enhance, not destroy, Aston Martin's unique image and reputation in Britain. Far from dropping their own four-cam 5.3-litre V8 — a very fine engine indeed now after a long and troublesome period of gestation — they in-tend retaining and developing it for existing and future models. Mr Willson confirmed, however, that they had been exploring the possibility of using a big American V8, probably a Chrysler, for cars sold in America. This, he indicated, may be the only way that Aston Martin can afford to keep a foot in the American market. That Rover have pulled out of America altogether, he said, reflected how difficult it was for small manufacturers to keep up with ever-changing legislation. It will not be until September that the latest cars comply with US regulations, though cars built to the earlier spec are still being sold there.

And a BRM-engined two seater? No more, it seems. This project was the brainchild of an earlier managing director before the takeover, and has now been abandoned for a variety of reasons, among them the con-tention that Aston Martin can get more power from their own road-going engine than BRM could from a detuned F1 unit modified for road use.

At the moment, Aston Martin cannot afford to go racing, said Mr Willson, but the possibility of doing so has certainly not been dismissed from future plans. "We hope to get back in a limited way."

And on that bright note we'll leave the new AM team to get on with the job, with our very sincerest best wishes. **Roger Bell**

**FOR** : very fast ; good steering, handling and brakes ; fairly quiet ; very satisfying to drive
**AGAINST** : heavy clutch ; inadequate headlights ; heating and ventilation hard to control ; poor steering lock

# ASTON MARTIN V8

The Aston Martin V8 is not only the fastest production car manufactured in the UK today but, with its outstanding handling and braking, is perhaps one of the safest. Small wonder then, that everyone breathed a sigh of relief when Company Developments Ltd decided to rescue the sinking Aston Martin company from its 24-year association with the David Brown organisation. The first revised version of the car to emanate from Newport Pagnell after the new regime took over was very similar to the DBS, but with certain detailed improvements. The full-width slatted radiator grille and its four 5in headlights were replaced by a neater mesh version incorporating two 7in lamps. The auxiliary light clusters were set under the bumper and protected by thick over-riders with rubber inserts. At the rear a modified fuel tank has resulted in a larger and more usefully shaped boot. Internal modifications include a much-needed revision of the control layout with better use of the fingertip stalks, and slimmer seats.

The car tested here, however, is a still newer version revealed for the first time today. It has four twin-choke Webers in place of the Bosch fuel injection, giving a worthwhile improvement in low-speed running and tractability. When combined with the Aston's very high cornering powers this makes the V8 one of the most satisfying road cars we have driven for some time.

Unfortunately some of the car's original faults still remain, including the indifferent action and poor synchromesh of the five-speed ZF gearbox, the intolerably heavy clutch and the uncontrollable heating and ventilating system. Moreover, like our previous road-test Aston, this one was not very reliable. During our test the bolts retaining the final drive unit came detached, the transistorized ignition amplifier failed as did the air-conditioning thermostat, some swarf was found in a carburetter and the clutch required attention.

## PERFORMANCE

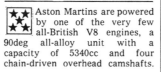 Aston Martins are powered by one of the very few all-British V8 engines, a 90deg all-alloy unit with a capacity of 5340cc and four chain-driven overhead camshafts. Four twin-choke Weber 42 DCNF carburetters nestle in the hollow of the "V", replacing the original expensive Bosch mechanical injection system and constituting one of the major changes to the car since its conception. Though hardly lacking in performance, the earlier cars did suffer from surge and poor torque at low speeds.

Since Aston Martin do not release power output figures, we cannot directly compare the two engines. However our performance figures suggest a slight improvement in low and mid-range torque. What the figures do not convey is that the car will now pull without snatch from as low as 600 rpm on part throttle, something it would not do before. Full throttle can be used from 1350 rpm without fear of "drowning" the engine, and the power really starts to surge forth as the needle passes the 1500 rpm mark.

As before the acceleration is quite breathtaking and the Aston makes some of its competitors look slow. Its 0-60 mph time of 5.7 seconds, for instance, leaves the Lamborghini Espada two seconds adrift.

Like its predecessor, the V8 will cruise all day on Continental motorways at 130-140 mph, though (rather academically), its mean maximum speed was " only " 154.8 mph compared to the 160.1 mph we got from the previous car. During our maximum speed runs the tread of one of the GR 70 VR 15 Avon tyres fitted to a rear wheel separated from its carcase. Although the tyres had been correctly inflated for high-speed work, all were found to be very hot when the car was finally brought to a halt. The cause of this failure is still being investigated.

The engine started almost instantaneously from cold after two dabs of the throttle to prime the Webers, and warmed quickly to its work. Once hot it restarted best with the throttles just cracked open. The starter itself however was not so reliable ; apart from making unpleasant grating noises (even after the engine had fired) it failed to engage on occasions.

The car is commendably free of unpleasant noise, that emanating from the engine being largely confined to the remarkably restrained waffle of the twin exhausts. The engine rattles some-

what when starting from cold and vibrates slightly between 1000-1500 rpm. But from then on it remains smooth and unstrained to its limit of 6000 rpm. The misfiring evident at high engine speeds after a lengthy spell in town traffic, which presumably fouls the plugs, quickly disappears.

## ECONOMY

 With an overall consumption of 13.2 mpg, the Aston could hardly be described as economical. It is however less thirsty than many comparable cars and fractionally less thirsty than the injected version which returned 12.9 mpg. When considering the 14.7 mpg " touring " consumption one should note that the Aston will cruise a good 10 mph faster than most of the other cars in the comparison chart.

The two interconnected fuel tanks hold a total of 21 gallons and give the Aston a range of just over 300 miles. The 9 : 1 compression ratio requires five star fuel on which we detected no running-on or pinking.

## TRANSMISSION

★★★★ Finding a gearbox to transmit the torque of a high-output 5.3 litre engine and to give five well spaced ratios for a 150 plus mph car is not really difficult—if you don't make your own you use the German ZF unit. There really aren't any other alternatives for road cars.

As fitted to the Aston, the ZF has a gate like the old Porsche box with first down and away to the left and the upper four ratios in the normal H pattern. This inevitably makes the first to second change slightly ponderous, though ours was more positive than many in its action. In fact for normal driving we found the gearbox quite pleasant. However it does not take kindly to being rushed, and a hurried change often results in heavy baulking and/or crunching as the synchromesh fails to cope, that of third gear being particularly weak on our test car.

The ratios are excellent for progressive acceleration though first and second are perhaps a

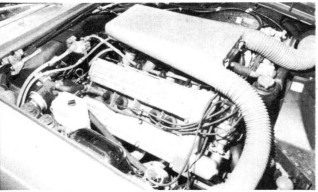

Engine accessibility is much better with the new carburation, the plugs in particular being much easier to get at

Redesigning the fuel tank has allowed space for another 1.7 cu ft of luggage

shade wide for regular town driving. With the 3.54:1 axle ratio (3.31:1 is an option) 47, 77, 112 and 136 mph are available in the lower gears.

An operating pressure of no less than 64lb (one of the highest we have recorded) makes the clutch intolerably heavy in traffic. Fortunately it is particularly smooth in its action so you don't have to feather the changes up or down the box, though that on our test car did need pressing right to the floor for full disengagement. We also noticed slight slip after repeated standing starts, but this disappeared when the unit had cooled.

Although fairly free from whine, the gearbox chattered noisily at idle. There were no noises from the final drive unit.

## HANDLING

★★★ / ★★★ Despite its size and great weight, the Aston is so controllable and rolls so little that it can be thown about with the abandon normally reserved for cars half its size and power.

Much of this is due to the Adwest power-assisted steering which unlike the similar Jaguar system, feels like any good unaided set-up because Aston Martin have not made it too light. The slight kickback merely adds to the already high degree of feel available through the steering wheel. The lock however, is poor, nearing 39ft in one direction.

The front suspension is by conventional unequal length wishbones and coil springs, that at the back by a full de Dion system with Watt linkage and parallel trailing arms. The handling from this set-up is tremendous. Turning into a medium speed bend, one is aware of slight reassuring understeer. Flooring the throttle, the car merely adopts a slightly tighter line and "digs in" more firmly at the back. Lifting off in mid-corner has a similarly safe effect, as there's a gradual and controllable tuck-in at the front. Naturally full power in a tight bend will send the tail adrift, but even with quite brutal use of the throttle, the transition to oversteer is gentle and controllable. We found the adhesion of the Avon radials quite astonishing both on wet and dry roads.

## BRAKES

★★★ / ★★★ In both power and reassurance, ie, feel—the Aston's brakes are almost beyond reproach. Massive ventilated discs are used all round, the rear ones being mounted inboard. Despite twin servos the pedal pressures are quite high, 100lb being required to make a 1g stop from 30mph.

Our standard 20-stop test caused the pedal pressure to go *down* slightly, not up, so the brakes actually un-faded. After repeated high-speed stops however the pedal travel seemed to increase slightly, something we also noticed on the road. This phenomenon was accompanied by a certain amount of drumming and juddering. At no point did the efficiency deteriorate, though, nor was it affected by a thorough soaking in the water splash.

The excellent fly-off handbrake gave a passable 0.38g stop from 30mph on the level and successfully held the car on a 1 in 3 slope, though the lever was by then at the limit of its travel.

## ACCOMMODATION

★★★ / ★★ Inevitably, the classic fastback styling of the V8 limits rear seat accommodation somewhat. However the Aston is a genuine four-seater and considerable thought has obviously been given to accommodating rear seat passengers and their luggage in an area rather dominated by the mechanics of the de Dion and its inboard braking system.

Getting in to the back is straightforward as the opening for the wide doors extends beyond the edge of the seat cushion. The chromed catches for tilting the front backrests are unnecessarily fiddly though. Once installed, six footers will find their head a little near the rear screen, and not too much kneeroom, though the seats themselves are comfortable enough. Padded and contoured wheelboxes and a central armrest supply the necessary lateral support.

As a two-seater there is more than enough space for both driver and passenger, with plenty of fore-and-aft adjustment to the

seats and even an adjustable toe board on the passenger's side. Oddments space is also quite generous with large map pockets in the back of both front seats, a long but shallow lockable glovebox in the facia, a lipped tray at the base of the gear lever, and a large parcel shelf.

By modifying the shape of the fuel tank, a larger and more usefully shaped boot has been created, and it is now possible to lay quite large cases flat where previously they had to be upright. We squeezed in 8.9 cu ft of our Revelation suitcases.

## RIDE COMFORT

★★★ / ★★ Around town the ride is quite harsh and road shocks can become obtrusive, with noticeable crashings from the front end in particular.

Slimmer leather-covered reclining seats offer good support, though we did find the cushions just a little flat. Access to the rear is good thanks to the forward-tilting backrests and wide doors

·UKX 50L·

The rear seats are surprisingly comfortable and head and knee room is just sufficient for an average-sized adult

The release catches for the backrests are ridiculously fiddly

Going faster the ride is significantly better with only the occasional bump catching the suspension out. At high speed on main roads it is very well controlled and comfortable.

There is a great deal of bump thump from the fat tyres and road-roar can be bad on motorways, but a far worse fault is the lack of clearance under the front wheel arches which the tyres occasionally foul when negotiating undulating surfaces at speed. The same can also occur at the rear when travelling four-up.

## DRIVER COMFORT

★★ / ★★ Our testers had few complaints about the driving position, which remains comfortable after 500 miles of consistently fast motoring, even though the telescopically adjustable leather-rimmed steering wheel is set a mite too high. The offset pedals are about right though, that of the brake and the organ-type throttle being well positioned for heel and toe operation. There is a useful foot rest to the left of the clutch.

The seats in the V8 are slightly slimmer than those of the original DBS, and offer more lateral support. There is plenty of fore-and-aft adjustment, and in fact most of us could not reach all the pedals with the seat in its rearmost position. The fully-contoured backrest offers

## PERFORMANCE

### CONDITIONS
| | |
|---|---|
| Weather | Dull, overcast ; wind 7-15 mph |
| Temperature | 55-57° F |
| Barometer | 29.95 in hg |
| Surface | Dry tarmac |

### MAXIMUM SPEEDS
| | mph | kph |
|---|---|---|
| Mean of opposite runs | 154.8 | 249.1 |
| Best one way kilometre | 155.4 | 250.0 |

Terminal speeds :
| | | |
|---|---|---|
| at ¼-mile | 101 | 163 |
| at kilometre | 126 | 203 |

Speed in gears (at 6000 rpm) :
| | | |
|---|---|---|
| 1st | 47 | 76 |
| 2nd | 77 | 124 |
| 3rd | 112 | 180 |
| 4th | 136 | 219 |

### ACCELERATION FROM REST
| mph | sec | kph | sec |
|---|---|---|---|
| 0-30 | 2.3 | 0-40 | 1.8 |
| 0-40 | 3.2 | 0-60 | 2.9 |
| 0-50 | 4.6 | 0-80 | 4.5 |
| 0-60 | 5.7 | 0-100 | 6.1 |
| 0-70 | 7.2 | 0-120 | 7.9 |
| 0-80 | 8.9 | 0-140 | 10.3 |
| 0-90 | 11.2 | 0-160 | 13.6 |
| 0-100 | 13.6 | 0-180 | 17.3 |
| 0-110 | 16.8 | Stand'g km | 25.2 |
| 0-120 | 20.5 | | |
| Stand'g ¼ | 14.1 | | |

### ACCELERATION IN TOP
| mph | sec | kph | sec |
|---|---|---|---|
| 30-50 | 7.0 | | |
| 40-60 | 6.9 | 60-80 | 4.0 |
| 50-70 | 6.7 | 80-100 | 4.3 |
| 60-80 | 6.2 | 100-120 | 4.0 |
| 70-90 | 6.4 | 120-140 | 4.2 |
| 80-100 | 6.8 | 140-160 | 4.1 |
| 90-110 | 7.5 | 160-180 | 4.9 |
| 100-120 | 8.7 | | |

### ACCELERATION IN 4TH
| mph | sec | kph | sec |
|---|---|---|---|
| 20-40 | 5.8 | | |
| 30-50 | 5.5 | | |
| 40-60 | 5.0 | 60-80 | 4.0 |
| 50-70 | 4.8 | 80-100 | 4.3 |
| 60-80 | 4.8 | 100-120 | 4.0 |
| 70-90 | 5.0 | 120-140 | 4.2 |
| 80-100 | 5.2 | 140-160 | 4.1 |
| 90-110 | 5.4 | 160-180 | 4.9 |
| 100-120 | 6.8 | | |

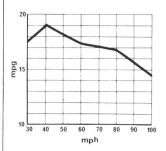

### FUEL CONSUMPTION
| | |
|---|---|
| Touring* | 14.7 mpg / 19.2 litres/100 km |
| Overall | 13.2 mpg / 21.4 litres/100 km |
| Fuel grade | 100 octane (RM) / 5 star rating |
| Tank capacity | 21.0 galls / 95.4 litres |
| Max range | 309 miles / 496 km |
| Test distance | 1670 miles / 2680 km |

* Consumption midway between 30 mph and maximum less 5 per cent for acceleration.

### BRAKES
Pedal pressure deceleration and stopping distance from 30 mph (48 kph).
| lb | kg | g | ft | m |
|---|---|---|---|---|
| 25 | 11 | 0.19 | 158 | 48 |
| 50 | 23 | 0.66 | 45 | 14 |
| 75 | 34 | 0.96 | 31 | 9 |
| 100 | 45 | 1.00+ | 30 | 9 |
| Handbrake | | 0.33 | 91 | 28 |

### FADE
20½ g stops at 1 min intervals from speed midway between 40 mph (64 kph) and maximum (97 mph, 156 kph).
| | lb | kg |
|---|---|---|
| Pedal force at start | 40 | 18 |
| Pedal force at 10th stop | 39 | 18 |
| Pedal force at 20th stop | 38 | 17 |

### STEERING
Turning circle between kerbs
| | ft | m |
|---|---|---|
| left | 38.4 | 11.7 |
| right | 38.8 | 11.8 |

Lock to lock 3.0 turns
50ft diam circle 1.15 turns

### CLUTCH
| | in | cm |
|---|---|---|
| Free pedal movement | 2.0 | 5.1 |
| Additional to disengage | 2.0 | 5.1 |
| Maximum pedal load | 64 lb | |

### SPEEDOMETER (mph)
| | | | | | | | | |
|---|---|---|---|---|---|---|---|---|
| Speedo | 30 | 40 | 50 | 60 | 70 | 80 | 90 | 100 |
| True mph | 31 | 40 | 51 | 60 | 70 | 80 | 90 | 100 |

Distance recorder: accurate.

### WEIGHT
| | cwt | kg |
|---|---|---|
| Unladen weight* | 34.7 | 1762 |
| Weight as tested | 38.4 | 1952 |

*with fuel for approx 50 miles.
Performance tests carried out by Motor's staff at the Motor Industry Research Association proving ground, Lindley.

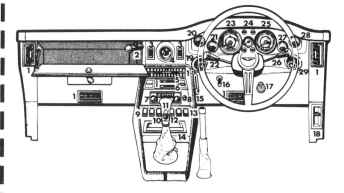

| | | |
|---|---|---|
| 1 fresh air vents | 14 ashtray | |
| 2 map reading light | 15 vent control | |
| 3 window switches | 16 trip reset knob | |
| 4 clock | 17 ignition switch | |
| 5 air conditioning control | 18 bonnet release | |
| 6 fan control | 19 windscreen washer control | |
| 7 radio | 20 ammeter | |
| 8 radio aerial switch | 21 fuel gauge | |
| 9 hazard warning switch | 22 horn | |
| 10 interior light switch | 23 speedometer | |
| 11 gear lever | 24 warning lights | |
| 12 lights switches | 25 rev counter | |
| 13 handbrake | 26 flasher/indicator | |
| | 27 water temperature | |
| | 28 oil temperature | |
| | 29 panel lights | |

## COMPARISONS

| | Capacity cc | Price £ | Max mph | 0-60 sec | 30-50* sec | Overall mpg | Touring mpg | Length ft in | Width ft in | Weight cwt | Boot cu ft |
|---|---|---|---|---|---|---|---|---|---|---|---|
| Aston Martin V8 | 5340 | 9057 | 154.8 | 5.7 | 7.0 | 13.2 | 14.7 | 15 3.0 | 6 0.0 | 34.7 | 8.9 |
| Jensen SP | 7212 | 7320 | 140.0 | 7.6 | 2.8 | 11.0 | 15.2 | 15 8.0 | 5 10.0 | 35.1 | 8.5 |
| Maserati Indy 4.7 | 4719 | 9587 | 143.0 | 7.5 | 2.8 | 12.5 | 15.1 | 15 7.8 | 5 9.5 | 32.8 | 6.6 |
| Jaguar V12 E-Type | 5343 | 3580 | 146.0 | 6.4 | 6.0 | 14.5 | 16.1 | 15 4.0 | 5 6.8 | 28.8 | 3.8 |
| BMW 3.0 CSL | 3003 | 6899 | 132.5 | 7.2 | 7.3 | 17.2 | — | 15 7.78 | 5 9.5 | 32.8 | 6.6 |
| Lamborghini Espada | 3929 | 12453 | — | 7.8 | 10.3 | 11.3 | 16.5 | 15 6.5 | 6 1.5 | 34.6 | 4.6 |

*In top—fifth for the Aston Martin, Lamborghini; kickdown for the Jensen and Maserati.

STAR GRADE KEY  excellent  good  average  poor  bad

# MOTOR ROAD TEST No 46/73 ● ASTON MARTIN V8

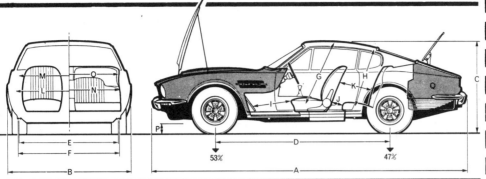

The old-fashioned pedals are wel spaced. When tired of pushing the 64 lb clutch pedal one can use the handy footrest

| | ft | in | cm | | | ft | in | cm |
|---|---|---|---|---|---|---|---|---|
| A overall length | 15 | 1¼ | 452 | J kneeroom | | | | |
| | | | | max | 1 | 0½ | 30 |
| B overall width | 6 | 0 | 180 | min | 0 | 4½ | 11 |
| C unladen height | 4 | 4 | 130 | K front to back | | | |
| D wheelbase | 8 | 6½ | 255 | seat max | 2 | 4½ | 70 |
| E front track | 4 | 11 | 147 | min | 1 | 8½ | 51 |
| F rear track | 4 | 11½ | 149 | L front elbow width | 3 | 1 | 152 |
| G com seat to | | | | M front shoulder | | | |
| roof, front | 3 | 1 | 92 | width | 4 | 8 | 140 |
| H com seat to | | | | N rear elbow | | | |
| roof, rear | 3 | 0 | 90 | width | 4 | 11 | 147 |
| I pedal to seat | | | | O rear shoulder | | | |
| max | 1 | 11½ | 57 | width | 4 | 9½ | 143 |
| min | 1 | 3½ | 38 | P min ground | | | |
| | | | | clearance | 0 | 5½ | 13 |
| | | | | Q boot capacity | 8.9 cut ft | | |

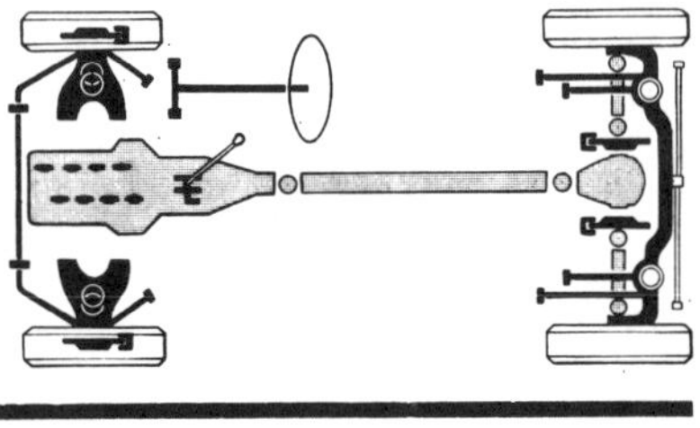

## GENERAL SPECIFICATION

### ENGINE
| | |
|---|---|
| Cylinders | V8 (90°) |
| Capacity | 5340 cc (326 cu in) |
| Bore/stroke | 100/85 mm |
| | (3.94/3.35 in) |
| Cooling | Water |
| Block | Aluminium alloy |
| Head | Aluminium alloy |
| Valves | 4-ohc |
| Valve timing | |
| inlet opens | 30° btdc |
| inlet closes | 64° abdc |
| ex opens | 65° bbdc |
| ex closes | 27° atdc |
| Compression | 9 : 1 |
| Carburetter | 4 downdraught twin-choke Weber 42 DCNF |
| Bearings | 5 main |
| Fuel pump | Twin SU electric type AVF 412 |
| Max power | Not available |
| Max torque | Not available |

### TRANSMISSION
| | |
|---|---|
| Type | 5 speed ZF manual |
| Clutch | 10.5 in dia Borg and Beck diaphragm spring |
| Internal ratios and mph/1000 rpm | |
| Top | 0.845 : 1/26.9 |
| 4th | 1.000 : 1/22.7 |
| 3rd | 1.220 : 1/18.6 |
| 2nd | 1.780 : 1/12.8 |
| 1st | 2.900 : 1/7.9 |
| Rev | 2.630 : 1 |
| Final drive | Salisbury L.S.D. 3.54 : 1 (3.31 : 1 option) |

### BODY/CHASSIS
| | |
|---|---|
| Construction | Steel platform chassis, with steel superstructure and aluminium panels. |
| Protection | Chassis sprayed with red-oxide and underseal. Aluminium panels are etched, primed and sealed before spraying. |

### SUSPENSION
| | |
|---|---|
| Front | Ind. by unequal length wishbones, coil springs, telescopic dampers and anti-roll bar. |
| Rear | Ind. by de Dion axle, located by parallel links and Watt linkage, coil springs and lever arm dampers. |

### STEERING
| | |
|---|---|
| Type | Adwest rack and pinion |
| Assistance | Yes |
| Toe-in | 1/16 in |
| Camber | 0°-30′ positive |
| Castor | 2° 30′-3° |
| King pin | 5° 30′ |
| Rear toe-in | None |

### BRAKES
| | |
|---|---|
| Type | 10.75 disc F ; 10.38 disc R (inboard) |
| Servo | Twin |
| Circuit | Dual |
| Rear valve | None |
| Adjustment | Self adjusting |

### WHEELS
| | |
|---|---|
| Type | 7 in aluminium alloy |
| Tyres | Avon GR 70 VR 15 |
| Pressures | 35 F ; 35 R or 40 all round for cont. high speeds. |

### ELECTRICAL
| | |
|---|---|
| Battery | 12V, 68 Ah |
| Polarity | Negative earth |
| Generator | Alternator |
| Fuses | 12 |
| Headlights | 2 QH sealed beam 60/55W. |

## STANDARD EQUIPMENT

| | | | | | |
|---|---|---|---|---|---|
| Adjustable steering | Yes | Head restraints | No | Parcel shelf | Yes |
| Anti-lock brakes | No | Heated rear window | Yes | Petrol filler lock | No |
| Armrests | Yes | Laminated screen | Yes | Radio | Yes |
| Ashtrays | Yes | Lights | | Rev counter | Yes |
| Breakaway mirror | Yes | Boot | Yes | Seat belts | |
| Cigar lighter | Yes | Courtesy | Yes | Front | Yes |
| Childproof locks | No | Engine bay | Yes | Rear | No |
| Clock | Yes | Hazard warning | Yes | Seat recline | Yes |
| Coat hooks | Yes | Map reading | Yes | Seat height adjuster | No |
| Dual circuit brakes | Yes | Parking | No | Sliding roof | No |
| Electric windows | Yes | Reversing | Yes | Tinted glass | Yes |
| Energy absorb. steering col. | Yes | Spot/fog | No | Combination wash/wipe | Yes |
| Fresh air ventilation | Yes | Locker | Yes | Wipe delay | No |
| Grab handles | No | Outside mirror | No | Vanity mirror | Yes |

## IN SERVICE

### GUARANTEE
Duration **12 months or 12,000 miles**

### MAINTENANCE
| | |
|---|---|
| Schedule | **Every 2500 miles** |
| Free service | **At 500 and 1000 miles** |
| Labour for year | **£116** |

### DO-IT-YOURSELF
Sump ........ **20 pints, SAE 20W/50**

| | |
|---|---|
| Gearbox | 3½ pints, EP 90 |
| Rear axle | 3½ pints, EP 90 LS |
| Steering gear | 3½ pints ATF-A |
| Coolant | 32 pints 80% antifreeze |
| Chassis lubrication | 6 pints every 2500 miles, 4 every 10,000 |
| Contact breaker gap | 0.022 in |
| Spark plug type | Champion N9Y |
| Spark plug gap | 0.025 in |
| Tappets (cold) | inlet 0.008/0.009 exhaust 0.012/0.013 |

### REPLACEMENT COSTS
| | |
|---|---|
| Brake pads/linings (front) | £17.40 |
| Clutch unit | £61.49 |
| Complete exhaust system | £101.50 |
| Engine (new) | £1850 |
| Damper (front) | £10.74 |
| Front wing | N/A |
| Gearbox (new) | £786.04 |
| Oil filter | £1.05 |
| Starter motor | £42.65 |
| Windscreen | £58.75 |

**Make : Aston Martin**
**Model : V8**
**Makers :** Aston Martin Lagonda Ltd, Newport Pagnell, Buckinghamshire
**Price :** £8050 plus £670.84 car tax, plus £872.08 VAT equals £9592.92

excellent lumbar support and reclines right back. Some people complained of poor thigh suppor though, as the cushion is a little too flat.

A pair of column-mounted stalks now look after most o the auxiliary controls, that on the left operating the excellen two-speed wipers and electric washers, that on the right the di and flash for the headlights a well as the horn and indicators The main lights switch, a clearly marked rotary knob, is situated on the facia to the right of the wheel. There is a matching for the panel light rheostat the left. Large rocker switche which operate the electric win dows are placed either side o the centrally positioned clock Most of the remaining switche are found on the console belov the excellent radio/stereo unit the electric aerial for which i operated by a toggle switch o the facia. A rocker switch se into the front of the driver's arm rest operates the remote contro for the passenger door-lock. A traditional feature is the fly-of handbrake which is ideall situated to the right of th transmission tunnel.

## VISIBILITY

★★★ Forward vision throug the Sundym laminate screen is excellent, though neither the "power bulge" no the forward curvature of th wide bonnet assist parking. No does the high waisting of th rear screen which puts the tai out of sight. Thick pillars an seemingly unnecessary quarter lights reduce the otherwise ex pansive area of glass on each side of the driving seat.

The four-shot headlamp system has now been replaced by a pai of 7in QH units which are quit inadequate for high-speed cruising

## INSTRUMENTS

★★ A full complement of dial
★★ grace the Aston's facia The large circular speedo meter and rev counter sandwich the oil pressure gauge in th centre. Those for oil and wate temperature are offset to the right and the fuel gauge an ammeter are balanced in sym metrical fashion on the left. A the instruments were unusuall accurate and we liked the cal brations on all but the re

counter; its mass of thick white lines became a blur when attempting a quick glance at speed. When the speedometer reads 150mph however, it means it.

The oil pressure release valve prevents the oil pressure exceeding 80 psi on the cold start, but it does rise to 100 psi at times once the engine is fully warm. Tickover pressure was a mere 10lb on our test car.

## HEATING AND VENTILATION

★★ There have been at least three different types of heating and ventilating system installed in the V8 since its introduction, none of which we have liked. The control layout is now better, consisting simply of three levers, a vertical one for the four-speed blower switch, a horizontal one for the temperature control, and one for the distribution.

Unfortunately the system would only supply freezing cold air or the sort of stifling hot atmosphere that sends one groping for the window switch. Moreover, it sometimes made a very efficient job of misting the entire windscreen. The vent layout is also mystifying in that the two large fan-boosted vents are located very low on the facia in the proximity of one's knees, while the side vents which presumably should supply most of the fresh air to the face have such a poor

ram effect as to be virtually useless. Fortunately a further fan-aided strip vent in the centre of the console largely makes up for this deficiency, for by having the fan on one of its higher settings, cold air can be made to reach the driver's and passenger's faces. No less than six openings on the top of the facia direct air to the screen when the distribution lever is in the demist position. A heated rear screen is standard equipment.

## NOISE

★★ Wind noise is astonishingly low, increases very little with speed, and allows one to make full use of the stereo. Even at 150 mph there is little more than a slight whistle around the windscreen

pillars. Engine noise, too, never really rises above a pleasant but distant howl, though not so pleasing are the poppings and bangings that occur on the overrun.

Undoubtedly the biggest offender is the road noise. Minimal compliance in the suspension pivots, which undoubtedly helps to give the car its wonderfully taught handling, probably has much to do with the constant transmission of road roar to the interior which is made all the more noticeable by the lack of wind noise.

## FITTINGS AND FINISH

A price of £9000 is difficult to justify for any car, but the finish of the Aston is no more likely to disappoint than its performance. Extensive use of leather helps to project that air of quality one has come to expect from the Newport Pagnell firm. Sensible stainless steel kicks run the length of both door sills and a similar strip protects the lip of the boot. Rich pile carpet is found along the transmission tunnel, at the rear of the back foot wells and in the boot as well as on the floor. Contrasting felt lines the roof.

There is an abundance of auxiliary lighting with a swivel map light tucked neatly in the corner of the glovebox, automatic ones in both the bonnet and

The side vents are unaided by the blower and have poor ram pressure. Note the bonnet release below
The excellent inertia-reel seats belts pack away into the padded wheel-boxes. Right: although better the heating and ventilating is still difficult to control. Excellent illuminated buttons look after the minor auxiliary controls

the boot and a pair of automatic reversing lights. The interior lights are operated either by micro switches on the door pillars or by the "push-push" one on the console.

Smokers will find ashtrays set in both the doors as well as a large one on the console near the cigar lighter. Also on the driver's door is the remote switch for the passenger door lock. Such items as Radiomobile eight-track stereo with electric aerial, Sundym glass, twin-tone horns, heated rear screen and dipping mirror are all standard equipment on the Aston.

A traditional but most effective facia. The excellent instruments are not only well positioned, but unusually accurate

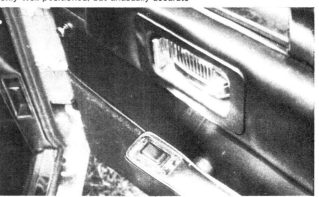

There is a remote switch for locking the passenger door set into the head of the driver's armrest

## IN SERVICE

The replacement of the fuel injection system by the considerably less bulky Weber set-up has resulted in much better underbonnet accessibility. The sparking plugs are now a lot easier to get at. Important service items like the distributor and hydraulic pump reservoirs are all readily available, as are the washer bottle reservoir, dipstick and oil filler cap.

A strict maintenance schedule calls for some chassis lubrication every 2500 miles and to a further four points every 10,000. Oil changes alone will result in quite a sizeable bill, the engine holding 20 pints.

The jack and comprehensive roll of tools is stored above the battery box in the nearside corner of the boot. The spare wheel is found under the boot floor.

A block of 12 fuses is located under the glovebox

If you start off with the well-hackneyed phrase "Will it fit your garage?" you probably wouldn't buy an Aston as the odds are that it may fit but you'll have to stay there all night. At 6 ft × 15 ft 3¾ in the V8 is a very large sports car but it is a sports car and will take four people in comfort with only a little compromise from those in front. With a foot and a half beyond the power bulge, which is the furthest forward that most people will see from the driving seat, it isn't the easiest thing to park and this isn't helped by a flat fast-back which leaves over two foot invisible beyond the base of the rear screen. Prominent ridges to the wing tops make it relatively easy to aim through gaps though. With that off the Editorial chest, there isn't much left on which to fault the mechanical concept of the new V8, the latest development of the DBS—the last of the David Brown products.

The remarkable thing is that it is still very much a post-war Aston whether you are used to a DB2, 4 or 6. All the controls have that reassuringly firm, solid even heavy feel of sound substantial engineering. The 5·3-litre quad-cam V8 gives phenomenal performance to 35 cwt with remarkably little effort and no temperament on its new 4-Weber set-up apart from the occasional spit at low throttle before the unit is fully warm; it starts easily with choke or the usual couple of dabs on the throttle once you have let the pumps fill the float chambers.

It is happy to pull from 1,000 rpm although the ZF box gives its usual nasal chatter up to 1,200 rpm, but the engine really gets into its stride from 2,500 rpm onwards and roars up to 6,000 rpm in the lower gears with no strain and not too much noise. The acceleration available in first gear is really too much to apply to an unsuspecting passenger, more particularly as the optional headrests weren't fitted; first takes you to 47 mph and second through the limit to 77 mph at which point you either slot it easily into fifth or carry on revelling in the sheer power, winding up to 112 and 136 mph in third and fourth—safe enough because no one else would be anywhere near you.
The actual

# Aston Martin V8

Latest in a long line of thoroughbreds the V8 is fast and safe transport for four in comfort

times are 0-60 mph in 5·7 sec, 0-100 mph in 13·6 sec and a maximum around 160 mph; although Aston Martin have given up quoting power figures we are told that the peak power on Webers is near enough the same as with fuel injection and Motor's DBS V8 achieved 160 mph. All the acceleration figures are better than before largely due to the much improved torque on Webers so we reckon the V8's maximum is still no less than 160 mph.

· Changing to Webers has stopped the idling surge that made traffic work unpleasant on the previous model; although the clutch is heavy the driving position makes this quite acceptable and the car will trickle along with the best, or worst, of them. You can potter along in fifth at 30 mph or even stay in third without being aware of the extra revs. The ZF box is remarkably good; first, back on the left, is easy to find and the change to second is a not uncomfortable dog-leg. Once on the move you use the upper four ratios as a normal box; the changes are always smooth however you want to play tunes—1 to 3 to 5 is a much used combination for normal motoring and for overtaking 5 down to 3 makes the manoevure safely rapid. Good

placing of the floor-hinged pedals makes heel and toeing a natural process although the change is well enough cushioned for this not to be essential. The box chatters a little in neutral but is otherwise faultless.

Around town with a lot of idling and low gear use consumption drops to around 10 mpg but our overall figure of 13 mpg is more representative—even at 70 mph it is only 17 mpg but a 21-gallon tank-full of five-star will allow about 250 miles between stops.

Such performance would be wasted and even unusable in soggy Americana but the Aston chassis is first-class and particularly good to make a large car behave like a well sorted two-seater. It is designed to be utterly safe up to its high limits; the Watts-linked de Dion with a limited slip diff puts all the power down on the road through the big Avons which grip astonishingly well in the wet as well. At the front, wishbone suspended wheels are controlled by the Adwest power-assisted rack and pinion, set up to Aston Martin requirements with a reasonable steering weight; it gives the right amount of assistance for parking but on the open road gives the reassuringly direct feel of ideally

chosen geometry. It is responsive and easy to place accurately; in first and second there is enough power to displace the tail if you try hard but you are more likely to get the typical understeer of a limited slip diff on tight corners. At speed it is nicely neutrally balanced and holds an arrow-like course on the straights. The lights are up to a cats-eyed road at 100 mph on main beam but the dipped beam is poor by contrast which limits safe cruising with oncoming traffic to around 70.

Brakes are well up to the performance; big ventilated discs all round require quite an effort despite twin servos but they are very powerful and seem fade-free. A long wet motorway drive soaked them noticeably and the first two or three stops were below par until they had dried out.

The only disadvantage of creating such response in such a car is that suspension compliance has been minimised, so low speed thump with the tyres set at the recommended 35 psi is very pronounced on ridgy town

UKX 50L

# Aston Martin V8...

*Back seats are shaped for two although there is room for three of this size.*

surfaces, almost to the extent of the front end sounding rattly on really poor surfaces. At higher speeds it takes all sorts of bumps and undulations in the comfortable well-damped way that one would expect in a car of the Aston's pedigree.

The driving position is virtually faultless; it can be made comfortable for all sizes and there is plenty of side support for driver and passenger to stay in place under hard cornering. Telescopic adjustment is provided for the steering column and the stalks stay within finger tip reach. All other switches and controls are easily found. Perhaps the gear lever is a shade far back for 5 ft 8 in but at least it can be reached easily by a wide variety of sizes. Electric windows work with the ignition key removed which saves a great deal of aggravation, and so too does the passenger's door lock switch on the driver's arm rest; it would have been nice to have had a driver's lock on the passenger door too, if one is going to remember the old world courtesies of opening your passenger's door—you have to lock your door first and use the key twice.

The interior smells as good as it looks with real leather upholstery; access to the rear is relatively simple with release catches at the seat-hinge but long-legged front occupants need to move the seats forward for rear passenger's feet. Once in, they have plenty of elbow room.

The cars are fitted with an air conditioning system which has three controls for temperature, direction and fan-speed; it is essential to use the fan, which should be quieter even on its slow setting, as no ram effect seems to penetrate the convoluted system. In other respects it worked well although the temperature adjustment was rather insensitive.

What the Aston does particularly well is to convey two or four people very quickly in comfort; grand touring boot space is just suitable for four now that the tank has been redesigned to enlarge the luggage space. It is fast, comfortable over long distances and exceptionally quiet with very little wind noise and only a muted growl from the engine that becomes distantly audible beyond 100 mph. Around town it is anti-social; it needs too much valuable parking space and uses a lot of valuable petrol. On the open road it is fun; it is immensely satisfying to drive smoothly but quickly and it is practical. The bad news is inevitably the price, which at £9,593 is expensive; we have judged it on that basis and it is still a superb but costly car. There is a strong case for using Aston Martin's leasing system through Forward Trust.

Two and a half years ago the DBS V8 cost £7,500—the firm was subsequently sold; however if one compares the 1971 car as a proportion of the cost of a house, the latest V8 will represent a lower proportion of the current cost of the same house. This Aston is demonstrably better in more than just detail and the company is back in business and there to provide service. No one can deny on these premises that the latest V8 is therefore much better value, if you can afford it. ○

*Now with four Webers in the Vee, the 5·3-litre V8 is a powerful untemperamental performer; compressor for air conditioning is on the left front. Interior is well laid out to transmit vital information and seats are comfortable.*

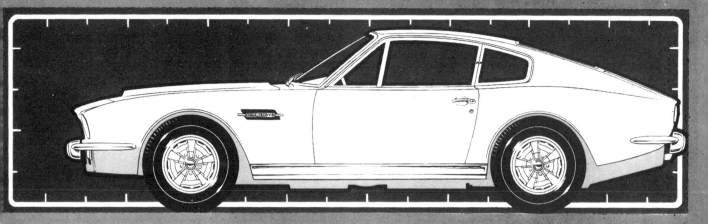

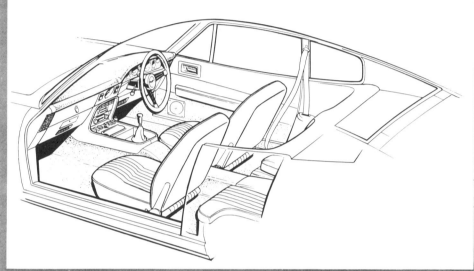

## PRICES

(Including car tax and VAT) : £9592·91

**Extras**

| | |
|---|---:|
| 1 Sliding roof, electric | 369·41 |
| 2 30-gallon tank | 57·20 |
| 3 Rear seat belts | 19·66 |
| 4 Two door mirrors | 22·88 |
| 5 Two detachable headrests | 47·68 |
| 6 Non-standard paint | 143·00 |
| 7 Non-standard trim | 143·00 |
| 8 Cosmic fire paint finish | 309·84 |
| As tested with 4, 8 | **£9925·63** |

## ENGINE

Capacity : 5,340cc (326 cu in)
Configuration : V-8 with dohc per bank
Bore×stroke : 100×85 mm
        (3·94×3·35 in)
Compression ratio : 9·0 : 1
       (100-octane RM)
Carburetters : Four Weber 42 DCNF
Power : Not given
Torque : Not given

## TRANSMISSION

| Gear ratios : | Top | 0·845 |
|---|---|---|
| | 4th | 1·000 |
| | 3rd | 1·220 |
| | 2nd | 1·780 |
| | 1st | 2·900 |

Final drive : 3·54 (3·31 option)
Mph per 1,000 rpm : Top 26·9
                 4th 22·7

## RUNNING GEAR

Suspension : Front, independent by wishbones, coil springs and anti-roll bar. Rear, de Dion located by 4 arms and Watt-linkage, coil springs.
Damper : Telescopic front, lever arm rear.
Brakes : Ventilated discs, inboard at rear.

## CAPACITIES

| | |
|---|---|
| Fuel tank | 21 gallons |
| Oil | 20 pints |
| Water | 32 pints |

## DIMENSIONS

Wheelbase : 8 ft 6¾ in
Track : 4 ft 11 in
Overall length : 15 ft 3¾ in
Height : 4 ft 4¼ in
Width : 6 ft 0 in
Weight : kerb with fuel for 50 miles
      34·7 cwt
Weight distribution : 53/47 F/R

# PERFORMANCE

**IN GEARS**

| MPH | Top | 4th |
|---|---|---|
| 20-40 | — | 5·8 sec |
| 30-50 | 7·0 sec | 5·5 |
| 40-60 | 6·9 | 5·0 |
| 50-70 | 6·7 | 4·8 |
| 60-80 | 6·2 | 4·8 |
| 70-90 | 6·4 | 5·0 |
| 80-100 | 6·8 | 5·2 |
| 90-110 | 7·5 | 5·4 |

**STANDING STARTS**

| | |
|---|---|
| 0-30 | 2·3 sec |
| 40 | 3·2 |
| 50 | 4·6 |
| 60 | 5·7 |
| 70 | 7·2 |
| 80 | 8·9 |
| 90 | 11·2 |
| 100 | 13·6 |
| 110 | 16·8 |
| SS. ¼m | 14·1 |
| SS. km | 25·2 |

**MAXIMUM SPEEDS**

| Top | 160 mph |
|---|---|
| Fourth | 136 |
| Third | 112 |
| Second | 77 |
| First | 47 |

(Third/Second/First) 6,000 rpm

**BRAKES** (from 30 mph in neutral)

| Pedal load (lb) | Retardation | Stopping distance |
|---|---|---|
| 25 | 0·19 | 158 |
| 50 | 0·66 | 45 |
| 75 | 0·96 | 31 |
| 100 | 1·00+ | 29 |
| Handbrake | 0·33 | 91 |

**FUEL CONSUMPTION**

(at steady speeds in top)

| | |
|---|---|
| 30 mph | 17½ mpg |
| 40 | 19 |
| 50 | 18¼ |
| 60 | 17½ |
| 70 | 17 |
| 80 | 16¾ |
| 90 | 15½ |
| 100 | 14½ |

Overall fuel consumption over 650 miles 13·0 mpg (21·8 litres/100 km)
Overall oil consumption 650 mpp

**STEERING**

Turning between kerbs : 38½ ft
Turns lock to lock : 3·0

# Lagonda name revived

### Four doors, better aerodynamics, and rivalry with Rolls-Royce are ingredients of new Aston model

Joining the ranks of the hand-built, four-door, super-luxurious ultra-high performance cars is a new car with a revived name: Lagonda. Although based on Aston Martin V8 the changes made are extensive enough to justify the title of "new car," for Astons are such a small specialist company that any major alteration is sufficient cause. At a price approaching £14,000 they make no secret of the fact that they regard the Rolls Silver Shadow as their main competition (although there are other rivals—the Iso Fidia, for example, or the Monteverdi) since they believe that the Shadow has been around long enough now for there to be a marketing slot for another expensive low-volume model. Their intention (provided their cash-flow problems can be overcome) is to produce only about one a fortnight (although to meet the initial demand they will make two a week for the first few weeks), so there can be no doubt that the Lagonda will be exclusive. The

original concept of the DBS Bill Towns-styled shape called for either a two- or four-door version so the re-engineering required was simplified by that much at least. One of the company's aims is to expand into world markets (60 per cent of the output will eventually go to America) and thus the new model will be called the Aston Martin Lagonda, linking it with a name that is more familiar through racing success rather than just plain Lagonda. The last Lagonda made, by the way, was the Rapide, dropped in 1963.

The major technical changes occur, naturally enough, to the body/chassis structure, the mechanical elements remaining basically the same. Both models are built up on a fabricated steel platform with load-bearing structures either end, but the Lagonda platform has been increased by exactly one foot, thus increasing the wheelbase (and overall length) by the same amount. Apart from being lengthened the chassis has

Styling very similar to the familiar Aston shape, but air flow should be better

been stiffened both in bending and in torsion by beefing up the side members of the frame: extra length means not just extra weight but also (because of the longer wheelbase) higher torsional loads. The suspension towers fore and aft are the same for both models, but of course the fabricated superstructure on to which the aluminium body panels are attached is altered to take the extra rear doors. All this has meant an increase in weight from about 3800 lbs to something approaching 4400 lbs, depending on individual specification. The extra length is all in the rear seat footwell area, while the roof line above the rear seats has been raised slightly: these changes mean that there should be more than sufficient space in all the relevant directions.

The engine is the well-known

four ohc (two per bank) all-alloy V8 in its latest Weber-carburretted form, and is identical to that in the V8 we tested last September except that the air-boxes for the intakes have been modified slightly to lower the line of the power bulge on the bonnet. Like their august competitors, Rolls-Royce, Aston Martin do not release power and torque figures, but the unit's output was sufficiently powerful to push our last test V8 to a mean maximum of 154 mph: the extra weight of the Lagonda will obviously have an effect on the performance, and Astons reckon on a figure of about 18 secs to 100 mph (the V8 took 13.6 secs) and a top speed around the 140 mph mark (although weight is up, the longer shape with the same frontal area should be aerodynamically more efficient). The Lagonda should

therefore be among the fastest of the specialist four-doors. Transmissions are either a five-speed ZF manual box or the Chrysler Torqueflite three-speed automatic.

Front suspension is by unequal length wishbones, coil springs, telescopic shock absorbers and an anti-roll bar, while a de Dion axle at the rear is located by parallel trailing arms and a Watts linkage, with coil springs and lever-arm dampers. Steering is power-assisted rack-and-pinion, and light alloy wheels take massive Avon GR 70 VR 15 tyres.

Aston Martin have great pride in the effort that is lavished on both the engineering and assembly of their cars—they would not fit a proprietary American V8 because they feel that they would not then be so exclusive and unique—and the standard of finish and comprehensive equipment of the prototype we saw more that justifies this pride. Power-assisted steering, a limited slip differential, electric door, boot and petrol filler cap locks, electric windows, a built-in radio/cassette player with microphone, all-hide seats, a fire extinguisher and (last but not least) a specially designed Coolaire air conditioning system are all standard. It would be tragic indeed if Astons were to go under in their present crisis (part of the cause of which was the development costs of the Lagonda) and we on *Motor* can only hope that the new model is not their swansong.

**Mike McCarthy**

Deeply-cushioned seats front and rear, with pockets in the seat-backs and console for rear seat passengers

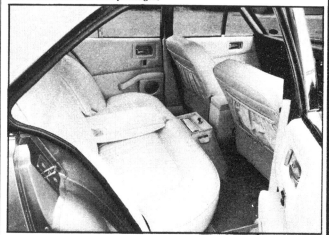

Comprehensive instruments and a good driving position, à la Aston. Below: engine bay is very crowded with Aston's own engine and ancillaries

# I TOLD YOU SO!

RAB COOK DRIVES THE LATEST ASTON MARTIN V8 AND FINDS IT IS EXACTLY THE WAY HE ALWAYS WANTED IT.

ASTON MARTIN

THERE ARE FEW things more flattering for a motoring journalist than to find that some manufacturer has not only taken heed of his criticisms, but actually done something about them. Even better when the manufacturer has ignored false-based praise from other writers (ya boo).

Thus it was when I drove the first Aston Martin DBS to reach the hands of the Press in Britain I thought it was a splendid car but . . . but . . . some things I didn't like at all. My colleagues all said that I was mad and that I didn't appreciate a real sports car and that the device was perfect and would I please go away and shut up and stick to things that I understood.

My contention was that they were still in a Austin-Healey 3000 frame of mind and that to them a sports car had to be a form of masochism. I felt that times were achangin' and there was no reason at all why high performance motoring shouldn't be allied with comfort. I have never been of the hairy knees and rucksack mentality.

My main criticisms of the DBS were that it was rather hot and stuffy inside and the engine was so inflexible that almost every change of speed called for a change of gear ratio in the five-speed box. It also looked a bit like a meat safe to the rear of the side windows.

Well, the years rolled by and the Aston Martin Lagonda company was sold to some people with a considerable amount of business know-how and a matching amount of money. That got the financial basis right. The first thing they did was to halt production completely (as well as sacking almost everyone within shouting distance) and then sit down quietly in a corner with the car in one hand and a sheaf of Press criticisms in the other. What our American cousins refer to as an agonising reappraisal.

When production started again, it was with a very different vehicle and the first 1974 models have just arrived here, imported by a new concern called Aston Martin Australia. I've just been driving one and I would like to say to the motoring writers of the world: "I told you so."

The Bosch fuel injection system has been replaced by four twin-choke Webers and that has had a magical effect on the flexibility. You can now motor away from 600 rpm on part throttle or give it the full gun from little over the 1000 mark.

Another major change is that the car has been fully "tropicalised" to make it suitable for hot country motoring. Thus it has enlarged water and oil radiators, extensive heat insulation, and full dehumidifying air-conditioning as standard.

The meat-safe louvres I objected to were replaced by glass earlier in the piece and a lot of minor improvements have been grafted in, such as a bigger boot and splendid seats with good mid-back support — in which connection, by the way, the pedals are two-position and the steering wheel is adjustable so, with the wide range of seat and back adjustment, you just can't fail to find the right position.

The minor controls have been brought up to date and even the dip-switch has climbed up off the floor on to a column stalk. There is flow-through venting with eight holes for the air to come in and there are none of the silly little things that shouldn't have been there in the first place.

Possibly the most welcome change is the incredible silence of the car. The original DBS had such a deep roar that it was physically tiring, mile after mile. Now, you can hear things working at low speeds but when you get over 50 mph or so there is this almost eerie silence — even well over the 100 there isn't the slightest trace of wind whisper, let alone rustle.

In other words, the Aston Martin has been completely civilised without in any way affecting the performance, which is what I'd always said was possible (yes, I know, but I feel so pleased about it). The manual version will hop from a standstill to 60 in 5.7 seconds with the auto only two-tenths behind it. Top speed is still in the 150 mph region and although AM don't release bhp and torque figures, its answer to enquiries can be one up on the R-R "sufficient". Aston can say: "More than sufficient."

Getting back to that 0 to 60 time, you'll find that only the manual De Tomaso manages to slot in between the two Astons, at 5.8 sec, and an automatic Lambo Espada is about a couple of seconds behind, which means the difference between right here and a speck in the distance.

The secret of the Aston Martin is, of course, the De Dion rear axle. It's all very well having a 5.43-litre V8 with twin overhead camshafts but you have to be able to pour the output on to the roadway.

This is where dear old M. De Dion comes into the picture. Every ft/lb of torque is turned into forward motion and if you take off after holding the car on the brakes, the automatic (which is what we'll be getting in Australia with the five-speed manual to special order only) makes an express lift seem like a high-hysteresis foam cushion.

# I TOLD YOU SO!

Wet roads, it goes just the same and even on a loose surface you can be pretty free with the weight of the right foot. The tyres, by the way, are Avon radial GR70/VR15, which is about as near as you can get to Formula 1 rubber on a normal car.

The brakes — Girling ventilated discs with triple-piston calipers — are every bit as startling. Not ultra-light in their initial application, they are beautifully progressive and, again, the car is so thoroughly clamped to the road that you can get away with almost anything.

The final attribute of the De Dion axle becomes evident when you come to a series of S bends. If you're a passenger you sit there in absolute terror thinking: "Bloody fool — he'll never make it — has he died at the wheel . . .?" Then

*Quad cam V8 engine now has Weber carburettors rather than fuel injection. Cook claims it is more flexible and far easier to manage in traffic.*

# I TOLD YOU SO!

you're through and thinking: "Blimey — I must have imagined the bends." As the driver in such circumstances you won't think that you've done anything at all unusual because nearly two tons of motorcar and people just stays dead flat and goes where it is pointed. The sideways g can be very considerable. But it just goes through, relentlessly.

Bumps you hear as tyre plop at low speeds, feel a little at town speeds, and don't feel at all once the car is cruising. Otherwise, the silence is broken only by the tape stereo speakers or the radio. Whisper sweet nothings to your girlfriend in the rear seats and the driver will hear you!

These are the main points of the car. Getting down to other matters, we have the aluminium body panels on a steel frame which is built on a box-member platform chassis. There are fuel fillers at each side and if you open them both — one to let petrol in and the other to let air out — you can top up the 21 gallons at a furious rate. That's a good point.

Rear seat room is much more than it looks and you can fit four grown men in the car — the doors are wide so there's no struggling. Every "extra" you care to think of isn't extra at all and here, too, commonsense has taken over. Like — you can operate the electric windows when the engine is switched off, how about that? Others please copy. And on the nose of the driver's armrest there is a switch which locks or unlocks the passenger door with a loud click.

What noises there are become more noticed in the general silence and, especially if you are standing outside the car, the starter makes a fair old clamor. Starting is instant from cold without using the choke, and can be just as quick from hot if you remember to open the throttles just the merest fraction and hold them there. If not, you have a typical V8 churn. The viscous-coupling fan whirs a bit at low speeds but goes quiet once the revs are up. Nothing sounds really rorty and sporty — it's more of a whispering giant.

The Aston Martin V8 is going to sell in Australia at under $30,000 complete with all doohickies such as heated window, Sundym glass, stereo player/radio, air-conditioning, the lot, and it is unique in having classically simple lines with no hint of spacecraft about them. It is a product of evolution rather than whim or sudden inspiration and you can somehow sense the 60 years of history behind it from the moment you get behind the wheel.

For people with that kind of money I'd regard it as a particularly sensible buy because I can't see it having heavy depreciation; it is an extremely practical car rather than merely a show-piece; it clings to the road so well that it is surely tops in the primary safety stakes; the alloy body should see out the century after this one; it is outstandingly swift (which is quite different from merely being fast) and very unobtrusive in the manner of its going, both to occupants and outside observers, and it is backed by sound organisations, here and in Britain, which must remove a lingering doubt from quite a few minds.

One other thing — it is exceptionally easy to drive and although the steering is powered it has the minimum assistance necessary and there is ample feel. Other than deliberately driving it over a cliff I just cannot see how it is possible to get into trouble with it.

This is just an appetite whetter — WHEELS will be carrying a full road test in due course once a test car is fully run in. For now, welcome back, Aston Martin, and congratulations on listening to the lone voice of one crying in the wilderness.

I *told* them — I said to them, I said . . .                                    *

# Aston Martin V8

**Now coming back into production, the Aston V8 is tried in its latest Canadian form.
Tremendous performance, even with lowered compression and an air pump.
Good gear ratios, though awkward change, and all controls positive if a little heavy.
Fuel consumption rather disconcerting, and range could be better**

AT THE turning point of Aston Martin's future it was known that extensive testing of their V8 engine in a form adapted to meet America's emission control laws was nearing an end. Subsequently, they have passed all the stringent tests, and the future sales potential of the car will be in the North American market, earning dollars for Britain.

At the same time, a restricted number of cars will sell in Europe, where the choice of exotic machinery has already been severely reduced by the demise of such names as ISO and the big question mark currently hanging over Maserati and Jensen. The important question for the potential buyer of an Aston is, how appropriate is it now for Europe?

Knowing the model well, as we do from three Road Tests of the body style dating back to the DBS, we have to confess that in some respects it has been slightly spoilt. In particular, ultra-safety devices required for America proved an infernal irritation, and by the time we returned the car we were heartily sick of buzzers to tell us to remove the key or close the door

or whatever, and the sheer stupidity of having to fasten the seat belt before the engine could be started – even if only to move the car a few yards. This

*The car tested was to Canadian specification, with seat belt interlock in the ignition circuit and impact absorbing bumpers. These items are not fitted for the UK market*

GMJ 313N

# Aston Martin V8

interlock is not fitted to UK cars, and is already redundant, even for America.

On the other hand, we were lucky enough to be able to take the Aston to Germany for the recent Frankfurt Motor Show, and had the opportunity to drive the car really fast, to pack large distances into limited time, and generally put the car to its real purpose for grand touring. In these conditions the car which seems so bulky and unwieldy in town or congested areas, really comes into its own.

## Performance

Since our test of the automatic version just two years ago, the compression ratio has been reduced from 9 to 1, and is now 8·3 enabling Regular grade 2-star fuel, to be used – inappropriate though this may seem for such a car. One or two petrol attendants raised their eyebrows somewhat when they saw us draw up at the "commercial" pump, Occasionally the engine ran on for a second or two after switching off but at no time did we detect any detonation, even under full throttle acceleration test conditions, in the higher gears.

Aston do not publish power or torque figures for the engine, so we can only surmise at the probable 15–20 bhp this has cost, in conjunction with other changes in the interests of reduced pollution. There is further loss of power in driving an air pump.

Four twin-choke Weber carburettors are fitted, as before, and although no doubt set for lean mixture, we found it was never necessary, even after quite a cold night, to use the choke control. Cold starting was always prompt, and the engine pulls strongly without hesitance or stalling, almost as soon as it has fired up. What it will not do, is to start promptly when hot. All sorts of techniques were tried – full throttle, no throttle, part way and so on – but it would seldom start without three or four long churning-over attempts on its very clattery starter. To anyone who has admired the car and stands awaiting the spectacular getaway, the process is rather a let-down.

Once running, though, there is nothing lethargic about the way the Aston goes. We found it took practice and care to make the best standing start, which involved an engine speed about 4,000–4,500 rpm, and simultaneous engagement of the clutch and flooring of the accelerator. This would then "break" the grip of the rear tyres, sending the car fairly rocketing off the line, snaking

slightly as the tyres began to bite.

It was suggested that faulty plugs, found when we returned the car, may have taken the "edge" off the acceleration. However, at 15·2sec, the standing quarter-mile-time is only half a second slower than before; and from rest to 60 mph in 7·5sec is not too badly down compared with the former 6·2sec. The 18·4sec taken to reach 100 mph from rest is getting close to the time the previous car took to reach 110 mph. It is still not slow, for all that, and the ability to attain 120 mph in less than half a minute is always the hallmark of a very fast car indeed.

Maximum speed testing presented some problems, as the power begins to tail off once 130 mph has been exceeded and it takes quite a time – gobbling up several miles of straight – before the speed stops creeping up. After many frustrations with traffic and weather we were finally able to satisfy ourselves that it had stabilized each way, giving a mean top speed of 145 mph. This is only ½ mph below the top speed of the previous car, showing that the reduced power of the engine is compensated by the reduced power losses of a manual instead of automatic transmission.

## Transmission

As fitted to the test car, a five-speed manual gearbox, with first gear offset to the left, and familiar H-pattern layout for the four upper gears, is the car's standard transmission. Although it is an awkward, clumsy change, we have to confess to coming to like it in time, perhaps because of the challenge it offers to the driver. The gear positions are very close together, and a little offset; the movement from first to second, in particular, is very exacting and does not take kindly to being hurried.

A suggestion of lack of flexibility of the V8 engine is really just a reflection of the very high gear ratios. Thus, one may feel irritated that the engine seems a bit lifeless at 30 mph in third gear, until it is remembered that this same gear will give a top speed of 110 mph. Frequent use of the lower gears has to be made around town; but on the open road the superb span of performance in each ratio is really appreciated, as indicated by the maxima of 48, 77 and 110 mph in the three lower gears. Fourth gear looks after most overtaking situations, but if the driver wants to be ready to sprint past something in minimum distance it is worth getting that rather awkward U-shaped change from fifth down to third done in advance, and then the car really answers magnificently on demand.

There is some not unpleasant gear whine in the lower gears, and some gravelly clatter if the

*A single air pump is fitted to the engine for emission control. Despite the cramped compartment, accessibility to almost all components is surprisingly good*

Aston is left running too slowly in fifth. The clutch pedal load is very heavy at 60lb effort; but apparently this, too, was a fault on the test car.

## Steering, ride and handling

Power assisted steering is standard, and works unobtrusively and effectively. One is aware that the steering effort is fairly considerable, without actually feeling heavy; and the accuracy is good. On some of the very narrow stud-marked lanes past roadwork areas on the German *autobahnen*, there is slight wander and a sense of uneasiness in passing heavy lorries in the adjacent lane, but this is accentuated by the great width of six feet. Directional stability is very good and blustery sidewinds have little effect on the car. The many miles we covered at extremely high speeds were all with complete confidence in the steering and straight-line precision.

Turning or parking, the power assistance enables one to switch locks quickly and without a struggle, but the actual turning circle at over 40ft is deplorable. If one has to turn in the road, at least the answer is known in advance: it won't lock round in one!

The enormous weight of 35½ cwt is well distributed, and the strong understeer is no doubt owed more to the steering geometry than to the presence of 18½cwt on the front wheels. The car sits down very well on corners, with no roll; if it is pushed through very hard there

*The basic flowing shape of the Aston has altered little. Rear quarter windows are fixed; the side windows are electrically operated*

is a slight corkscrew sensation as the back of the car tends to lift slightly on its de Dion suspension. The understeer is marked on tight motorway bends taken at high speed when one feels aware of having to pull the front round rather firmly. In all these conditions, the handling remains easily manageable and the driver feels fully in control. Wet grip of the Avon tyres also is good; if a slide is provoked it is of the kind which is graceful and easily checked.

Once or twice on the Continent, torrential rain was experienced, sufficient to reduce visibility seriously. In these occasions, aquaplaning of the huge tyres was felt, but even then there was no anxiety.

Although levelling out at speed, the ride is pretty harsh,

and there is a lot of wheel thump over bad bumps, accompanied by quite severe jolting. This harshness of the suspension was accentuated by inflating the tyres to the high pressures (40 psi) needed for sustained fast driving.

**Brakes**

Big Girling disc brakes are fitted, with internal ventilation both front and rear. They have divided hydraulic circuits and a twin-vacuum booster, and response is very reassuring. Pedal loads are fairly high, giving a slightly dead feel to the brakes at first, but if they have to be used in earnest from three-figure speeds they do their job magnificently. Fade tests produced a very moderate increase in pedal load, showing that in spite of the heavy demands made on them, they are well up to the task.

This is one of the few cars to retain a fly-off handbrake. It is well-placed beside the console and gives good leverage; in general use it is effective and convenient to use. On a steep gra-

dient, however, it has to be applied very hard indeed, and was even then barely able to cope with the 1 in 3 test hill. On this gradient, incidentally, a restart proved tricky because of carburation difficulties with the angle of the car. Also, due to the high bottom gear, a restart was possible only with controlled clutch slip.

**Fuel consumption**

In the early stages of the test we were rather alarmed to return a fuel consumption of only 8·6 mpg, but this was with some local running in dense London traffic, where the weight penalty plays havoc with the figures. Given the opportunity for full use to be made of the high gearing in fifth, the figures improved to a more tolerable 11 mpg in sustained cruising around or above the 100 mph mark, and nearing 14 mpg if the speed was kept around the 85 mph mark. Overall fuel consumption at 11·7 mpg is almost the same as we obtained from the automatic model.

One cannot hope for much more than about 13–14 mpg in ordinary driving, and for this rate of consumption a 21gal fuel tank should be just about adequate, but we question whether it really holds as much as is claimed. The greatest quantity ever put in was 15·6gal, after the gauge had snown Empty for some time and the fuel warning light had been on for some 30 miles. When filling up, both caps can be opened, and as they enter into a common tank, the unused one serves as a vent for rapid filling. Even with this aid, it takes a long time to get the last two or three gallons in to obtain a genuine "brim".

*Below left: Upholstery is in leather and the quality of finish is very good*

*Below: Rear seat headroom is rather limited but otherwise the seating in the back is comfortable*

# Aston Martin V8

## Maximum speeds

| Gear | mph | kph | rpm |
|---|---|---|---|
| Top (mean) | 145 | 233 | 5,400 |
| (best) | 147 | 237 | 5,450 |
| 4th | 136 | 219 | 6,000 |
| 3rd | 112 | 180 | 6,000 |
| 2nd | 77 | 124 | 6,000 |
| 1st | 47 | 76 | 6,000 |

## Acceleration

| True mph | Time secs | Speedo mph |
|---|---|---|
| 30 | 2·5 | 28 |
| 40 | 3·6 | 38 |
| 50 | 5·9 | 48 |
| 60 | 7·5 | 58 |
| 70 | 9·3 | 67 |
| 80 | 12·5 | 76 |
| 90 | 15·2 | 87 |
| 100 | 18·4 | 96 |
| 110 | 23·7 | 105 |
| 120 | 29·3 | 115 |

**Standing ¼-mile:** 15·2sec 90 mph
**Standing kilometre:** 27·9sec 118 mph

| mph | Top | 4th | 3rd | 2nd |
|---|---|---|---|---|
| 10–30 | — | — | 7·1 | 4·6 |
| 20–40 | 10·8 | 8·1 | 6·4 | 3·9 |
| 30–50 | 10·5 | 7·6 | 5·7 | 3·5 |
| 40–60 | 9·0 | 6·6 | 4·8 | 3·1 |
| 50–70 | 8·3 | 6·1 | 4·6 | 3·2 |
| 60–80 | 7·8 | 6·3 | 4·8 | — |
| 70–90 | 8·0 | 6·3 | 5·1 | — |
| 80–100 | 8·5 | 6·3 | 5·6 | — |
| 90–110 | 9·0 | 7·3 | 7·1 | — |
| 100–120 | 11·3 | 8·8 | — | — |

## Consumption

### Fuel

**Overall mpg** ..11·7 (24·2 litres/100km)
Calculated (DIN) mpg
15·9 (17·8 litres/100km)

**Constant speed:**

| mph | mpg |
|---|---|
| 30 | 18·7 |
| 40 | 19·9 |
| 50 | 20·2 |
| 60 | 19·4 |
| 70 | 17·5 |
| 80 | 16·1 |
| 90 | 14·7 |
| 100 | 13·2 |

**Autocar formula:**
Hard driving, difficult conditions
10·5 mpg
Average driving, average conditions
12·8 mpg
Gentle driving, easy conditions
15·2 mpg

Grade of fuel: Regular
2-star (90RM)
Mileage recorder: Accurate

### Oil

Consumption (SAE 20/50):
800 miles/pint

## Brakes

**Fade** (from 70 mph in neutral)
**Pedal load for 0·5g stops in lb**

| | start/end | | start/end |
|---|---|---|---|
| 1 | 40–35 | 6 | 40–35 |
| 2 | 40–35 | 7 | 40–35 |
| 3 | 40–35 | 8 | 45–35 |
| 4 | 40–35 | 9 | 50–35 |
| 5 | 40–35 | 10 | 50–35 |

**Response** from 30 mph in neutral

| Load | g | Distance |
|---|---|---|
| 40lb | 0·37 | 81ft |
| 60lb | 0·75 | 40ft |
| 80lb | 1·04 | 28·9ft |
| 100lb | 1·05 | 28·7ft |
| Handbrake | 0·42 | 72ft |

Max. gradient 1 in 3

## Clutch

Pedal 60lb and 5·5in.

## Test Conditions

Wind: 0–5 mph
Temperature: 18 deg C (64 deg F)
Barometer: 30·1in. Hg
Humidity: 30 per cent
Surface: Dry asphalt and concrete
Test distance: 2,294 miles

*Figures taken at 12,500 miles by our own staff at the Motor Industry Research Association proving ground at Nuneaton, and on the Continent.*

*All Autocar test results are subject to world copyright and may not be reproduced in whole or in part without the Editor's written permission.*

## Regular Service

| Change | Interval (miles) | | |
|---|---|---|---|
| | 2,500 | 5,000 | 10,000 |
| Engine oil | Yes | Yes | Yes |
| Oil filter | No | Yes | Yes |
| Gearbox oil | Yes | Yes | Yes |
| Spark plugs | No | No | Yes |
| Air cleaner | No | No | Yes |
| C/breaker | No attention necessary (Opus ignition) | | |

| **Total cost** | £28.75 | £52.81 | £79.03 |
|---|---|---|---|

*(Assuming labour at £4.30/hour)*

## Parts Costs

*(including VAT)*

| | |
|---|---|
| Brake pads (2 wheels) – front | £19.01 |
| Brake pads (2 wheels) – rear | £5.28 |
| Silencer(s) | £213.62 |
| Tyre – each (typical advertised) | £38.25 |
| Windscreen | £86.40 |
| Headlamp unit | £9.83 |
| Front wing (complete) | £249.48 |
| Rear bumper | £86.40 |
| Warranty Period | 12 months/ 12,000 miles |

## Weight

**Kerb,** 35·6cwt/3,990lb/1,811kg
(Distribution F/R, 52·0/48·0)
As tested, 38·9cwt/4,350lb/1,975kg

**Boot Capacity:** 8·9 cu. ft.

**Turning Circles:**
Between kerbs
L, 41ft 1in.; R, 41ft 4in.
Between walls
L, 43ft 4in.; R, 43ft 5in.
Turns, lock to lock 2·9

OVERALL LENGTH 15' 11·75"
OVERALL WIDTH 6' 0"
OVERALL HEIGHT 4' 4·5"
GROUND CLEARANCE 5·5"
WHEELBASE 8' 6·75"
FRONT TRACK 4'11"
REAR TRACK 4'11"

## Test Scoreboard

*Average of scoring by Autocar Road Test team*

**Ratings:**
7 Outstanding
6 Excellent
5 Good
4 Better than average
3 Worse than average
2 Poor
1 Bad

| | |
|---|---|
| POWER UNIT | 4·83 |
| STEERING AND HANDLING | 4·75 |
| BRAKES | 5·20 |
| COMFORT IN FRONT | 4·00 |
| COMFORT IN BACK | 3·29 |
| DRIVERS AIDS | 4·38 |
| *(instruments, lights, wipers, visibility etc.)* | |
| CONTROLS | 3·50 |
| NOISE | 4·17 |
| STOWAGE | 3·00 |
| ROUTINE SERVICE | 4·40 |
| *(under-bonnet access: dipstick etc.)* | |
| EASE OF DRIVING | 4·00 |
| **OVERALL RATING** | 4·18 |

## Comparisons

| Car | Price £ | max mph | 0–60 sec | overall mpg | capacity c.c. | power bhp | wheelbase in. | length in. | width in. | weight cwt | fuel gall | tyre size |
|---|---|---|---|---|---|---|---|---|---|---|---|---|
| **Aston Martin V8** | 12,765 | 145 | 7·5 | 11·7 | 5,340 | — | 103 | 184 | 72 | 35·6 | 21·0 | GR70/V15 |
| BMW 3·0CSi | 7,657 | 139 | 7·5 | 20·7 | 2,985 | 200 | 103 | 183 | 66 | 27·0 | 16·5 | 195 VR 14 |
| Ferrari 365 GT4 2+2 | 14,584 | 150 | 7·0 | 11·2 | 4,390 | 340 | 106 | 189 | 71 | 29·6 | 26·0 | 215 VR 15 |
| Mercedes Benz 450SLC | 11,271 | 136 | 9·0 | 14·1 | 4,520 | 225 | 111 | 187 | 71 | 32·9 | 19·8 | 205/70 VR 14 |
| Porsche Turbo 3-litre | 14,749 | 153 | 6·1 | 18·5 | 2,994 | 260 | 89 | 169 | 70 | 22·4 | 17·6 | 205-225/50 VR 15 |

**ENGINE**

| | |
|---|---|
| Cylinders | 8 in 90-deg vee |
| Main bearings | 5 |
| Cooling | Water |
| Fan | Viscous |
| Bore, mm (in.) | 100 (3·94) |
| Stroke, mm (in.) | 85 (3·35) |
| Capacity, c.c. (in.³) | 5,340 (326) |
| Valve gear | Dohc per bank |
| Camshaft drive | Chain |
| Compression ratio | 8·3 to 1 |
| Octane rating | 90RM |
| Carburettors | 4 twin choke Weber downdraught 42DCN F2T |
| Max power | Not quoted |
| Max torque | Not quoted |

**TRANSMISSION**

| | | |
|---|---|---|
| Clutch | Borg and Beck | |
| Gear | Ratio | mph/1,000 rpm |
| Top | 0·845 | 26·9 |
| 4th | 1·000 | 22·8 |
| 3rd | 1·220 | 18·6 |
| 2nd | 1·780 | 12·8 |
| 1st | 2·900 | 7·8 |
| Final drive gear | Hypoid bevel, limited slip | |
| Ratio | 3·54 to 1 | |

**SUSPENSION**

| | |
|---|---|
| Front – location | Wishbones |
| springs | Coil |
| dampers | Coaxial telescopic |
| anti-rollbar | Yes |
| Rear – location | De Dion, with parallel trailing links and Watt linkage |
| springs | Coil |
| dampers | Double-acting telescopic |
| anti-roll bar | Yes |

**STEERING**

| | |
|---|---|
| Type | Rack and pinion |
| Power assistance | Adwest, standard |
| Wheel diameter | 15in. |

**BRAKES**

| | |
|---|---|
| Front | 10·75in. dia. ventilated disc |
| Rear | 10·38in. dia ventilated disc |
| Servo | Two, vacuum type |

**WHEELS**

| | |
|---|---|
| Type | Cast light alloy, ventilated |
| Rim width | 7in. |
| Tyres – make | Avon |
| – type | Radial ply tubed |
| – size | GR 70VR 15in. |

**EQUIPMENT**

| | |
|---|---|
| Battery | 12V 68Ah |
| Alternator | 75 amp CAV 4C5A 12/D821 |
| Headlamps | Halogen 120/110 watt |
| Reversing lamp | Standard |
| Hazard warning | Standard |
| Electric fuses | 24, in passenger knee roll |
| Screen wipers | 2-speed with touch wipe |
| Screen washer | Electric |
| Interior heater | Water valve |
| Interior trim | Leather seats, Leather headlining |
| Floor covering | Wilton carpet |
| Jack | Hydraulic pillar |
| Jacking points | Two each side under sills |
| Windscreen | Laminated Sundym |
| Underbody protection | Undersealed over rust protection |

**MAINTENANCE**

| | |
|---|---|
| Fuel tank | 21 Imp gallons (95·5 litres) |
| Cooling system | 32 pints (inc. heater) primer |
| Engine sump | 18 pints SAE 20/50 |
| Gearbox | 3½ pints SAE 80 |
| Final drive | 3½ pints SAE 90 |
| Grease | 6 points every 2,500 miles 4 points every 10,000 miles |
| Valve clearance | Inlet 0·008in. (cold) Exhaust 0·012in. (cold) |
| Contact breaker | Opus (no attention needed) |
| Ignition timing | 10 deg BTDC (static) 30 deg BTDC (stroboscopic at 3,000 rpm) |
| Spark plug type | Champion N9Y |
| gap | 0·025in. |
| Tyre pressures | F 35; R 35 psi (normal driving) F40; R 40 psi (high speed) |
| Max payload | 750lb (340kg) |

*A lockable cubby box provides storage for cassettes and oddments as well as serving as an armrest; but it tends to get in the way of the driver's elbow when gear changing. The speedometer includes a trip mileometer and is calibrated to 200 mph, and is matched by a rev counter with red zone beginning at 6000 rpm. As well as an oil pressure gauge there are an oil temperature gauge and an ammeter. A Kienzle clock is mounted in the centre between switches for the electric window lifts. The wipers are controlled by a column lever on the left*

Care has to be taken not to open the boot when the filler caps are open, otherwise the forward edge of it fouls the open cap.

**Fittings and equipment**

Seat upholstery is in leather, and the general interior appearance is reasonably well up to the standard expected in a car at this price. In the practical test of long hours of travel the seats proved rather hard to sit on, but lateral support is good. Softer upholstery, and more support in the small of the back, would help for further comfort. The backrests are adjustable, though the hand wheel which controls them is rather inaccessible. Seat belts, with their inertia reels neatly concealed in the side trim, are standard. For access to the rear seat, the front seat backrests are released by a small chrome catch, and then tip forward to lie flush with the cushion. Rear seat leg and headroom is very much a compromise with the attractive fastback shape of the car; but usually rear passengers accept the slight restriction of space without grumbles, for the privilege of riding in an Aston.

Air conditioning is standard, with a switch marked Summer and Winter to put it into or out of action. There is no regulation of the amount of cooling provided, and it might prove rather marginal for some hot countries; but for use in Europe in hot September weather it was very satisfactory. The same cannot be said of the ventilation, which seems to lack adequate through-flow, and in rain it was always difficult to try to get the windscreen demisted. Even with full heat to the screen, misting up in the wet was a major problem. The rear window is well cleared by the heating element, although once the glass has been wetted by a moment of reduced speed, it is not subsequently cleared by the slipstream.

Instrumentation is comprehensive and includes an oil temperature gauge and an ammeter. The speedometer is rather small and calibrated only in 20 mph stages. It under-reads throughout the range by some 5 mph, so the driver who sticks at an indicated 75 mph on a British motorway makes quite good progress.

Good areas of the screen are cleared for the driver by the wipers, but on the passenger side there is a large unswept triangle. The worst feature of the wipers is their slowness – only 50 strokes a minute at fast setting, and 41 at slow position. The wipers are controlled by a column lever, which is pulled back to give a single wipe to clear spray.

A puncture involved us in a wheel change which was accomplished quite easily although the wheel is a huge weight to lift, and we had some reservations about the strength of the welded arm on the pillar jack.

**Conclusion**

Before contemplating an Aston Martin, one must be in the position to allocate an enormous outlay to both running and purchase costs. For those in such a position, the undoubted irritations and inconveniences of the car might come as a disappointment. But every time there was need to undertake some major journey, the real merit of the car would really come into its own, the more so if time was short giving need to press on at speed. For others who can only admire and pipe-dream, it is good to see this historic British car firm back in production and maintaining former standards.

---

**MANUFACTURER**
*Aston Martin Lagonda (1975) Ltd, Newport Pagnell, Buckinghamshire MK16 9AN*

| PRICES | | | Number plates | £9.72 | *Rear seat belts | £48.86 |
|---|---|---|---|---|---|---|
| Basic | | £10,910.00 | **Total on the Road** | | Headlamp washer/wipers | £105.30 |
| Special Car Tax | | £909.17 | **(excl. Insurance)** | **£12,814.42** | Detachable headrests | £42.12 |
| VAT | | £945.53 | | | *Door mirror | £21.06 |
| **Total (in GB)** | | **£12,764.70** | Insurance | Group 7 | *Side marker lights | £28.08 |
| | | | | | *Fitted to test car | |
| Seat belts | | Standard | **EXTRAS** (incl. VAT) | | | |
| Licence | | £40.00 | Electric sliding roof | £421.20 | **TOTAL AS TESTED** | |
| Delivery charge (London) | | Included | Overriders | £63.00 | **ON THE ROAD** | **£12,912.42** |

# ASTON MARTIN OF NEWPORT PAGNELL

*Motor Sport* visits the home of a great British sporting *marque*, recently saved from extinction

*Fred Hartley, Managing Director of Aston Martin Lagonda (1975) Ltd., left, with his lates product and former Technical Director Harold Beach (now Engineering Consultant), wh engineered the chassis and suspension of the DB4, DB5, Lagonda Rapide, DB6, DBS and V8*

THERE WERE TIMES last year when the demise of one of the most famous sporting car names, Aston Martin, looked not just possible, but a *fait accompli*. The Newport Pagnell company was in the hands of the Receiver after the post-David Brown owners, William Willson's Company Developments, had found their backs against the wall in respect of their small, though renowned, motor manufacturing interests. Most of Aston's special breed of craftsmen had been laid off, leaving just a skeleton staff to control clearing-up operations and restricted spares and service facilities. All attempts to rescue the company had either failed or been rebuffed by the Receiver, including a last-ditch effort made by the Aston Martin Owners' Club at the instigation of the late Dudley Coram.

But Aston Martin is made of much more resilient stuff than surely the Receiver could have envisaged. After all, it had survived many such vicissitudes since its Lionel Martin origins (as distinct from the earlier Bamford and Martin cars) almost sixty years before. This time good fortune smiled in the shape of North American businessmen Peter Sprague and George Minden, Aston Martin *afficionados* both. Their first attempts were shunned; finally, an offer of £1,050,000 persuaded the Aston remains from the Receiver's hands last June. Subsequently, further recapitalisation help came from Sheffield industrialist and well-known Aston Martin-owning motorist Denis Flather and another British industrialist, Alan Curtis. Lest we British take offence at yet another of our great traditions falling into the hands of foreigners, Peter Sprague anxiously points out that almost half Aston Martin remains British-owned.

With purchase, the new owners' problems had only just begun. All they had was a name and a shell; no cars in production, no men to produce them, suppliers who, with fingers burned once, were interested in recommencing business with Aston only on a strictly cash-on-the-nail basis. Their one big asset, though he would be loathe to admit it, must have been the former Director an General Manager, now Managing Director Fred Hartley, who had stayed on to worl with the Receiver and provided the nev owners with the essential continuity.

Whilst all the financial haggling an picking-up-of-pieces went on, there wer many, myself included, who thought any sucl rescue attempt was doomed, all the more se when the grapevine from Newport Pagnel went quiet for many months. Communication were re-opened at the beginning of last Marcl by Luton journalist Geoff Courtney, Aston' newly-appointed Press and PR Officer; ai open-day for the Press coincided with th first week of full production for Astoi Martin Lagonda (1975) Ltd. Re-recruitec workers had previously completed 40 car from parts produced before the collapse, bu that week five cars were completed fron scratch, a heart-warming exercise for the b now less-cynical journalists to watch.

Since then, a five car a week average ha been maintained and another visit I paid t the factory with Geoff Courtney recentl confirmed that production and enthusiasm amongst the work-force is back in full swing Fred Hartley aims for a peak of seven car a week to be produced by the current work force of 230, of which 50 per cent are shop floor workers. This contrasts pointedly witl the pre-collapse average ratio of six car from 490 people! In fact the factory capacity with an enlarged work-force, would be 1 cars per week, but Hartley believes tha Aston's success must lie in producing less thai customer demand to foster that very demand which depends so much upon exclusivity Presumably, such a policy must ensure a les problematical cash flow, too. A 70-30 pe cent export/home production ratio is being maintained, including the satisfying of ai order for 80 cars over a two-year period fron Japan, and the re-opened US market.

*Ninety-seven hours' work results in this stee platform chassis and superstructure.*

*Fred Waters, above left, puts 20 years' Aston engine-building experience to work on a V8, which will be tested later by Charles Haycock, left, on a test bed. Engines are carefully mated with chassis halfway down the production line, above.*

As befits something of a shrine for admirers of high performance, hand-built cars, Aston Martin's Newport Pagnell factory has history and character, if you can call character the fact that it is split in twain by the A50 main road leading from the M1, a mile away, into the Town. On the northern side lie the Enginering, Service, Spares, Engine Test Department and the all-important canteen, while south of Suicide Alley are all the production facilities and the Edwardian black and white house containing the offices. Production has been based upon this factory since 1963, when David Brown moved it from Feltham to the premises of the old Tickford Motor Body Works. Previous to Tickford occupancy, Salmon Bros., the coachbuilders, had been established there.

What is so admirable about Aston Martin is that practically everything is produced, or at least assembled or machined, by hand by their own craftsmen in this one factory: aluminium body; steel chassis and superstructure; that beautifully-engineered, four-overhead camshaft, all-aluminium V8 engine; most of the suspension, including the hubs and the De Dion rear axle; the exquisite, hand-crafted trim. Kent Alloy supply the 7 in. wide alloy wheels, Avon the GR70 VR15 Turbospeed tyres, Coolaire the air-conditioning, Lucas the electrics, Connolly the leather, ZF the 5-speed manual and Chrysler the Torqueflite automatic gearboxes, Girling the brakes, Ad-West the steering, Salisbury the limited-slip differential, Birmid or Aeroplane and Motor Aluminium Castings

*Bert Brooks applies nearly 50 years of craftsmanship to an aluminium front body section, below left. With the aluminium panels fitted to the chassis/superstructure, the body is ready for the first of 20 coats of paint, below right.*

the cylinder block and head castings, Hepworth and Grandage the pistons, Smethwick Drop Forgings the nickel chrome molybdenum steel forged connecting rods, to name but a few of the component suppliers who feed the craftsmen's hands.

Though Aston Martin Lagonda (1975) Ltd. cars look identical to the Company Development cars, some subtle and useful changes have taken place beneath the skin. These have been engineered by Mike Loasby, who rejoined the reformed company last October as Chief Engineer, a post with great traditions behind it in which this comparatively young engineer had been steeped as an Aston Martin employee up to 1969 when, while Development Engineer, he left to join Triumph, latterly as Manager of Engine Design. If necessary he can call on the services of Harold Beach, the former Technical Director, who is retained as Engineering Consultant. Loasby found much over-engineering in the existing car, particularly in the chassis area, to the detriment of production costs and ease and cost of servicing. For instance, as somebody who has never worked, nor paid for work, on an Aston I was astounded to learn that the rear seat trim and a metal panel have to be removed to change the pads on the inboard rear discs! The new Chief Engineer has re-sited the calipers on future production cars so that the pads can be changed from underneath.

The basis of an Aston Martin V8 ("DBS" went out when Company Developments came in), the only model in current production, is a 16-gauge sheet-steel platform chassis upon which is welded an integral box-section steel superstructure. The "production line" starts at the sheet-steel stage; this is guillotined and hand formed into the multiplicity of separate chassis parts, which are welded together by arc and gas upon an assembly jig. The complexity of construction is painfully apparent, another challenge for Loasby, who says, "I'm trying to get rid of this complexity, trying to make bits and pieces fit accurately instead of filling holes up with weld, which takes hours to do. I'm trying to avoid the

time-wasting hand production of tiny metal parts, too. The floor-pan structure alone took 60-65 hours to make. I've taken about 25 per cent out of that."

From the assembly jig the floor-pan goes to an inspection jig, after which the superstructure is welded up and closed over, by which time no less than 97 hours have been expended upon the chassis. Until Loasby took over there were different chassis for the UK market and the US market, the latter having a modified floor to take the emission catalyst in the exhaust system. Now the chassis, symmetrical in any case, before steering columns and pedal boxes are added, are identical, to US pattern. Small panels are pressed out on a rubber press.

From the jig, each chassis goes to a spray booth to be rust-protected and sprayed with a black finish. Then, almost magically, the black lump of steel complexity takes on the shape of an Aston Martin as pre-assembled front and rear aluminium panel structures are riveted on, clenched around the doors and welded on to the screen pillars. Fred Hartley pointed out that a great deal of

money has been spent on specialised arc welding equipment for the 16-gauge aluminium, to avoid the re-activation of fluxes which used to be a problem on Astons: "We shan't save initially with this equipment, but we shall save on warranty work."

Perhaps the most fascinating part of Aston Martin production is the hand-forming of those gleaming silver, aluminium body panels watching the virgin alloy take curvaceous shape around the confidently smiling grill aperture and the thirstily open-mouthed bonnet power bulge. This is craftsman's work indeed, typified by the oldest of the panel beaters, Bert Brooks, who started work in the same premises for Salmon Bros. in 1929, stayed when Tickford took over, worked on aircraft production during the War and has worked in this factory ever since, save for a brief and disillusionary period with Rolls-Royce between last year's collapse and the new company's formation. During my first visit, Peter Sprague had been quite eulogistic about Bert Brooks' craftsmanship on some cowls for aerobatic aircraft commissioned by the aeronautically-bent Director, Alan Curtis, adding that the company would probably produce more complicated aerofoil structures if these aerobatic aircraft proved successful. "We're looking for diversification if it will bring in money, but this won't be allowed to interfere with our main aim of Aston production. And micro-processing machines can't replace craftsmen in our sort of work." Sprague, it should be said, produces micro processing machines in the States, amongst many other interests. Indeed, this tall, affable and modest man, a truly Quiet American with an obviously genuine enthusiasm for Aston and all it stands for, has a fascinating background; his multi-lingual capabilities include fluent Russian, a reminder of his journalistic career with the United Press in Moscow in 1959/'60. Most of Sprague's time is spent running his businesses in the States, but his flying visits to Newport Pagnell for Board

:eetings and policy decisions are frequent.
:e's a sort of less flamboyant parallel to
nsen's former boss, the Californian Kjell
:vale. I wish Peter Sprague more success
ith his British motor industry venture . . .
:eorge Minden, equally quiet, but Cana-
an, the Aston Martin importer to
:anada with an undisguised admiration for
:errari too (and why not?), has settled in
:ritain where he spends at least three days
: week on Aston business. As Ferraris are
:ccasionally "chopped in" against Astons at
:e company's own London retail outlet in
loane Street, he can happily indulge in driv-
:g both his fancies.

But this is digressing. Once body panels
ive been fitted, the chassis/shells are pushed
: trolleys to one of two spray booths, one a
:ew gas-heated one from Air Industrial De-
:lopments and the other a Lee-Beesley, for
>raying with primer and a first top coat.
:p to 20 coats will have been applied by the
:me the finished car has been finally road-
:sted. The paint, from General Industrial
:aints, is sprayed on with hand-held guns
:d each coat is baked on in the aforemen-
:oned ovens. Always-exacting standards are
:ing improved still further under the new
:gime, for Fred Hartley spotted areas for
:nprovement.

From the spray booths the shells head for
:e assembly lines, little more than two long
:ts in the floor. Along the first south-pointing
:it the car acquires its suspension, slave
:heels, brakes and numerous sundries. At the
:uthern tip lies a most impressive bench-full
:f four-cam V8s, some with twin emission
:r pumps, denoting American emission en-
:ines, which will also have catalytic units
: the exhausts, others single air pumps, des-
:ned for the less stringent British and
:apanese markets. All have an exciting array
>efore being hidden by the air filters),
: four, twin-choke, downdraught, 42 mm.
Weber carburetters. Designed in the 'sixties
:y Tadek Marek, the then Manager of Re-
:earch and Development, firstly as a 4.8-litre
:nit, uprated to 5-litres for racing use in the
:wo Le Mans Lola-Astons in 1967, it was pro-
:uctionised at the end of 1969 as a 5,340 c.c.
:nit, initially on Bosch fuel injection. This
:ngine apparently copes easily with American
>w-lead fuel because of the alloy cylinder
:ead construction with valve-seat inserts.
.ower compression ratios are used on Ameri-
:an and Japanese engines. Mike Loasby
:laimed proudly that the engine's power is
:uch that it does the entire American emission
:st cycle on the idle cycle. The ratio of auto-
:natic transmission to manual vehicles is
:0/40 on average, but, "Occasionally we're
:aken by surprise and suddenly most Ameri-
:ans want manual again," said Loasby.

Once the engines and transmissions have
:een lowered in by block-and-tackle, the cars
:re pushed in a northerly direction up the
:arallel assembly line where trim, instrumen-
:ation and what-have-you are added gradu-
:lly, "gradually" being a euphemistic sub-
:titute for "with painstaking thoroughness".
Once the final details have been checked
:ut, oil, water and fuel added, the bonnet
:tted and a slave driving seat and slave steer-
:ng wheel fitted, to match the slave road
:wheels and tyres, the car is ready for road

testing by one of a team of four testers super-
vised by Bill Bannard. Each car is tested for
a minimum of 50 miles, sometimes rising to
120 miles if problems arise, on a variety of
road types in the Newport Pagnell area. Once
the car has been signed off as mechanically A1
it is checked finally for detail flaws, receives
a final coat of paint if necessary, has its correct seats, steering wheel and road wheels
fitted and instantly adopts the shining grace
of a £15,000 motor car. Such perfection will
have taken no less than 10 weeks to achieve.

While the bulk of the car takes shape, other
smaller assemblies are built up alongside the
main track. The De Dion tube is built up,
the Salisbury differential is mated to its inboard ventilated disc brake assembly and then
the whole axle assembled, and the front wishbone suspension prepared for mounting on
the car. Talking of suspension, the Armstrong
lever-type rear shock-absorbers are shortly to
be replaced by telescopic versions; a kit will
be available to convert existing cars. Also
alongside the track is the trim shop, where
the all-leather trim is meticulously crafted,
the recently re-designed front seats around
frames supplied by Deciform of Luton.
Interestingly, there is a service for rebuilding
seats for older Astons to original specification in this trim shop, a refurbishing facility
which is duplicated for mechanical parts by
the Engineering Department.

Astons rely on a general purpose machine
shop, their multifarious demands making
special purpose machines impractical. In here,
where Mike Loasby has employed a planning engineer with the intention of cutting
production time by 10 to 15 per cent overall,
practically everything for the car is machined.
An £80,000 Dixi transfer machine machines
the blocks, which then have iron liners
installed and other precision machining is
carried out on such things as con-rods, hubs,
wishbones, bearing caps.

In spite of the fascinating activities elsewhere in the works, the enthusiast's main
altar on his visit to this shrine must be the
engine shop. Three long-serving engineers,
Fred Waters, Sid King and Fred Osborne
(the man in the Duckhams advertisement has
left) build all the engines from the bare block
upwards, each man responsible totally for
an individual engine. One marvels at the
exquisite sculpture taking shape laboriously
on each engine stand, built to racing standards and capped proudly by four Aston
Martin Lagonda cam covers. Once built, each
engine is shipped across the A50 for testing
by Charles Haycock on a couple of old Heenan
and Froude dynamometers. During three
hours of running-in and testing, each engine
is run up to 4,500 r.p.m. after two hours and
to maximum revs for a full power reading
at the end of three hours. Full power? Like
Rolls-Royce, Aston Martin refuse to quote
power outputs, even in confidence, but I see
that Dudley Gershon, Aston's Deputy
Managing Director until 1972, quotes 345

*Phil Hill in Project 215, Le Mans 1963.*

b.h.p. at 5,800 r.p.m. for the earlier Bosch
injection engines in his fascinating book
*Aston Martin 1963-1972* (Oxford Illustrated
Press 1975). If rectification is needed, the
engine's own builder makes it before the
unit is finally signed off after 55 hours of
work. Sadly, Peter Sprague scotched the
legend that Aston's engine tester can tell
which man has built it just by listening to it.

The vast size of the service department
reflects its vital importance, "One of the
most important facets of the Aston Martin
image", says Gershon, in his book. Most
owners insist on factory servicing, especially
for more comprehensive work and prefer
the personal contact with the factory. This
was obvious during my last visit from Aston
V8s bearing number plates from as far afield
as the Middle East, Portugal, Switzerland,
Spain and the USA. From Aston's point
of view the practice is not only profitable
but ensures a direct feed-back from owners.
A service is offered for all post-war Astons
and Lagondas, while an occasional pre-war
example is tended, such as the 1936
Lagonda I saw on my last visit, which
was in good company with Peter Sprague's
mint, supercharged 4½-litre Bentley. Of
equal fascination was the last factory-built
racing Aston, Project 215, which had arrived
for conversion to road use (without detracting
from originality, I must add) for its present
owner, Malcolm Calvert, an Isle of Wight
hotelier. This was the Phil Hill/Lucien
Bianchi 1963 Le Mans car, reputed by Geoff
Courtney to be the first car to exceed 300
k.p.h. (186 m.p.h.) on the Mulsanne Straight,
though I have been unable to confirm this.
Perhaps readers can? The car retired from
Le Mans after two hours with its rear-
mounted gearbox broken.

So far I have made no mention of production Lagondas. In fact only eight of the four-
door Lagonda V8s introduced at the 1974
London Motor Show were produced, the last
one in the first week of March whilst I was
there. That one was to be taken to the
Aerobatic Championships at Kiev in August
by Messrs. Sprague and Curtis. Apparently
there were too many production engineering
difficulties to make this Lagonda viable for
production. But the name Lagonda is not
being allowed to die: wait for the Motor
Show for details!

A rather ugly, white, fixed-head sports car
observed from a distance proved to be not
an Aston prototype, but one of the ill-fated,
Canadian-built Bricklins, on which Aston
have been carrying out a £15,000 evaluation
contract for the New Brunswick Government,
to decide whether the bankrupt company is
worth rescuing.

Peter Sprague and his co-directors have no
intention of either following their Aston predecessors or Bricklin down the yawning chasm
of financial disaster. Nor have they any
ulterior motive such as asset stripping. "We're
doing it because we believe this car and name
should never die. We've acquired a tradition
and have a responsibility to see it go on."
That the tradition does and should live on
was obvious from my tour of this fascinating
factory, where visitors are welcome by prior
appointment. I am not the biggest fan of the
current product, though I am of its pedigree;
but to see the quality of construction has left
me with overwhelming respect—C.R.

# A GIANT STEP IN TO THE PRESENT

Great publicity stunt, they said (so did we) but it will never go. We're delighted to report that Aston Martin proved us wrong by connecting the back wheels to the V8 up front to start their development tests on the new Lagonda. Edward Frances has driven it

**HIS WORSHIP** the Mayor of Newport Pagnell may have been forgiven for interpreting the outburst of clapping and cheering when he appeared to switch on the town's Christmas lights as evidence of his own popularity.

Down the road at Aston Martin Lagonda they read it differently. The Mayor had unusual transport for the function, and Aston reckon it was that which drew the roar of public approval. It was their new Lagonda — theirs and Newport Pagnell's — making its first public appearance under its own motive power.

Even at this little Bucks town, where they are used to the odd miracle such as the survival of Aston, they had been worrying quietly about post-Motor Show murmurs here and there in the Press that doubted the seriousness of the Lagonda project. It had, after all, not turned a wheel at the time of the show. Was it, after all, just a brilliant publicity stunt?

So Aston decided to reassure the town that the Lagonda really did exist — and that it was no cardboard replica powered by an elastic band either. A couple of days later I drove it myself, and lived to tell the tale.

One cannot expect a prototype in its earliest development stage to reveal the whole truth about the car to be, of course. Only

days had passed since the essentials had been screwed into place, and the whiff of the adhesive they use to locate sound insulation still hung inside. Also all the flash gas-plasma analogue and digital displays were stripped out and mounted on a separate jig for the devising of a printed-circuit-and-jack-plug system suitable for the £25,000 production models. The first of those is due in the spring, production being at a rate of two a week initially, perhaps rising to four, with 100 orders already for which deposits have been paid, including 36 by British customers.

So — no intriguing touch-switch tickling, no digital figures to blink over or average speeds and fuel consumptions to command at the tip of a finger, no instant conversion of miles to kilometres and back again at will. This was the chassis and mechanical tuning test bed, and being newly assembled for road use (only 40 miles on the speedo when I caught up with it) it was being run quite slowly to keep Aston chief engineer Mike Loasby happy.

Since it was his decision to allow journalistic hands on his baby at this absurdly early development stage (has any other manufacturer ever let an outsider in so soon?), keeping Loasby happy was rather important. . . .

Not that this quietly-spoken yet

Above: stylist Bill Towns (left) and engineer Mike Loasby looking justifiably pleased that PUR 101R is now a runner, below

Above: as motor show visitors saw the new Lagonda with its unfinished but striking cockpit and disconnected engine, left

Left: the digital instruments as they will be when installed in the car. The running prototype uses conventional slave dials (not shown) and is the same car as that originally shown to the Press, below. Note the changed number plate

conversationally agile engineer is over-sensitive about the Lagonda. He readily agrees that touch-switches and digital displays are in no way futuristic or even man-in-the-moonish, though their presence in the specification did lead some observers to suggest that the car was some sort of escapee from NASA. Even Aston's own press-release writer allowed that silly word "futuristic" to creep into his enthusiastic handout.

"Yes, this technology has been around for some years," says Loasby. "You can find touch switches in hotel lifts and digital displays in cheap pocket calculators and wrist-watches. A touch switch is the same price as a push-push these days, and an analogue display costs the same as a conventional speedometer. It simply needed someone to package it all in an automotive context, and though this packaging is going to be expensive, with the Lagonda we have merely taken a giant step into the present."

Aston's size, structure and flexibility make it possible for the firm to conceive and design very much for the present, points out Loasby. Other companies design for launches five years away, and have to bear in mind what the public will want 10 years hence. But not Aston — they can react very quickly, probably more quickly than anyone else.

The short history of the Lagonda bears Loasby out. Only eight months elapsed between basic conception and the triumphant Motor Show appearance, and now, another six weeks on, the running chassis/bodyshell is doing roadwork, bringing practice to bear on theory, teaching its creators a thing or two.

The initial results? With no suspension tuning done, the car is extraordinarily smooth, level and quiet. I mean *really* smooth despite the scrap Avons doing duty at each corner: *impressively* level despite the efforts of that nasty bit of North Crawley road near Newport Pagnell which Aston use to test ride: and *genuinely* quiet despite the odd rub of rubber against wheelarches awaiting clearance modification.

In real terms, all that came through was the dull crackle of tyres on the road and a fine-grained tremor from the bitchy surface. For an undeveloped chassis the standards achieved were impressive, and a considerable tribute to the Loasby slide-rule.

I must emphasise the car's levelness. The moment you enter it, the Lagonda imposes a feeling of the horizontal — the strong flat facia line does that — while its interior dimensions both look and prove to be generous for four. And airy with it — although this is a long low car, glass areas and window width lend a fair greenhouse effect, heightened by the glass roof over the rear seats.

I had the oddest impression that the interior reached more or less to the limits of the body. Yet I enjoyed a very physical closeness of the type associated with a well set up sporting car. This intimation that I had the total span of the car within reach added con-

siderably to my awareness that the Lagonda sat imperturbably foursquare over a rutted surface and through bends.

And though in truth we were not really flying round the corners, such a flat ride achieved with so little suspension work remains as an abiding memory of the car.

This said, the deepest impression of all was left on me by the steering. Two turns lock to lock sounds like hard work in certain conditions, but variable-rate power steering evens the score, be the car in urban traffic or cruising the motorway, and I did some of both.

Probably only a driver who has weighed in his fingers and palms a tacky, draggy, positive, dead accurate steering which ing system knows fully what I mean, but the Lagonda has a dead acurate steering which points the car so accurately that you practically think the thing round rather than steer it.

This is a toothsome yet relaxing state of affairs, with a wholly comfortable but still attentive driving position that allows the forearms to purchase on the thighs with the hands located at 20 past eight. As a result of all this — plus the dimensional thing — the Lagonda "drives small" in a way that no other large car in my experience does. There was a bit of rattly feedback on harsh bends and the single-spoke wheel seemed rather bendy to me, but so many adjustments are under way that I am probably already out of date.

The exhaust system produced no low-frequency drumming and the William Towns body—which Towns himself sees as a conventional three-box job, plus some interesting detail, and certainly not as a rocket-ship on wheels — created no windnoise, at least up to the 80 mph I permitted myself on the M1.

The shape takes into account everything that Towns and Aston know about aerodynamics, and though these have been kept subservient to aesthetics, the drag coefficient is said to be very low and the turbulence extremely slight owing to the substantial wheel trims and their near-flush location. Loasby is keeping the photographs of tunnel testing and the resulting figures to himself, but he admits to being inordinately pleased that, in terms of Lagonda shape, theory and practice have proved compatible.

I was asked not to thrash this new-born prototype, so Loasby's thoughts on performance must at this stage suffice. But he is given to understatement, so his assessment of 0-60 mph in under 7s is probably modest.

The Lagonda kerb weight should be about the same as that of the V8 whose mechanical specification it shares, but since the drag coefficient is lower and the final drive ratio is 3.07 to 1 to get quieter cruising and a 140 rather than 155 mph maximum, the new car may have a sprinting edge on the V8 (which *Motor* timed from rest to 60 mph in 5.7s).

It was certainly impossible to remain unaware of the firmness of purpose lurking in the rumbled response to the throttle.

# 1984 for sale

*With apologies to George Orwell, we bring you
a car of the future, today. Dev Dvoretsky
reports from the home of Aston Martin . . .*

*ASTON MARTIN'S reliable 5.3 litre V8 powers the luxury "wedge."*

*OVERHEAD view shows the neat and unusual sun-roof.*

*CAPACITY is very generous, loads of legroom and a 16cu ft boot.*

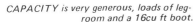

THE NEW Aston Martin Lagonda limousine is a remarkable car, produced by a remarkable company formed by five remarkable men.

Fifteen months ago the company was derelict. It was broke. It had failed. No one but those five unlikely men and a handful of others reckoned it could be revived. Even the receiver had his doubts!

Then in late June last year a young Canadian resteranteur-cum-car distributor and an even younger American chairman of an electronics group of companies, put up less than $1.5-million to buy the company. They were joined by Aston's one-time marketing director Fred Hartley 46, who had become managing director under the receiver, and two other enthusiastic Englishmen — aviation man Alan Curtis 49, and retired steelman and car enthusiast Denis Flather.

With what was left of a depleted and morally whacked workforce (some had left to work at Rolls-Royce and the now defunct Jensen), the Canadian, George Minden 39, a one-time philosophy and English student, and Peter Sprague 37, chairman of a number of companies including the National Semi-Conductor Corporation of California (22,000 employees world wide), and those three Englishmen set about putting Aston Martin back on the map.

They simplified and streamlined what is probably the only individual handbeaten metal production car line left in the world, gave it new heart and its workers new impetus. By March this year they'd got it working and were on their way (despite the critics who never thought they'd get there) to producing their break-even figure of 4.9 cars a week of the two door, two-plus-two sports limousine.

By the time they introduced the new Aston Martin Lagonda in October production was running at more than six cars a week — and the order books were full and expanding for months ahead.

*CONTROLS are all-electronic including a speed/distance computer.*

*STYLING is clean, angular and shows definite traces of Guigiaro.*

*NATURALLY the seats are power-adjustable, with electronic touch controls.*

ASTON MARTIN'S new super-luxury, 225 km/h, $30,000 plus, electronic Lagonda limousine takes the super-car from the drawing boards of the 1980's into the showrooms of the seventies. It jumps ahead that far!

It is a practical, safe, four door, four/five seater which can get to 100 km/h in 7 seconds and stop with the impeccable manners of its DBS sports car bred stablemate.

Its wedge-shaped wind-cheating angular styling, its excellent proportions and its modern internal electronic instrumentation and control are bound to make it a pace setter in design and function for years to come.

What makes it even more remarkable is that from the time the company's new chiefs gave the go ahead for a new four door limousine to the time it was shown with all its electronic gadgetry and specialised styling, took only seven months! And that included the initial styling dreamt up by DBS designer privateer William Towns.

When you think Astons were down the drain, virtually derelict only 15 months ago, that makes it a fair entry for the Guinness Book of Records. Built on a wheelbase of 2915mm the new Aston Martin Lagonda (to give it its full badge title) is 5280 mm long, 1816 mm wide and only 1302 mm high. It weighs 1727 kgs, and has a turning circle between walls of 11.5 m.

(Comparative figures for say a Holden Caprice or de Ville are wheelbase 2890mm, length 5180mm, width 180mm and height 1370mm. Weight of the Caprice is 1535kgs.)

Power unit is the now reliable eight-year-old 5340cc all light-alloy block and head, quad overhead camshaft Aston Martin V8 power unit. Fed by four twin choke Webers (Astons dropped the troublesome injection version even before the receiver walked in) and a 9:1 compression ratio, its output is "sufficient "!! (to borrow a Rolls-Royce cliche).

Leastways with those standing start and top speed figures its academic anyway and the makers won't reveal them. The AML comes fitted with three-speed Chrysler Torqueflite automatic which, like every other form of instrumentation and function, is 'touch' button controlled from a flat, figure-illuminated, glass panel on the right of the dashboard.

Like the rest of the controls and instruments they operate by a 'touch' of the fingers.

A limited slip differential and a final

drive ratio of 3.07:1 are standard. A five speed all-synchro gearbox is optional — but frankly I just can't see any prospective Lagonda customer wanting it.

Suspension differs only slightly from the DB 2-door with higher rate springs and the inclusion of self-levelling electronic ride control. There's independent with unequal length wishbones and ball-jointed king pins with co-axial coil springs and large diameter telescopic shock absorbers at the front with anti-roll bar.

At the rear the de Dion axle is located by parallel trailing arms and Watts linkage. The self-levelling system incorporates coil springs and telescopic dampers.

Steering is rack and pinion with variable ratio power assistance and only two turns lock-to-lock of the single-spoke, 14 inch, leather-trimmed, steering wheel. One interesting feature is that hydraulic pressure from the power steering which decreases as speed increases, is also diverted to turn a hydraulic cooling radiator fan.

Chief engineer Mike Loasby doesn't think there will be any problem with cooling the power unit though it "might be necessary to fit an air dam and provide air extraction in excessively hot climates". For the most part Astons believe no oil baron will have any trouble from the Lagonda which comes with electronically controlled air conditioning as standard equipment.

Brakes are ventilated discs front and rear with independent front and rear hydraulic circuits. There's a tandem master cylinder with integral servo and hydraulic fluid level, (fly off) handbrake and pad — wear warning lights.

Boot size of the prototype was 13 cubic feet — big enough for most but AML plan lowering the boot floor to increase capacity.

All doors, the boot and bonnet lids are hydraulic-strut assisted. The central 'B' pillar goes straight down from roof to chassis member giving just the extra inch or so to make for easier entry into the futuristic interior of the rear seat.

The seating, padded in soft, luxury leather, was designed for the Lagonda by KAN of Toronto. The seats are fully adjustable fore and aft, tilt of squab and seat and height.

The electric motor controls which make the adjustments to the seats appear beneath a black perspex trim running the length of the door in the form of a lower door capping. This applies in both front and rear compartments.

A touch of the required illuminated 'switch' will set the motors operating. But if you think that's something, you ain't heard nothing yet!

The entire instrument panel and all anciliary switches for lights, wipers, indicators et-al, plus the dual (digital as well as dials) rev counter and speedometer is hidden beneath the black glass — until the ignition is turned on. Then some of the magic comes to life.

The instrument panel includes a speedo with mph/kph changeover operated by a touch switch. The rev counter, oil pressure and temperature gauges, water temperature and fuel guages, voltmeter and ammeter gauges are all electronically displayed and controlled.

There are interior and exterior temperature gauges, a digital clock which also shows the date, and an electronically controlled display showing the average speed and fuel consumption on a journey, combined with a speed/instantaneous fuel consumption reading.

This display also has an elapsed time and distance reading and can tell the driver his average for the journey so far and what his average speed for the total journey will be at the speed control setting he has selected!

If you're not accustomed to the 20mm high digital readout for speed reading you can keep an eye on the circular spread dials for both revs and speed provided.

Sensitive 'touch' switches (the amount of sensitivity can be adjusted which amounts to getting a larger part of the finger pad on to the glass, thus providing 'pressure') control the side, head, spot, fog fascia and interior lights, the electric windows, door locks and the front and rear seat adjustment.

Additionally they also control the cruise control, the air conditioning, the two speed wipers which also have flick and intermittent facilities, horns, indicators and hazard warning light. And, of course, the Torqueflite automatic has

*SUPER LONG super-low, super-fast and super-comfortable — Aston's new luxury sedan took only seven months to come to life from the drawing board. Production is scheduled at two per week. Power is from Aston's own V8.*

fail-safe touch switches near the right finger tips to change gear if required.

The car abounds with great ideas — though strangely not yet with fault-finding interface under the bonnet for external investigation.

System's designer John Willis of Fotherly Willis Electronics of Leeds who adapted the touch switch controls and electronic circuitry says the computer box can be made to handle many other functions in the future. And that will include diagnostic parameters.

The idea of the touch switches came to Engineer Mike Loasby when he selected his floor by operating one in the elevator of a London Hotel. Later, on a visit to Peter Sprague's California electronics group, he was introduced to the company that makes them.

The new Lagonda also has a control of the steering column to adjust the position of the brake and accelerator pedals to suit the length of leg of individual drivers. There is a radio-stereo unit fitted as standard.

The armrests incorporate illuminated ashtrays and cigar lighters are located on all four doors. There are four reading lights and four further interior lights including footwell illumination.

Pop-up halogen headlamps provide the main illumination ahead but there are also two fog and two spotlights fitted behind a glass screen which can be used as "flashers" and provide in-town illumination.

The aluminium body is mated to a rigid steel superstructure and safety platform chassis. Sundym glass is fitted to the roof for rear seat passengers and used throughout the big glass areas of the car.

There are day-night intensity control for brake lights and indicators and red safety lights on the opening edges of all doors.

My only reservation to the electronic touch switchery is for night driving. So that the driver's eyes never leave the road ahead, I would prefer the glass panels in front of the switches to be indented or provided with some 'touch' recognition feature.

Aesthetically the flat glass panels maybe terrific, but they do require 'eye' recognition to locate. That, to my mind, is not safe, but I reckon the designer and the engineers haven't done a bad job — and indented panels with recognition notches built into them, shouldn't be too difficult to devise by the men who have pushed us through into the 1980's with car design. ∎

# LAGONDA: A FITTING REVIVAL

## Aston Martin brings back a great name in superb form by JOHN BLUNSDEN

The story goes that in 1897 Wilbur Gunn left his home in Springfield, Ohio, and headed for England to further a career as an opera singer, that apparently his voice turned out not to be so good after all, and that he ended up making automobiles.

He found a modest shed in Staines, about 20 miles west of London, built his first cyclecar there in 1900 and called it a Lagonda, which was a French derivation of the Indian name for Buck Creek, the stream near his old home. Lagondas were built at Staines right up to 1947, when the company joined Aston Martin as part of the David Brown Organization and moved to nearby Feltham. Later came a move to Newport Pagnell, 50 miles to the north, where Aston Martins have been built ever since but where the last true Lagonda was made in 1963.

Since then, several efforts have been made to revive the name, but each time the car (there have been eight of them) was simply a "stretched" 4-door version of the Aston Martin. Until a few months ago.

The Lagonda is back, as a car in its own right, with a completely separate identity and as a concept so ambitious and original that it took the London Motor Show at Earls Court by storm. The story had turned full circle, for once again the man behind it all was an American (Peter Sprague), in partnership this time with a Canadian (George Minden).

In 1975, when Aston Martin Lagonda Limited was liquidated, Sprague, head of National Semi Conductor Corporation of California, and Minden, whose car-sales interests in the Toronto area include the Canadian franchise for Aston Martin, joined forces and bought the company's assets for close on $2 million (the UK price was 1,050,000 pounds). With their three British board members,

managing director Fred Hartley, Alan Curtis and Denis Flather, they took stock, costed a return to production with an improved version of the Aston Martin V-8, went to the British Government for a loan, and when they were turned down by Industry Secretary Anthony Wedgewood Benn they decided to go it alone, taking a stand at the 1975 Earls Court Motor Show (before they had produced a car) as an act of faith.

By mid-1976 they had passed the production target of 4.7 cars per week to break even, were soon to put the 124-strong workforce on a promised bonus for hitting 6 cars per week, and were able to tell Rex Woodgate, president of Aston Martin Lagonda, Inc., that he would be getting more than the promised first-year allocation of 85 cars through his premises at King of Prussia, Pennsylvania, for distribution through the 14 reactivated United States dealerships. It was a remarkable turnaround for a company which so many had written off.

"The greatest spur we had," said Sprague and Minden at the new Aston Martin Lagonda's unveiling, "was Tony Benn's inference that we were not worthy of any government assistance, that we had nothing worth saving. That made us determined to prove, as quickly as possible, just how wrong he was. We've got back together some of the finest craftsmen in the British motor industry, they've done a fantastic job for us, and we've got a spirit, an enthusiasm and a will to work going for us that we just couldn't have believed was possible."

Right from the start the new board dismissed the idea that a Lagonda should be merely an elongated Aston Martin. The two makes were to be aimed at clearly defined, different markets and would therefore have their own individual identities. The Aston Martin would cater to the traditional 2 + 2 sector, the Lagonda would offer a new conception of luxury 4-door, 4-seater transportation.

With this in mind, William Towns, the industrial designer who styled the Aston Martin DBS when he worked for the company between 1966 and 1968, was commissioned to create a new product type which would integrate highly sporting characteristics with new standards of style, refinement, space, detail and finish.

The result, which took a mere seven months to convert from lines on a drawing board to a drivable reality, is arguably one of the most elegant wedges yet seen on four wheels. But if the styling is exciting, the interior and its equipment are remarkable. The latest Lagonda offers a new concept of luxury car accommodation and car control, including electronically controlled instrumentation incorporating both graphic and digital displays and elevator-type touch switches for all the controls apart from the steering wheel, handbrake and pedals. Mike Loasby, the company's chief engineer, is the man who has brought the technology of the electronics laboratory and the mini-computer into the driving compartment.

In place of a conventional instrument panel there is a strip running the full width of the fascia, with a further rectangular "read-out" panel above the steering column, coupled to a series of touch-sensitive control surfaces. Ribbon-style scales have replaced needles in creating the graphic displays.

Full advantage has been taken to exploit the wide scope which such a

sophisticated system offers. For example, the speedometer has a touch-operated mph/kph changeover, and there is an electronically controlled display showing average speed and fuel consumption throughout a journey, linked to elapsed time and distance, and instantaneous speed and fuel consumption readings.

A wide range of "conventional" information is provided, including engine revs, oil pressure and temperature, water temperature, fuel content, volts and amps, plus interior and exterior temperature, a digital date clock and a row of 16 warning lights.

More touch switches control the dual lift-up headlights, the side, spot, fog, dash and interior lights, electric window lifts, door locks, and the powered adjustment of rake, height and reach of the front seats and of the rake of the individual rear seats. The same goes for the automatic cruise control, air conditioning, automatic transmission selector and the screen-cleaning equipment. There is even a control on the steering column for adjusting the position of the pedals. In other words, there has probably never been such a complex list of information or control facilities offered to a driver in a car which, paradoxically, requires so little effort to drive.

Top-quality hides have been selected for the upholstery and much of the interior trim, and an interesting feature is a glass panel recessed into the roof above the rear compartment.

Each door has an armrest incorporating an illuminated ashtray and a cigar lighter. There are four reading lights, four more interior lights (including footwell illumination) and lighting for the glovebox, engine compartment and trunk. Tinted glass is used throughout.

By using the Aston Martin's 4-overhead-camshaft 5340cc engine, the Lagonda has been given a top speed potential of over 140 mph coupled to a 0-60 mph acceleration time of approximately 7 seconds. The choice of Torqueflite automatic or ZF 5-speed manual gearbox and the provision of a limited-slip differential, independent front and De Dion rear suspension, rack-and-pinion power steering and ventilated brake discs all around also follow the Aston Martin specification in general layout, although there are many detail differences. For example, the engine sits notably lower in the steel platform-type chassis of the Lagonda, to which the aluminum-paneled body is attached through a steel superstructure.

At 17 ft, 4 in., this is one of the longest cars produced in Britain in recent years, and at 5 ft, 11½ in., it is one of the widest, though a height of only 4 ft, 3¼ in. makes it one of the lowest-ever 4-door sedans. The wheelbase is 114 ¾ in., and the car weighs approximately 3800 lb.

Bearing in mind the incredibly short gestation period, I'm not at all surprised that production versions of the Lagonda may differ in a few minor respects from the prototype car which appeared at Earls Court. I expect, for example, that the trunk capacity will be increased beyond the current 13 cu ft, which is barely adequate for an otherwise so spacious 4-seater. At the present time the trunk dimensions are constrained by the huge 28-gal. (Imperial) fuel tank mounted ahead of it and the large cradle for housing the spare wheel underneath, and it is almost certain that the floor panel can be lowered to give some needed additional depth. It could be, too, that the center part of the radiator grille will be made just a little less austere, perhaps by incorporating a bolder name badge; this, incidentally, carries both the Aston Martin and Lagonda names, in view of the wider international awareness of the former.

The plan at Newport Pagnell is to build one car per week to start with, as a "market tester," then to up the output as necessary and establish a regular mix between Aston Martin and Lagonda production. If the costing works out the way the board hopes, then the price tag in the United States could be under $40,000, or about half the cost of a Rolls-Royce Camargue. In the ultra-exclusive world of automotive exotica, that must make it something of a bargain. Meanwhile, it's one heck of a car with which to revive the classic name Lagonda. If old Wilbur Gunn were alive, he'd be singing in the bath! ∎

# AMazingV8

**Forty per cent more oomph, tauter handling and equal the Vantage, the latest and most breathtaking version aerodynamic aids plus all the standard Aston luxurie of our home-grown supercar. Gordon Bruce reports**

BRITAIN came perilously close to losing a vital part of her motoring heritage in June 1974 as, but for the Eleventh Hour intervention of American and Canadian interests, Aston Martin and Lagonda would have faded into history. Since then our New World cousins have rekindled the spirit that won Aston Martin their coveted Le Mans victory and are accelerating the re-juvenated firm back to the fore of the automotive world.

What the company needed more than most was a new model, a prestige carriage to tap the interest and custom of the rich. Realising this a new generation Lagonda appeared almost overnight to steal the 1976 London Motor Show. In the shadow cast by the star studded attraction stood the model with which the company's fortunes had oscillated since October 1967: the Aston Martin V8 (née DBS).

Dismissed as anachronistic by the uninitiated and almost unknown to many, the V8 is worshipped by those lucky enough to have driven one. Perhaps it doesn't bear the sharp aggressive lines of the futuristic looking Lamborghini Coutach, or the relatively light, efficient frame of a Lotus Elite. But it does possess outstanding performance, and extraordinarily high levels of handl-

ing and adhesion which it combines with the traditional craftsmanship for which British cars were once renowned and after which many still hanker. Such comments are never more valid than when applied to the V8 Vantage, the latest and most electrifying version of the Aston Martin V8 yet.

The Vantage has considerably more power than even the standard car though as Aston never quote power figures, we're reduced to making an educated guess. Uprated camshafts, larger inlet valves and carburetters and special inlet manifolds must have raised the output by around 40 per cent however — meaning phenomenal power by any standards. Supporting the theory is the fact that when committed to the rigours of standing start accelerations AM V8 was said to be 37 bhp down on power yet still returned almost identical figures to our old pre-emission car of 1973!

Feeding the clutch in sharply with the engine howling in excess of 5000 rpm the Aston stormed off the line leaving a weaving trail of spent rubber in its wake. It takes bags of power and not a little adhesion to do that. The car reaches 30 mph in a mere 2.2 sec and in fact the number of current production cars that will scorch to 60 mph in under 6 sec can

44

The handling is a joy on any surface

be counted on one hand. What's more the experience is the type that sets your nerves tingling however often you do it.

Helped by the sheer precision of the superb ZF gearbox, the Aston's acceleration is relentless. There's only a hint of a pause between changes before you're pressed firmly back in the seat once more. Before braking for the ends of MIRA's one mile straights the car was pulling close on 140 mph.

Its ultimate speed? Well, it will pull its red line of 148 mph with disdain and has more than enough power to cap its predecessor's best of 154.8 mph, despite its special low final drive ratio. To match Aston's claim of 167 mph it would be pulling nearly 6800 rpm, a figure we have no reason to doubt.

Just as impressive as the flat-out acceleration is the uncanny pull in top gear. At a mere 1000 rpm in fifth, the throttle can be floored, opening wide all eight chokes of the fat Weber carburetters. So instantaneous is the response that cog swopping is often needless even round town. Even in its high state of tune the Aston's British-built V8 is totally untemperamental. It bursts into life with just a few pumps of the throttle whatever the ambient temperature, and when warm settles to an unfussed 900 rpm.

One of many minor changes that comprise the Vantage package is the raising of the fuel capacity from 21 to 30 gallons (an option on the standard car), a very necessary tweak when you realise that Aston's new road burner averaged exactly 10.0 mpg. Obviously we made full use of the available acceleration but were never able to cruise at sustained high speed. It seems reasonable to assume that fast trans-continental runs would have brought the figure even lower! However, we strongly suspect that the problems that caused the loss of performance also affected the consumption — 13–14 mpg being a more likely average.

We could find nothing but praise for the handling of our last V8 test car and if anything the behaviour of the Vantage was even more satisfying. Happily Aston Martin have done their uprating thoroughly and with the extra power come suspension and brakes to suit. Rubber has been used to give progressive springing at the rear and the diameter of the front anti-roll bar has been

A dated but none-the-less workmanlike cockpit. Little niceties include telescopic steering and town/country horn

increased. Koni telescopic dampers are now standard all round. Even wider section tyres on the standard 7 in alloy rims ensure further adhesion and a deep air dam for the front and boot lid spoiler for the rear are aimed at reducing lift and giving superior high-speed stability. The net result of these changes is a car that evoked fresh enthusiasm for driving on our over-crowded roads.

The Adwest power steering — full of feel on and off lock — combined with the predictability of the well sorted chassis, gives the effect of a car half the Aston's size and weight; a car that can be driven hard and with confidence. So adhesive are the fat, 60 series Pirellis that most drivers will rarely find themselves in true poses of understeer or oversteer. Suffice to say that if pushed to the limit in the dry or wet the weighty nose will cling on grimly, as will the rear, until deliberately provoked by the tremendous power. Only in torrential rain does the considerable width of the high-grip tyres call for respect, lest they aquaplane.

Huge ventilated disc brakes, slotted and set outboard at the front, inboard at the rear, wrench the Aston down from speed without any hint of strain glazing, noise or fade. The pedal is heavy, even a mite dead in feel, but the power of the dual circuit system is never in doubt.

Outwardly the Vantage is recognisable by its deep bib spoiler, the

blanked-off intake and radiator grille with its inset lights and the boot-lid spoiler. Some thought the aids detracted from the gracious lines of the original William Towns design, others felt they just endowed the car with an even more masculine, purposeful air. The sight of the car's bulbous nose is sufficient to move even the laziest of drivers from the overtaking lane of our motorways.

Inside there is little or nothing to give the game away. The seats are the same hide-covered recliners we enjoyed in the last car, and even the bank of instruments and bevy of switches all looked familiar. Time has changed and improved some items, however. The clutch was notably lighter than before, and the ZF box no longer baulked, proving sheer joy to use despite its old-fashioned dog-leg first to second change. The organ throttle pedal has been changed for a pendant type while the others still sprout from the floor.

Despite the auxiliary driving lamps the total light power seemed insufficient for a car of such extreme performance — perhaps they needed re-setting. Other lights exist in abundance, however, with courtesy operated ones for the interior, bonnet and boot, automatic ones for reversing and a swivel one for map reading. Other nice touches include the traditional fly-off handbrake, the town/country horn, the battery master switch, the telescopic steering column and the pair of fillers for the vast petrol tank.

At £19,998.81 the Vantage specification adds just over £4000 to the price of the everyman's V8. What's more, had that elusive 37 bhp been on tap at the time of our test the figures would more than have justified the cost. As it was the car completely re-awakened our almost unbounded enthusiasm for cars of its ilk. Far from being just a show-piece the Vantage is a true thoroughbred that combines the very best in performance and road manners with quality of workmanship.

Maybe it is both heavy and thirsty by modern standards, but it has more than enough power to overcome its bulk and has that feeling of longevity and well-being that is lacking in many rival supercars.

Exciting though their space-age Lagonda is, we hope Aston Martin continue to unleash their V8s on the world for many years yet. Speed restrictions or no, life wouldn't be quite the same without them.

One of the very few all-British V8s. despite its considerable output it is totally untemperamental. A joy to sit behind

## PERFORMANCE

### MAXIMUM SPEEDS

| | mph |
|---|---|
| Banked Circuit | See text |

Speed in gears (at 6000 rpm):

| | |
|---|---|
| 1st | 43 |
| 2nd | 70 |
| 3rd | 103 |
| 4th | 125 |

### ACCELERATION FROM REST

| mph | sec |
|---|---|
| 0-30 | 2.2 |
| 0-40 | 3.1 |
| 0-50 | 4.4 |
| 0-60 | 5.8 |
| 0-70 | 7.2 |
| 0-80 | 9.1 |
| 0-90 | 11.1 |
| 0-100 | 13.6 |
| 0-110 | 17.0 |
| 0-120 | 20.7 |
| Stand'g ¼ | 14.0 |
| Stand'g km | 25.2 |

### ACCELERATION IN TOP

| mph | sec |
|---|---|
| 40-60 | 6.9 |
| 50-70 | 6.8 |
| 60-80 | 6.6 |
| 70-90 | 6.4 |
| 80-100 | 6.4 |
| 90-110 | 7.2 |
| 100-120 | 8.2 |

### ACCELERATION IN 4TH

| mph | sec |
|---|---|
| 30-50 | 5.8 |
| 40-60 | 5.3 |
| 50-70 | 5.1 |
| 60-80 | 4.8 |
| 70-90 | 5.2 |
| 80-100 | 5.0 |
| 90-110 | 5.9 |
| 100-120 | 7.2 |

### FUEL CONSUMPTION

| *Touring | See footnote |
|---|---|
| Overall | 10.0 mpg |
| | 28.3 litres/100 km |
| Fuel grade | 100 octane |
| | 5 star rating |
| Tank capacity | 30.0 galls |
| | 136.4 litres |
| Max range | 300 miles |
| | 483 km |
| Test distance | 780 miles |
| | 1255 km |

### SPEEDOMETER (mph)

| Speedo | | | | | | | |
|---|---|---|---|---|---|---|---|
| 30 | 40 | 50 | 60 | 70 | 80 | 90 | 100 |

| True mph | | | | | | | |
|---|---|---|---|---|---|---|---|
| 27 | 36 | 45 | 54 | 64 | 74 | 84 | 94 |

Distance recorder: accurate

**Performance tests carried out by Motor's staff at the Motor Industry Research Association proving ground, Lindley.**

*Test Data: World Copyright reserved; no unauthorised reproduction in whole or part.*

## GENERAL SPECIFICATION

### ENGINE

| Cylinders | V8 (90°) |
|---|---|
| Capacity | 5340 cc (326 cu in) |
| Bore/stroke | 100/85 mm (3.94/3.35 in) |
| Cooling | Water |
| Block | Aluminium alloy |
| Head | Aluminium alloy |
| Valves | 4-ohc |
| Compression | 9:1 |
| Carburetter | 4 downdraught twin-choke Webers |
| Bearings | 5 main |
| Fuel pump | Twin electric |
| Max power | Not available |
| Max torque | Not available |

### TRANSMISSION

| Type | 5-speed ZF manual |
|---|---|
| Clutch | Sdp, diaphragm spring |

Internal ratios and mph/1000 rpm

| Top | 0.845:1/24.7 |
|---|---|
| 4th | 1.000:1/20.9 |
| 3rd | 1.220:1/17.1 |
| 2nd | 1.780:1/11.7 |
| 1st | 2.900:1/7.2 |
| Rev | 2.630:1 |
| Final drive | 3.77:1 |

### BODY/CHASSIS

| Construction | Steel platform chassis with steel superstructure and aluminium panels |
|---|---|
| Protection | Chassis sprayed with red-oxide and undersealed |

### SUSPENSION

| Front | Ind. by unequal length wishbones, coil springs, telescopic dampers and anti-roll bar. |
|---|---|
| Rear | Ind. by de Dion axle located by parallel links, with linkage, coil springs and telescopic dampers. |

### STEERING

| Type | Adwest rack and pinion |
|---|---|
| Assistance | Yes |

### BRAKES

| | Ventilated with radial slots, rear |
|---|---|
| Servo | Yes |
| Circuit | Dual |
| Rear valve | None |
| Adjustment | Automatic |

### WHEELS

| Type | 7in Aluminium alloy |
|---|---|
| Tyres | 255/60 VR 15 Pirelli CN12 |
| Pressures | 40    30 all round, ous |

### ELECTRICAL

| Battery | 12V, 68Ah |
|---|---|
| Polarity | Negative earth |
| Generator | Alternator |
| Fuses | 12 |
| Headlights | 2×QH sealed beam 60/55W plus 2 auxiliary driving lights |

# Aston Martin V-8

Each one is five months in the making.

PHOTOGRAPHY: ROBIN RIGGS

• As long as there are gentlemen, there will be gentlemen's cars. The grand marques of the world somehow survive all odds, perpetuated by sheer devotion long after their commercial franchises have expired.

Aston Martin is a classic case in point. The world's bad times finally reached this old-guard maker three years ago, and drastic action had to be taken. A plea to Parliament for financial aid only served to demoralize creditors, and when loans were denied the company was forced into receivership. But fate was not so cruel to permit the dissolution of 60 years of craftsmanship overnight. Two wealthy Aston Martin aficionados materialized from nowhere to rescue the honor of their marque, and this latest surge of enthusiasm is now propelling the firm somewhere in the gener-

al direction of tomorrow once again.

Anyone with the proper credentials can join this hearty fraternity. At $34,250 the dues are stiff, but this buys you more than a factory-fresh Aston Martin. You'll also own part of a legacy that dates to the original philosophy of 1913: "A quality car of good performance and appearance, a car for the discerning owner/driver with fast touring in mind." This creed stands for just the kind of social order any honorable individual could aspire to. There is no claim to being the world's quickest, the most up-to-date or the most expensive. Demanding recognition as the "best" is just not a gentlemanly thing to do, and Aston Martins are first and foremost gentlemanly.

This decade's Aston Martin is simply known as the V-8, and it's built exactly as past models. "Handmade" has real

meaning in this context—perhaps more so here than anywhere else in the world now that Rolls-Royce Silver Shadow panels are stamped by the same presses that make MG fenders. Mass production is just not good enough for Aston Martin. In fact, this company is so dedicated to perfection that its output volume is less than that other paradigm of British cottage industry, the Morgan Motor Company Ltd.

At Aston Martin, body panels start as aluminum sheets hand-beaten over wooden forms—because, well, that's how they've always done it. You may never appreciate such a detail under 26 coats of paint nor the dedication involved in a car that spends over five months in the hands of its makers. Nonetheless, the Aston Martin heritage is reason enough to build a car this way.

America's throw-away society may have difficulty coming to terms with an aluminum-bodied grand-touring original like the Aston Martin V-8, but the affordable replicas are in strong demand. The whole covey of Grand Prix, Monte Carlo, Thunderbird and Cordoba personal-status-mobiles owes its existence to the Aston Martin philosophy of motoring. The twenty-grand bracket contains additional subscribers to the four-passenger concept laid down with Aston's DB2 through 6 series of the 1950s and '60s: Mercedes-Benz, Jaguar and now BMW. Meanwhile, Aston Martin's original competition in the coach-built realm—Ferrari, Lamborghini, Maserati and Jensen—have all faded, leaving the V-8 as the sole survivor. It is one of the few remaining links to a grander era.

Speed was not so socially unacceptable yesterday, so the V-8 has a strong heart and long legs to carry it great distances quickly. Actually, this car started life with a broad mix of priorities that shaped it with great flexibility. The chassis came from the "steel safety plat-

---

**Driving is treated as serious business in the Aston, and the sweep of needles across dials tell you there are things you must know and do to be worthy of command**

---

form" introduced on the DB4 in 1959. A four-cam V-8 engine was tooled up for power, and prototypes were built in an aggressive-looking sedan configuration. This four-door, known as the Lagonda, gave way to a shortened-wheelbase design which is today's V-8 coupe. However, the sedan's influence did succeed in making this the roomiest and most comfortable Aston Martin ever.

This genesis took place in the late 1960s, and today the Aston Martin is ready for an American presence in the era of fuel efficiency, crashworthiness and near-zero emissions. It stands surprisingly undaunted by our tangle of regulations. The delicate bumpers have been granted a DOT exemption from the five-mph pendulum test. However, guard beams are buried deep within the doors, and other occupant protection paraphernalia is up to snuff. Catalysts and air pumps have been added to the exhaust

## ACCELERATION standing ¼ mile, seconds

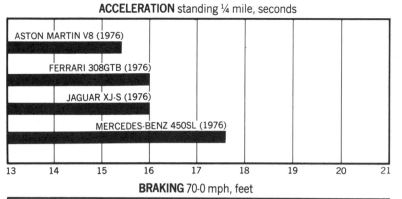

- ASTON MARTIN V8 (1976)
- FERRARI 308GTB (1976)
- JAGUAR XJ-S (1976)
- MERCEDES-BENZ 450SL (1976)

13  14  15  16  17  18  19  20  21

## BRAKING 70-0 mph, feet

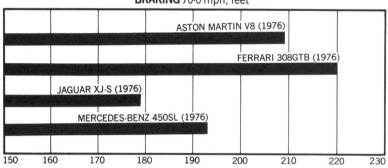

- ASTON MARTIN V8 (1976)
- FERRARI 308GTB (1976)
- JAGUAR XJ-S (1976)
- MERCEDES-BENZ 450SL (1976)

150  160  170  180  190  200  210  220  230

## FUEL ECONOMY C/D mileage cycle, mpg

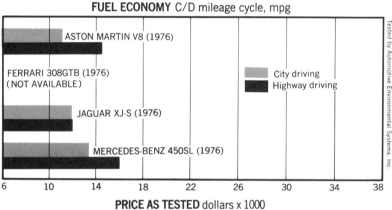

- ASTON MARTIN V8 (1976)
- FERRARI 308GTB (1976) (NOT AVAILABLE)
- JAGUAR XJ-S (1976)
- MERCEDES-BENZ 450SL (1976)

City driving
Highway driving

6  10  14  18  22  26  30  34  38

## PRICE AS TESTED dollars x 1000

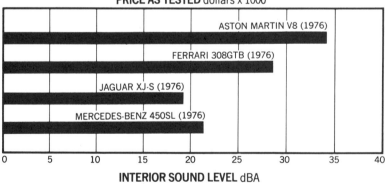

- ASTON MARTIN V8 (1976)
- FERRARI 308GTB (1976)
- JAGUAR XJ-S (1976)
- MERCEDES-BENZ 450SL (1976)

0  5  10  15  20  25  30  35  40

## INTERIOR SOUND LEVEL dBA

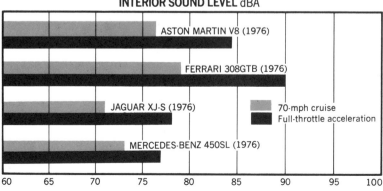

- ASTON MARTIN V8 (1976)
- FERRARI 308GTB (1976)
- JAGUAR XJ-S (1976)
- MERCEDES-BENZ 450SL (1976)

70-mph cruise
Full-throttle acceleration

60  65  70  75  80  85  90  95  100

Tested by Automotive Environmental Systems, Inc.

---

HEINZ MAURER

## ASTON MARTIN V-8

**Importer:** Aston Martin Lagonda Inc.
650 Clark Avenue
King of Prussia, Pennsylvania 19406

**Vehicle type:** front-engine, 2 door coupe
rear-wheel-drive, 4-passenger

**Price as tested:** $34,250
(Manufacturer's suggested retail price, including all options listed below, dealer preparation and delivery charges, does not include state and local taxes, license or freight charges)

**Options on test car:** Aston Martin V-8, $33,950; dealer prep, $300.

**ENGINE**
Type: V-8, water-cooled aluminum block and heads, 5 main bearings
Bore x stroke . . . . . . . . . . . 3.94 x 3.35 in., 100.0 x 85.0mm
Displacement . . . . . . . . . . . . . . . . . . . 326 cu in, 5340cc
Compression ratio . . . . . . . . . . . . . . . . . . . . . 8.3 to one
Carburetion . . . . . . . . . . . . . . . . . . . . . 4x2-bbl Weber
Valve gear . . . . . . . . . . . . . chain-driven double overhead cams
Power (SAE net) . . . . . . . . . . . . . . . . . . . . . . . . . . NA
Torque (SAE net) . . . . . . . . . . . . . . . . . . . . . . . . . NA
Max. recommended engine speed . . . . . . . . . . . . . . 6000 rpm

**DRIVETRAIN**
Transmission . . . . . . . . . . . . . . . . . . 5-speed, all-synchro
Final drive ratio . . . . . . . . . . . . . . . . . . . . . 3.31 to one

| Gear | Ratio | Mph/1000 rpm | Max. test speed |
|------|-------|--------------|-----------------|
| I | 2.90 | 7.6 | 45 mph (6000 rpm) |
| II | 1.78 | 12.3 | 74 mph (6000 rpm) |
| III | 1.22 | 18.0 | 108 mph (6000 rpm) |
| IV | 1.00 | 22.0 | 132 mph (6000 rpm) |
| V | 0.84 | 26.0 | 135 mph (5200 rpm) |

**DIMENSIONS AND CAPACITIES**
Wheelbase . . . . . . . . . . . . . . . . . . . . . . . . . 102.7 in
Track, F/R . . . . . . . . . . . . . . . . . . . . . . . 59.0/59.0 in
Length . . . . . . . . . . . . . . . . . . . . . . . . . . . 183.8 in
Width . . . . . . . . . . . . . . . . . . . . . . . . . . . . 72.0 in
Height . . . . . . . . . . . . . . . . . . . . . . . . . . . 52.2 in
Ground clearance . . . . . . . . . . . . . . . . . . . . . . 5.5 in
Curb weight . . . . . . . . . . . . . . . . . . . . . . . 4100 lbs
Weight distribution, F/R . . . . . . . . . . . . . . . 51.2/48.8%
Battery capacity . . . . . . . . . . . . . . . . 12 volts, 68 amp-hr
Alternator capacity . . . . . . . . . . . . . . . . . . 1050 watts
Fuel capacity . . . . . . . . . . . . . . . . . . . . . . . 25.2 gal
Oil capacity . . . . . . . . . . . . . . . . . . . . . . . . 10.8 qts
Water capacity . . . . . . . . . . . . . . . . . . . . . . 19.2 qts

**SUSPENSION**
F: . . . . . . . . . . . . . . ind, unequal-length control arms, coil springs, anti-sway bar
R: . . . . . . . . . De Dion, 4-trailing links, Watts linkage, coil springs

**STEERING**
Type . . . . . . . . . . . . . . . . . . rack and pinion, power-assisted
Turns lock-to-lock . . . . . . . . . . . . . . . . . . . . . . . . 2.9
Turning circle curb-to-curb . . . . . . . . . . . . . . . . . . 38.0 ft

**BRAKES**
F: . . . . . . . . . . . . . . . 10.8-in dia vented disc, power-assisted
R: . . . . . . . . . . . . . . . 10.4-in dia vented disc, power-assisted

**WHEELS AND TIRES**
Wheel size . . . . . . . . . . . . . . . . . . . . . . . . 7.0x15-in
Wheel type . . . . . . . . . . . . . . . . . . cast aluminum, 5-bolt
Tire make and size . . . . . . . . . . . . . Avon Radial, GR70VR-15
Tire type . . . . . . . . . . . . . . . . fabric cord, radial ply, tube-type
Test inflation pressures, F/R . . . . . . . . . . . . . . . . 35/35 psi
Tire load rating . . . . . . . . . . . . . . . . . 1830 lbs per tire @ 40 psi

**PERFORMANCE**

| Zero to | Seconds |
|---------|---------|
| 30 mph | 2.7 |
| 40 mph | 3.9 |
| 50 mph | 5.5 |
| 60 mph | 7.7 |
| 70 mph | 9.6 |
| 80 mph | 12.8 |
| 90 mph | 15.9 |
| 100 mph | 19.6 |

Standing ¼-mile . . . . . . . . . . . . . 15.4 sec @ 88.9 mph
Top speed (observed) . . . . . . . . . . . . . . . . . . 135 mph
70-0 mph . . . . . . . . . . . . . . . . . . . . 209 ft (0.78G)
Fuel economy C/D mileage cycle . . . . . 11.0 mpg, urban driving
14.5 mpg highway driving

system, but otherwise this Aston is pretty much as the Britishers think it should be. Craftsmanship pervades the whole car, so the view under the hood is just about as mechanically elegant as any automobile made in the last five years. Four two-barrel Webers stand neatly ordered on top of things, and the engine beneath has that fully-machined look of a Bugatti. Extraneous plumbing is at a bare minimum, and the necessities are neatly located and routed in such a way that the underlying beauty is intact.

The internal design of the engine is just as classical. Piston displacement is 326 cubic inches with a very over-square bore/stroke ratio. The block and heads are aluminum alloy with wet iron cylinder liners. Valves are operated by four overhead cams driven by double-row chains, and combustion chambers are hemispherical. Passages are almost a perfect tube per cylinder, from the throat of the Webers to the mouth of the catalytic converter. Horsepower and torque figures are not disclosed in another Olde English tradition, but the might is there to accelerate this 4100-pound machine through the quarter-mile with muscle-car dispatch. Interestingly enough, the landmark claim of 0–100 mph—0 in 20 seconds is just beyond reach. We clocked the Aston Martin V-8 at just over 25 seconds in this test.

You may choose a manual or automatic transmission to complement the well-mannered engine. The manual is a five-speed by ZF with but a single flaw: The "racing" shift pattern with first down and to the left of the H makes the one-two upshift cumbersome. The automatic is a familiar Chrysler Torqueflite.

The rest of the car is assembled with one predominant 1960s philosophy all but extinct now: Roadworthiness outranks ride comfort. Even though the engine is ahead of the driver, it's well back in the chassis to improve weight distribution. The suspension is unequal-length control arms in front matched to a De Dion rear axle located by four trailing links longitudinally and a Watts linkage laterally. Coil springs are used at each corner with concentric shock absorbers in front and lever-type units in the rear.

Suspension settings are decidedly firm, right up from the 35 psi tire inflation pressures up through the stiff spring rates and shock calibrations. Rubber bushings are very solid at control points, so there is little compliance over bumps. This results in a surprising degree of harshness on rough or grooved pave-

CONTINUED ON PAGE 143

Craftsmanship pervades the whole car, from the ordered intricacy of the engine to the hand-formed grace of the aluminum fenders.

# Driving Impressions

# ASTON MARTIN VANTAGE

*World's quickest production car?*

**BY DOUG NYE**

JUST THE NAME Vantage tells it all. It sounds like a cross between advantage and vintage and it's a perfect description of Aston Martin's upgraded V-8. I had previously driven the futuristic new Lagonda which Chief Engineer Mike Loasby calls "the bestest," and now in the modified Vantage V-8 he has tried to produce "the quickest." The object was to build a supercar that would out-accelerate and perhaps out-handle such confirmed exotica as Ferrari's Berlinetta Boxer, Lamborghini's Countach and even Porsche's Turbo.

It would be nice to record that the Vantage is everything Aston Martin claims it to be. Unfortunately I can't quite do that, but my reasons have nothing to do with either the car or its manufacturer. Instead I have to fall back on the British weather. After the harshest drought on record, we had the wettest winter since 1700-and-something. During the six days I ran the Vantage it rained pushrods virtually nonstop. When the clouds briefly parted I tried to record the kind of 5.3-sec 0-60 mph acceleration figures Aston claims, but every attempt floundered in runaway wheel-spin on greasy road surfaces.

Even so, my best times of around 6.1 sec were still shoulder-blade bruising enough to compare very favorably with the competition—0.6 sec quicker than R&T's Porsche Turbo time, 0.8 sec quicker than the Countach and more than a second faster than the Berlinetta Boxer! On a dry surface in still air there can be no doubt that the Vantage will blow them all into the weeds.

but dry figures are only part of the story. They provide the comparisons, but it's the feel which provides the fun.

That surely is what a supercar is all about, and in a heavy metal and decidedly masculine manner the Vantage is great fun. For example, on my first morning with the car it didn't actually rain when Geoff Goddard and I drove up to Donington Park circuit for its official opening. We left Geoff's Ascot home and arrived at Donington, 138 miles away along country roads, just 1 hour and 43 minutes later! Don't work out the average, it bends the rules a little, but that was a drama-free morning's motoring which left an indelible impression of the Vantage's advantage.

Loasby's initial targets were to find 40 percent more power from his 5.3-liter V-8 engine allied to 10 percent more torque. To avoid "odious comparisons," Aston has never released output figures for its standard V-8, but great attention to the Vantage unit's breathing must have boosted it to perhaps 475 bhp. Four 48-mm Webers replace the standard 42-mm units and revised-profile camshafts lift larger inlet valves, aspirated through re-shaped inlet manifolds. A new airbox sits above the rack of four Webers and with colder plugs than standard, the modified V-8 has a 9.0:1 compression ratio demanding 97-octane fuel.

Chassis developments include a heftier than standard front anti-roll bar, Koni shocks front and rear and a geometry change on the De Dion rear end to promote a different roll-steer effect. Slotted as well as ventilated disc brakes are used, derived directly from the V-8 which Loasby raced briefly in British club events last season. Wheels are 7-in.-wide cast aluminum 15-inchers carrying podgy Pirelli CN12 tires. Transmission is ZF 5-speed manual with a 3.54:1 final drive. A 3.77:1 ratio is optional.

To prevent this little lot from rising gracefully into the air, a fiberglass air dam is hung beneath the nose, slotted for brake and oil/water cooling, while the hood-mounted air intake is blanked off along with the standard radiator grille. In the wind tunnel, Mike's men found that only some 15 percent of the total airflow passed above the bumper in a standard shell, and of this only about 2 percent actually entered the radiator opening. With this intake blanked off to minimize drag, the engine still cools effectively on air entering beneath the bumper through slots cut into the air dam. The same holds true for the carburetor airbox. A pair of dipping spotlights are mounted on the radiator intake blanking plate, while the headlights are neatly fared in behind perspex covers. A small and unobtrusive tail spoiler fits onto the

trunk lid to balance the air-dam's effect up front.

The result is a handsome but decidedly brutish-looking machine which evidently means business. Inside it's a mid-Fifties racing driver's dream, with antiquated-looking chrome-bezeled instruments residing behind very reflective glass on a black-trimmed dash. One sits quite high in the hide-covered seats, but even so the commanding forward view is all hood bulge and lapped-up fender edges; the extreme nose is invisible. The fascia roll itself is high and a cowl forms up chin-high ahead of the adjustable 3-spoke steering wheel.

Vital instruments dead ahead of the driver include a 200-mph speedometer on the left, a tachometer redlined at 6000 rpm to the right and an oil-pressure gauge bang in the middle.

Down beside the driver's right shin is a fly-off handbrake (what a delight to use) while the lengthy ZF gearshift on its high center tunnel falls handily into one's palm. It has a typically Germanic gate, with 1st over to the left and back, leaving 2nd/3rd and 4th/5th in a normal 4-speed pattern, spring-biased into the lower plane. Reverse is to the extreme left and forward and in a sleepy moment it's possible to select reverse instead of 1st which makes for spectacular happenings as the traffic lights change.

Cold starting is no problem. A brief pump on the throttle pedal primes that rack of Webers and at a key turn the quad-cam V-8 whoops into life. Instant throttle response and an abbreviated overrun indicate a light flywheel, and blipping the unit as it warms up sends curtains twitching right down the street. The Vantage could be an exhibitionist's dream car but its muted gunmetal color and quiet exhaust make it more civilized than a $36,000 boy racer.

On first acquaintance I just couldn't sort out the gearshift. There's no distinct gate, its movements are long and limp and my first few miles were fraught with pregnant pauses as I searched around for the next cog. I was trying to guide the lever rather than allow its spring-loading to do the job for me. Once I realized this and simply began open-palming the lever forward and fingering

it back, allowing the spring to center it whenever 2nd or 3rd was required, the change became delightfully precise, marred only by a slight balkiness into those two ratios.

At low speeds, when not pulling, the V-8 burbles softly and almost inaudibly, but the high-price image is spoiled by an intrusive thump-thump from the tires and rattles from the suspension and body. Bumps and patches on the road surface snatch and tug at the steering which joggles the wheel against one's palms and such first acquaintance is frankly disappointing.

The steering is sufficiently power-assisted to make parking possible with that massive footprint, but it is heavy because sufficient natural feel has been retained to make it acceptable in high-speed motoring. The brake pedal has a very solid feel and at low speeds requires a great deal of pressure. In short, the whole car feels as though it weighs two tons, which it does, and feels and looks antiquated, which it is, up to a point.

That point is discovered on a better-surfaced road as speed builds up to 60-70 mph without wind noise, the road noise leveling away and a mild-mannered waft mutedly rumbling from those twin tailpipes.

Blipping down from 4th to 3rd is easy once one has mastered the gearshift's peculiarities. The V-8 gives a bloodtingling bark

surface.

Neither is there anything antiquated about the Vantage handling, for although it has a very mild initial understeer its characteristics become almost perfectly neutral with a tiny nudge of throttle. When its Pirellis let go they go as one and the car tends to slide bodily sideways in a predictable and totally controllable manner. The Vantage seems to be a victim of its own weight in that its outright cornering power is probably lower than that of a Turbo Porsche, for example, but it is essentially a magnificent example of balance.

Through all these maneuvers the driver is working fairly hard. This is no skippy little car that can be flicked about with wrist movements. The steering action has to come from the shoulder and after a long cross-country drive the effort required must do wonders for the circulation. It's not a car to take liberties with, although this is a function of its size rather than of any particular vice. In fact, it seems virtually vice-free, apart from a disconcerting tendency to weave when braked hard over bumps, deflecting the steering. I have no praise high enough for the difficult-to-obtain Pirelli CN12s, however, and even in streaming rain their drainage was beaten only once, and that was by hitting a puddle at least 2 in. deep at very high speed. Then the left front took off

## ASTON MARTIN VANTAGE SPECIFICATIONS

### GENERAL
| | |
|---|---|
| Curb weight, lb | 4000 |
| Wheelbase, in. | 102.8 |
| Track, front/rear | 59.0/59.0 |
| Length | 183.0 |
| Width | 72.0 |
| Height | 52.3 |
| Fuel capacity, U.S. gal. | 30.0 |

### ENGINE
| | |
|---|---|
| Type | dohc V-8 |
| Bore x stroke, mm | 100.0 x 85.0 |
| Displacement, cc/cu in. | 5340/326 |
| Compression ratio | 9.0:1 |
| Bhp @ rpm, net | est 475 @ 6000 |
| Torque @ rpm, lb-ft @ 5000 | est 440 |
| Carburetion | four Weber (2V) |

### DRIVETRAIN
| | | |
|---|---|---|
| Transmission | | 5-sp manual |
| Gear ratios: 5th (0.85) | | 3.01:1 |
| 4th (1.00) | | 3.54:1 |
| 3rd (1.22) | | 4.32:1 |
| 2nd (1.78) | | 6.30:1 |
| 1st (2.90) | | 10.27:1 |
| Final drive ratio | | 3.54:1 |

### CHASSIS & BODY
| | |
|---|---|
| Body/frame | steel platform with aluminum body panels |
| Brake system | 11.5-in. vented & slotted discs front, 10.4-in. vented & slotted discs rear; vacuum assisted |
| Wheels | cast alloy, 15 x 7 |
| Tires | Pirelli CN12, 255/60VR-15 |
| Steering type | rack & pinion, power assisted |
| Turns, lock-to-lock | 2.8 |
| Front suspension: | unequal-length A-arms, coil springs, tube shocks, anti-roll bar |
| Rear suspension: | De Dion axle on trailing arms & Watt linkage, coil springs, tube shocks |

on the blip, then the progressive clutch grabs, and as the right foot floors the throttle, the Vantage simply powers for the horizon with an unashamed bellow. Shoulder blades are slammed into the seat back. One's head literally jolts rearward. A finger-flick forward against the spring-loading grabs 4th and the Vantage is still pulling undiminished g. Staring eyeballs flicker to the tach—white needle nudging red—finger-flick back for 5th and, my God, there's still more to come. The Vantage's tail is still tucked down and its nose is looking into the turn which ends what was once a long, long straight.

Go in deep, bury the brakes, flick down through the gears and the Vantage has just about stopped! It's as bald and undramatic as that. The firm brake pedal feels unreassuring at first touch, but as those slotted discs heat up they bite with disconcerting ease. In fact, without locking a wheel, brake reaction through those fat Pirellis is sufficient to dust black marks down onto the road

for some yards before its sipes conquered and the tread bit down again.

Indications are that Aston Martin's performance claims for the car (0-30 mph in 2.2 sec, 0-100 in 12.7 sec) are perfectly accurate. Certainly the way it thumps itself up to 46 mph in 1st gear, then to 75 in 2nd, 109 in 3rd and 133 in 4th leaves little doubt in the driver's mind of what he has beneath his hands and feet. Still accelerating hard in 5th, it must run well beyond 160 mph and yet even at speeds doubling the British legal maximum the car's aerodynamic aids are extremely effective in maintaining a very stable platform. Crosswinds are of no significance and with those amazing brakes and easily neutralized cornering characteristics this is a supercar of considerable merit.

The Vantage has the Aston Martin image going for it, but against it must be its dated style and fittings, its heavyweight feel and perhaps its slowish ZF gearbox. I can't imagine the James Hunts and Jackie Stewarts of this world investing in a Vantage road car, but for a Mike Hawthorn or a Juan Manuel Fangio or a Froilan Gonzalez it would seem ideal. It's a hairy-chested man's car of surprising sophistication.

# A~M LAGONDA
## MOVE OVER
## ROLLS-ROYCE

The men of Newport Pagnell have never stooped to producing cheap or high volume cars in their pursuit of profits. They prefer to build big cars, fast cars and luxury cars — and the new Lagonda wedge is the grandest in the line. We drive the $250,000 prototype.

Even the greatest names in motoring are not safe from Aston Martin's latest effort to carve itself a secure and permanent niche. Today Aston's management is aiming at the Rolls-Royce and Mercedes limousine market with the striking Bill Towns' styled Aston Martin Lagonda model, which carries both these classic marque titles largely because Lagonda is not well-known outside the UK.

The new car is similar mechanically to the existing V8s, sharing the 5.3-litre light alloy V8 with a steel platform chassis, aluminium bodyshell, coil-and-wishbone front suspension and a De Dion rear end. But the wheelbase has

CONTINUED ON PAGE 56

PUR 101R

# MARTIN EIGHTIES

# VANTAGE
# WORLD'S FASTEST ACCELERATING PRODUCTION CAR

The format of Aston Martin's fastest road cars — big engine up front, bulky coachbuilt body and driven rear wheels — hasn't changed for many years and this has been a point of criticism of Aston. Nevertheless, with the Vantage, Aston Martin has built what it says is the world's fastest-accelerating production car. Doug Nye says it's also one of the very best . . .

"Vantage" — a word sounding like a cross between Vintage and Advantage tells it all. The old-established Aston Martin model name for a highly-tuned version of their basic product goes way

CONTINUED ON PAGE 57

# LAGONDA

been stretched 300 mm and Burman two-stage power steering has been specified for production to give finger-light parking yet allow some sensitivity at higher speeds.

SCW drove the prototype Lagonda, the very car which had reigned as queen of the last London Motor Show. Since its Show appearance the new car had been gutted and rigged with all manner of test instrumentation for its high-pressure development period. Nevertheless, we were grateful to chief engineer Mike Loasby for the chance to drive his valuable and (then) still unique baby. It wasn't disappointing.

This is remarkable, for the whole car was designed and built from a clean piece of paper to the London Show success in a little more than seven months. Loasby and Towns wanted a controversially-styled high performer which was lighter, simpler to build, quieter, more aerodynamic and

better-riding than its predecessors. The intention was to build a car to what people habitually describe as "Rolls-Royce standards" though Loasby points out that Aston Martin coachwork won the London Show Gold Medal in four straight years from 1972-1975 and so A-M feels it is Rolls-Royce that is trying to build its cars to *Aston Martin* standards!

Towns was responsible for the DBS and the earlier four-door DBS-based Lagonda four-door when employed by the company during the '60s and he now works as a freelance consultant. Loasby was head of Aston's experimental department from 1967-1969 before going to Triumph for six years. He returned as A-M Chief Engineer in 1975, at the time of the company's reformation.

The new Lagonda is based on a massive sheet steel structure built up around a beefy centre backbone which

encases the transmission line. Massive front bulkhead and rear axle tunnels form on to this structure, while a robust tubular framework is erected on this completed pan to accept the aluminium body and provide roll-over protection. A front subframe is bolted rigidly to the main structure.

While this chassis was being built in the experimental shop on one side of the road at Newport Pagnell, the bodyshell was being hand-crafted on the other. Production Lagonda bodies will almost certainly be produced by a new process using "superplastic" aluminium alloys which can be extended more than 10 times their original length when moulded at the correct temperature. This allows panels to be vacuum-formed in a single die. Tooling costs are roughly equal to Aston's normal cold-forming requirements but this system allows harder-grade aluminium to be moulded
CONTINUED ON PAGE 58

*Bulky but surprisingly light body of the new Aston Martin Lagonda. It takes some getting used to, but no-one can say it isn't different! Designers have tried very hard for optimum interior room with the best in aerodynamics.*

*Lagonda wedge uses A-M V8 engine. It has four camshafts, 42 mm Weber carburettors and drives through a Chrysler automatic gearbox. Performance is said to be commensurate with 5.3 litre capacity . . .*

# VANTAGE

back into the mists of the DB2/4 era in the early '50s, but the latest model to carry the name is an affirmation of the Newport Pagnell concern's ambitions to be, as chief engineer Mike Loasby puts it, "the quickest and the bestest".

Loasby returned to the Aston Martin fold following the company's salvation led by George Minden and Peter Sprague on June 27, 1975. He had spent some years with Leyland and was glad to return where individuality reigns supreme. In the Aston Martin Lagonda and the Vantage, Loasby's individuality emerges in the metal. During 1976 he raced his own Aston V8 and some of the experience he gained has been built into the Vantage. The result is a masculine modern sports car with real hairs on its chest, which simply outperforms such foreign exotica as Ferraris, Lamborghinis, Maseratis and — from a standing start — even a Porsche Turbo!

The works Vantage — carrying their "AM V8" registration — began life many moons ago as a standard V8 but it has been Vantage-ised in Mike's compact development shop to one side of the main road which bisects the Newport Pagnell works area.

Initial targets were 40 percent more engine power and 10 percent more torque than standard. To avoid "odious comparisons" the power output figure of Aston's standard V8 has never been released, but great attention to the Vantage unit's breathing must have boosted it to perhaps 320 kW. Four 48 mm Webers replace the standard unit's 42 mm throats, and revised camshafts lift larger inlet valves aspirated through reshaped inlet manifolds. They are fed by a revised airbox sitting atop the Webers, and so the 100 mm x 85 mm (5341 cm$^3$) quad-cam engine is just asking for harder plugs than standard — which it receives. With a compression ratio of 9:1, the Vantage demands 97-octane fuel.

Other modifications from standard include a heftier front anti-roll bar, Koni shocks front and rear and a "demon tweak" on the De Dion rear end to promote a different roll-steer effect. Slotted front discs derive directly from racing experience while chunky seven-inch wide cast aluminium 15-inch wheels carry podgy Pirelli CN12 255/60-15 tyres. The five-speed all-syncromesh ZF manual gearbox drives to a 3.54:1 final drive with an optional 3.77 available.

To prevent this little lot rising gracefully into air at speed, a fibreglass front air-dam is hung beneath the nose, slotted for brake and radiator cooling, while the bonnet-top air intake is blanked off and a GRP tail spoiler sprouts from the boot lid. The radiator air intake of the standard shell is also blanked off, the blanking plates also housing a pair of dipping spotlights which effectively form another pair of headlamps. The headlamps themselves are neatly faired-in behind perspex covers.

The result is a handsome but decidedly brutish-looking machine which evidently means business. Starting cold is no problem. Just a brief pump on the throttle pedal primes that rack of Webers and at a key-turn the V8 whoops into life. Instant throttle

response and abbreviated over-run indicate a light flywheel, and blipping the unit as it warms up sends curtains twitching right down the street! It should make the Vantage an exhibitionist's dream car, but out on the road AM V8's muted gunmetal color and effective silencing made it a civilised sports car rather than a boy's racer.

One sits quite high in the leather seats, but only commands a view past rather than over the bonnet-top bulge. The facia roll is quite high and a cowl forms up over the instrument panel ahead of the adjustable steering wheel. The panel itself is black-lined, carrying antiquated-looking instruments with chrome surrounds and unfortunately highly-reflective glasses. The oil pressure gauge is placed squarely before you

CONTINUED ON PAGE 59

Vantage is styled in the typical Aston way but extra-fat tyres and great big front air dam give a clue that this car is capable of even bigger things than "ordinary" Astons.

Vantage interior is vintage Aston — leather and carpeting in the old Pom tradition and instruments whose faces haven't changed for years. Author Nye says it even smells right.

# LAGONDA

into more complex but more easily-assembled shapes.

Target weight for the Aston Martin Lagonda is under 1720 kg, or around 40 kg less than the much smaller two-door V8 and approaching 320 kg less than the preceding four-door Lagonda. Front suspension geometry has been altered to keep the heavily-laden outside wheel vertical in corners. Each front suspension assembly is 10 kg lighter than before as part of Mike Loasby's war on weight in general and on unsprung weight in particular. In production, aluminium brake calipers may be adopted to reduce weight still further. The De Dion tube is located by parallel radius rods and a transverse Watts linkage at the rear, while the coil-springs are co-axial with Koni self-levelling shock absorbers. Rear disc brakes are mounted inboard with independent front/rear hydraulics, servo-boosted.

The quad-cam V8 is standard, running 42 mm Webers and mated to a Chrysler Torqueflite three-speed auto transmission. A ZF five-speed manual will also be offered in production. Gear selection for the Torqueflite will be made by touch switches in the production cars. This brings us to the car's space-age instrumentation and switch gear which has attracted so much publicity.

Mike first saw gas plasma instrument displays during a visit to Aston co-chairman Peter Sprague's Californian electronics factory in 1975. The touch switches are actuated simply by brushing a finger tip against the appropriate section of a fixed illuminated panel. The difference in resistance as moist skin touches the panel is sufficient to trip its associated switch gear. Glowing graphic and digital instrument displays can provide alternative mph or km/h speedo readouts, plus instant average speed and fuel consumption calculations if you want them. Add all the usual instruments, all displayed on what is just a black translucent panel with the ignition switched off, and 16 warning lights and you have one of the best-instrumented cars in history.

Touch-switch panels set into the doors provide window-lift, door-locking and seat adjustment, while both steering column and foot pedals positions are also adjustable. A monster 136-litre fuel tank wraps over the rear suspension bay and there are gas control struts on every door to prevent injurious slamming!

When I found myself seated in the driver's seat of the prototype I felt tense. Gazing through that panoramic wrap-round of a windscreen at the misty, slippery outside world my thoughts tumbled over each other. Obviously it was my duty to extend the thing, to explore its abilities, but should I bend it or have someone drive into me, Aston's programme would be hamstrung and valuable time would be lost. Mike Loasby fussed like a mother hen and I must say I sympathised with him. He'd had bad experiences of journalists, he said, and he eyed me with undisguised suspicion.

So I tried to reassure him, explained my feelings, turned the key and away we motored. Lagonda number one was a rolling testbed after its brief Earls Court glory. All the futuristic instrumentation had been removed, and there weren't even proper door seals to kill wind and road noise. An experimental valve fitted to the hydraulic fan that morning

CONTINUED ON PAGE 60

PUR 101R

58

# VANTAGE

between the left-hand 200 mph speedometer and the right-hand tacho red-lined at 6000 rpm. Water and oil temperature gauges reside to the right while ammeter and a rather depressingly fast-moving fuel gauge sit to the left. A right-hand column stalk operates indicators and headlamp dip/flash while the left-hand lever provides wiper control.

The long ZF gearchange lever falls handily into your palm on the humped centre tunnel, with its first gear to the left and back, reverse to the left and forward, and second/third gear spring-loaded into the centre plane, forward and back. There is no distinct gate in this change, and my first few miles were fraught with pregnant pauses as I searched around for a cog. My problem was that I was trying to guide the lever rather than allowing its spring-loading to do the job for me. Once I twigged the problem and simply began open-palming the lever forward and fingering it back the change became delightfully quick and precise, marred only by a slight syncro baulk into second and third.

The steering is power-assisted sufficiently to make parking possible with those massive tyres, but with sufficient natural feel retained to make it acceptable in high-speed motoring it is heavy. This isn't a nimble little thing which can be leaned through esses with a flick of the fingers. The steering movement has to come from the shoulders, and a long cross-country drive leaves your arms tired.

At slowish speeds when not pulling the V8 burbles almost inaudibly, though a thump-thump from the tyres and suspension spoils the opulent air. Bumps and road surface patches snag and tug at the steering which joggles against your hands, and such first acquaintance is disappointing. Then on to a better road, speed building up to 100-110 km/h, no wind noise at all, the road noise has gone and there's a mild-mannered waft from those twin exhaust tail pipes.

Knock the shift lever forward out of fifth, allow it to centre on its spring-loading into the second/third plane and tap it neatly back into third. This is a slick movement. The V8 doesn't so much bark as *shout* on the blip, then the progressive clutch takes up drive again, right foot floors the throttle and with an unashamed bellow the Vantage powers for the horizon. Shoulder blades slam back into the seat squab, one's head jolts back, the car's bulbous nose is lifting and the road is streaming faster and faster beneath that air-dam as long straights become fleeting blasts, gentle curves become corners.

Tap the gearlever towards the steering wheel rim for fourth. The same effect, pulling like a Trojan. Up to the red-line, flick back for fifth and still there's more to come, that gunmetal nose still up in the air and searching for the horizon.

Now a blind hairpin approaches, at 4500 rpm in fifth, that's 190 km/h. Go in deep, bury your foot in the brakes, flick down through the gears. The brake pedal is firm and at first not too assuring as the slotted discs heat-up. They feel unprogressive but the Vantage is squatting firmly, trying to bury itself in the road surface. We are slowed and set-up long before the corner so you roll off the brakes and *accelerate* into it! A check later shows four even black lines dusted on to the road surface by braking reaction through those superb

CONTINUED ON PAGE 61

# LAGONDA

proved noisy and began to moan immediately the engine fired. Mike had explained that he was aiming for Rolls-Royce-like quiet and refinement, but in these circumstances it wasn't obvious. At low speeds the Lagonda was quiet, just the same.

The good news was the car's unbelievable ride quality, combined with quite the best power steering I have used. Even without the intended two-stage assistance the new front-end geometry allows light steering but retains ample feel. In fact the Lagonda felt more like a light car than a large and relatively hefty limousine. It felt more like a well-developed rack and pinion, and I was deeply impressed.

Mike then pointed out that we were on one of the roughest roads in Buckinghamshire. I slowed to a crawl and sure enough the Lagonda had to climb and bump over an endless succession of ripples and potholes. Accelerating away smoothed the ride into a very well-controlled vertical motion, devoid of pitch or shock.

Unfortunately the roads were just too slick and slippery to instil any confidence and in tight turns I found the Lagonda nosing into a gentle understeer with that superb steering giving fingertip warning the instant those front tyres threatened to break adhesion. Gentle treatment of the throttle balanced it out and the car settled into an effortless 5.3-litre squirt to the next turn. As I gained confidence so the whole $250,000-worth began to drift controllably across the cambered road surface. Slowly I became aware of Mike's staring eyes and white knuckles in the passenger seat and when he pointed out that we had just negotiated a very tight and slippery roundabout at a steady 70-80 km/h I backed off,

apologised for worrying him and said "you needn't worry, your car's doing it all for me". At that point I had accepted that Loasby and Aston Martin had got their sums right, and that the new Lagonda had all the potential to become a real rival for Rolls-Royce and Mercedes Benz.

Still, the Lagonda's controversial styling attracts extreme opinions — you either love it or you hate it. I can only say that I hated the thing when I saw it in two-dimensional photographs, yet when it lay before me in the three-dimensional metal it looked surprisingly compact, very low, and quite beautiful.

Production of the new car should be starting at Newport Pagnell this year. The price will be around £25-30,000 (at least 60 grand in Australia) and unless Loasby's team unaccountably lose their

CONTINUED ON PAGE 62

*Car looks almost like a mobile light platform with main headlights exposed. The lights below are for parking, turn signalling and flashing.*

*Not one of the car's prettiest angles. Lines are very square but couldn't be called cluttered. Even exhaust tailpipes fit styling theme.*

# VANTAGE

Pirellis. And that without ever having locked them up.

Through such a bend a strong understeer can be balanced out on power, and then the Vantage's nose is rising, the tail is beginning to slide in perfect balance with the front and the whole two tons is hurtling out of the bend and hammering out its quad-cam song away on to another straight.

On the first morning I had the car I drove it from Ascot — to the west of London — up to Donington Park near Derby. That's about 223 km door-to-door, and leaving at 7.30 in the morning we arrived 1 hour 43 minutes later, after only the last 32 kilometres or so on motorway, and the rest cross-country through several towns. That average of over 130 km/h for a fuel consumption of 5 km/l was a highly impressive morning's motoring.

While a Vantage is not a foolproof Ford Escort type car in which one can take maniacal liberties, it is a true Grand Tourer which rewards driving concentration with superfast averages.

Aston Martin claims acceleration as follows: 0-48 km/h (30 mph) in 2.22 secs; 0-64 (40) in 2.94; 0-80 (50) in 4.21; 0-96 (60) in 5.30; 0-112 (70) in 6.62; 0-129 (80) in 8.57; 0-145 (90) in 10.46 and 0-160 (100) in 12.67 secs. To 193 (120) from rest is claimed to take just 18.88 secs, and we were hoping to check out the whole list. We hadn't bargained for British weather, however, and apart from brief periods during which the roadways were drying after showers it rained throughout our six days with the car. Attempts to set representative times foundered in runaway wheelspin on greasy roads, and the best 0-96 (60) time we managed was just on six seconds dead, and 0-129 (80) was nearer 11 seconds.

Aston claims the Vantage is the fastest-accelerating production car on the strength of a 5.3 sec 0-96 time compared to something like the Ferrari Daytona at 5.4 secs or the slow-off-the-mark Porsche Turbo at 6.1 secs.

Times may be the measure of performance but they don't put across the impression of sheer "grunt" which sitting in the Vantage's driving seat gives you. With that sensational — but externally always civilised — exhaust note sending the adrenalin coursing through your veins the Vantage almost literally rockets up to 73 km/h in first, to 121 in second, 175 in third and 214

in fourth. Still accelerating hard when pulling fifth gear it must run on to a maximum well in excess of 256 km/h, and yet even at speeds doubling the legal maximum (whisper it) the car's aerodynamic aids are extremely effective in maintaining a perfectly stable platform. Crosswinds lose significance even at such high speeds, and with those great brakes and easily neutralised cornering characteristics this is one exoticar which breathes security, in all but one condition. I found that heavy braking on a patched or rippled surface upset the car considerably, and fightback through the steering with that light rear end set up some rather exciting dodging and weaving which wasn't exactly calculated to soothe a nervous passenger!

In the wet those grooved Pirelli CN12s instil a deep trust and only once — upon hitting a puddle which must have been a good 5 cm deep — did their drainage prove inadequate and provoke a brief moment's aquaplaning.

Through corners the Vantage is immensely predictable except over unexpected bumps, but with such weight it can be seen off by lighter performance cars such as the Lotus Esprit or a well-driven Porsche.

With a 113.6-litre fuel tank residing in the luggage boot the space available there looks limited, but will swallow rather more than one might suppose, while the cabin itself will carry even its rear-seat passengers in a considerable degree of refined comfort despite the "G" which the Vantage can pull fore, aft and sideways!

CONTINUED ON PAGE 62

*Tyres are Pirelli 60-profile and give the car such a grip on the road that it needs a madman or a monumental misjudgement to unstick it. Extra lights are standard — and needed to match the car's rocket-like performance.*

*Twin fuel fillers give a clue to the car's sizeable tank capacity (114 litres) and to its healthy fuel consumption rate. Buyers of this car won't quibble for long over the fuel price . . .*

# LAGONDA

way somewhere between this very promising prototype and the production version it is going to be something of a bargain, even at that.

The Lagonda is very much Aston Martin's challenge for the '80s, and if it develops as it should I am going to have a very proud memory of being one of the first ever to experience it. □

# VANTAGE

For an asking price of £20,000 the Aston Martin Vantage offers what buyers of '78 expect of a truly exciting motor car. It's a traditional car, not a modern, mid-engined coupe. But with its boot and fairly roomy interior, many enthusiasts will find it more practical. Whatever your point of view, it's a great car. □

# THE RESCUERS OF ASTON

Aston Martin Lagonda Ltd was forced into receivership in 1975, just a few years after the fragmentation of David Brown's empire and its acquisition by Company Developments Ltd. It was tragic because at that time it seemed that profitability was within the grasp of the production side (as distinct from service and parts) — for the first time since Brown's had sold it off.

The production side of the works was closed on December 31, 1974 and managing director Fred Hartley worked with the UK government to find somebody to rescue the company as a whole. Many businessmen came to Newport Pagnell to see if Aston Martin had any prospects. Some made bids but it was not until two Aston Martin Owners' Club members from across the Atlantic met in the Aston works that rescue became certain.

Fred Hartley introduced Canadian George Minden and American Peter Sprague for the first time as they were visiting the stilled factories. Sprague, born in 1939, is the youthful and dynamic boss of America's National Semiconductor Corporation, a huge Californian-based electronics undertaking. Married with four sons, he lives in Massachusetts and New York City, and he lists his hobbies as photography and "driving Aston Martins". During 1959-60 he had in fact been a UPI staff photographer in Moscow.

George Minden, born June 2, 1937, studied Philosophy and English at Toronto University in Canada and in 1962 took an interest in a Toronto hotel and restaurant chain. In 1972 he set up a major Aston Martin, BMW and Rolls-Royce dealership in the city, and became Aston's Canadian importer.

He and Sprague hit it off from their first meeting at Newport Pagnell and their offer of £1,050,000 for the whole place was accepted — at the last minute — on June 27, 1975.

A hard-core of Aston's skilled workers had stayed with the company despite its problems and the acute uncertainty of its survival, and with Fred Hartley continuing as managing director, two other British directors were appointed to assist co-chairmen Sprague and Minden.

One of the Englishmen is Alan Curtis, a director of six companies including George House Holdings, a major property group. Curtis also has considerable aviation interests and owns 12 aircraft, including two Tiger Moth biplanes. As an enthusiastic private pilot and an Aston Martin owner-driver for nine years he was not prepared to see the company die, and in March, '77 when Fred Hartley left Newport Pagnell to become a self-employed marketing consultant, Curtis became managing director in his place.

Finally Denis Flather, retired head of his family's steel business, threw his whole-hearted support behind Aston Martin. Flather had been managing director of the business in 1947. He was one of the industrialists approached by Raymond Mays to give support to the original BRM V16 project and he became its first chairman. Today he lives in retirement in Derby but in addition to his Aston Martin interest he is also active on the main committee of the Royal Automobile Club, is deeply involved with the British Trials and Rally Drivers Association and is an enthusiastic member of the Veteran Car Club. He owns a 1898 Daimler — one of the oldest surviving British-built horseless carriages, and a 1913 Rolls-Royce Silver Ghost.

The rescuers of Aston Martin are intensely enthusiastic. Happily, it shows in their newest products. □

# Driving the new Lagonda

T was a long time a-coming and few believed that the 1976 Show Lagonda would turn from dream-car to reality, but it has and in substantially as-shown form. Put simply, the car is a lengthened and developed Aston Martin V8 with elaborate electronic touch-sensitive switchgear and digital read-out instrumentation clothed in a striking and possibly timeless creation by William Towns. It is, in fact, hard to believe that the delicate wedged nose allows a substantial V8 to fit underneath the broad flat bonnet, but it does and visibility over it is good.

Inevitably the first drive in the Lagonda comes in two parts, tackling the daunting switchgear then appreciating the rest of the car. Obviously the layout is logical once your mind has been programmed to that of the layer-out, but you also have to bear in mind that the Lagonda provides you with far more information than any other car, and incorporates far more features over which you have individual control, so there have to be more controls. If everything were to be transferred to orthodox switches and dials, there just wouldn't be room and the whole facia would be a confusing flight-deck mess to any but the most initiated. As it is, the facia and cockpit design looks particularly neat and stylish apart from the ugly Blaupunkt radio/stereo stalk, conveniently placed and undoubtedly excellent though it is.

There are a large number of controls which you don't require often while driving and these are grouped in the door panel and on the central console; if necessary you can easily find the air conditioning switches and the instrument check switch in the centre or the window lift switches on the door, but the rest that you really need are on the steering column pod. Facing you in the pod are automatic transmission controls on the left; on the right you have cruise controls and a headlamp wiper. The left face has wiper controls and the right face, horns. The right top surface has lighting controls and right indicator while the bottom surface carries the left indicator. Further away on top right are all the lighting switches.

For instruments you get illuminated arcs for speed and revs with a digital display giving the figures, while all other instruments record in figures only. There are warning lights in addition.

On an 80-mile run I played with very few. Having adjusted my seat all ways, closed the windows and locked the doors I left the door switches alone. On the move I only required the indicator switches although I played with the transmission ones, checked the wipers and tried a headlamp flash although the car is sufficiently striking to make even the most obstinate move over. It was in fact, surprisingly easy to get into and drive off in daylight; further knowledge could come gradually. I think one could probably know roughly where all the buttons are within a 250-mile afternoon to dark drive, but you may not always find them first time without checking the symbols; much the same distance is required to assess a Citroen SM against the 50 miles or so for most cars.

The car itself is a delight to drive. It is extremely quiet, has almost all the expected Aston performance and the high-geared steering earns full marks for weight and general feel. The ride is substantially softer than that of an Aston V8, and you really feel that the suspension is working, as the body maintains an effortlessly even progress, while the wheels follow the road contours, whatever the surface. With familiarity you can begin to take it through corners at surprising speed with no lurch and little apparent roll, despite the softer springing and damping. As far as the instruments were concerned once on the move, I would rather have some figures on the two dials, as constant reference to the digital figures for town speed limits was an irritation, although more experience would probably remove the need for that. Figure read-outs for oil, water, voltmeter etc require more concentration than watching a needle creep nearer the red, as you have to remember danger figures or trust the warning lights.

But really you have all you want in the ultimate barouche supercar; it's a pity that Jaguar got there first with the "Grace, Space and Pace" slogan because the Lagonda is very comfortable indeed for four people, although the rear seat is not in the taxi-cab class for legroom, and the transparent roof panel adds a welcome touch of airiness, which those who design claustrophobic rear seat areas could usefully follow.

There are so many features still not mentioned like average speed and fuel consumption computation and which all have a useful if esoteric function, but space prevents a total description. I have always been an advocate of the 'black box' to control injection, ignition, transmission and anti-lock braking but it has yet to be done; it seems that the Lagonda is most of the way there but approaching it from a different angle. I think that fewer people would have labelled the car's electronickery as gimmickry, if the computer had started on "my" theme and added the rest because the facilities were already there – electronic anti-lock braking has been just round the corner for so long now and this would have been an additional safety-car feather in an already very well plumed cap.

One of the reasons behind the delay that Mercedes have put forward over the Teldix system is that drivers of their cars would use such a feature so rarely – I agree – that they would never know if it had actually ceased to function, and perhaps subsequently blame the manufacturer if they had the accident with locked wheels. The Lagonda level of electronic sophistication could surely monitor that one, couldn't it Mr. Designer Loasby?

No, the Lagonda is not a four-wheeled gimmick looking for someone to impress, it is a serious super barouche. ●

*Top, selecting a gear at rest. Left, all systems open. Right, head and kneeroom are just adequate for those over six foot.*

# LAGONDA

*Lord Tavistock of Woburn is first to receive the new Lagonda. Superb design now in production, with two-a-week target. Design analysis of the final format*

**By Stuart Bladon**

*Photographs by Ron Easton*

that the car really is now in production, albeit on a very limited scale. Each one takes up to 13 weeks to build, and Aston Martin are anxious not to rush things and risk mistakes as the programme gets under way. Completion of only one a month is likely at the outset, building up to one a week and eventually two cars a week.

It may be true that we have already allocated a lot of space in *Autocar* to accounts of the progress, out of all proportion with the sales volume prospects of the model — a car for "the few, and the very few", as Churchill would have said. Yet we see it as not only a design of fascinating interest, but also as one of great technical significance, bringing a lot of refreshingly new thought to the evolution of the big car. It marks, in particular, the beginning of what we see as a new era in the use of electronics in cars.

Former technical director Mike Loasby has now been appointed managing director of Aston Martin Engineering — a new company formed to exploit the company's

talents. With half an eye on the weather, to see whether he was going to be able to take his test for a private pilot's licence that afternoon, he filled in the gaps for me, explaining what had changed since I last drove the car, and how the Lagonda will finally be built.

In the event, the weather turned for the worse, the flying test was postponed; but one could not help wondering how someone so involved with such a time-consuming and in

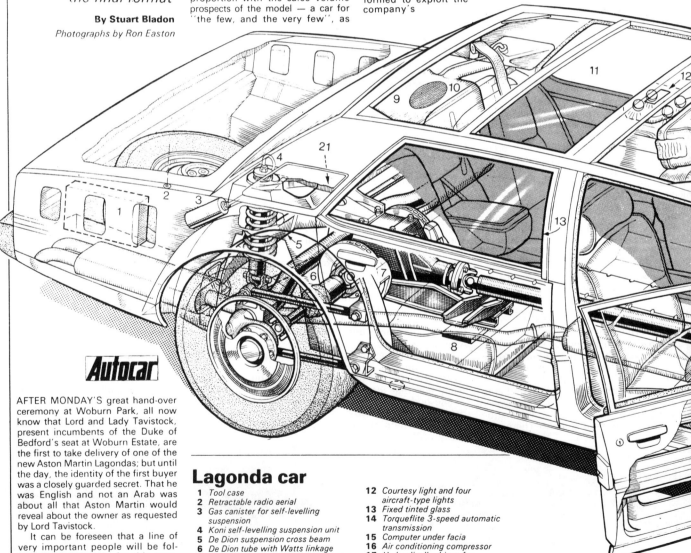

*Autocar*

AFTER MONDAY'S great hand-over ceremony at Woburn Park, all now know that Lord and Lady Tavistock, present incumbents of the Duke of Bedford's seat at Woburn Estate, are the first to take delivery of one of the new Aston Martin Lagondas; but until the day, the identity of the first buyer was a closely guarded secret. That he was English and not an Arab was about all that Aston Martin would reveal about the owner as requested by Lord Tavistock.

It can be foreseen that a line of very important people will be following as recipients for this magnificent car — not necessarily household names, but at least all people of immense wealth and able to meet the formidable purchase bill of £32,620. The significant aspect is

## Lagonda car

1  *Tool case*
2  *Retractable radio aerial*
3  *Gas canister for self-levelling suspension*
4  *Koni self-levelling suspension unit*
5  *De Dion suspension cross beam*
6  *De Dion tube with Watts linkage*
7  *10⅜ dia. ventilated Girling inboard disc brake*
8  *Computer power supplies (each side)*
9  *30-gallon fuel tank*
10 *Radio speaker (each side)*
11 *Tinted glass roof panel*
12 *Courtesy light and four aircraft-type lights*
13 *Fixed tinted glass*
14 *Torqueflite 3-speed automatic transmission*
15 *Computer under facia*
16 *Air conditioning compressor*
17 *Hydraulically-driven fan*
18 *Transmission oil cooler*
19 *Engine oil cooler (each side)*
20 *Exhaust emission air pump*
21 *Main and subsidiary batteries (on boot floor)*

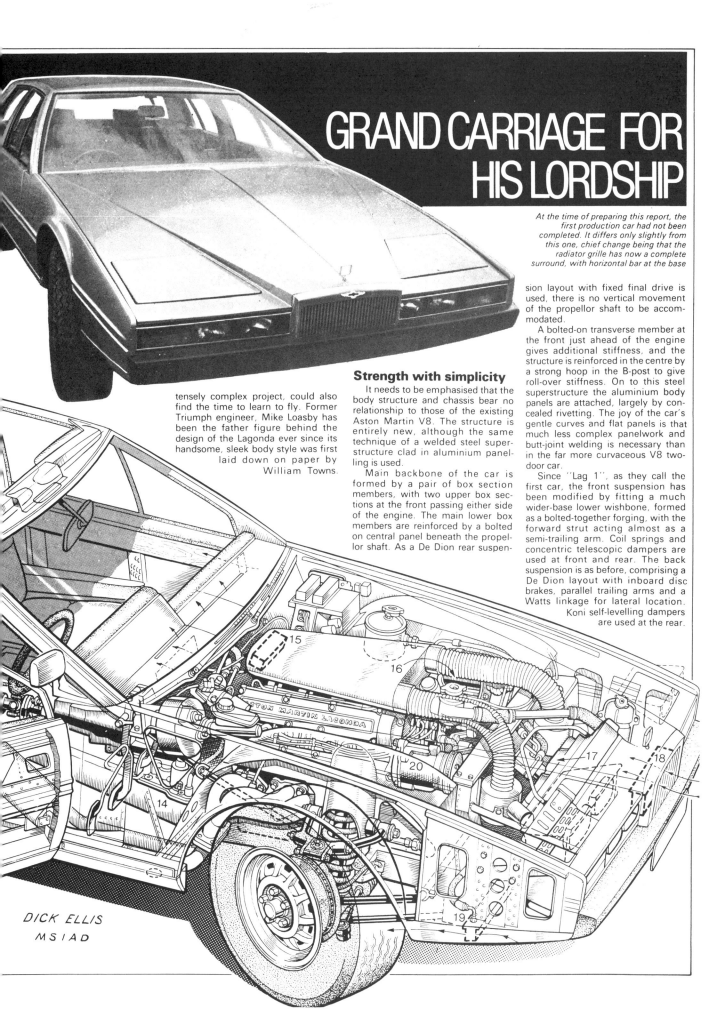

# GRAND CARRIAGE FOR HIS LORDSHIP

*At the time of preparing this report, the first production car had not been completed. It differs only slightly from this one, chief change being that the radiator grille has now a complete surround, with horizontal bar at the base*

tensely complex project, could also find the time to learn to fly. Former Triumph engineer, Mike Loasby has been the father figure behind the design of the Lagonda ever since its handsome, sleek body style was first laid down on paper by William Towns.

## Strength with simplicity

It needs to be emphasised that the body structure and chassis bear no relationship to those of the existing Aston Martin V8. The structure is entirely new, although the same technique of a welded steel super-structure clad in aluminium panelling is used.

Main backbone of the car is formed by a pair of box section members, with two upper box sections at the front passing either side of the engine. The main lower box members are reinforced by a bolted on central panel beneath the propellor shaft. As a De Dion rear suspen-

sion layout with fixed final drive is used, there is no vertical movement of the propellor shaft to be accommodated.

A bolted-on transverse member at the front just ahead of the engine gives additional stiffness, and the structure is reinforced in the centre by a strong hoop in the B-post to give roll-over stiffness. On to this steel superstructure the aluminium body panels are attached, largely by concealed rivetting. The joy of the car's gentle curves and flat panels is that much less complex panelwork and butt-joint welding is necessary than in the far more curvaceous V8 two-door car.

Since "Lag 1", as they call the first car, the front suspension has been modified by fitting a much wider-base lower wishbone, formed as a bolted-together forging, with the forward strut acting almost as a semi-trailing arm. Coil springs and concentric telescopic dampers are used at front and rear. The back suspension is as before, comprising a De Dion layout with inboard disc brakes, parallel trailing arms and a Watts linkage for lateral location. Koni self-levelling dampers are used at the rear.

DICK ELLIS
MSIAD

# LAGONDA

Both the Editor and the Deputy Editor have the dubious distinction of having grounded the Lagonda, which perhaps shows that something was not quite right, and this has now been modified by gaining another 1½in. ground clearance. The former separate sub-frame at the front is now welded solid with the structure, and it is claimed this has given more strength without introducing any road noise problem. The anti-roll bar now has a vertical link each side to allow movement.

We recently published a picture of the compulsory ECE crash test being carried out on Lag 2. Before this was done, two additional angled struts had been introduced each side at the front to give additional energy-absorbing strength. The results of the test are described as very satisfactory indeed. There was a dummy in the car during the test, and "he might have been a bit shocked and sur-

*Mike Loasby points out a feature of the new Lagonda to the author, using* Autocar's *cutaway drawing reproduced here*

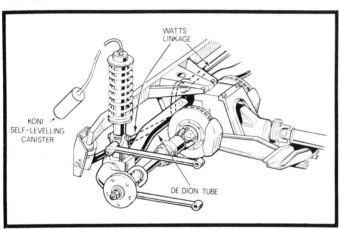

WATTS LINKAGE

KONI SELF-LEVELLING CANISTER

DE DION TUBE

prised" says Mike Loasby, "but he would have survived if a real person had been there".

The former intention to use Burman two-stage varying ratio steering had to be abandoned as it did not become available, and instead the steering is a Burman-powered rack and pinion unit, the same as is supplied for the Rover SD1. However, with near-90 per cent Ackerman steering geometry it gives a very high rate of response, and there are only just over 1.8 turns from lock to lock.

## Speed slightly reduced

A problem with tyre availability has led to a necessary reduction in the speed potential of the new car to 130 mph; but it is felt that this is more than compensated by the extra torque provided by the engine in its form as turned out for the Lagonda. Details of valve timing are different from those of the two-door, but as usual no power or torque figures are revealed for publication.

Engine design is mainly unchanged, featuring all-aluminium construction, with cast iron cylinder liners and twin overhead camshafts for each bank of the 5,340 c.c. V8. The engine sump is also an aluminium casting, and for the Lagonda the drain plug has to be

repositioned on the bottom instead of the back because of the relationship to a cross-member. Main modification to the engine was redesign of the air filter box and other changes to reduce its height by some four inches to clear the very low bonnet.

Each engine is individually assembled by one fitter, and a nice touch is that a little plate is now fitted on the righthand upper camshaft cover giving the name of the man who assembled the unit. This is done, incidentally, for all Aston engines now.

A toothed belt drive is taken off the front of the engine to drive a small hydraulic pump, solely to power the fan. The complication of the hydraulic drive seems rather elaborate but was considered

*Above: Telescopic rear dampers have Koni self-energising units to restore correct static height when laden. The suspension at the back is otherwise the same as for the Aston Martin V8*

*Right: One man builds each complete engine for all Astons and Lagondas, and has his name on one of the camshaft covers to encourage pride in the job. Fred Waters, shown here, built the engine for the first Lagonda to be sold*

ASTON MARTIN LAGONDA

ENGINE BUILT BY FRED WATERS
ASTON MARTIN LAGONDA (1975) LTD

necessary to provide adequa cooling at low speeds and in cou tries of high temperatures. It provid a constant fan speed of 2,500 rp regardless of engine speed. Since th first car, the fan has been redesigne with fewer blades acting as larg scoops to pull a lot of air through th forward-inclined radiator. An electr fan was discounted on grounds noise and particularly for conce about its current consumption.

Carburation is by four big twi choke Webers, and there are no plar to make any further adventures alor the fuel injection road. Chrysler Tc queflite automatic transmission standard, with touch control ele tronic selection. Five speed manu gearbox would be provided, sa Mike, only if someone really insiste on it.

A Salisbury limited slip differenti with final drive ratio of 3.31-to-1 used, giving a top gear mph p 1,000 rpm figure of 24.5. Equ length splined half shafts with u versal joints at each end take t drive to the rear wheels.

## Now a foot-operated parking brake

Because it seemed neater ar offered greater efficiency, a foo operated parking brake is used, wc king on the rear discs. The brakes a ventilated discs front and rear wit twin hydraulic circuits and direc acting servo. Very good brakin efficiency is claimed, and althoug there is no anti-dive geometry it ha been found that there is no proble with plunge on braking since th front suspension link was raised b 1½in. and moved forward.

Exhaust requirements for bot noise and emissions have been m for the ECE, but not yet for America pollution laws; Aston are going start working on that next. Th exhaust system is entirely in stainles steel, with a complex layout. Fo separate pipes of the manifold eac side go into twin pipes which the pass into a single silencer box in th centre of the car. This does away wit a lot of the characteristic V8 exhau beat. Twin pipes then emerge goir to a separate tail silencer each sid with two outlets from each.

The fuel tank, built into the cave nous space between the rear whee and over the fixed final drive un contains a lordly 30 gallons. Th snap fastening filler on each side the wide D-post is for ease of venti and fast refuelling, and their cove have a facia release switch each sid There are twin fuel pumps and separate switched reserve.

## Why it needs two batteries

Aston believe they are the fir in Europe to fit the Del maintenance-free Freedom batter which is located in the floor of th boot, just ahead of the spare whe well. There is also a small Varle accumulator which is als maintenance-free. Its function solely to power the electronic cor puter while the starter motor is action. When the starter is used, t main battery powers the motor ar the ignition circuit, but the comput is automatically switched over to th mall Varley. This is solely to avoid a "spike" or surge of current which ould damage the computer. The arley is recharged from the alternar in the usual way.

The computer is located in the cia above the front passenger's nees, and governs the electronic strumentation with its ingenious uel consumption calculator and verage speed indicator.

A two-position memory is proided for the Keiper electric seat echanism. The driver can use the dividual adjust buttons to set the ke, tilt and height of the seat to his king; and then a touch on the emory "button" records these setngs. Another driver, Lady Tavistock erhaps, can do the same for her deal seat position. Then as either ets in the car, a touch on the door utton sends the seat to the nosen position for its occupant. Peraps the Mark 2 model will even etermine by weight analysis which river is getting in, and set the seat ccordingly.

One speaks of buttons for the mior controls, but of course most of nem are concealed touch-sensitive witches in a single panel on the oor, with illuminated identity.

### nter, the Retractile

In the small diameter steering heel there is a wide central boss on hich are dispersed four rows of witches; and there are two more nderneath. At the top, nearest the cia, are the pad switches for the ruise control. In the next row are vin pads for left and right indicators. own and country horns are in the ext row, and nearest the wheel rim re switches for wipers on/off (with eed or intermittent selection on the ain panel), and the headlamps dip witch. Two pads are concealed beeath the panel for finger-tip opera-

Toothed belt drive powers a hydraulic pump, which is solely to power the fan, to cope with Middle East temperatures without fear of putting too much load on the battery

Headlamps swing up automatically when switched on, and they are now carried complete with the lifting mechanism, as part of the bonnet structure

tion for the screenwashers or to flash the headlamps.

Thus we count at least 10 wires emerging from the central area of the steering wheel; but the steering wheel is going to turn in either direction, and you can't bend wires indefinitely, nor is there much reliability in having ten sliding contacts. So how is it done?

The answer is the Retractile — a section of flexible printed circuit like a piece of flat plastic, which emerges sideways from the column and goes into what is called a "false coil". It is not easy to visualise, but imagine that you take a piece of paper and fold it, then roll it up from the folded end. Now, you can roll and unroll the coil, and this is what happens with the Retractile. The springy plastic is set in the shape of the coil, and as the steering is turned one way or the other the Retractile either winds up or unwinds. So simple, yet as Mike says, without it they simply could not have located these minor controls on the steering wheel boss. It has enabled them to dispense with column-mounted levers in a way even neater

than Citroen, and the Retractile is an inexpensive standard component used in photo-copying machines, with proven reliability.

Front windows are electrically-operated, but the rear windows are fixed. With air conditioning it is argued that there is no reason for them ever to be opened, and it has been found that on many American cars the same dodge is used. Central locking is standard and programmed to operate with a predetermined delay, every time the door is closed after removing the ignition key. Footlights in the doors light the step-out area.

Fog and spot lamps are built in at the front in the narrow panel above the deep, rubber-faced bumper. The retracting main headlamps are lifted and lowered electrically, and are now attached to the bonnet. This system was preferred as it overcame any problems of opening the bonnet with the headlamps up, and the bonnet (forward hinged) is so firmly located that there is no problem with bonnet "shiver".

At the rear, the lamps, including

are all built into the rear face of the boot panel. This way it is ensured that there is no sill to get in the way when loading up. Repeater tail lamps built in on the underside of the lid are angled so that when the boot lid is up, they face rearward at the correct angle. There are four aircraft-type reading lights in the centre of the roof, and an overall roof courtesy light. It cuts out with delayed action fade, after the last door is closed.

The air conditioning unit is by Frigiking — an American unit with automatic temperature control and air blending mix for the heater unit which is incorporated with it. Radio and tape unit will be to choice of the buyer, but since the earlier designs the loudspeakers have been repositioned on the rear parcels shelf instead of on the back doors.

Another small, rather regrettable change is that the gas plasma instruments to give an analogue display of speed and revs have been deleted. There will now be only digital indication of these readings.

# Lagonda Facia — Key

1 Hazard warning
2 Second gear and Drive
3 First gear
4 Visual gear legend for night driving
5 Neutral, Reverse, Park
6 Left fuel filler
7 Heated rear window
8 Right fuel filler
9 Fuel reserve
10 Fast wipe
11 Bonnet
12 Start/stop
13 Reset
14 Date
15 Set clock
16 Hours/months
17 Interior lights
18 Set date
19 Trip
20 Minutes/days
21 MPH/KPH

22 Average consumption
23 Average speed
24 Mode
25 Test
26 Essential instruments
27 Headlamps
28 Side lamps
29 Spot lamps
30 Fog lamps
31 Display
32 Dimmer
33 Cruise control switches
34 Indicators
35 Headlamp flash
36 Screen wash
37 Dip/main beam
38 Wiper on/off and single wipe
39 Town and country horns

Aim of the complex-looking switch layout is to put related controls together with logical grouping. A switch for "essential instruments" cuts out all supplementary information from the facia, leaving only speed, revs, oil and temperature indicators still alight, to avoid confusion, especially at night. Vital switches, such as horns, lights, wipers are all logically arranged on the steering wheel boss

# LAGONDA

## The world's most advanced production car

As well as inheriting the great Woburn Estate, Lord Tavistock has the satisfaction of knowing that he is the owner of what is undoubtedly the most advanced production car in the world. Its revolutionary approach to many familiar problems intrigued us greatly when the broad details of the design were first revealed, just as it does now with the further refinements introduced for the production model.

Its completion marks a great achievement for British engineering, styling, craftsmanship and inventiveness, all rolled into one. It should do much for our industry's prestige, not to mention serving as a major confidence boost for the small and now-thriving Newport Pagnell concern Aston Martin Lagonda (1975) Ltd.

This important milestone is not the end of the Lagonda road for us. A firm promise has been given that the world's first full road test of the Lagonda will be published in *Autocar*.

Left: Chassis forming jigs are here being used to position the steel superstructure ready for welding
Above: Aluminium panelling forms the outer skin, secured to the main structure by concealed riveting

Above: The huge fuel tank holding nearly 30 gallons has twin fillers and a positive reserve with separate facia switch

Right: A fitter working inside the boot reveals the size of the luggage compartment; the spare wheel and two batteries are stowed on the floor of the compartment

Left: With such a wide opening and a forward-hinged bonnet, there should be very good access to the engine
Above: Seats are softly upholstered and trimmed in leather

## Specification

### ENGINE
| | |
|---|---|
| | Front, rear drive |
| Cylinders | 8 in 90 deg vee |
| Main bearings | 5 |
| Cooling | Water |
| Fan | Hydraulic |
| Bore, mm (in.) | 100 mm (3.94 in.) |
| Stroke, mm (in.) | 85 mm (3.55 in.) |
| Capacity, cc (in³) | 5,340 c.c. (326 cu in.) |
| Valve gear | dohc each bank |
| Camshaft drive | Chain |
| Compression | 9.5-to-1 |
| Octane rating | 97 RM |
| Carburettors | Four Weber twin-choke 42 DCNF |
| Max. power | Not quoted |
| Max. torque | Not quoted |

### TRANSMISSION
| | | |
|---|---|---|
| Type | | Chrysler Torqueflite automatic |
| Gear | Ratio | mph/1000rpm |
| Top | 1.0 | 24.5 |
| 2nd | 1.45 | 16.8 |
| 1st | 2.45 | 10.0 |
| Final drive gear | | Hypoid bevel, limited slip |
| Ratio | | 3.31-to-1 |

### SUSPENSION
| | |
|---|---|
| Front-location | Independent, wishbones |
| springs | Coil |
| dampers | Telescopic |
| anti-roll bar | Yes |
| Rear — location | De Dion with Watts linkage |
| springs | Coil |
| dampers | Telescopic with Koni self-levelling |
| anti-roll bar | No |

### STEERING
| | |
|---|---|
| Type | Rack and pinion |
| Power assistance | Yes |
| Wheel diameter | 15 in. |

### BRAKES
| | |
|---|---|
| Front | 11.1 in. dia. ventilated disc |
| Rear | 10.4 in. dia. ventilated inboard discs |
| Servo | Yes, direct acting |

### WHEELS
| | |
|---|---|
| Type | Pressed steel |
| Rim width | 6 in. |
| Tyres — make | Avon |
| — type | Radial tubeless |
| — size | 235 HR 15 |

### EQUIPMENT
| | |
|---|---|
| Batteries | 12 volt 68 Ah (main), 12 volt 8 Ah |
| Alternator | 75 amp |
| Headlamps | 110/220-watt, with electric lift |
| Reversing lamp | Standard |
| Hazard warning | Standard |
| Electric fuses | 28 |
| Screen wipers | 2-speed with touch wipe and intermittent |
| Screen washer | Electric |
| Interior heater | Air blending with air conditioning unit |
| Interior trim | Leather seats, PVC headlining |
| Floor covering | Carpet |
| Jack | Screw pillar |
| Jacking points | Two each side under sills |
| Windscreen | Laminated |
| Underbody protection | Wax and PVC |

### MAINTENANCE
| | |
|---|---|
| Fuel tank | 28 Imp. galls (127 litres) |
| Cooling system | 25 pints (inc. heater) |
| Engine sump | 20 pints SAE 10W/30 |
| Transmission | 14 pints TZ Dexron |
| Final drive | 4 pints SAE 90 Hypoy LS |
| Grease | 13 points |
| Valve clearance | Inlet 0.014 in. (cold) Exhaust 0.016 in. (cold) |
| Contact breaker | None (electronic ignition) |
| Ignition timing | TDC at 850 rpm |
| Spark plug — type | Champion N10PY |
| — gap | 0.03 |
| Tyre pressures | F28, R28 psi (normal driving) |
| Max. payload | 1,054 lb (478 kg) |

### DIMENSIONS
| | |
|---|---|
| Length | 17ft. 4in. (528 cm) |
| Width | 5ft. 10½in. (179 cm) |
| Height | 4ft. 4in. (132 cm) |
| Wheelbase | 9ft. 7in. (291 cm) |
| Weight | 4,365 lb (1,980 kg) |

# ROAD TEST
# The Aston Martin Vantage

## An exhilarating fireball, exquisitely crafted

A NEW PERFORMANCE standard has been set amongst so-called "super-cars". And it originates not in Modena or Stuttgart, but in urban Newport Pagnell. For the most breathtakingly exciting, adrenalin churning example of all that rarefied breed, indeed the fastest accelerating current production car in the World is the Aston Martin Vantage.

I can sense some readers scoffing right now. "Aston Martin – b...... great lorry." It happens all the time. But this "b...... great lorry" accelerates from 0-60 m.p.h. in 5.3 seconds, has been timed by Astons at 180 m.p.h. and, for all its weight and girth, handles superbly. Into the bargain it carries four people and adequate luggage in absolute luxury and is exquisitely hand-built. Like Rolls-Royce, Aston Martin refuse to disclose brake horsepower figures, but a good authority intimates that another journalist's estimate of 425 b.h.p. was pretty near the mark, making the Vantage's four-cam, 5,340 c.c. 100 mm. x 85 mm. V8 the most powerful current production car engine in the World.

I too was sceptical. I have not been the most ardent admirer of modern Astons, although I have nothing but admiration for the craftsmanship involved in their manufacture. Now, after testing the Vantage, I am lost for adequate superlatives. I have driven most of the

World's fastest, most expensive production sports cars, but I can't think of one that has surprised me, excited me quite so much as the Vantage. It does not have the supreme chassis characteristics of the new Porsche 928 (a 928 fitted with the Vantage engine would be the absolute ultimate!), the uncanny smoothness of the Turbo, the silence of the XJS, or the charismatic styling of the Boxer and the Countach. But it will out-perform them all in a manner which is as untemperamental as it is shattering, and makes no sacrifices for the sake of outrageous styling and the current mid-engine cult. Such power is

*The incredible Aston Martin Vantage, the World's fastest accelerating production car, in company with a remarkable machine of yesteryear, a De Havilland Mosquito, shrouded for the winter. The photographs in this article were taken at Salisbury Hall and the Mosquito Museum, London Colney, near St. Albans, by kind permission of Mr. Walter Goldsmith. The historic Hall and Museum are open to the public on Sundays from Easter to the end of September, Thursdays from July to September and Bank Holiday Mondays.*

not for the faint of heart or muscle, or for the unskilled, but allowing for those obvious strictures this Vantage is remarkably vice-free and forgiving, another bonus from conventional layout.

It is heartening to be able to lay such praise at the door of a so very British company which three years ago had floundered over the brink. Not many people would have projected success for the Anglo-American consortium of individuals which rescued Aston Martin in that disastrous year. Yet now the company is back in profit, with a full order book and with the first, production, revolutionary Lagonda scheduled for delivery to the customer at the end of this month.

Aston Martin resurrected the Vantage name and its theme of being a higher performance version of the standard car early last year as an aid to polishing the tarnished image. It is built to special order only, an average of one per week, sells for £23,000, by no means immodest in super-car terms and has had apparently the desired effect by reflected image of attracting customers for the standard V8, itself a vastly improved motor car since 1975.

MOTOR SPORT should have had a Vantage for test last year; two bad crashes in which Aston's Press test car – a converted standard V8 – was involved prevented this. Aston had not replaced the car on their fleet, but thanks to the cooperation of Aston Martin Sales in London's

Sloane Street, we were able to borrow their 3,600 mile-old demonstrator, a proper production Vantage. It was certainly worth waiting for.

The Vantage makes no bones in appearance about its performance purpose in life. A deep front spoiler, a high tail spoiler contoured smoothly into the coachwork, a blanked-off power bulge in the bonnet, a blanked-off grille carrying two dipping, long-range Cibie auxiliary lamps, massive 255/60 x 15 in. Pirelli Cinturatos on 7 in. GKN alloy wheels, give this six-foot wide monster an air of wickedly muscular purposefulness which is not belied. Its appearance in the mirror moves dawdlers out of the way faster than anything I can recall, including the Countach.

When the Vantage was introduced last year it boasted a 40% power increase over the then current V8. Improvements to the V8's engine gave that 15% boost in mid summer and at the same time the V8 adopted the same suspension revisions which had been essential to cope with the Vantage's extra power. The most important improvement was to fit Koni telescopic shock-absorbers all round. Early Vantages had stiffer front anti-roll bars; this was found unnecessary and the model now has the standard V8 item. A change in castor angles has given more steering feel to the Vantage, which has a standardised-effort, Adwest power-assisted steering rack mid-way between the heavier and lighter choices which used to be available to Aston customers.

At the heart of this astonishing car is that 90 degree V8 engine, built in that small factory at Newport Pagnell. Each engine is built by one man, as I described in an account of the Aston Martin factory in the September, 1976 issue of MOTOR SPORT. I liked the personal touch on the offside cam cover of the test car's engine: a little brass plate announcing "Engine built by Fred Waters". By chance, he was the long-serving engine builder we portrayed in that 1976 colour feature. This mainly cast aluminium engine has two overhead camshafts per bank, driven by twin two-stage Duplex chains with automatic and manual adjustment (they need

attention every 10,000 miles – servicing intervals on the car as a whole have been extended from 2,500 to 5,000 miles). The heads have hemispherical combustion chambers and the block contains chrome vanadium iron wet

liners. The nitrided crankshaft runs in five main bearings and is fitted with forged steel conrods.

The Vantage differs from the standard V8 engine in having bigger inlet valves, new cam profiles with increased overlap on the induction side of things and a redesigned inlet manifold.

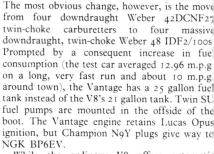

The most obvious change, however, is the move from four downdraught Weber 42DCNF27 twin-choke carburetters to four massive downdraught, twin-choke Weber 48 IDF2/100s. Prompted by a consequent increase in fuel consumption (the test car averaged 12.96 m.p.g. on a long, very fast run and about 10 m.p.g. around town), the Vantage has a 25 gallon fuel tank instead of the V8's 21 gallon tank. Twin SU fuel pumps are mounted in the offside of the boot. The Vantage engine retains Lucas Opus ignition, but Champion N9Y plugs give way to NGK BP6EV.

While the ordinary V8 offers automatic transmission as an option, the Vantage comes only with the ZF five-speed gearbox with ratios of: 1st, 2.90:1; 2nd, 1.78:1; 3rd, 1.22:1; 4th, 1.1:1; 5th, 0.845:1. The Salisbury differential contains a Powr-Lok limited slip device and a 3.54:1 final drive ratio, slightly lower than the V8's ratio. This gives 26 m.p.h./1,000 r.p.m. in fifth.

Bodywork changes are restricted to the aforementioned aerodynamic and cosmetic aids. This Vantage retains the modern Aston tradition of hand-formed aluminium alloy panelling over a rigid steel superstructure integral with a platform chassis. It seems almost superfluous to add that this magnificent bodywork receives over 20 coats of paint.

Suspension modifications have already been detailed. The basic design is unchanged, with unequal length wishbones, ball-jointed king pins, co-axial coil springs and shock-absorbers and an anti-roll bar at the front, and that substantial De Dion located rear end, located by parallel trailing links and a Watts linkage and suspended by coil springs and, nowadays, telescopic Konis instead of the old Armstrong lever shock-absorbers. The all-disc brakes are outboard at the front, inboard at the rear.

The wide doors, which have automatic warning lights in their trailing edges, open smoothly and clunk satisfyingly to entrap one in an interior which will be condemned as old-fashioned by some, praised as one of the few remaining bastions of traditional, hand-made

*A true four-seater, the Aston has luxurious accommodation for rear passengers.*

map-reading light. The centre console carries a large ash-tray and a cigar lighter.

One of the most admirable aspects of this Aston Martin performance package is that it is a genuine four-seater. The contoured rear seats, with fold down centre arm rest, are a work of art in the execution of their leather trim. True, a tall driver would leave little room for anything but the legless, but with the driver's seat in my own position I could sit behind it in absolute comfort and, into the bargain, gain entry through the wide doors without having to tip the front seat.

The driver's seat lacks height and cushion tilt adjustment facilities and may be too short in the cushion for tall drivers. However, Aston could no doubt come to some sort of bespoke arrangement for first-owners. The steering wheel has telescopic adjustment for reach and the old-fashioned, pivot-on-the-floor, brake and clutch pedals can be set in two alternative positions. As a concession to modernity, the old organ throttle pedal has given way to a pendant device. One thing which hasn't changed, thank goodness, is the good old fly-off handbrake by the driver's left leg, so convenient and effective.

To sit behind the Vantage's dished, leather-trimmed wheel for the first time is awe-inspiring. The massive power bulge towers at the base of the screen and the vast expanse of bodywork seem to confirm that lorry simile. The bellow as those four-hundred-plus horses spring to life is edifying, even more so because they become rampant so easily; no choke is fitted and two prods of the throttle when the engine is cold suffices to prime the carburetters adequately for first-time starting. After a short warm-up period the engine runs without a splutter. Hot starting is just as undramatic.

First gear in the ZF box is selected on a dog's leg down to the left, the other four being in H-pattern (with reverse on another dog's leg up to the right). Modifications have been made to lighten the clutches on current manual Astons and the test car's was a shade lighter and a good deal more positive and progressive than that of my old Jaguar 3.8. It gave my left leg no qualms in heavy traffic. The big ZF 'box displays the

**CONTINUED ON PAGE 187**

luxury, a reminder of almost forgotten qualities of life, by others. A lovely smell of hide pervades the air, from the Connolly products which so neatly cover the luxurious seats, the door trims, centre console, rear quarter panels and even the screen pillars. Wilton carpets cover the floor and a smooth, cloth headlining has replaced the ribbed lining of earlier V8's. The doors carry substantial leather-trimmed arm-rests, the driver's containing a remote lock for the passenger door. There are neat, leather map pockets in the doors and in the tip-up, reclining backs of the front seats. The big, high, fascia is a little bit overpowering, but functional. The instrumentation, recently revised, is contained in a cowled, crackle-black oval ahead of the driver. A clearer, 170 m.p.h. speedometer has replaced the impressive, but cluttered, 200 m.p.h. device of earlier cars and has been juxtaposed with the 7,000 r.p.m. tachometer, which no longer bears a warning line. Other instruments include a battery condition indicator, fuel gauge, water and oil temperature gauges and a precise oil pressure gauge mounted prominently between the two main instruments. These recent current Astons have been given sensible rows of warning lights above and below the instruments. Matching light master switches and panel switches are on the fascia on each side of the steering column. Headlight, flash and dip, winkers and horn are controlled by a positive right-hand column stalk and two-speed wipers/washers by the left-hand stalk. Although the wipers have a facility for flick-wipe they do not have an intermittent wipe facility. A row of auxiliary switches is contained in the leading edge of the centre console. These include a changeover switch for the electrical or air horns and another for the auxiliary lamps, which are wired through the dip switch. Switches for electric windows operation flank a Smiths clock in the centre of the fascia. Below these are the controls for the Coolaire air conditioning, a standard fitment. A Pioneer stereo AM/FM radio/cassette player is fitted though there is no storage place convenient to the driver for cassettes. A wide, lockable cubby hole on the passenger side contains a vanity mirror and a

*Vantage recognition factors are the front and rear spoilers, blanked off power bulge, blanked off grille and spotlights and Perspex cowls over the headlights.*

# Volante-Voila!

### Aston Martin take the top off the V8; America only for new convertible at first; UK deliveries next year — at £32,500

#### By Stuart Bladon

EVERYONE thought the convertible market in America was completely dead, and that nothing so dangerous-looking as a car without a roof would be allowed to squeeze through the ever-tighter safety regulations. On these grounds, Jaguar did not even bother with an open version of the XJ-S, and nor at first did Aston Martin with their V8. But to general surprise, convertibles are still allowed, and to take advantage of the latent interest, Aston Martin are now launching a drophead version of their V8.

Appropriately they have resurrected the famous Volante name, last used when the DB6 convertible went out of production in 1970. Aston say their American subsidiary has been clamouring for a convertible for some three years. The first 80 cars are already committed to the States, but the intention is to make the Volante available in UK in about a year's time.

*Autocar* are the first of the Press to have been allowed to drive the Volante in rare right-hand drive form — a prototype built specially for Aston Martin's managing director, Alan Curtis. Even on a rather chill day, that extraordinarily enjoyable thrill of speed, rushing air and freedom of the open road could be relished in a way that is never quite possible with any sort of closed car.

Rear seat passengers asked to have the side windows up, but were then not too badly blown about. In the front of the car, with the hood down, there is enough breeze to blow the hair about but one does not feel badly buffetted, and if anything the wind in the front at speed improves as the flow over the screen stabilises.

With the driving seat in normal adjustment for ample leg length, there was still sufficient room for a passenger in the seat behind.

It is claimed that the slight extra weight low down, and less weight high up where the roof would be on the GT, has improved the handling. Such gains would be rather marginal and need a lengthy comparison of both cars to analyse. In the brief run we were able to take in the prototype, which had covered only 270 miles, the important aspect was that the car seemed every bit as manageable as is remembered from former tests of the V8, with no feeling of structural looseness.

*As nice a view as anyone could wish for, outside the front door on a sunny morning: from all angles, the Aston Martin Volante looks magnificent. The makers have bravely shunned off any fixed upper structure; "you can t roll an Aston anyway, so who needs a roll-over pillar?" is the line taken*

## Volante-Voila!

The deep, purposeful exhaust note, always very marked with the [V]8, is even more noticeable with no metal or glass to dampen the sound. [It] was rather pleasing to hear the [s]light change in note as the [a]utomatic transmission made its [g]ear changes. The Volante will be [a]vailable with automatic or manual [tr]ansmission.

Adaptation of the body to a [co]nvertible style has been very [co]mpetently done, and either open [or] closed, the Volante looks most [e]legant. The hood is of Everflex PVC, [w]ith a flexible plastic rear window. [In]evitably the rear quarters are blind [w]ith the hood up, but Aston have [m]anaged to make the hood fold back [m]uch lower than with, for example, [th]e former Jensen convertible. [W]hen the leather tonneau cover is in [pl]ace, the top of the cover is out of [vi]ew of the rear mirror.

Hood operation is almost entirely [a]utomatic using the Smiths electric [a]nd hydraulic lifting rams. The [o]perating switch on the facia is [is]olated, once the handbrake has [be]en released, to safeguard against [ac]cidental operation while the car is [o]n the move. To lower the hood, the [se]at over-centre catches at the [sc]reen rail are released, tonneau [c]over pulled clear of the hood well, [an]d the hydraulic mechanism does [th]e rest. Only a faint whirring from [th]e region of the boot is heard [d]uring the operating procedure, and [it] is not necessary to turn on the [ig]nition.

Raising the hood is slightly more [c]omplicated, as the tonneau cover

*Hood operation is automatic at the touch of a button, but inevitably the leather tonneau cover has to be fitted or removed by hand. Above: The Volante retains the elegant looks of the Aston even with the hood up. Below: The higher and flatter boot panel enhances the rear aspect.*

with its dozen or so lift-the-stud fasteners must be released first. The cant rail rises vertically initially, then comes down with a ''clunk'' on to the top of the screen.

To compensate for the loss of the rigid roof, the sills are reinforced by additional welded-on open box members. There is also reinforcement for the screen pillar at its base and sides. Aston claim that the Volante body is even a little stronger than the ordinary GT. There is certainly no trace of scuttle shake — that bugbear of many convertibles — to feel through the steering, though just a trace of lateral shimmy is discernible to the eye on certain surfaces.

The former boot panel line would have looked unhappy with the convertible, so a completely different shaped lid is used for the Volante.

Also exclusive to the new convertible is embellishment of the facia, window sills and the flat part of the console behind the gear selector with highly polished burred walnut fillets. Some of the purists may consider this out of place on a functional car such as the Aston Martin V8, but there is no denying that the work is beautifully done to the highest standards of coachbuilding art.

When the Volante goes on sale in America it will be priced at 66,000 dollars (£32,790 at current rate of exchange). A UK price of £32,500 has been predicted by Alan Curtis, if the Volante becomes available in Britain in a year's time. Standard equipment includes leather upholstery, air conditioning, electric windows, and Pioneer's excellent KP8300 stereo radio-cassette unit.

*[A]lways a problem of open cars, the seat belts are built into the rear quarter trim, with a high pivot to take the belt over the shoulder. Burr walnut trim on the facia, door cappings [a]nd behind the transmission selector are special to the Volante and there's a neater one-piece capping to the padded top of the facia*

# Viceless Vantage

*Breeding makes Aston's straightforward charger almost perfect*

THE ASTON MARTIN Lagonda factory is old-fashioned and in need of a repaint. Look into the eyes of a tester, development engineer, or even one of the service staff and you will see bright enthusiasm. The visitor has his coffee served in a cup and saucer — the vending machine has yet to take over. Out of it all comes a remarkable car.

Perhaps it was a lack of financial muscle, or just plain common sense — the latter I think — that dictated the simple supercar conception that is the Vantage. No power outputs are quoted for the very oversquare, all-alloy, 100mm by 85mm bore and stroke, 5,341 c.c. chain-driven, four cam V8, but a genuine 375 bhp at around 6,200 rpm should not be too far away from the truth. Fred Waters, one of the four engine builders put "mine" together; his name plate sat on the right-hand cam cover to prove it.

The engine looks clean, weighs a mere 500 lb, and practically sits over the front wheels. Its light weight must have some bearing on the Vantage's considerable 36 cwt kerb weight being distributed an ideal 50.5/49 5

front to rear. On these grounds alone traction and natural stability would be difficult to suppress. Add a de Dion rear axle to keep the rear sprung-to unsprung weight ratio favourable and the wheels upright in a corner, and the package is beginning to look very promising.

The key to Aston Vantage appeal i its simplicity. It goes straight to the top of the class where driveability and practicality are concerned. Looking out over the humped bonnet its six foot width (nearly three inches wider than a Daytona) is well defined. The boot is large enough, the handbrake works well, all the controls fall to hand, and legroom is only a problem for the rear seat passengers who still sit in acceptable Capri-like discomfort. Understated leather-bound quality describes the interior, however I would have expected the front seats to be more suited to such a car. Lateral support and head restraint were lacking, they were like the fly of handbrake — unmistakably Aston. Like so many current cars fan assistance is needed to push any fresh air through, but it is quiet, and the inside spacious — it's a good car to work in

It was lovely to read the name Smiths on all the instruments even if the speedometer **was** 10 per cent optimistic—by error or design? But I'm getting diverted — this is a thoroughbred. Only a British thoroughbred would have an effective but obviously home-brewed front spoiler attached to a superbly finished car, black sticky stuff oozing from inside the headlight fairings, and a rather crude radiator blank. The petty finish shortcomings almost add to the character, because somebody has laboured to make and fit the parts — not the same thing as poor mass production finish at all.

I didn't even think of looking for a choke (there isn't one anyway). It seemed natural to give the throttle a couple of pumps in the morning to start and then nurse the eight for a few hundred yards until the chill was off. The stupendous muted growl of a big, mildly-tuned V8 breathing through four 48 IDF Weber carburettors on full throttle is pure machismo. Yet with what must be well over 350 lb. ft. torque at around 4,500 rpm — when the real kick in the back starts — its pure unfussyness and massive low down bite at least equals all the screaming Italian horses in the world. Vantage performance is well documented; a standing quarter mile in 13.7 sec, 0-100 mph in 13.0 sec, 0-60 in a shattering 5.4 sec all involve no more than the first three gears. Using 6,500 rpm there is still the 144 mph fourth and estimated 170 mph top to be used — very occasionally in anger, but mostly in peace.

Although in outright terms Vantage performance is not quite up to Daytona standards, it is equally effortless, and much quieter than the Ferrari on the road at least. Through to speeds in to the 120 mph bracket there is only the muted engine, and ever present, but not unpleasant, noise, generated by Pirelli 255/60 CN 12 VR tyres.

I could fall in love with the Aston because it's British, and hand-made. I could cope with its faults, and get reasonably priced bits for it if it went wrong. Dammit, a competent owner driver could look after the thing. The rear differential is out of Salisbury, the gearbox by dependable ZF — what else could go wrong except the trivial things? Lucas Opus electronic ignition has always been reliable, but Italian words like Marelli spell midnight failure and parts scarcity to me.

Thankfully and at the last minute "my" Vantage was supplied by supercar brokers Autosearch who have the car for sale. The first owner can have had little emphathy with it. Lack of first service, or possibly factory attention had left the Koni dampers far too soft, and I wondered if the immediately apparent, joggly ride could really be right. Even in its floppy state for the photographic session, the Vantage stopped well, and steered better. Ideally geared with 2.8 turns from lock to lock the Adwest-AC Delco power steering was hard to fault and enticed me on to power oversteer the Vantage from second gear corners with utter confidence, and also balance the big beast oversteering round and round the steering pad at MIRA.

The Aston factory did what they could to taughten the car in a couple of hours, and managed to transform the rear. "You will have to live with the front for the moment — we need more time," they said. Time I did not have. The open road beckoned.

While I was at Aston, they lent me their sometimes raced, stiffly set-up works development car for a quick trip around the lanes. It confirmed "my" car's tendency to wander very slightly at high speed, but more on a countrylane, was only due to the maladjusted front dampers. I could live with it, and even so my subtle green Vantage was utterly predictable through the fast corners, understeering as the conception suggested and mildly tightening its line on a trailing throttle.

The Vantage rolls a lot in a corner (something we remarked on in our *Autotest*, (9 April, 1977), but it confirms a feeling that I have had for some time that within sensible limits, the more roll you have, the more roadgoing predictability there is, and of course the nicer the car is in the wet. Had Aston Martin chosen an independent suspension system for the rear — all too sensitive to incorrect setting up — lots of driver-confusing camber change would have been needed to compensate for the present amount of roll, or much less roll designed in. A car like the roadgoing Daytona (independently sprung at the rear) has less "on limit" predictability than the Aston, and only much stiffer front-engined cars like the Maserati Khamsin, with an excellent independent rear end can match the Aston's chassis balance. I haven't driven a 400 GT Ferrari which should be good, but the point is, all lack the Aston's rugged simplicity, and all-weather predictability.

After four days and 700 miles, I felt exactly the same way about the Vantage as I did about my Triumph Bonneville. Loving its British sanity and honestness; also the little touches, like the driver-operated passengers door lock, and electric windows that worked with the ignition switched off for forgetful people like me. Yet using the viceless braking, steering, handling and sheer urge to the full, the motor ran over 90 deg. C. water termperature. Our Road Test car did that too and no harm resulted. An average fuel consumption figure of 12.9 mpg should be of little concern to somebody with £24,500 for a new Vantage and could be improved on. But who would want to with all that usable performance?

Empiric development for the 30 or so Vantages built has left small quality gaps, and Aston recognise that there is room for further suspension tuning. No Porsche would sport a "bolt on" spoiler and radiator blank (if they had radiators), nor would the dampers need tuning at the first service. But could you fall in love with a Porsche? I doubt it. The very soul of the people at Aston Martin is built into the Vantage. Either you are sympathetic or not. To me the Vantage is the most simple, predictable, quiet, four-seat thoroughbred available today — it also happens to be the fastest.

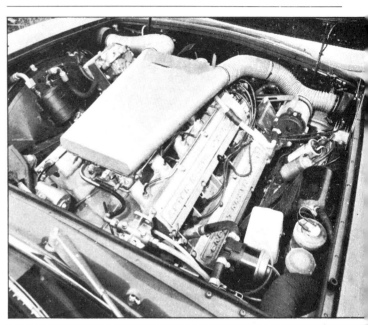

# A true grand tourer

**SIMON TAYLOR recounts a memorable trip to Le Mans in a traditional British grand tourer, an Aston Martin V8.**

I can't claim to share John Bolster's *penchant* for horses for courses when it comes to Continental motoring, for almost all my fortnightly trips for BBC Radio to the European Grands Prix during the season use efficient, boring aeroplanes. But I have had one highly memorable drive to a motor race in the past year, when Aston Martin kindly loaned me their V8 demonstrator for a hectic haul to the race they finally won 19 years ago — the Le Mans 24 Hours.

Borrowing any of the classic supercars is an exciting experience, but so often a dream car turns out to be a disappointment in reality. Either its swoopy lines clothe a cockpit which is impossible to see out of and fatiguingly noisy over long distances; or its designers — or more likely its marketing men — have had to sell out to the middle-aged bracket who are probably the only customers able to afford their car, so that soft suspension and power-assisted silence have taken precedence over gut-feel.

Not having driven an Aston since the days when they had six cylinders, I was curious to learn into which category fell the latest cars from the healthily reconstituted Newport Pagnell factory. What I discovered was that the Aston, almost uniquely perhaps, avoids both pitfalls. It has all the creature comforts, the air conditioning, the power steering, the beautifully detailed interior; 'my' car was even an automatic. But it also has a hard feel of total solidity and tautness, allied to superbly surefooted roadholding and handling, with none of the apparent fragility associated with the Italian exotics. It is a big brute of a car, but a brute which responds sweetly to authoritative commands.

The Aston is six feet wide and at first seems almost ungainly in traffic, but on further acquaintance the width brings an extraordinary feeling of stability. The power steering is light enough for parking but at high speeds gives a very definite message back from the big Avon tyres. The brakes too, despite their considerable servo assistance, need a very firm prod in an emergency, but then the effect is totally reassuring.

The view over the high-humped bonnet is impressive, and the dash is neatly laid out with all the dials visible with one's hands on the wheel — it's an obvious point, but so few dashboards achieve this. The seats deserve the highest praise because, without a sporty shape, they manage to supply support for the back and shoulders and remain comfortable over long periods at the wheel. There are proper back seats, but with a straight-arm driving position, leg room for the passenger behind becomes marginal; and the boot, though wide and deep, is very short, so for really grand touring the Aston is a two-seater.

Everything is beautifully made. The smell of leather on opening the door evokes a bygone era. The leather-rimmed steering wheel with its rim depressed to accommodate the thumbs, the neat switchgear, the passenger footrest, the faultless carpeting and trim, all exude a quality which used to be thought to be British. In fact, this is above all a traditional British car: its lines graceful but restrained, its exhaust note purposeful but subdued. What reputations could be rescued if all British cars were Aston Martins!

Under the bonnet the four-cam 5.3-litre alloy V8 is a joy to behold, and it certainly produces a lot of power. Just how much Aston won't tell us, but even in automatic form there was a smooth rush of acceleration up to and beyond 140mph every time even a short stretch of *autoroute* presented itself. We were travelling, not testing; but zero to 60 in six seconds, and to 100 in a quarter of a minute, which is what the proper road tests have shown for the automatic, felt easily believable. Even those figures don't quite convey the big Aston's effortless swoop towards the horizon in instant obedience to a poke at the loud pedal. Around 5000 rpm, roughly 125 mph, felt an easy gait on the less crowded roads.

If I were fortunate enough to be able to afford an Aston Martin I would specify the manual version to take full advantage of that wonderful engine, even though the excellent Chrysler Torqueflite transmission accentuates the effortless character of the car. On crowded, narrow French roads, when needing to dart in and out of a queue of *poids-lourds,* the kickdown wasn't quite responsive enough — and in any case

*A rather shorter, but no less impressive, journey was undertaken by the Assistant Editor when he travelled to Wiscombe in Devon for the Aston Martin Owners Club's annual hillclimb. The car, an automatic V8, was kindly provided by HWM Motors of Walton-on-Thames. The Aston is pictured down on the coast close to Wiscombe (above) and in the paddock among the competition cars (below). The AMOC badge proudly displayed on the radiator grille is that of Mike Harting of HWM, whose personal transport the car was. On more recent Aston Martins the bonnet line has been lowered slightly and a few other detail changes made.*

tended to unleash more power than was needed for the manoeuvre — so the second gear hold got used pretty frequently.

Except at very low speeds the suspension is not uncomfortably hard, even on the bad surfaces of Northern France, yet on long, sweeping corners the Aston feels as steady as a rock even at fairly unmentionable speeds. It is only when driving fast through a series of undulating S-bends that one remembers that this is a big, heavy car and understeer intrudes, but it never began to feel insecure — which helped to keep fatigue at bay when hurrying northwards up the RN1 to catch the hovercraft after a sleepless 24 hours. And thanks to the excellent air-conditioning the windows never need be opened, and the body's smooth shape and the total lack of creaks and rattles mean that this is a very quiet car at speed.

There was something rather splendid about taking

so British a car to Le Mans, where British cars used to do so well, and where apart from that 1959 win Aston Martin won their class so many times. At an overnight stop in Alençon our car (with Aston's cherished number AMV8) shared the car park in front of the hotel, quite coincidentally, with a DB4GT and a DB4GT Zagato which had travelled down to the race in convoy. Certainly the French enthusiasts and even the *gendarmerie* showed their appreciation by treating us with exaggerated courtesy.

Since our trip the Aston range has had detail changes, including a lower bonnet line and revised damper settings. But nothing can improve the basic concept: a big, powerful, responsive, handmade touring car which its lucky owners surely find worth every penny of the £23,000 they've had to pay for it, and every drop of each gallon they have to pump into it every 14 miles. What a car the Vantage must be . . . ∎

# THE POWER AND THE GLORY

B et this month's front cover gave you a bit of a shock, didn't it? Well don't worry too much, we haven't sold out and gone over to biking — it's too difficult finding somewhere to fit the Halda.

Nevertheless, whether you're into motorcycles or not, you can hardly have failed to notice that interesting things have been happening on the two-wheel scene over the last decade. Not only has bike racing achieved deserved acclaim as one of the most exciting, colourful and refreshingly uncorrupted sports around, but big changes have also been taking place on the roads.

It seems like only yesterday that the stock biker image was of evil Hell's Angels — denims stained with every kind of foul and filthy exudation — biting the heads off young virgins and raping chickens. In fact, as far as your average county

magistrate goes it *was* only yesterday, but in general the motorcycle has recently attained a greater degree of public acceptance. This has largely been due to the increased "civilising" of two-wheeled transport. Electric starting devices are now *de rigeur* on all but the humblest hack or sparse trail bike, and hitherto neglected areas such as instrumentation, lighting, reliability and rider comfort have been developed to make the modern bike a practical and exhilarating means of getting about.

On the technical front the modern multi-cylinder machine enjoys the very latest in technological sophistication — light alloy castings, overhead cams, four valves per cylinder, adjustable height suspension, even automatic gearboxes in some cases. The result is that the majority of current production motorcycles feature quick,

efficient engines and light, responsive handling.

The really big bikes — 750cc and up — are tagged "superbikes", and rightly so. In terms of outright performance they're little short of shattering, developing power outputs which ten years ago were the sole preserve of highly specialised racing machines. These days most of the major bike manufacturers compete fiercely with each other for the honours of producing the fastest, most powerful production bike in the world. A couple of years ago the crown was worn by the fiery Kawasaki Z1, followed by the notorious Laverda Jota. Right now these honours undoubtedly fall upon the Godzilla of motorcycles — Honda's new CBX, a veritable loin-grabber of a machine, boasting an all-alloy six cylinder transverse unit with twin overhead cams, 24-valves, 1050cc and a

power output of 105bhp. The darned thing looks so downright mean that the average bloke would think twice about standing next to it, let alone climbing aboard and trying to harness that power to public tarmac.

But just how fast *is* a machine like this? Is it as difficult to handle as its looks would suggest? How practical is it and, more important from our point of view, how does it compare in terms of handling and performance with its four-wheeled counterpart?

Faced with a parcel of questions like that, there's only one thing to do — get in there and find the answers first-hand by organising a comparative test with a suitable car. Which is just what we did.

After much deliberation, the car we chose was Aston Martin's glorious Vantage, the best looking and quickest chunk of automotion you're likely to find anywhere.

Powered by Aston Martin's own 5340cc, 4-ohc, triple Webered V8, the Vantage is a superbly engineered piece of equipment, combining as it does sheer performance and handling with classically understated styling — the very best of British. Agreed, there are cars with greater flash — but superfluous pizazz wasn't what we were after. Sure, there are a couple of cars which perform better in certain specifics — but we were looking for top performance throughout the range.

The best average, if you like, although average is far too mundane a word to be applied to the Vantage. Huge thanks are due to Ian Webb, who loaned us the car through his Autosearch company of Station Garage, East Horsely, Surrey, a company which specialises in all manner of mouthwatering exotica from AC Cobras to Ferraris and even Lola T70s. If you've got a few grand with no home to go to, the 'phone number is 048 65 2741.

Now it's all very well getting hold of machinery like the Honda and the Aston, but to get the very best from them it's obvious that you need someone pretty adept behind the wheel or handlebar. Everyone here would quite happily have plummeted around in the Vantage but we felt it important to get a driver who *really* knows what high speed driving's all about and whose opinion would be totally unimpeachable. And the thought of anyone on our staff trying to get to grips with the Honda was in the realms of fantasy.

So who did we choose? The best, of course; the very best.

For the Honda, no less a bike *meister* than Phil Read, eight times World Motorcycle Champion and current Honda works' Formula 1 rider, a motorcyclist of immense and unquestionable skill and phenomenal experience. As one of the world's greatest ever bike racers and a superb development rider, Phil Read was ideal.

The mighty Aston was trusted into the splendidly capable hands of Derek Bell — 1975 Le Mans winner, former Ferrari F1 driver and one of the best sports and saloon car racers of all time. With his current position as this magazine's No 1 test driver, his choice was almost automatic.

The venue chosen for this grand extravaganza of power, talent and pound notes was our customary test track near Chertsey in Surrey. This offers a fast, two mile outer circuit

within which can be found various facilities, including a tricky, tortuous section of tarmac aptly called the "Snake mountain course".

For the timing we used an excellent Heuer electronic-eye set-up incorporating three sets of timing lights and an automatic data print out.

Before going into details of the tests and their results, a brief run down of the vehicles:

ASTON MARTIN V8 VANTAGE
This is a high performance version of the Aston Martin DBS V8, boasting quadruple 48mm Weber downdraught carbs which breath expensive mixes of fuel and air into a 90° Vee engine of 5340cc. Power output is around 435bhp (Aston's simply claim that it is "adequate", without going into greater detail), with a power/weight ratio of 243 bhp/ton. This is transmitted to the road courtesy of a five-speed gearbox, torsion bushed propshaft and a hypoid final drive with limited slip and a ratio of 3.54:1. The 7 X 15in dia wheels are shod with

Pirelli CN12 radials which, for the purpose of the test, we inflated to 40psi all round.

The front suspension features coil springs, telescopic dampers and an anti-roll bar; rear suspension is by Aston's renowned De Dion axle located by parallel trailing arms and a Watts linkage. Once again, telescopic dampers and coil springs are used.

Top speed for the car is estimated at 170mph, with 0–60 acceleration of 5.4 secs. Price? A meagre £24,500.

HONDA CBX
Christened "The Super Sport King" by Honda's publicity men, the CBX is without argument the world's fastest and most powerful production motorcycle.

The six-cylinder, all-alloy, transverse engine is an air-cooled giant which developes a meaty 105bhp from 1047cc, yielding a power/weight ratio of 398.5 bhp/ton and a top whack of 135mph.

Drive is via a multi-plate wet clutch, five-speed constant

mesh gearbox and heavy duty chain to the 18in diameter rear wheel. Tyres as tested were the standard Japanese Dunlop Gold Seal, well scrubbed in for the purpose of the test and inflated to 28 psi front, 42 psi rear.

A particularly interesting feature of the CBX is the adoption of a "diamond frame" configuration chassis. Instead of the more common tubular frame, which cradles the engine in one or two down-tubes, the CBX utilises the engine as a stressed unit, suspending it from the three top tubes. By doing this the forks can be positioned closer to the engine — no down tubes to get in the way — thereby reducing the wheelbase and, as a consequence, improving response and handling.

The price, for those who want to take a ride on the wild side, is £2560 incl VAT.

THE TESTS
In order to achieve a fair comparison between the two machines — which, after all, was the object of the exercise

— we were careful to put them through tests which would emphasise their individual characteristics, and which would, in the final analysis, show no overall bias towards either vehicle.

All tests were carried out on a dry but overcast day, on a dry but slightly dusty track.

## TIMED LAPS
To set the scene and to gain an initial indication of how the machines would perform at very high speeds, we timed bike and car over several

flying laps of the 2-mile outer circuit. Both Phil and Derek were instructed to drive quickly but safely, ie. at about eight-tenths of maximum potential.

The outer circuit comprises mainly fast curves, including a banked 180° corner and a fast but difficult esses.

After a couple of shakedown laps to become accustomed to their respective steeds, Phil and Derek cracked the timing beam for the first of their timed laps.

Now we're a pretty blasé

crew at *Triple C* — spending our working lives immersed in high performance motoring of one kind or another it's only to be expected — but none of us was prepared for the sheer fury of bike and car exploding into view as they completed that first timed lap. The bike was narrowly in front, Phil hunched low over the tank, his head tucked down out of the slipstream, his right hand winding the throttle up against its stop. Looming in his wake came the Aston, squatting down hard on its offside tyres, the low thunder of its exhausts setting up a bass rumble to counterpoint the muted shriek of the Honda Six.

And then they were gone, dragging us forward from the trackside in the swirling vacuum of their slipstreams.

Barely had we recovered from this brain-numbing spectacle when they were with us again. This time the Aston was leading, Derek looking his usual cool self as he meticulously harnessed the power of the Aston thoroughbred, and sent it throbbing out of the bend at 130mph. But tucked right behind and fighting for every inch of tarmac between car and bike was Phil Read, his racer instinct taking over as he wrestled with the bucking Honda. Even from the trackside we could see the back wheel of the bike whipping and snaking across the track as the rider fought to keep it in line. A speedway slide at 125mph? Now *that* takes skill.

After several more laps even Phil's bravery could do nothing to prevent the long-legged Aston Martin drawing away. With the car pulling 150mph at the end of the straight, there was little Phil could do but breathe in the dust and hang grimly on. For the Honda, it was a losing battle.

Derek: "That car's just great. The more I use it the better it feels. It may look big and clumsy, but it's a joy to drive. Hey Phil, why did you keep wagging your backside at me?"

Phil: "Oh, that bike's a real handful at speed. It weaves all over the place at anything over 105mph, even on the straight. I can't work out whether it's the frame, the dampers, the tyres or a combination of all three. It's It's most likely the tyres, I think — wish I had a set of Formula 1 bike racing tyres on it. It's a shame I couldn't stay in front of the car — once I was behind, it kept throwing crap off the track at me, which didn't help much."

## STANDING START ¼ MILE
If the timed laps were a perfect exercise in flat-out

performance, the standing starts proved to be a lesson in the instantaneous translation of latent energy into surging motion. Time and technical difficulties prevented us from achieving a full range of acceleration figures, but the ¼-mile test sufficed to highlight the straight-line differences between car and bike.

Side by side the Honda and the Vantage lined up at the timing lights. Derek and Phil swapped grins, then fixed their eyes on our starter as he raised the flag. (Well, white hanky actually but it served the purpose.) The ground shook gently beneath our feet as driver and rider built up revs, then the flag dropped and they were away, leaving the line simultaneously with a howl of tormented rubber.

The Aston, with its massive power, sunk momentarily to its haunches as the rear wheels spun against the track then took off to a pulsing throb of V8 music, leaving thick black lines behind. At the same time Phil dropped the clutch of the Honda, leaning his weight forward over the bars as the rear tyre smoked then bit, and the front wheel lifted a foot off the ground. The rear end snaked slightly, but there was no chance of Phil allowing the beast to better him. For the rest of the ¼-mile the best Derek could do was to try to extract the most he could from the Aston; the only sight he had of his adversary was the rapidly diminishing name "Phil Read" written across the back of the scarlet and white leathers, as bike and rider drew inexorably away.

The average times told their own story — the bike had scored a time nearly 2½ seconds better than the metallic green Aston, popping the lights at a shattering 11.7 seconds — a respectable enough time for a Pro Street drag bike let alone an unmodified production machine.

Despite the Honda's recurring habit of weaving along the straight Phil was much happier now that the bike had gone some way towards avenging its defeat on the circuit. His smile was to broaden even more as the day progressed.

Derek: "With the Aston's power/weight disadvantage I knew there was little chance of beating the bike so I simply concentrated on getting away as cleanly as I could and making the gearchanges as slick as possible. The gearchange is notchy but not at all stiff, and there was no let up of power the whole length of the strip. It just kept accelerating."

Phil: "Fantastic! This bike's got the power and acceleration of a Grand Prix racer, but of course it's much heavier so you have to be a bit careful. People have said that it can be tricky on standing starts but I found it was more willing to spin the rear wheel than to do a lurid wheelie."

## SLALOM

This test, with the machines timed two ways over a zig-zag course delineated by eight road cones, was used in an attempt to highlight the manoeuvrability and response of each vehicle, and its ability to make sudden directional changes. Would the stability of four wheels compensate for the size and width of the Aston? Would the narrowness and speed of the Honda negate the effort of hauling its mass from bank to bank?

Derek was the first to go, squealing the Aston off the line in a flurry of dust, and chucking the big car through the first "gate" with deceptive ease. At each stab of the throttle the nose of the Aston lunged upwards, snarling at each cone as it slipped past only a couple of inches from the side of the car. The biggest problem was at the halfway point, where Derek was forced to make a wide U-turn in order to line himself up for the return run. The car looked quick and nimble — unbelievably so for a vehicle of such considerable bulk. No-one could really imagine the bike bettering this virtuoso performance — no-one but Phil, that was.

Now as bikes go, the Honda is a biggie. Six cylinders of engine plus all the paraphernalia to go with it makes for a pretty hefty chunk of metal to be stuck on two wheels. The thing is, someone must have forgotten to tell Phil Read that you can't chuck big, heavy bikes around like lightweight racers. As if it were a high speed moped he weaved the Honda between the cones with a skill and dexterity which suspended belief. As the bike banked one way, Phil was already leaning in the opposite direction to bring the bike over for the next change of course. Bike and rider became a single, sinuous entity, which treaded its way through the gates as if attached to an invisible rail. To save time at the halfway U-turn, Phil would stab the rear brake pedal to send the tail skating round, steadying the bike during its subsequent slide by stabbing his foot onto the ground. His times were *bloody* quick — a crushing 4 secs better than the Aston, and Derek certainly hadn't been

hanging around.

Derek: "Hey, my arms really ache after that lot! There's so much car you can't just flick it about. Half the time I couldn't even see where I was in relation to the cones. Steering and throttle response are very very good, which makes it easy to point the car, but you have to get a rhythm going so as not to be caught out by roll-steer delay. Once you've got it rocking nicely it's okay, but this car's basically a high speed performer and its ride and suspension characteristics don't really allow for the kind of low speed response you need for this sort of test."

Phil: "That was amazing. It's a big bike all right, but it responds really well, considering. And of course, on a test like this I'm not suffering from that high speed weave. I'm pretty sure now that it's caused by the tyres. The annoying thing is there are far better tyres available in this country — not necessarily British ones — and it's a shame that Honda have to put their bikes out on rubber which isn't up to the job. To be polite, the tyres make it 'slightly unstable', but otherwise it's magic."

## SNAKE

As mentioned earlier in the feature, The Snake is designed to emulate a mountain pass, with tight and winding bends all jumbled up with adverse cambers, dips and brows. Pretty scarey stuff and, we felt, a chance for the Aston to redress the balance by virtue of its better stability.

However, this wasn't to be, for despite Derek's absolute mastery of the car and his copybook driving, he was still nearly 2 secs adrift of Phil, who rode the fiery Honda through the twists and turns with heart-pounding verve. On each bend he banked the bike down as low as it would go, the footpegs scraping the tarmac, the rear wheel constantly trying to scrabble outwards.

Over a particularly wicked blind brow, where the Aston was rising high on its suspension and almost — but not quite — becoming airborne, the front wheel of the Honda would rise a full three feet into the air in a terrifying 70mph wheelie, staying up on its rear tyre for what seemed like an age. No wonder that, after performing his stint, Phil refused a couple more laps for photographic purposes. "If I go round again," he said with sardonic candour, "I'm going to fall off." Who were we to try and persuade him otherwise?

Derek: "That was more like it. I had enough room before

# Honda CBX

MAKE & MODEL: HONDA CBX 1000   PRICE £2560

**PERFORMANCE**
Maximum Speed — 138mph
Standing Quarter Mile — 11.7sec at 117mph
Fuel Consumption — Hard Riding — 28.7 mpg
Cruising — 35.5mpg
Best Full-Tank Range — 156miles

**ENGINE**
Type — air-cooled transverse in-line four stroke; six cylinders, double cams, four valves per overhead
Displacement — 1047cc   Power — 105bhp at 9000rpm
Torque — 62lb/ft at 8000rpm      Bore & Stroke — 64.5 x 53.4mm
Compression Ratio — 9.3:1
Induction — six 28mm Keihin VB constant velocity carbs
Exhaust — six-into-two
Oil System — wet sump, 9.7 pint capacity
Ignition — capacitive discharge, pointless

**TRANSMISSION**
Clutch — 13 plates, wet. Primary Drive — Hy-Vo chain, 2.27:1
Final Drive — ⅜in chain   Gears — five

**CHASSIS**
Frame — triangular spine type incorporating three top tubes and using engine as a structural member
Front Suspension — Showa tele forks, 6.3in travel
Rear Suspension — Showa FVQ spring shocks; five position spring preload, position compression damping, three position damping; 3.9in travel
Wheelbase — 59in
Ground Clearance — 7.5in
Trail — 4.72in
Castor angle —62.5 degrees
Seat Height — 32.25in
Weight (wet) — 562lbs
Fuel Capacity — 4.4galls
Tyres — Dunlop Gold Seal tubeless, 3.50 x 19 front, 4.25 x 18 rear
Brakes — twin 10.75in discs front, single 11.75in disc rear

**INSTRUMENTS**
150mph speedo with trip; 11000rpm rev counter, red lined at 9500rpm; vol warning lights for high beam, neutral, oil pressure, indicators

**EQUIPMENT**
Electrical 12v-14Ah battery and 35
Lighting 60/55w quartz halogen headlamp

# Aston Martin V8

Make and Model: Aston Martin V8 Vantage    Price: £22,999

**Performance**
Maximum speed: 170mph    Standing quarter mile: 14.2 sec
Fuel consumption: 14mpg

**Engine**
Type: V8 with double overhead chain driven camshafts. Pistons set at 90' vee and crank has five main bearings.
Displacement: 5340cc        Power: 425bhp (estimated)
Torque: Not available        Bore and stroke: 100mm x 85mm
Compression ratio: 9:1        Induction: 4 Weber 48IDF's
Oil system: Wet sump holding 20 pints.
Ignition: Electronic system.

**Transmission**
Clutch: 26.67mm single plate diaphragm spring, hydraulically operated and self adjusting.
Final drive: Hypoid drive unit, chassis mounted in rubber supported cradle. LSD standard. Ratio: 3.54:1.
Gears: Five speed with synchro on all forward ratios. Reverse 2.63:1, 1st 2.90:1, 2nd 1.78:1, 3rd 1.22:1, 4th 1.00:1, 5th 0.845:1.

**Chassis**
Front suspension: Independent with transverse unequal length wishbones and ball jointed king pins. Co-axial coil springs and large diameter telescopic shock absorbers. Anti-roll bar.
Rear suspension: De Dion axle located by parallel trailing arms and Watt linkage. Coil springs and telescopic shock absorbers. Roller spline drive shafts.
Steering: Power assisted rack and pinion. Collapsible column and turning lock of 2.9 turns.
Tank capacity: 25 gallons with reserve warning light indicating 3 gallons left.
Brakes: Servo assisted ventilated front and rear discs with independent hydraulic circuits. Floor mounted fly-off handbrake.
Length: 15ft 3¾ins    Width: 6ft    Height: 4ft 4¼ins
Wheelbase: 8ft 6¾ins    Kerb weight: 3,800lb
Wheels and tyres:    Light alloy ventilated wheels with 7inch wide rims. 250x60x15VR radial tyres.

**Instruments**
Tachometer, speedometer, oil pressure gauge, water temperature gauge, ammeter.

**Equipment**
68 amp hour battery with master switch, custom designed air conditioning with two 4 speed heavy duty blowers, stereo radio and cassette player. Electric windows HRW, high and low intensity horns with changeover switch, under bonnet and boot lights. Usual stalks for wipers, lights, indicators, washers and horns.

each bend to use the weight of the car. If you have enough time to set the thing up then it's solid as a rock. There's no noticeable dive under braking so you can power into a bend and balance the car with throttle and steering. You *know* that there's a lot of car to slow down and you wait for the weight to have an unpleasant effect, but it doesn't. The brakes are immensely powerful, yet there's no sensation of weight suddenly transferring to the front of the car under braking.

"Handling is basically very neutral, going into understeer when you're really pressing on; this can easily be countered on the throttle if necessary, and it's no trouble to put the car into a slide if things get tricky."

Phil: "The tyres are still the

limiting factor, but at least you don't get the weave below about 105mph so it was okay on the Snake. The brakes are very powerful, but it doesn't pay to forget that this is a heavy machine and it's possible to lock the wheels up if you're not careful. It handles remarkably well, although it's too heavy to be termed a sports bike; what it is is a terrific 110mph open road cruiser.

"That 70mph wheelie? Well, after The Mountain at Cadwell Park it's easy. You just have to remember to keep the front wheel straight when it comes down."

SUMMARY
In the tests which we carried out, the Honda CBX was unquestionably the faster package. No doubt the Aston Martin Vantage has more going for it at the top end of the spectrum, but under normal conditions, speeds in that zone are purely academic.

In terms of price related to performance, the Honda is once again the winner. At 2½ grand it offers an incomparable combination of speed, acceleration and manoeuvrability, and there can't be anything to touch it on four wheels or two when it

comes to clocking up fast road averages. It has the pace for motorways, the acceleration for safe overtaking, and the handling to make ferreting through traffic jams an absolute joy. A fantastic machine.

Thus far, though, we've only talked about end results — the bare bones of speed and handling. Other equally important factors come into play when considering that we're talking about modes of transport, not specialised racing machinery. An F1 Lotus would have outperformed both of our test machines — but it would make a lousy car to live with from day to day. What we have to take into account is the *means* by which our two vehicles deliver the goods, and it's in this area that the Aston shows its true worth.

Despite giving best to the Honda on three out of four tests, the Aston has so much more going for it than the figures alone would suggest. The Honda, like any motorcycle, is a raw, pared down package, carrying little which doesn't contribute directly towards performance. And that's what biking is all about.

The Vantage, on the other hand, is not only an outstanding performer — it's more than that. With its superb engineering and design, its luxurious trim and appointments, its sheer civility and breeding, the Aston Martin demonstrates a supreme combination of power and style. The end result and the means of achieving that end are fused inseparably to create a work of automotive art rather than a simple mode of transport.

You can't fall off an Aston Martin, and you can't get wet in one — what's more, you can stay dry and safe at high speed *and* in glorious luxury.

Of course, the ideal solution is an Aston Martin Vantage for everyday use and a Honda CBX for sunny weekends. You should be so lucky . . . .

**TG**

# ASTON MARTIN V8 auto

**Recent improvements have brought Aston's magnificent performance car close to perfection. This automatic version offers staggering acceleration in the mid-range allied to superb handling and braking; sumptuous interior lives up to beautiful exterior finish; gearbox rather slow to react to kickdown**

LIKE most cars costing more than the average man earns in four years, the Aston Martin V8 is surrounded by myth and legend. One of the legends is that, because it's a big car weighing almost 35 cwt, it must therefore be difficult and unwieldy to drive, whereas anyone who has ever had the privilege to drive a modern Aston will vigorously refute any such suggestions.

The Bill Towns-designed aluminium body, which cloaks the current coupé, originally appeared in 1968 as the DBS (using the straight six engine). Ten years later, with only minor visiual changes, it doesn't look in the least bit dated. More important than that, Aston Martin-Lagonda (1975) Ltd, which rose from the ashes of a company in disarray, shows every sign of having effected a full recovery, and the quiet enthusiasm and determination of the entire workforce, from shop floor personnel up to the managing director, is immediately apparent to anyone who visits the Newport Pagnell factory.

This new spirit has translated

itself not only into new models, such as the Vantage, Lagonda and Volante convertible, but also into detail refinements and improved quality control in the existing range. As unashamed Aston Martin fans, we are delighted to report that the latest model offers a standard of finish unsurpassed in the supercar league: this magnificent car is now assembled as magnificently as it deserves.

Apart from the Volante, which is not yet available in Britain, and the Lagonda, Aston Martin's range now consists of three models: the V8 five-speed manual, the V8 Auto (which is the subject of this test) and the manual Vantage.

A three-year improvement plan, instituted when the new company was formed, has just reached fruition. External differences are the new bonnet shape incorporating a smaller "power bulge", the fitting of overriders on the bumpers and the built-in rear spoiler previously fitted only to the Vantage. The exhaust is now stainless steel.

Some fine tuning of the suspension has been carried out with the aim of improving the ride: the front spring rates have been reduced and the rubber used to give progressive-rate damping in the Vantage is no longer used in the standard car. Low speed damping has been reduced, although overall damping has more than doubled.

The brakes have been modified. The radially slotted front discs, introduced on the Vantage to eliminate judder induced by glazing, are now used on all the cars, and a g-conscious pressure limiting valve has been developed to replace the previously used line pressure limiter. The new valve only limits rear braking when locking point is approached.

The majority of the revisions are to the interior. The leather-trimmed panels which were used for the instrument surround, clock housing, glovebox lid, central console and door cappings, have been replaced by polished walnut. The lower door panel is now trimmed in carpet, new-style headrests are fitted as standard, the cloth headlining is replaced by leather and a new central console provides a glovebox and cigar lighter for rear seat passengers.

The air conditioning system has been extensively improved, and new demister vents are fitted to the top of the facia. The speakers for the standard radio/cassette player have been repositioned, a new clock is fitted, illumination has been provided for the air conditioning panel, a delay mechanism for the interior light has been installed, and there's now a tyre pressure extension for the spare wheel.

All these modifications indicate a new attention to detail which perhaps in the past was not meticulous enough. With Aston Martin's restored pride, there is no reason why the steady flow of six cars a week (each taking three months to build) should not continue for the forseeable future. Total production of V8s, incidentally, recently topped the 1,000 mark.

Does the Aston have any rivals? Either you are an Aston Martin fan or you are not, so any contemplation of alternatives is perhaps pointless; to that select band capable of spending £22,998.69 (the manual gearbox version costs a fraction over £1,000 extra), any suggestion that cars like the Jaguar XJ-S (£15,149 or the Mercedes-Benz 450 SLC (£18,250) offer better value for money may well be dismissed with contempt. One rival that may come into the reckoning is Porsche's 928 (£19,499 in either manual or automatic form) but it isn't nearly so fast in equivalent form.

Aston Martin do not publish power or torque figures for their four-camshaft all-alloy 5,340 cc V8, but they claim that development carried out last year has increased

maximum power by some 20 per cent. Suffice to say that there is more than enough brake horsepower for the job.

As we have pointed out in past road tests of high performance cars, our desire to retain our driving licences precludes us from obtaining two-way maximum speed figures on the public road, while MIRA's banked circuit is unsuitable for speeds in excess of 130 mph.

Occasionally we have the opportunity to verify manufacturers' claims on a rapid continental journey; in the case of the Aston this was not possible. However, we consider Aston Martin's claim of "at least 140 mph" to be on the conservative side ("at least 150 mph" is claimed for the manual gearbox car) and that the true figure is more like 145 mph, at which speed the engine is doing less than 5,700 rpm.

With a slight flat spot adding to the disadvantages of its heavy weight and its automatic gearbox, our Aston didn't rocket off the line. By super car standards its 0-30 mph time of 3.6 sec is mediocre, while 0-60 mph in 7.5 sec is by no means outstanding. However, once its great mass is rolling, it really picks itself up and *goes* in no uncertain terms: from a standing start to 100 mph in 16.4 sec and to 120 mph in 25.7 sec is fairly dramatic by any standards (though obviously it cannot compare with the startling performance of the manual version).

Unless all your driving is in town, standing start acceleration is less important than what happens once you're on the move, and the Aston Auto really delivers the goods in kickdown: 30-50 mph in 2.3 sec, 50-70 mph in 3.3 sec, and 100-120 mph in 9.3 sec. Enough to make most other cars on the road dissolve into tiny specks in the rear-view mirror.

Apart from that flat spot (at around 1,800 rpm) we didn't think the Aston Auto's engine was as sweet as those of others we have driven in the past, and a slight tendency to spit back through the four twin-choke Webers on the overrun suggests that it was possibly a touch out of tune.

In other respects well mannered, and in our experience untemperamental, the big V8 may be burbled around at low speeds without fear of fouling the plugs, and once it's into its stride it pulls smoothly all the way to its rev limit of 6250 rpm (not actually marked on the rev counter). The muffled roar under full power will in no way be a disappointment to the majority of owners — the Aston cannot compete with the astonishing XJ-S for refinement, but the way in which it breaks the silence is music, to our ears at least.

We had no problem at all starting the engine in the recent mild weather, adopting the usual technique for Weber-carburetted cars of one stab on the throttle for priming and then turning the key. It was necessary on a couple of occasions, however, to choke the engine slightly before moving off.

As enthusiastic drivers, we prefer a manual gearbox in a car developing a lot of power, but if we are to use an automatic, the Chrysler

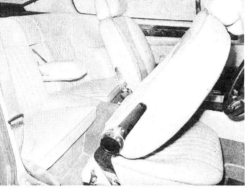

**Above: the leather trimmed seats are as comfortable as they look, giving good support in all areas. Left: there's just enough room for four adults in the Aston**

**Below left: an exquisite blend of walnut and leather, and all the panels fit perfectly. Below: air conditioning and the radio/cassette player (with speakers and automatic aerial) are standard**

Torqueflite is generally as good as any. We were a bit disappointed with the installation in the Aston: upward changes are virtually imperceptible apart from the change in engine note, and manual downchanges are equally smooth, but the kickdown is not what it might be. A delay of some two seconds intervenes before response to either full or part-throttle kickdown, though we would at least praise the part-throttle kickdown for its availability at higher speeds than is customary in most automatic boxes. Another fault we found was that the downward change following this delay comes in with an appreciable jolt, which can be unsettling on a wet road.

Using the lever and revving to 6250 rpm gives maximum speeds in the intermediates of 65 and 111 mph, but there is little to be gained from this, and one might as well allow the box to take care of the changes, which it does at around 57 and 97 mph.

It's advisable to have a credit card when you drive an Aston Martin, otherwise you need to carry huge bundles of pound notes to fill up the 25 gallon tank at fairly short intervals. Our overall consumption of 10.7 mpg reflects rather more enthusiastic driving than the average owner will indulge in, but in any case the "average owner" of an Aston is unlikely to have sleepless nights over anything as trivial as fuel consumption.

Considering the car's great weight and enormous power, the touring consumption of 14.6 mpg and the steady speed figures (interestingly, it's more frugal at 50 mph than at 30 mph) are really not too bad. A range of up to about 365 miles is possible on a full tank, and even our leaden-footed testers found no difficulty in passing the 250 mile mark with fuel to spare.

The Aston Martin's chassis, an excellent original design, has been carefully developed over the years. The aluminium body is non-structural, and all the strength is provided by a steel platform and superstructure, the most sensible choice for low-volume production. Front suspension is by unequal length wishbones and the de Dion rear end is located by parallel links with a Watts linkage to restrict lateral movements.

Without the slightest shadow of a doubt, the Adwest rack and pinion fitted to the Aston must be the finest assisted system in the world. The only time one is at all aware of it is at parking speeds, when it takes the effort out of moving the big Avon GR 70VR 15 tyres (the Vantage has Pirelli CN12s) on to lock. On the move it is exactly like an excellent unassisted system in a light car, informing the driver exactly where the front wheels are pointing and inspiring great confidence.

The grip bestowed by the wide tyres (on 7 in rims) is outstanding on dry surfaces, and remains surprisingly good in the wet, though (as with all high-powered motor cars) it is necessary to exercise caution on slippery surfaces.

Still fairly neutral in high speed bends, this Automatic Aston understeered more than others we have driven when hustled through tighter corners. It's a fairly easy matter, though, to provoke the tail out of line if need be.

The Aston has no significant faults in the handling department, proving that a well-engineered front engine/rear drive configuration is still highly desirable in a road car, even ignoring the practical aspects. Bumps in mid-corner barely affect it despite its great bulk, lifting off in a bend causes only a gradual and easily controlled reduction in understeer, and the overall responsiveness and impeccable stability make this a remarkably easy yet satisfying car to drive rapidly.

Efficient braking has always been a strong point in Astons, and the recent modifications have made the stopping power better than ever. The system on the automatic cars is exactly the same as for the manual versions.

Pedal pressure is high, and until the pads have warmed up the pedal feels lifeless. Once up to working temperature, however, they impart superb feel and are beautifully progressive. At no point during our test, despite some fairly hard driving, was there any trace of fade.

The Aston's immense bonnet, with its power bulge as imposing as ever, even if it has been reduced in height, and its classic lines, do not make for ideal visibility when parking. On the move, though, it's very easy to aim, and all-round visibility is at least adequate. Only in narrow streets, where it's hard to judge the width, does it begin to seem like a bulky motor car. The interior mirror and door mirror between them supply a comprehensive view of the road behind.

Standard lighting equipment on the Aston features a pair of 7 in Halogen headlamps, which we found more than adequate for most circumstances, giving a good spread of light on dip. Sensitive to criticisms that these are not as good as the old DBS system of four 5 in lamps, Aston offer the twin Cibié auxiliary lamps (standard equipment on the Vantage) as an extra. If the price of £210.60 sounds horrifying, bear in mind that extensive surgery to the grille is necessary to accommodate them. With these lamps on it's almost like driving in daylight, though they didn't seem to cause any discomfort to oncoming drivers.

The wipers clear the whole screen, do not lift even at very high speed, and the delay mechanism is very useful in light rain.

The design of the Aston, and in particular its de Dion rear suspension and inboard rear discs, conspires against outstanding accommodation. However, there is plenty of space for two, and just sufficient for four to travel in comfort, though leg and head room in the back seats is not generous. Similarly, the boot is fairly small in relation to the overall length of the car, but 8.9 cu ft of luggage may be squeezed in, thanks to careful design of the well for the spare wheel.

Stowage space inside the Aston is fair. Apart from the locker, now with a walnut lid (on the inside of which is a flip-up vanity mirror), there's a lidded oddments box in the central console behind the gear lever, and pockets in the backs of both front seats.

The suspension modifications already referred to have benefited the handling, but not at the expense of ride comfort. It remains firm, and it is still a bit jiggly at low speeds, but the faster the car is driven, the better it becomes. At high speeds bumps and potholes may be traversed with barely any crashing and no excessive movements — an excellent sporting compromise.

The relationship between the driver's seat and the major controls in the Aston has always been excellent. The siting of the gear lever, for example, is as near to ideal for drivers of varying height as is possible, the steering wheel is adjustable for height and the pedals are ideally placed. This automatic version retains the left footrest of the manual, while the throttle pedal is designed to obviate ankle strain and the large brake pedal permits comfortable left-foot, even dual-foot braking. The fly-off handbrake is set quite far forward, but even tall drivers need lean ahead only slightly to operate it.

The twin stalk arrangement is retained in the updated model, as are the push-push buttons for minor controls. An intermittent wipe control (with an infinitely variable delay ranging from one to 20 sec) is mounted separately on the central console.

All seven dials are now set into a single curved walnut panel, and their positions have been changed somewhat, so that the rev counter is now to the left of the speedometer. The symmetrical arrangement is so designed that the steering wheel does not obscure any of the gauges and the layout is at one time traditional, functional and pleasing to the eye. The speedometer, incidentally, is absolutely accurate at 100 mph.

One of our criticisms of Aston Martins in the past concerned the mediocre performance of the heating and ventilation system. The

Coolaire air conditioning system, as used in a lot of American cars, overcomes many of the shortcomings. Very soon after starting the engine from cold it is possible to obtain a powerful blast of warm air into the interior, and it is easy to adjust the flow to obtain a desired temperature. Directional control is good too, and fresh air ventilation through the well-sited outlets under ram pressure alone is excellent. On a hot day this may be greatly increased by the four-speed booster fan, which is quiet and powerful on its lowest setting.

Where the air conditioning loses out to other systems we have tried — such as the superb one in current Rolls-Royces — is that it can only supply an overall temperature and is not capable of delivering cool air at face level and warmed air to the footwells simultaneously.

From the beginning of its production run the Aston's suppression of wind noise has been excellent, and the current model is no exception. Engine noise at tickover and at cruising speeds (up to about 120 mph) is also well restrained, though the familiar V8 burble is always noticeable in the background. Open wide those four twin-choke Webers and get the camshaft chains flying around driving the four camshafts, and the expensive sound ("noise" seems too vulgar a word in this context) builds up to a crescendo; it isn't deafening by any means, but it is undeniably loud, though it doesn't ever becoming tiring even on a long journey.

With such big wheels and tyres, it isn't surprising that there's a fair amount of bump-thump. On most surfaces this isn't too noticeable, transverse ridges on motorways (where there's also a fair measure of tyre roar) apparently having the worst effect.

By replacing many of the leather-trimmed panels with polished walnut, Aston may be said to be reverting to tradition. We cannot imagine that anyone will quarrel with them for doing so, since the result is excellent. It isn't only the expensive materials that are used — the walnut, the Connolly hide (now used as a roof lining as well) and deep-pile carpeting — nor just the tasteful colour combination which impressed us: one of the chief aims of the new regime at Newport Pagnell has been to improve the quality of the product, and the fulfilment of this desire is immediately apparent both inside and outside the new cars.

Above: locking mechanism for the passenger's door, set in the driver's armrest. Below: the best pedal layout we've seen in a car with automatic transmission

The paint finish of the bodywork is beyond reproach, and the rear spoiler and bonnet scoop look far neater now that they are blended in. The doors close with a solid clunk, and all the panels and trim edges have been finished with care. The overall effect is so excellent that many cars which compete on price seem absurdly expensive alongside this fine example of British craftsmanship.

The list of standard equipment fitted to the Aston is as impressive as one would expect for the high price. Almost all the expected items are there, plus a few more, and among the rarer fittings are air conditioning, central locking, stereo radio/cassette player with automatic electric aerial, an engine bay light, and a delay mechanism to the courtesy light. We were a little surprised to find that locks to the twin filler caps are only an option, while other options include headlamp washers, rear fog lights, rear seat belts, and a sliding sunroof. In the boot, the owner will find an impressive tool kit sufficient to cope with minor difficulties. There's a useful cut-off switch for the boot-mounted battery so that electrical work may be carried out in safety.

Lift the front-hinged bonnet, and all you can see is engine, with a large air box covering the carburetters which nestle in the Vee. The engine bay, as always in Astons, is very neatly laid out, with most ancillaries accessible (the plugs being especially easy to get at), but in any case, if you can afford an Aston you can afford to have a man work on it for you.

Where it all happens — the magnificent V8 occupies all the available space under the bonnet, yet the ancillaries remain accessible

## PERFORMANCE

### CONDITIONS
| | |
|---|---|
| Weather | Overcast, wet; wind 10-25 mph |
| Temperature | 56°F |
| Barometer | 29.4 in Hg |
| Surface | Damp tarmacadam |

### MAXIMUM SPEEDS
| | mph | kph |
|---|---|---|
| Estimated | 145 | 233 |
| Terminal Speeds: | | |
| at ¼ mile | 97 | 156 |
| at kilometre | 123 | 198 |
| Speed in gears (at 5500 rpm): | | |
| 1st | 57 | 92 |
| 2nd | 97 | 156 |

### ACCELERATION FROM REST
| mph | sec | kph | sec |
|---|---|---|---|
| 0-30 | 3.6 | 0-30 | 2.9 |
| 0-40 | 4.7 | 0-60 | 4.4 |
| 0-50 | 5.9 | 0-80 | 5.8 |
| 0-60 | 7.5 | 0-100 | 7.9 |
| 0-70 | 9.2 | 0-120 | 10.1 |
| 0-80 | 11.2 | 0-140 | 12.8 |
| 0-90 | 13.5 | 0-160 | 16.3 |
| 0-100 | 16.4 | 0-180 | 21.3 |
| 0-110 | 20.5 | | |
| 0-120 | 25.7 | | |
| Stand'g ¼ | 15.4 | Stand'g km | 27.2 |

### ACCELERATION IN KICKDOWN
| mph | sec | kph | sec |
|---|---|---|---|
| 20-40 | 2.4 | 40-60 | 2.0 |
| 30-50 | 2.3 | 60-80 | 2.6 |
| 40-60 | 2.8 | 80-100 | 3.6 |
| 50-70 | 3.3 | 100-120 | 4.3 |
| 60-80 | 3.7 | 120-140 | 4.8 |
| 70-90 | 4.3 | 140-160 | 6.5 |
| 80-100 | 5.2 | 160-180 | 8.8 |
| 90-100 | 7.0 | | |
| 100-120 | 9.3 | | |

### FUEL CONSUMPTION
| | |
|---|---|
| Touring* | 14.6 mpg |
| | 19.3 litres/100 km |
| Overall | 10.7 mpg |
| | 26.4 litres/100 km |

| | |
|---|---|
| Govt tests | Not applicable |
| Fuel grade | 98 octane |
| | 4 star rating |
| Tank capacity | 25.0 galls |
| | 113.7 litres |
| Max range | 365 miles |
| | 587 km |
| Test distance | 883 miles |
| | 1421 km |

*Consumption midway between 30 mph and maximum less 5 per cent for acceleration.

### SPEEDOMETER (mph)
Speedo
| 30 | 40 | 50 | 60 | 70 | 80 | 90 | 100 |
|---|---|---|---|---|---|---|---|
True mph
| 30 | 40 | 50 | 60 | 69 | 77 | 90 | 100 |

Distance recorder: 2 per cent fast

### WEIGHT
| | cwt | kg |
|---|---|---|
| Unladen weight* | 34.8 | 1767.9 |
| Weight as tested | 38.5 | 1955.9 |
*with fuel for approx 50 miles

Performance tests carried out at 5200 miles by Motor's staff at the Motor Industry Research Association proving ground, Lindley.

Test Data: World Copyright reserved; no unauthorised reproduction in whole or part.

## GENERAL SPECIFICATION

### ENGINE
| | |
|---|---|
| Cylinders | V8 |
| Capacity | 5340 cc (325.6 cu in) |
| Bore/stroke | 100/85 mm (3.94/3.35 in) |
| Cooling | Water |
| Block | Aluminium alloy |
| Head | Aluminium alloy |
| Valves | Dohc per bank |
| Cam drive | Chain |
| Valve timing | |
| inlet opens | 28° btdc |
| inlet closes | 64° abdc |
| ex opens | 66° bbdc |
| ex closes | 26° atdc |
| Compression | 9.0:1 |
| Carburetter | Four downdraught twin-choke Weber 42 DCNF |
| Bearings | 5 main |
| Max power | Not available |
| Max torque | Not available |

### TRANSMISSION
| | |
|---|---|
| Type | 3-speed Chrysler Torqueflite automatic |

Internal ratios and mph/1000 rpm
| | | |
|---|---|---|
| Top | 1.00:1 | 25.6 |
| 2nd | 1.45:1 | 17.7 |
| 1st | 2.45:1 | 10.4 |
| Rev | 2.20:1 | |
| Final drive | 3.07:1 | |

### BODY/CHASSIS
| | |
|---|---|
| Construction | Steel platform chassis with steel superstructure and aluminium panels |
| Protection | Chassis sprayed with red oxide and baked PVC |

undersealant. Aluminium panels etched, zinc-primed and sealed before spraying

### SUSPENSION
| | |
|---|---|
| Front | Ind. by unequal length wishbones and coil springs; anti-roll bar |
| Rear | Ind. by de Dion axle located by parallel links and Watts linkage; coil springs |

### STEERING
| | |
|---|---|
| Type | Adwest Rack and pinion |
| Assistance | Yes |

### BRAKES
| | |
|---|---|
| Front | Disc, 10.75 in dia |
| Rear | Disc, 10.38 in dia (inboard) |
| Park | Fly-off, on rear wheels |
| Servo | Yes |
| Circuit | Dual, split front/rear |
| Rear valve | Yes |
| Adjustment | Automatic |

### WHEELS/TYRES
| | |
|---|---|
| Type | Light alloy 7J |
| Tyres | Avon GR 70 VR 15 |
| Pressures | 30/30 psi F/R (normal) 35/35 psi F/R (full load) |

### ELECTRICAL
| | |
|---|---|
| Battery | 12V, 68 Ah |
| Earth | Negative |
| Generator | Alternator, 80 Amp |
| Fuses | 12 |
| Headlights | |
| type | Two QH Lucas H4 |
| dip | 110 W total |
| main | 230 W total |

Make: Aston Martin
Model: V8 Automatic
Maker: Aston Martin-Lagonda (1975) Ltd, Newport Pagnell, Bucks MK16 9AN. (Newport Pagnell 610620)
Price: £19,657 plus £1,638.08 car tax plus £1,703.61 equals £22,998.69. Extra fitted to road test car: auxiliary headlamps (£210.60). Total as tested: £23,209.29

# The Rivals

## ASTON MARTIN V8 (AUTO) — £22,999

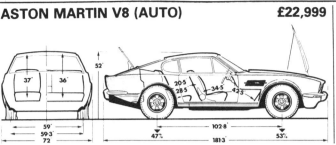

| | |
| --- | --- |
| Power, bhp/rpm | Not available |
| Torque, lb ft/rpm | Not available |
| Tyres | 225/70 VR 15 |
| Weight, cwt | 34.8 |
| Max speed, mph | 145† |
| 0-60 mph, sec | 7.5 |
| 30-50 mph in kickdown, sec | 2.3 |
| Overall mpg | 10.7 |
| Touring mpg | 14.6 |
| Fuel grade, stars | 4 |
| Boot capacity, cu ft | 8.9 |
| Original Test date | Oct 21, 1978 |
| †Estimated | |

A superb motor car, and now it is superbly made. Recent revisions have made vast improvement to interior, and overall quality is noticeably better. Otherwise as before: excellent handling, astounding performance, powerful and progressive brakes, ride reasonable at low speeds, good at high speed. Very expensive and rather thirsty, but if you can afford it, it's worth it. At the top of the supercar league.

## BRISTOL — £27,097

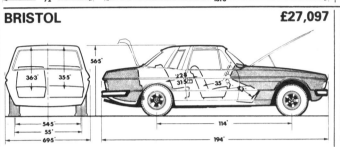

| | |
| --- | --- |
| Power, bhp/rpm | Not available |
| Torque, lb ft/rpm | Not available |
| Tyres | 205 VR 15 |
| Weight, cwt | — |
| Max speed, mph | 140† |
| 0-60 mph, sec | 7.4 |
| 30-50 mph in kickdown, sec | 2.8 |
| Overall mpg | — |
| Touring mpg | — |
| Fuel grade, stars | 2 |
| Boot capacity, cu ft | — |
| Test date | March 2, 1977 |
| †Estimated | |

Aimed at the sporting owner/driver, the bespoke Bristol's key offerings are an excellence of manufacture and exclusivity — only 6000 have been built in 30 years. With its American V8 engine the 412 is a unique amalgam of stirring performance (achieved on two-star fuel) and the ultimate luxury of wood and leather that only the British understand. There is no shortage of customers for this rare car.

## JAGUAR XJ-S — £15,149

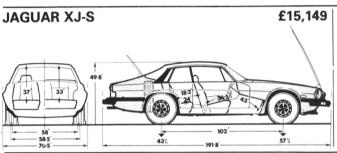

| | |
| --- | --- |
| Power, bhp/rpm | 285/5500 |
| Torque, lb ft/rpm | 294/3500 |
| Tyres | 205/70 VR 15 |
| Weight, cwt | 33.4 |
| Max speed, mph | 155† |
| 0-60 mph, sec | 6.7 |
| 30-50 mph in 4th, sec | 6.6 |
| Overall mpg | 12.8 |
| Touring mpg | 14.4 |
| Fuel grade, stars | 4 |
| Boot capacity, cu ft | 8.4 |
| Original Test date | Feb 21, 1976 |
| †Estimated | |

In true Jaguar tradition, the XJ-S combines exceptional performance and refinement at a very competitive price. The styling may not be to everyone's taste and the rear seat accommodation is cramped for so large a car. But if you can afford the fuel bills, the XJ-S is without doubt one of the world's most desirable vehicles. We've only tested the manual but it's available in auto form as well.

## MASERATI KYALAMI — £21,996

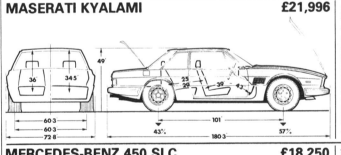

| | |
| --- | --- |
| Power, bhp/rpm | 270/6000 |
| Torque, lb ft/rpm | 289/3800 |
| Tyres | 205/70 VR 15 |
| Weight, cwt | 33.3 |
| Max speed, mph | 147† |
| 0-60 mph, sec | 7.6 |
| 30-50 mph in 4th, sec | 6.2 |
| Overall mpg | 11.6 |
| Touring mpg | 14.7 |
| Fuel grade, stars | 4 |
| Boot capacity, cu ft | 8.9 |
| Test date | July 22, 1978 |
| †Estimated | |

Notchback 2 plus 2 has De Tomaso-derived body, but the engineering is pure Maserati. Not as quick as some rivals, but more thirsty. Excellent high speed cruiser, handling good until limit is approached, but ride only fair. Engine less refined than those of many rivals, sounding strained at high revs; gearchange slow. Powerful, progressive brakes. Interior finish leaves much to be desired. A disappointment — not in the same league as the Aston.

## MERCEDES-BENZ 450 SLC — £18,250

| | |
| --- | --- |
| Power, bhp/rpm | 225/5000 |
| Torque, lb ft/rpm | 278/3000 |
| Tyres | 205/70 VR 14 |
| Weight, cwt | 33.0 |
| Max speed, mph | 134† |
| 0-60 mph, sec | 8.5 |
| 30-50 mph in kickdown, sec | 3.3 |
| Overall mpg | 15.1 |
| Touring mpg | |
| Fuel grade, stars | 4 |
| Boot capacity, cu ft | 8.9 |
| Test date | May 1, 1976 |
| †Estimated | |

A magnificent motor car, and one of our favourites. Typically Mercedes, which means an exceptionally high standard of finish allied to engineering that is second to none. Performance is more than adequate while the automatic transmission sets new standards. A limited slip diff would improve roadholding and handling by increasing traction. The 5.0-litre version has been sold on the Continent for some time, but is not yet available here.

## PORSCHE 928 — £19,499

| | |
| --- | --- |
| Power, bhp/rpm | 240/5500 |
| Torque, lb ft/rpm | 257/3600 |
| Tyres | 225/50 VR 16 |
| Weight, cwt | 28.9 |
| Max speed, mph | 140† |
| 0-60 mph, sec | 7.0 |
| 30-50 mph in 4th, sec | 5.4 |
| Overall mpg | 14.9 |
| Touring mpg | |
| Fuel grade, stars | 2 |
| Boot capacity, cu ft | 7.3 |
| Test date | Full test next week |
| †Estimated | |

Porsche's all new luxury sports car hasn't the mind-blowing performance you'd expect, but it's no sluggard. Super-refined engine and low wind noise but potential refinement let down by excessive tyre roar. Superlative road holding, and excellent handling in all but the most extreme conditions, with mediocre ride. Excellent brakes. Beautifully made and lavishly equipped. Very spacious for two, but cramped rear seat.

# LAGONDA...

## IS THIS THE NEW BEST SEDAN IN THE WORLD ?

Mel Nichols has been driving Aston Martin's new Lagonda. He calls it lithe and luxurious, elegant and eager, refined and rakish, exclusive and certainly expensive. From its astonishing electronic systems to the stunning styling, here is a car of tomorrow.

I THINK we can forgive Aston Martin its miscalculation of the time it would take to get the Lagonda into production, don't you? The Italians do it habitually, and it has never stilted their customers' enthusiasm. And, after all, three years ago the people who now own Aston Martin were faced not only with the task of resurrecting a factory that had collapsed but had no previous experience of the motor industry to light their path. In retrospect, that appears to have caused it no real difficulty: it may have led to its over-optimism but that is about all.

Within 18 months of buying the factory from the receiver, Aston's new owners were unveiling a new car sufficiently stunning to steal the show at Earl's Court. They took it from design to prototype in less than 10 months, and if it had gone into production as intended in April, then that too would have been an achievement bordering on the miraculous. As it is, the final kick-off in October was impressive enough: just as it will be for Maserati's new Quattroporte — the Lagonda's most obvious rival — itself the

first properly-new product from a company which died and was reborn about the same time as Aston Martin Lagonda.

The Lagonda, you see, is *good* — perhaps indecently good — for a car taken from conception to creation in such a short time. It begins with styling that is as different as it is effective: here is a big sedan that looks to be what it is — luxurious but lithe, elegant but eager, refined but rakish, exclusive and certainly expensive. It is conservative and yet somehow notably a car of tomorrow. It is a design, I would expect, that Bill Towns had firmly in his mind and was merely waiting for the opportunity to release. I do not know whether it is an expensive body to make, but it is almost exactly the way Towns drew it. Happily, his concept is aerodynamically sufficiently efficient to require little modification there and aesthetically commanding enough to demand no changes there either. That alone must have saved Aston a great deal of time.

It has benefited, too, by using the familiar 5.3-litre V8 engine, that great alloy brute

whose power it has never disclosed but which, in its Vantage form, provides around 340 kW. The tamer engine, the one used for so long in the basic V8, is less potent — 245 kW — but still capable not only of providing sufficient power for a car the Lagonda's size but apparently adequate reliability too; it is a known quantity. Equally important in these times of phenomenally high developmental cost, it is sufficiently clean to be acceptable in North America. Nor was there need for Aston Martin to be concerned with development of a transmission — it was already using the superlative Chrysler Torqueflite automatic and if customers cared to insist upon a manual it could simply install the not-very-nice but nevertheless faithful big-power ZF five-speeder so familiar in Maseratis as well as Astons; here is yet more common ground which links the two companies.

A new steel sub-structure had to be built to carry the Lagonda's body and mechanicals, but Aston were freed of the time and cost of creating new suspension. Chief

# LAGONDA...

Engineer Mike Loasby made changes to geometry and there are obvious differences in things like wheelbase and weight, but he was able to take the suspension from the V8 and apply it to the Lagonda without fuss. That gives the Lagonda unequal length wishbones, coil springs, fat telescopic dampers and an anti-roll bar at the front with Aston's De Dion axle at the rear. It is located by parallel trailing arms and a Watt linkage; coils look after the springing and there are self-levelling dampers. At the front, the altered geometry rids the Lagonda of the heavy and slightly unstable feel of the standard V8. Steering angles were re-thought and re-applied, and so were spring and damper settings; relatively small changes but ones which have made all the difference.

If all this required a very careful study and then a long process of tuning and proving to hone the balance, it was relatively straightforward to Aston's designers, engineers and construction craftsmen. But they pushed into new territory when they chose to work as many of the Lagonda's systems as possible electronically. It was Mike Loasby's idea but it met with ready approval by his masters. Peter Sprague, some of whose American interests concern electronics, was especially keen.

So the Lagonda was given all-electronic instrumentation with digital read-outs in place of conventional dials and needles, sophisticated to the point of having a speedo switched at the touch of a button from a mph reading to km/h. Another display covers average speed and fuel consumption, combined with a speed/instantaneous fuel consumption readout and elapsed journey time and distance. Touch switches — tiny, fingertip-size pads — work all the minor controls from selection of the transmission mode to the wipers, air conditioning and windows. Further touch buttons in the driver's door-mounted panel look after fore and aft movement of the seat, squab angle, cushion height and tilt, and things like automatic door locking and the bonnet and fuel cap locks. While Aston was able to find the electronic systems to institute these functions it had, it was to discover, great trouble getting sufficient reliability from them, especially in extremes of temperature.

It was, in fact, the electronics that caused such embarrassment in April when Aston endeavored to deliver the first Lagonda, on schedule, to the Marchioness of Tavistock. The car couldn't be driven and Aston had to announce to the gathered press a postponement of further deliveries until October, and take the Tavistock's car back. Now Aston has given up its attempts to use European electronics and has a car in the United States being fitted with a new system, and so far the American electronics are doing the job without trouble. The engineers are confident they have solved the problems this time, and of getting deliveries under way in 1979 (initially, they'll be building one Lagonda a week; it will rise to two a week when production of the electronics systems comes

*Lagonda's interior (left) is plush, comfortable and unique in that rear passengers get a overhead glass panel. Digital readouts (below) use new US electronics. Styling is both aesthetically pleasing and aerodynamically efficient (bottom).*

fully on stream this year in Aston's new department).

With the electronics systems, you slide into the Lagonda, touch your forefinger to the white-on-black symbol you require and get your seat precisely right: it is moved quickly and accurately by electric motors. The steering wheel, too, is adjustable. You're then sitting perfectly comfortably in a long, wide car that does not seem as big as it looks, with a deep windscreen to peer through and the narrow, raised edges of the

mudguards to make placement of the car easy. Start the car normally with an old-fashioned key and figures dance before you — the tachometer flicking out its message: you are doing 750 rpm at idle, 760, 750, 760, 770. There is another figure for the charge going into the battery, another for oil pressure, another for temperature and one more for the gallons in the tank. The speed readout comes after you've touched the tiny button marked D in the row on the edge of the dash that control the transmission.

# LAGONDA...

There is a bleep of acknowledgement and you feel the transmission engage.

The speedo and tachometer figures start flicking silently upwards as you ease up the road, not so furiously that they are annoying and you will find that it takes very little time to get used to the system. The car itself is silky. The big V8 pulls it forward with enough ease to provide for 0-96 km/h in 7.0 secs if you floor the throttle, but progress, even then, is without drama. It feels at once a smooth, balanced, relaxed car — and poorly-surfaced backroads will prove that impression correct. Two things will impress you most: the sheer quality of the ride and the remarkable flatness with which the car corners. There is no mistaking its cornering ability but nor is there any doubting its aplomb. The car is tauter, crisper than a Jaguar XJ12 but its ride appears to be every bit as impressive and the suppression of road noise excellent.

This really is a car in which backseat passengers can snuggle down amongst the leather and enjoy themselves. They will not be thrown about even when the driver is pressing the car very swiftly along the road, nor even in roundabouts taken really hard;

the driver will know he isn't upsetting his passengers too, for the car feels precise, stable and accurate in the hands. The steering is, beautifully balanced and properly smooth, and the car responds to it precisely as one would wish; a fine throttle linkage, and, when necessary, equally progressive and informative braking completes the equipment he needs to drive as quickly and smoothly as he might wish. Bumps encountered mid-bend are absorbed without the car being deflected; it just continues going where the driver points it, without real understeer and without oversteer (unless, of course, you ram it into low and stand on it in a really tight bend).

What you *will* need to get used to is placing the car properly into the kerb or the white line on tight right-hand bends. The A-pillars are quite thick and can obstruct the view in tight bends; you need to learn to cock your head around the pillar and once you've picked up your reference point on the road ahead, the car is easy to place and hold through the bend.

Conditions prevented us travelling much beyond 180 km/h, but at that speed the car is stable, easy in the hands, quiet and smooth, with plenty of power left to send it streaking forward if one could unleash it further. Again, it's just as impressive in the rear as in the front. Indeed, that glass panel

set into the roof above the rear passengers makes life there especially pleasant, removing any trace of claustrophobia and making the rear like a separate compartment.

If the developmental car we drove is anything to go by — and we are quite sure it is — Aston has, in short, one hell of a motor car. It is a car as delightful to drive as it is in which to be driven; it is a car to satisfy a fastidious driver with its cleanliness, its efficiency and its ability, and a finickity passenger with its stability, refinement and comfort.

If we can see anything to grumble about at this stage — and we are not in a position to pass full judgment until we spend some time with a production Lagonda — it is that the rear door opening may prove too restricted for fully-convenient access, and the boot too small for long four-person journeys.

Otherwise we're quite sure that not only Aston Martin but Britain will have a dashing new flagship with the ability to lay the rest of the world in the aisles. Here at last may be the car that displaces the Jaguar XJ12 as the world's best sedan (although it would be foolish to overlook the new Quattroporte); it is certainly the car that Rolls-Royce has to watch as it enters the final developmental stages with the new SZ series. *

---

# Luxury Lagonda is a smash hit

ASTON MARTIN'S remarkable Lagonda has progressed even further towards becoming a Rolls-challenger with its clean-sheet crash barrier safety tests. Despite the car being virtually a write-off after the crash tests, the windscreen stayed intact, all the doors opened normally and the passenger shell was not deformed.

The tests were at 48 km/h and the Lagonda was launched into a 200-tonne cement block. The test is equivalent to a 96 km/h head-on smash. For US regulations, there was a dummy wearing a seat belt in the front passenger seat.

Results proved that passengers wearing seat belts would have escaped the crash unscathed. As a spokesman for the company said: "The result was most satisfactory".

Front-end damage was estimated at more than $12,000 but the car was later turned around on its

launching rail and smashed backwards into the concrete block. The backwards tests were also impressive.

Every centimetre of the car was checked after the tests for distortion and metal fatigue.

Alan Curtis, the 51-year-old Managing Director of Aston Martin Lagonda, the company of two Britons, one Canadian and one American which saved Aston from going broke in 1974, was on hand to watch the tests.

"It's painful to see such a fine car smashed in this way," he said. "And it is also a very costly experience. But if we want to sell cars, we have to do it."

Apart from being safe, the Lagonda has the mind-boggling interior luxury of a Rolls-Royce challenger. Back seat passengers will even be able to play computerised games, flashed on to a television-type screen. That's style. *

# ASTON MARTIN VOLANTE

For this first of our new, tougher, more comprehensive road tests we put the first right hand drive example of the Aston Martin Volante through its paces. Our verdict? Read on . . .

IT IS ironic that one of the reasons for today's dearth of new convertibles was the fear a few years ago — now receded — that pending American regulations would soon outlaw them on grounds of inadequate roll-over protection. Yet the very reason for the Aston Martin Volante's somewhat belated arrival on the home market is that all the cars so far built have been sent across the Atlantic.

Since the Volante was unveiled last June it has accounted for half the Newport Pagnell factory's six-cars-per-week production, the remainder being one Lagonda and two V8 saloons. Only one right-hand drive Volante so far exists in England, the original prototype, and it is that which is the subject of this, the first full test of a Volante in Europe.

It should be said that the manufacturers were at pains to point out that this particular car has had a very hard life as a development hack, and in a few respects is not representative of the cars currently being assembled. If that is so, then the cars now coming down the line must be very special indeed, for we could find little to fault with the design, execution, or finish of the car we tested.

As its appearance would suggest, the Volante is based on the latest V8 saloon (about which we eulogised last October) with the same basic steel chassis and steel superstructure and front-mounted 5340cc V8 engine driving the rear wheels through a Torqueflite automatic or 5-speed ZF manual gearbox. For the drophead, however, the structure has been substantially strengthened (even more so on the production versions than on the prototype, which displayed occasional scuttle shake on bad bumps), and of course the hand-assembled aluminium bodywork has been revised to suit the Volante's power-operated folding hood.

If the standard saloon is an expensive car at £24,000, the price of the Volante's open-topped exclusivity may make even rich men blanche; £33,864. But if this seems exorbitant, bear in mind that the only other comparable genuine convertible is the Rolls-Royce/Bentley Corniche drophead and that costs £43,980. There is also the Mercedes 450SL, but that's only a two-seater, albeit much cheaper at £15,495.

There are a few other pedigree cars offering fresh-air motoring, but with 'targa' type detachable roof panels rather than genuine soft-tops; of these, only the Bristol 412 S2 can be considered a 'natural' rival at £29,264, others such as the Ferrari GTS (£18,169) or Porsche 911 SC Targa (£14,549) being smaller and less refined two-seaters. Other cars that would normally be considered as Aston rivals — Jaguar XJ-S, Maserati Kyalami or Porsche 928 — are all closed coupés and much cheaper.

When all is said and done the Volante must be considered as an all too rare convertible, and one with a very distinct character; and in those terms it is unique, which means if you can afford one, it's worth it. And evidently there are more than enough buyers who do see it in those terms, for Aston Martin has already taken over 40 orders in anticipation of the first right-hand drive cars becoming available on the home market this month.

## PERFORMANCE

Aston Martin still decline to quote any power or torque output figures for the all-alloy four-cam V8, which breathes through four twin-choke down-

**Make:** Aston Martin. **Model:** Volante.
**Maker:** Aston Martin Lagonda (1975) Ltd, Tickford St, Newport Pagnell, Bucks MK16 9AN. Tel: 0908 610620.
**Price:** £28,944 basic plus £2,412.00 Car Tax plus £2,508.48 VAT equals £33,864.48 total. Extras fitted to test car: electric passenger door mirror, £105.30; head restraints, £77.22.

 excellent  good  average  poor ★ bad

draught Weber carburetters and burns four star on a 9:1 compression ratio.

Evidently the power is more than sufficient, however, for even when fitted with power-sapping automatic transmission the acceleration of this heavy car is little short of stunning, and delivered with a semi-muffled bellow from beneath the bonnet that's as pleasing as the performance itself. In reality, the performance is even better than our recorded zero to 60 mph time of 7.7 sec (the best times were achieved by using manual override to hold the revs to 6000 rpm: peak power is at 5500 rpm, the recommended limit 6500 rpm) would suggest, for, as with the last Aston automatic we tested, a bad carburation flat-spot severely mars initial off-the-line acceleration. Hence the 0-30 mph time of 3.7 sec is at *least* half a second slower than it ought to be, and provides a deficit which is reflected in all the subsequent standing start figures. If the acceleration over those first few yards were in proportion with the rest of the car's performance, the Volante would probably have a 0-60 mph time of 7 sec or less.

For a truer appreciation of the Aston's capabilities, then, look instead at the 30-50 mph time of 2.4 sec; of our selected automatic transmission rivals only the Bristol comes anywhere near it with a time of 2.8 sec, the remainder taking 3 seconds or longer. Or consider the Aston's standing start times to 100

mph (17.3 sec) and 120 mph (28 secs), figures that the Porsche 928, for example, cannot match even with *manual* transmission (17.8 sec and 31.3 sec respectively). Of the automatic transmission rivals that we've quoted even the potent Bristol is lagging behind with corresponding times of 19.3 and 32.7 sec.

There is nowhere in the UK that the maximum speed of a car like the Aston can safely (or legally) be measured; unfortunately our deadlines left us no time to take the Volante to the Continent, so we have quoted the manufacturer's claim of 150 mph. Since we recorded 155 mph on a manual version in 1973, and Aston claim a 20 per cent power increase since then, this seems a credible figure.

In any event, such academic figures matter less than how a car performs as daily transport. Starting from cold during our test — whether we used the choke or pumped the throttle to prime the Webers — was always reliable though never instantaneous. Warm-up was characterised by flat spots, however, unless you kept the choke fully on for the first mile or so. Even when warm, the low-speed flat spot that hampered our tests at MIRA was also apparent on the road, so that it paid to avoid full throttle below 20 mph. But from then on, the acceleration (and exhilaration) is such that we doubt if any other current automatic transmission car — and certainly none that we have tested — could stay with the Volante in full flight.

## ECONOMY

The fuel consumption of any car costing £34,000 is rather academic; a buyer is hardly going to be concerned about petrol costs. In any event, the 11.8 mpg overall that we recorded for our hard-driven test is not significantly worse nor better than any of the Aston's rivals would manage. What is of greater interest is the range on each tankful of four-star; on the basis of our computed Touring consumption of 13.6 mpg, the Volante should be capable of some 340 miles on each filling of its twin-filler 25-gallon fuel tank.

## TRANSMISSION

In spite of Aston Martin's strong ''performance'' image, the majority of cars sold have 3-speed automatic transmission, as had our test car.

As on the saloon we tested last year, this combination of automatic transmission and the engine's low-speed flat spot makes the Volante rather sluggish (relatively speaking) from standstill, but once 20 mph is passed it hurtles forward at a prodigious rate with automatic change-ups occurring at 4900 rpm (51 mph) and 5400 rpm (96 mph).

For catapult-like overtaking ability, full-throttle kick-down into first is available at up to 40 mph and to second at up to 80 mph. Part-throttle kickdown is also available over an unusually wide speed range. The tunnel-mounted gear selector lever has a smooth yet positive action, and allows second gear to be selected manually without pressing the detent button in the top of the lever; there is a detent between second and first, however, and also between ''D'' and Neutral.

Upward gearchanges from second to top are at all times smooth, but first-to-second changes on our test car were a little inconsistent: under gentle acceleration the gearbox tended to hang on to first gear rather too long and then change up with a distinct thump, while, unusually, the brisker the acceleration, the smoother were the changes. Similarly, automatic downchanges to first can be rather abrupt and require care when accelerating out of a corner, especially in the wet, if the sudden massive increase in torque at the rear wheels is not to cause an unintended power slide.

## HANDLING

The Volante's suspension is well tried and superbly developed, employing double wishbones, coil springs and an anti-roll bar at the front, and a de Dion rear axle located by parallel links and a Watts linkage, again with coil springs.

Where the Aston really stands out from its rivals, however, is its superb Adwest power-assisted rack-and-pinion steering. This system is not only sensibly weighted to give good feel, it also still provides enough assistance for reasonably easy parking (though the turning circle of almost 40 ft is poor).

Of its behaviour on the move, we can only repeat what we said in our last test, that the steering is exactly like an excellent unassisted system in a light car. There is ample self-centring; it writhes gently in your hands in response to bumpy surfaces; and it has real feel (as the steering torque figures in the data panel show), becoming steadily and detectably heavier as cornering speeds increase, and lightening to inform the driver when the tyres lose grip on a slippery surface.

With over 1.1 turns required to scribe a 50 ft circle the figures indicate that the mechanism is a shade low-geared, but this hardly seems apparent on the road, such is the car's response and poise; it can be cornered with a verve that quite belies its bulk and massive weight. The ultimate roadholding is impressively high in the dry, still good in the wet, and the behaviour as the limit is approached is entirely predictable. Strong ultimate understeer is the normal characteristic, while lifting off the throttle will reduce the understeer without any inclination to sudden oversteer. A tail out attitude can, of course, be induced with plenty of throttle, the transition to oversteer being both progressive and, often, virtually self-correcting.

Overall the Volante's cornering behaviour is as safe as it is entertaining, and the feeling of security thus engendered is further strengthened by the arrow-like stability at speed on a motorway and on bumpy roads.

## BRAKES

If considered purely from the point of view of the driver who likes to drive hard and fast, the Aston's braking — by ventilated discs all round with twin servos — is outstanding, being immensely powerful, perfectly progressive, and seemingly immune to fade. Even our new, much tougher fade test — explained in detail on p 23 of this issue — had no effect whatsoever on the braking efficiency of this heavy car, apart from a trace of rumble and judder.

By modern standards, however, the required pedal pressures are high, particularly at low speeds when the brakes are still cold, as indicated by the 125 lb pedal pressure required for a maximum stop from 30 mph. Moreover, the handbrake on our test car proved feeble when used as an emergency brake and was unable even to hold the car on the 1-in-4 slope, let alone the 1-in-3. But as past Aston V8 test cars have had very effective handbrakes, we are prepared to accept that the Volante's may simply have been in need of adjustment.

## ACCOMMODATION

While nobody is likely to buy an Aston in search of maximum four-seat accommodation, the Volante is roomier than just a 2 plus 2, and has no *less* passenger accommodation than the fixed head versions. Thus there is an enormous amount of legroom available in the front, with generous head-room, and if you set the driver's seat for a male of average height there remains just sufficient legroom for a similarly-sized passenger behind. The rear seats are rather upright, however, and headroom is only fair, while shoulder room is limited. The front seats' backrests can be tipped forward without disturbing their settings, to allow easy access to the rear.

Interior stowage is fair, with a glove locker, a box under the central armrest, and map pockets in the backs of the front seats. There is also a large, deep trough behind the rear seats which accommodates the folded down hood, but which can be used when the hood is erect to compensate for the Volante's rather small boot — at 5.1 cu ft it is a lot smaller than the saloon's, a consequence of the revised rear coachwork necessitated by the folding hood.

To lower the hood you simply release two over-centre catches on the windscreen header rail and push the "power-hood" button. Electric motors do the rest, though we found it needed a slight helping push to get it moving. The whole operation can thus be accomplished without leaving the driver's seat, though for a neat appearance you do need to step out to button down the hood cover, a reasonably easy task. A tonneau cover is available as an extra cost (£196.56) option.

## RIDE COMFORT

★★★ In the past we have always found Aston Martins to ride rather harshly at low speeds, but to compensate with a remarkably well controlled high speed ride; on the whole this remains true of the Volante, though the small-bump harshness at low speeds seems to have been reduced. The ride remains essentially firm around town, however, and prominent bump-thump sometimes makes progress *sound* less smooth than it really is. Even so, little disturbance is transmitted to the occupants most of the time; the occasional scuttle shake on bad bumps that we experienced in "our" Volante test car has apparently — as the manufacturers were at pains to point out *before* we drove the car — been all but eliminated on the production cars, which have strengthening of the chassis over and above that carried out on the prototype.

## AT THE WHEEL

★★★ The front seats — which have a wide range of adjustment and infinitely variable backrest recline — are superbly shaped, giving good support in all areas, and, with well placed armrests on either side, an almost armchair-like effect. Similarly, the relationship between the driver's seat and the major controls is hard to fault. The steering wheel is adjustable for reach, and the gearlever and pedals are all well situated, while a left footrest is provided. There are two column stalks, for wash/wipe on the left and indicators/dip/flash/horn on the right. Unfortunately these are fixed in position and can be a long hand's

stretch away if the steering wheel is set near to the driver

There is a large easily found rotary knob on the facia for the lights, with push-push buttons on the centre console for other minor functions. The choke control is a large vertical slider on the facia.

## VISIBILITY

★★ Shorter drivers complained of difficulty in seeing out of the Volante because of the very low seating position. The bulk of the enormous bonnet bulge, in particular, creates a large blind area to the front nearside of the car, and drivers of all heights complained about the severe rear three-quarter blind spot created by the heavy side panels of the hood when it is up, which requires a van driver's technique at T-junctions. The relatively small rear window also makes parking or reversing a little difficult.

More praiseworthy are the excellent electrically adjustable door mirrors (an extra-cost option on the nearside) and the effective wash/wipe system incorporating a variable delay intermittent wipe facility. The headlamps, in contrast, are not nearly powerful enough for the car's performance potential (our Volante was not fitted with the optional Cibié auxiliary lamps that we praised on last year's saloon test car).

All round visibility is, of course, much improved with the hood down, in which condition the car can be cruised with some draught but no buffeting at the legal limit, with the radio still audible over the rush of the wind.

## INSTRUMENTS

★★★ The Volante has a comprehensive display of traditionally styled round-dial instruments with clear white-on-black calibration, which look splendid, though reflections off the glass covers can be a problem. There is a speedometer calibrated to 170 mph, a tachometer (which has no red line), oil and water temperature gauges, a voltmeter, an oil pressure gauge, and of course a fuel gauge. These are positioned on a single walnut panel so that they are not obscured by the wheel itself, though some of the minor gauges may be at least partly blocked from view if you drive with your hands on the wheel at the ten to two position.

There is a panel lighting rheostat for night driving, and a Kienzle clock mounted on the centre of the facia.

## HEATING AND VENTILATION

★★★ Both heating and cooling of the Volante's interior are provided by the standard Coolaire air conditioning. This incorporates a four-speed fan and has two easy-to-use horizontal slide controls for temperature and distribution, the latter providing a choice of throughflow or recirculating modes.

In the freezing weather that prevailed throughout our test we found

Above: sumptuous front seats allow plenty of legroom and tip forward for easy access to rear, below left, which is roomier than appearances suggest

Above: the narrow, slot-like boot took only 5.1 cu ft of test luggage

Above: the driving position is excellent, the seats extremely comfortable, and the finish, in Connolly hide and polished walnut, looks exquisite

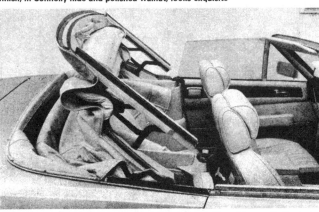

Above: the power hood is wired through the parking brake so it can only be operated at a standstill; it works smoothly, quietly and simply

the maximum heat output to be modest, though within its limitations the temperature was progressively controllable. As with many others, the Aston's system is only able to provide an overall setting with air at the same temperature through all its vents; there is no way to obtain warm feet and a cool face simultaneously. In practice the flow of air (whether heated or cooled) through the central waist-level vent or the two outer face-level ones is generous in volume and easily aimed. Although there is a vent in each footwell — aimed at your knees rather than your feet — the flow through these is meagre.

## NOISE

You can certainly buy quieter cars than the Volante, but we doubt if any true enthusiast would ever complain. Even at low speeds the engine is not especially quiet — the burble of the exhausts is ever present — and it develops an awe-inspiring bellow at high revs guaranteed to delight even the most blasé enthusiast; with a recorded peak of 83 dB at maximum revs in second gear it is by no means the loudest engine we've measured, but it certainly isn't silent.

When cruising at speed, exhaust noise gets "left behind", and there is very little mechanical fuss even at speeds far in excess of any speed limit. Instead it is (not surprisingly) wind noise that dominates at speed; a fairly even rushing sound that becomes apparent at quite low speeds and steadily increases thereafter, though you would have to be travelling at very illegal speeds to drown out the radio, and only above about 110 mph does it become uncomfortable with the hood up; with the latter down, this point is reached at 90 mph.

Tyre roar, well muted normally, also becomes much more prominent with the car fully open, and there is appreciable bump thump at all times, though it doesn't reach excessive levels.

## FINISH

One of Aston Martin's major priorities under its present management has been to improve standards of finish and consequent reliability; if our V8 saloon test car of last October was an apparent testament to the success of this policy, this latest car provided an even more convincing demonstration, for the hard-used Volante prototype performed near-faultlessly throughout our test and was superbly finished inside and out.

Although traditional almost to the point of being old-fashioned, we found the interior's combination of polished walnut, beige Connolly hide and deep pile carpet to be quite exquisite, and assembled to a standard fully in keeping with the quality of the materials used.

## EQUIPMENT

Although such standard items as a power-operated hood, stereo radio/cassette player, electric window actuation, air

## PERFORMANCE

### CONDITIONS

| | |
|---|---|
| Weather | Foggy, wind 15-20 mph |
| Temperature | 32°F |
| Barometer | 28.75 in Hg |
| Surface | Damp tarmacadam |

### MAXIMUM SPEEDS

| | mph | kph |
|---|---|---|
| Banked Circuit | 150† | 241 |
| Terminal Speeds: | | |
| at ¼ mile | 95 | 153 |
| at kilometre | 120 | 193 |
| Speed in gears (at 5500 rpm): | | |
| 1st | 57 | 92 |
| 2nd | 97 | 156 |

†see test

### ACCELERATION FROM REST

| mph | sec | kph | sec |
|---|---|---|---|
| 0-30 | 3.7 | 0-40 | 3.0 |
| 0-40 | 4.8 | 0-60 | 4.5 |
| 0-50 | 6.1 | 0-80 | 6.1 |
| 0-60 | 7.7 | 0-100 | 8.1 |
| 0-70 | 9.6 | 0-120 | 10.5 |
| 0-80 | 11.7 | 0-140 | 13.3 |
| 0-90 | 14.1 | 0-160 | 17.0 |
| 0-100 | 17.3 | 0-180 | 22.8 |
| 0-110 | 21.9 | | |
| 0-120 | 28.0 | | |
| Stand'g ¼ | 15.6 | Stand'g km | 27.8 |

### ACCELERATION IN KICKDOWN

| mph | sec | kph | sec |
|---|---|---|---|
| 20-40 | 2.4 | 40-60 | 1.5 |
| 30-50 | 2.4 | 60-80 | 1.6 |
| 40-60 | 3.1 | 80-100 | 2.3 |
| 50-70 | 3.8 | 100-120 | 2.6 |
| 60-80 | 4.1 | 120-140 | 2.8 |
| 70-90 | 4.7 | 140-160 | 4.5 |
| 80-100 | 6.4 | 160-180 | 6.1 |
| 90-110 | 8.5 | | |
| 100-120 | 11.2 | | |

### FUEL CONSUMPTION

| | |
|---|---|
| Touring* | 13.6 mpg |
| | 20.8 litres/100 km |
| Overall | 11.8 mpg |
| | 23.9 litres/100 km |
| Govt tests | Not applicable |
| Fuel grade | 97 octane |
| | 4 star rating |
| Tank capacity | 25.0 galls |
| | 114 litres |

| | | |
|---|---|---|
| Max range | 340 miles | 547 km |
| Test distance | 780 miles | 1255 km |

*Consumption midway between 30 mph and maximum less 5 per cent for acceleration.

### BRAKES

Pedal pressure, stopping distance and average deceleration from 30 mph (48 kph).

| lb | kg | g | ft | m |
|---|---|---|---|---|
| 25 | 11 | 0.26 | 114 | 34.8 |
| 50 | 23 | 0.52 | 58 | 17.9 |
| 75 | 34 | 0.62 | 48 | 14.6 |
| 100 | 45 | 0.79 | 38 | 11.6 |
| 125 | 57 | 0.97 | 31 | 9.5 |
| Handbrake | | 0.23 | 133 | 40.6 |
| From 70 mph (113 kph) | | | | |
| 88 | 40 | 0.80 | 206 | 62.8 |

### FADE

Twenty 0.6g stops at 45 sec intervals from speed midway between 40 mph (64 kph) and maximum (95 mph, 153 kph) with vehicle laden to maximum payload

| | lb | kg |
|---|---|---|
| Pedal force at start | 52 | 23.6 |
| Pedal force at 10th stop | 50 | 22.7 |
| Pedal force at 20th stop | 50 | 22.7 |

### STEERING

Weighting at wheel rim on parking and when cornering on 108 ft diameter circle

| | lb ft |
|---|---|
| Parking | 12 |
| Cornering at: | |
| 0.1g | 3 |
| 0.3g | 3.5 |
| 0.6g | 4 |

| Turning between kerbs | ft | m |
|---|---|---|
| left | 39.4 | 12 |
| right | 40.0 | 12.2 |
| lock to lock | 2.9 turns | |
| 50ft diam. circle | 1.15 turns | |

### NOISE

| | dBA | Motor rating* |
|---|---|---|
| 30 mph | 66 | 12 |
| 50 mph | 69 | 15 |
| 70 mph | 74 | 21 |
| Max revs in 2nd | 83 | 40 |

(1st for 3-speed auto)
*A rating where 1=30 dBA and 100=96 dBA and where double the number means double the loudness

### SPEEDOMETER (mph)

Speedo
30 40 50 60 70 80 90 100
True mph
30 39.5 49.5 60 69 78.5 88.5 98.5

Distance recorder: 2 per cent slow

### WEIGHT

| | cwt | kg |
|---|---|---|
| Unladen weight* | 35.3 | 1793 |
| Weight as tested | 39.0 | 1981 |

*with fuel for approx 50 miles

**Performance tests carried out by Motor's staff at the Motor Industry Research Association proving ground, Lindley.**

*Test Data: World Copyright reserved; no unauthorised reproduction in whole or part.*

## GENERAL SPECIFICATION

### ENGINE

| | |
|---|---|
| Cylinders | 8 in Vee |
| Capacity | 5340 cc (326 cu in) |
| Bore/stroke | 100/85 mm (3.94/3.35 in) |
| Cooling | Water |
| Block | Alloy |
| Head | Alloy |
| Valves | Dohc per bank |
| Cam drive | Chain |
| Compression | 9.0:1 |
| Carburetter | 4 Weber downdraught twin-choke 42 DCNF |
| Bearings | 5 main |
| Max power | Not available |
| Max torque | Not available |

### TRANSMISSION

| | |
|---|---|
| Type | Torqueflite 3-speed |
| Internal ratios and mph/1000 rpm | |
| Top | 1.00:1/25.6 |
| 2nd | 1.45:1/17.7 |
| 1st | 2.45:1/10.4 |
| Rev | 2.20:1 |
| Final drive | 3.07:1 |

### BODY/CHASSIS

| | |
|---|---|
| Construction | Steel platform chassis with steel superstructure and aluminium panels |
| Protection | Zinc-phosphated box members treated with stainless steel and wax spray; rubber-based underseal |

### SUSPENSION

| | |
|---|---|
| Front | Ind by unequal length wishbones, coil springs; anti-roll bar |
| Rear | Independent by De Dion axle located by parallel links and Watts linkage; coil springs |

### STEERING

| | |
|---|---|
| Type | Rack and pinion |
| Assistance | Yes |

### BRAKES

| | |
|---|---|
| Front | 10.75 in ventilated discs |
| Rear | 10.4 in ventilated discs (inboard) |
| Park | Fly off, on rear wheels |
| Servo | Yes, twin |
| Circuit | Split front/rear |
| Rear valve | Yes |
| Adjustment | Automatic |

### WHEELS/TYRES

| | |
|---|---|
| Type | Light alloy 7J x 15 |
| Tyres | Avon GR70 VR 15 |
| Pressures | 30/30 psi F/R (normal) 35/35 psi F/R (full load) |

### ELECTRICAL

| | |
|---|---|
| Battery | 12V, 68 Ah |
| Earth | Negative |
| Generator | 75A Alternator |
| Fuses | 12 |
| Headlights | |
| type | 2 Lucas halogen |
| dip | 100 W total |
| main | 110 W total |

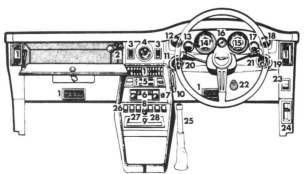

| | | | |
|---|---|---|---|
| 1 | Vents | 14 | Tachometer |
| 2 | Map light | 15 | Speedometer |
| 3 | Window winder switches | 16 | Oil pressure gauge |
| 4 | Clock | 17 | Water temp. gauge |
| 5 | Air conditioning controls | 18 | Oil temp gauge |
| 6 | Radio/cassette player | 19 | Light switch |
| 7 | Wiper delay | 20 | Wash/wipe stalk |
| 8 | Cigar lighter | 21 | Indicators / dip / flash / horn stalk |
| 9 | Ashtray | 22 | Ignition |
| 10 | Fly-off handbrake | 23 | Power hood switch |
| 11 | Panel light rheostat | 24 | Bonnet release |
| 12 | Voltmeter | 25 | Fly-off handbrake |
| 13 | Fuel gauge | 26 | Hazard flashers |
| | | 27 | Interior light |
| | | 28 | Air/wind horn changeover switch |

The instruments are clear and comprehensive, but the glasses reflect and some can be obscured from view

conditioning, adjustable steering, and electric driver's door mirror indicate a level of equipment that is far from spartan, there are some surprising omissions; items like head restraints, lockable filler caps, a headlamp wash/wipe and rearguard fog lamps are available, but cost extra. For almost £34,000 you would think that such items — often found on cars costing one tenth the price — would be fitted as standard.

## IN SERVICE

After its free service at 500-1000 miles, the Volante requires servicing every 5000 miles, to a schedule that includes 14 different grease points. The electronic ignition requires no attention, and the spark plugs are unusually accessible for a V8, as are most other underbonnet items requiring regular attention.

The battery, however, is located in the boot (where there is also a battery cut-out switch) along with the jack and reasonably comprehensive tool kit. The spare is housed under the boot floor.

## CONCLUSION

We have long been fans of the current range of Aston Martins, and the Volante in no way diminishes our respect for the marque. The near-unique feature of a convertible top compensates for an inevitable increase in wind noise; the high speed cruising ability is otherwise relaxed and outstanding; the performance is stunning even with automatic transmission; and the handling is perhaps the most exploitable of all the current Supercars, with brakes to match. Some rivals ride more smoothly, and some are quieter, but few can match the finish of this fine example of British craftsmanship.

The splendid 90 deg V8 looks as good as it sounds and goes

# Comparisons

| PERFORMANCE | Aston** | Bristol** | Jaguar | Mercedes** | Porsche** | Rolls** |
|---|---|---|---|---|---|---|
| Max speed, mph | 150† | 140† | 155† | 134† | 138† | 116 |
| Max in 3rd | — | — | 116 | — | — | — |
|       2nd | 97 | 99 | 84 | 96 | 113 | 86 |
|       1st | 57 | 58 | 50 | 60 | 69 | 51 |
| 0-60 mph, secs | 7.7 | 7.4 | 6.7 | 8.5 | 7.9 | 10.7 |
| 30-50 mph in 4th, secs[1] | 2.4 | 2.8 | 6.6 | 3.3 | 3.0 | 4.3 |
| 50-70 mph in top, secs[1] | 3.8 | 4.3 | 6.9 | 4.4 | 3.7 | 6.5 |
| Weight, cwt | 35.3 | 34[2] | 33.4 | 33.0 | 29.6 | 43.5 |
| Turning circle, ft* | 39.7 | — | 34.2 | 30.4 | 34.1 | 34.9 |
| 50ft circle, turns | 1.15 | — | 1.1 | 0.9 | 1.05 | 1.15 |
| Boot capacity, cu ft | 5.1 | — | 8.4 | 8.9 | 7.3 | 12.7 |

*mean of left and right  **automatic  †estimated  [1]kickdown for automatics
[2]manufacturers figure

| COSTS AND SERVICE | Aston | Bristol | Jaguar | Mercedes | Porsche | Rolls |
|---|---|---|---|---|---|---|
| Price, inc VAT & tax, £ | 33864 | 29264 | 15996 | 15495 | 20498 | 43980 |
| Insurance group | † | 7 | 7 | 7 | 8 | 7 |
| Overall mpg | 11.8 | — | 12.8 | 15.1 | 13.6 | 11.6 |
| Touring mpg | 13.6 | — | 14.4 | — | — | 13.8 |
| Fuel grade (stars) | 4 | 2 | 4 | 4 | 2 | 4 |
| Tank capacity, gals | 25.0 | 18.0 | 20.0 | 19.8 | 18.9 | 24.0 |
| Service interval, miles | 5000 | 5000 | 6000 | 5000 | 12000 | 6000 |
| No of dealers | 27 | 1 | 316 | 95 | 18 | 82 |
| Set brake pads (front) £* | 39.35 | 13.40 | 21.91 | 15.58 | 52.83 | 22.44 |
| Complete clutch £* | — | — | 68.85 | — | — | — |
| Complete exhaust £* | 516.32 | 321.25 | 307.04 | 400.15 | 604.52 | 777.60 |
| Front wing panel £* | 405.24 | 237.60 | 88.02 | 125.09 | 220.37 | 55.51 |
| Oil filter, £* | 4.53 | 5.19 | 5.89 | 2.69 | 10.51 | 5.01 |
| Starter Motor, £ | 94.34 | 92.66§ | 67.87§ | 82.57§ | 214.22 | 82.08§ |
| Windscreen, £* | 237.36** | 194.40** | 38.61** | 161.47** | 266.76** | 94.90** |

*inc VAT but not labour charges  **Laminated  ††to be decided  §exchange

| STANDARD EQUIPMENT | Aston | Bristol | Jaguar | Mercedes | Porsche | Rolls |
|---|---|---|---|---|---|---|
| Adjustable steering | ● | | ● | | ● | |
| Air Conditioning | ● | | ● | | ● | ● |
| Alloy Wheels | ● | ● | ● | | | |
| Central door locking | | | ● | ● | ● | ● |
| Cigar lighter | ● | ● | ● | ● | ● | ● |
| Clock | ● | ● | ● | ● | ● | ● |
| Cloth trim | [1] | [1] | [1] | ● | ● | [1] |
| Dipping mirror | ● | ● | ● | ● | ● | — |
| Electric window lifters | ● | ● | ● | ● | ● | ● |
| Fresh air vents | ● | ● | ● | ● | ● | ● |
| Hazard flashers | ● | ● | ● | ● | ● | ● |
| Headlamp washers | | | | | ● | ● |
| Head restraints | | ● | ● | ● | ● | ● |
| Heated rear window | [3] | ● | ● | ● | ● | [3] |
| Intermit/flick wipe | ● | | ● | ● | ● | ● |
| Laminated screen | ● | ● | ● | ● | ● | ● |
| Locker | ● | ● | ● | ● | ● | ● |
| Petrol filler lock | | ● | ● | ● | ● | ● |
| Power steering | ● | ● | ● | ● | — | ● |
| Radio | ● | ● | ● | | ● | ● |
| Rear central armrest | | ● | | | ● | ● |
| Rear courtesy light | | | | | | |
| Rear fog light | | ● | | ● | ● | ● |
| Rear wash/wipe | | | | | ●† | |
| Rev counter | ● | ● | ● | ● | ● | |
| Reverse lights | ● | ● | ● | ● | ● | ● |
| Seat belts — front | ● | ● | ● | ● | ● | ● |
|     rear | | | | | ● | |
| Seat recline | ● | ● | ● | ● | ● | ● |
| Sliding roof | | [2] | | | | |
| Tape player | ● | | ● | | ● | ● |
| Tinted glass | ● | | ● | ● | ● | ● |
| Vanity mirror | ● | | ● | ● | ● | ● |

[1]leather  [2]Targa roof  †wipe only  [3]dhc

94

# The Rivals

Other open top cars that might be considered are the Bentley Corniche (£43,980), Ferrari 308GTS (£18,169), Cavalier Centaur (£7,548), Panther de Ville dhc (£44,321), Porsche 911 Targa (£14,549), TVR Turbo (£11,445)

## ASTON MARTIN VOLANTE £33,864

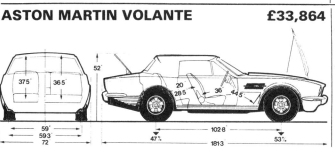

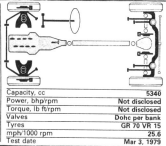

| | |
|---|---|
| Capacity, cc | 5340 |
| Power, bhp/rpm | Not disclosed |
| Torque, lb ft/rpm | Not disclosed |
| Valves | Dohc per bank |
| Tyres | GR 70 VR 15 |
| mph/1000 rpm | 25.6 |
| Test date | Mar 3, 1979 |

The essence of an Aston — stunning performance, excellent handling and outstanding braking — remains unchanged in the Volante, though an increase in wind noise has marred the easy cruising at very high speeds. The power-operated hood fits well and is easy to use, but vision to the rear is poor. Ride is fair at low speeds, good at high. Beautifully made and sumptuously trimmed. Very expensive, but a magnificent car with unique qualities.

## BRISTOL 412/S2 £29,264

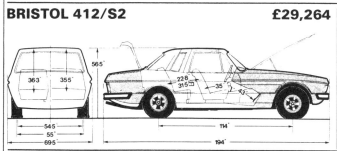

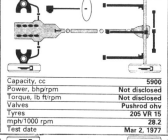

| | |
|---|---|
| Capacity, cc | 5900 |
| Power, bhp/rpm | Not disclosed |
| Torque, lb ft/rpm | Not disclosed |
| Valves | Pushrod ohv |
| Tyres | 205 VR 15 |
| mph/1000 rpm | 28.2 |
| Test date | Mar 2, 1977 |

Aimed at the sporting owner/driver, the bespoke Bristol's key offerings are excellence of manufacture and exclusivity. With its American V8 engine (smaller now than when we tested it, but the car is lighter too) the Targa-topped 412 is a unique amalgam of stirring performance (on two star fuel) and the ultimate luxury of wood and leather that only the British understand. There is no shortage of customers for this rare car.

## JAGUAR XJ-S £15,996

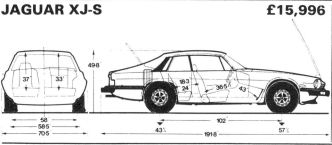

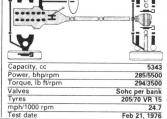

| | |
|---|---|
| Capacity, cc | 5343 |
| Power, bhp/rpm | 285/5500 |
| Torque, lb ft/rpm | 294/3500 |
| Valves | Sohc per bank |
| Tyres | 205/70 VR 15 |
| mph/1000 rpm | 24.7 |
| Test date | Feb 21, 1976 |

In true Jaguar tradition, the XJ-S combines exceptional performance, balanced handling and refinement at a very competitive price. The styling may not be to everyone's taste and the rear seat accommodation is cramped for so large a car. But if you can afford the fuel bills, the XJ-S is without doubt one of the world's most desirable vehicles. We've only tested the manual but it's available in auto form as well; no convertible version, however.

## MERCEDES 450SL £15,495

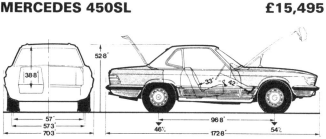

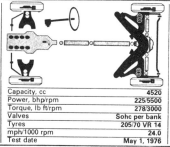

| | |
|---|---|
| Capacity, cc | 4520 |
| Power, bhp/rpm | 225/5500 |
| Torque, lb ft/rpm | 278/3000 |
| Valves | Sohc per bank |
| Tyres | 205/70 VR 14 |
| mph/1000 rpm | 24.0 |
| Test date | May 1, 1976 |

One of the few remaining true convertibles, the 450SL has typical Mercedes exceptionally high standard of finish, and engineering second to none. Performance is more than adequate (we've quoted figures for the fractionally heavier SLC) while the automatic transmission is one of the best around. No attempt to provide occasional rear seats so the boot is a very good size. The heavy hardtop can be removed and there's also a tight fitting hood.

## PORSCHE 928 £20,498

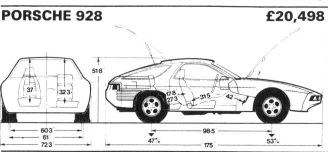

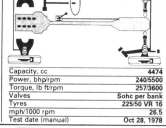

| | |
|---|---|
| Capacity, cc | 4474 |
| Power, bhp/rpm | 240/5500 |
| Torque, lb ft/rpm | 257/3600 |
| Valves | Sohc per bank |
| Tyres | 225/50 VR 16 |
| mph/1000 rpm | 26.5 |
| Test date (manual) | Oct 28, 1978 |

The 928 hasn't quite the mind-blowing performance you'd expect from a Porsche, but it's no sluggard — we quote figures for the auto, full test of which is yet to be published. Super-refined engine and low wind noise, but potential refinement let down by excessive tyre roar. Excellent handling and roadholding in all but the most extreme conditions, excellent brakes, but mediocre ride. Very spacious for two, but cramped rear seat, and no drophead version.

## ROLLS-ROYCE CORNICHE CONV £43,980

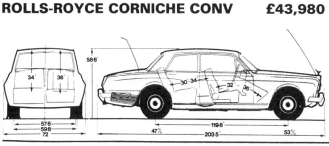

| | |
|---|---|
| Capacity, cc | 6750 |
| Power, bhp/rpm | Not disclosed |
| Torque, lb ft/rpm | Not disclosed |
| Valves | Pushrod ohv |
| Tyres | 237/70 HR 15 |
| mph/1000 rpm | 26.9 |
| Test date | Oct 4, 1975 |

Superb construction and engineering combine with a fabled finish, impressive noise suppression, smoothness and comfort to make an outstanding car. Transmission and brakes are praiseworthy too, but road noise is disappointing and the performance is below others of this class: the ride/handling bias is towards comfort rather than cornering. We tested the hard-top but a convertible is available.

# Lagonda Revisited

BY L.J.K. SETRIGHT

**What this product of British brains needs now is an American brain.**

*I called the New World into existence,* proclaimed George Canning in a speech in December 1826, *to redress the balance of the Old.* Next year he was prime minister of Great Britain—but in the light of what he said, that greatness was doomed to recede. The balance has yet to be struck: it was in search of an equilibrium of ends and means, of an idea in need of realization, that a prototype Lagonda went on an American tour last year. The idea was an English one, blossoming from the brain of Mike Loasby, former chief engineer of Aston Martin Lagonda, Ltd., who has recently gone to De Lorean; but the blossom wilted when it was found that Britain could not provide the technology to make his dream into a reality. For that, they had to go to America.

It was a mini-computer that was the stumbling block, a data-processing electronic thingummy intended to correlate speed and time and fuel flow, to present the driver on demand with information about running average speed, instantaneous or average fuel consumption, time to destination, remaining fuel range, and anything else amenable to calculation from the available premises. The computer was one of the three modernistic marvels of the original Lagonda facia, along with touch-sensitive proximity switches for all minor controls and gas-plasma displays of all mustered information. The digital feed-in and the digital readout were manageable: the first batch of Lagondas off the production line, numbering at least a dozen, incorporate these features. The computer made in Britain failed: those fir

cars cannot calculate. Since the summer of 1978, proving trials of a new American computer have been going on in an area of increasing radius centered on Dallas, Texas; but the softly sprung, well-insulated, smooth-running modern motorcar is apparently a much tougher environment for electronics than a combat aircraft or a space satellite, and until there is absolutely no doubt about the efficacity of the Texas instrument, Lagondas are not going to be put at risk any more.

The car has been compromised enough already. When I drove an early prototype a couple of years ago (*C/D*, June 1977) it still displayed all its first promise of enormous performance and boggleworthy roadhugging combined with luxury such as might give the sybaritic something new to covet. The chassis was a simpler and more coherent structure than the old and much-modified Aston Martin platform; the suspension and running gear, although superficially similar, suffered none of the installational constraints and approximations of

**A car that costs as much as an emerging nation's GNP should look it. The Lagonda does.**

the Aston Martin, so the geometry was better and the cornering power even greater; and with the same engine (losing only a few horsepower through a more muffled exhaust) in a body of much lower drag coefficient and significantly lower total drag, the thing was likely to go very fast indeed. The company originally claimed only 140 mph, but Loasby knew from the figures that it was capable of at least 160.

Alas, all trade tends to corrupt; selling corrupts particularly. There are in this world more rich men than racing drivers, and Lagonda was after the ones with the money. Such a customer might not notice, might never come within half a g of noticing, the exquisite feel of the steering relaying its messages from the tires as the car clung fastidiously to its line through a rousing corner; his idea of fastidiousness would more probably measure the smoothness of the powered seat adjustments, his concern with feedback would be to judge the fidelity of the stereo speakers. He would have to be indulged; but the Lagonda had such ex-

ceptional performance and roadworthiness that it could afford to sacrifice some in the cause of such comforts.

That is how the Lagonda put on weight. That early prototype weighed a scant 3800 pounds empty—but, in Loasby's sorrowful words, *luxury weighs heavy*. Electric motors that would reliably move the seat cushions and squabs in their four distinct modes were hard to find, and for a while it looked as though the only ones available to do the job were great lumpen things of Chrysler iron. To ward off noise and vibration from the wheel arches, thick wedges of lead-layered attenuator sandwich had to be laid everywhere. American needs (or tastes) in bumpers put more heft into the hull. At one stage in the car's development, the weight reached a disgusting 5800 pounds; furious concentration on materials and methods eventually brought the burden down again, to something like 5000 pounds, with 4400 the current goal; but the car had lost the edge of its acceleration, which in the early days had been lively enough to

## It's Touch-Tone driving with the Lagonda's space-age control console.

allow 60 mph to be reached from standstill in seven seconds.

The top speed was cut back, too, for a variety of reasons. The extra weight knocked the top off the acceleration curve; the nasal revisions required for bumpers and air intakes (more cooling air was needed, especially now that the engine and brakes were having to work harder) did some harm to the drag coefficient; and the tires posed another problem. Loasby and his development-engineering henchman Bill Bannard (since promoted to management of the service department, where he can get the best feedback from the customers and make the most sense out of it, but also responsible for quality control) tried all sorts of rubberware. On Pirelli CN12 tires, as fitted to the blisteringly powerful Aston Martin Vantage, the four-door Lagonda could outcorner the two-door Aston; but the ride was not good enough for the sort of customers who were expected to pay Rolls-Royce prices for a car that they expected to be better than a Rolls-Royce. The best tires

for ride were some Avons, very grippy but not especially responsive, that only had an HR rating, meaning that they could not be expected or required to sustain more than 130 mph. Recognizing with the idealist carmaker's familiar blend of sadness and cynicism that 130 mph was a lot faster than most customers would ever drive anyway, Lagonda left it at that. The result, at a projected $75,000, should be available in America early next year.

The car is no slouch, despite the lower top speed. Driving an early production specimen proved to me that, though the uncomputerized Lagonda may be brainless, it is by no means gutless. It is fast without apparent effort, very fast with only some slight indication of the four-camshaft V-8's working hard. The ride is superb, and the roadholding and steering still amazing for a car of such size. Hurtling along a winding, roach-backed country lane, all damp patches and puddles and muddied edges close to both flanks of the William Towns body, I spared a glance for the light-emitting

**Vehicle type:** front-engine, rear-wheel-drive, 4-passenger, 4-door sedan

**Price (U.K.):** $75,000

**Engine type:** V-8, water-cooled, aluminum block and heads, double overhead cams, 4x2-bbl carburetors

| | |
|---|---|
| Displacement | 326.3 cu in, 5340cc |
| Power (SAE net) | NA |
| Transmission | 3-speed, automatic |
| Wheelbase | 108.6 in |
| Length | 208.0 in |
| Front suspension | ind, unequal-length control arms, coil springs, anti-sway bar |
| Rear suspension | de Dion, 3 trailing links, Watt linkage, coil springs |
| Steering | rack-and-pinion, power-assisted |
| Brakes | vented discs, power-assisted |

diodes on the facia—to discover that we were doing well over 80 mph where nobody in his right mind would expect to exceed 60 in anything bigger than a Lotus Elan; and we were doing it comfortably, feeling completely secure and confident in the ability of the Lag to pick its path between the veering verges. Haring between flat, unposted fields, we were actually going as fast as we could see the road before us, yet that was well within the car's limits.

Only when I took the Lagonda to the roundabout where I had wrung out the first prototype did I realize what it had lost. Instead of two dozen back-straining laps getting closer and closer to the limit, I found that two laps were enough for me to find how far the car wanted to go. A faint groan from the outside wheels suggested that enough was as good as a feast, that the ultra-high-geared and pleasantly weighted steering was meant for direction, not for correction. The Lagonda is not so much of a driver's car anymore; but it is a far better passenger's car than it ever was.  ●

# IT'S TRUE, THE LAGONDA LIVES!

*It's like driving the world's fastest calculator*

**BY JOHN LAMM**

I N THE RAPIDLY fading light of day, the red digital instruments of the Aston Martin Lagonda were getting to be almost mesmerizing, particularly the one for speed as it continued to flash its way up to 100 mph. That may not seem like the best speed at which to find your eyes being drawn back from the highway, but despite the fact that it was a 2-lane road and not in the best of condition, I still felt quite secure with the Lagonda. That is one of the greatest attractions of European luxury automobiles: their uncanny ability to adapt to all road surfaces, smoothing out patches and lumps while staying steady at 100 mph or more. In a country with a 55-mph speed limit that sounds almost silly, but is it any less sensible than the car's $85,000 price tag?

Fantasy tends to beget fantasy, and so it would be unthinkable to try this new goatskin-lined flying wedge without topping the century mark, just to make sure Aston Martin is living up to its heritage. There's much more to recommend the Lagonda than just speed, of course, and getting past the styling is good for openers. The shape, you may recall, was drawn by William Towns, the man responsible for the Aston Martin DBS. And though some staffers were uncertain of the car's beauty when

they first saw photos of it more than two years ago, several were completely taken by the Lagonda's spectacular design when we finally had a chance to see it on the road. It is one of those shapes that only photographs well from about two angles, and then only with medium-length telephoto lenses. This is also an automobile that has to be seen on the road with other cars before it can be appreciated. First, because it dominates the scene just by its design. Second, because of its size, as the car is much larger than you'd think just by looking at photos of it. The Lagonda's overall length is 208.0 in., 1.4 in. less than a Mercedes-Benz 450SEL. The English car is also 2.1 in. narrower than the German make and 5.1 in. lower. I think one thing that makes it difficult to estimate the size of the Lagonda is the way those 235/70-15 Avon tires fill the wheelwells.

One dimension Lagonda owners are most concerned about is the size of other drivers' eyeballs when they spot the car. There it does famously. And if you can't lip read "What the hell is that?"

you'll be able to after 20 minutes in a Lagonda. The car we drove was prototype number 2 and had right-hand drive, which was quite convenient when we did have the chance to talk to other drivers.

The basic simplicity of the Lagonda's exterior design is carried over inside, and it might be easy to start an argument over whether the decor should be described as "simple elegance" or "plain." We prefer the former. The seats in the Lagonda were upholstered in medium-blue goatskin and are soft and cushy in the manner of the Jaguar and Rolls-Royce as opposed to the firmness of most German seats. There are no pretenses that this car might have room for five passengers and each of the four places has an individual feel to it. The view, inside and out, is

quite nice, the floor is covered with Wilton pile carpeting, the headliner is a soft fabric and in the ceiling just ahead of the rear-seat passengers is a non-removable sunroof. Also fixed on our car were the rear door windows, though it's said they will lower in production models.

Crowning touch of the interior is the instrument panel, which has been redesigned since the original prototype, but still has a bank of red light-emitting diodes (LEDs). On the upper left are the speedometer and tachometer with the largest of the figures. In the center top is a clock and below that a trip odometer, then ammeter. The column of LEDs on the right are, from top to bottom, percentage of fuel remaining, oil pressure, oil temperature, coolant temperature and ambient air temperature.

The whole system is fascinating, as you might guess, and a great toy to boot. They were not, however, the easiest instruments to read in daylight for some drivers who found them difficult to see easily, despite a switch to brighten or dim the display. It also takes a long time to read the instruments, as opposed to being able to just glance down and see a needle in about the right position. The original Lagonda display had bands or circles of light to do this in addition to the LEDs and we suspect that was a ➤➤➤

*Light-touch switches for door panel (left) and dashboard.*

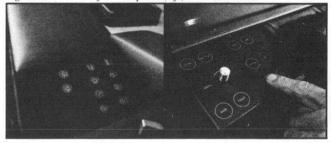

better system. To minimize confusion, it is possible to shut off all the instrument lights except the most critical—tach, speedometer, clock and fuel percentage—with the others coming on only in the case of an emergency in a critical system. In that case, the light displaying the problem will flash. This system, incidentally, was developed in this form by a Texas-based company named, strangely enough, Javelina, which means wild pig.

Just below the panel are a bank of pressure sensitive switches. The first Lagonda had touch-sensitive switches that reacted to the temperature of the driver's finger, but it was thought conditions such as temperature extremes might cause problems with this type of switch. Now just a light touch on any of the printed circles does the same job as it brings together two thin pieces of copper—the switches are only 1 mm thick—to close the circuit which then trips a relay. When you hear a little beep, the switch has switched. This array of circles allows you to turn on such things as the front lights (spot, fog and headlights), change the speedometer calibration from mph to km/h, check ambient temperature inside or out, change the tone of the horn, turn on the hazard light, reset the trip odometer and, at some future time, operate a trip computer. In the driver's door are similar switches to control the adjustable seats, windows and door locks. All the usual luxury car features are included, with cruise control, air conditioning (based on General Motors' rotary compressor) and a sophisticated sound system by Audiomobile.

The platform chassis on which all this is mounted is a development of the same one used for other Aston Martins. To this platform is added a tubular steel subframe over which is mounted the aluminum body. Initially, all the Lagonda bodies will be pounded out by hand, but AM hopes to eventually use the TI Superform vacuum forming system for the panels, as it allows the use of harder-grade aluminum. The body is finished with no lead or plastic filler and then covered with 16 hand-rubbed coats of lacquer and a layer of clear coating.

The suspension uses unequal-length A-arms, coil springs, tube shocks and an anti-roll bar up front, with the De Dion rear suspension having coil springs and self-leveling shock absorbers. Brakes are Girling ventilated discs front and rear, the back ones mounted inboard next to the Salisbury limited-slip differential. Steering is an Adwest power-assisted rack-and-pinion unit.

Aston Martin refuses to give horsepower figures, but we think their description of adequate is, well, adequate; it's the same two-cam-per-bank, cast aluminum, 5.3-liter V-8 used in the Aston V-8 coupe. Webers do the carbureting while a Lucas Opus II electronic ignition system provides the spark. Incidentally, each Aston Martin V-8 is handbuilt by one man and then run for nine hours on a dynamometer before being installed. It's said the dyno operator can tell who built which engine just by the sound of it. Behind the V-8 is a Chrysler Torqueflite automatic transmission with appropriately modified shift points and, eventually perhaps, pressure-sensitive buttons on the dashboard to operate it. A ZF 5-speed will be offered as an option, though it seems out of character with the car.

All this is assembled into an interesting contrast of what is and what isn't expected from a luxury car. For instance, if we discount the little faults in the finish of the interior because this is a prototype, I'd have to say the rear seat is very comfortable, and

certainly more so than that of a 6.9-liter Mercedes or a Rolls-Royce. And yet the doors don't quite open wide enough for me to get in or out of the Aston comfortably. (And then you have to consider the price of the Lagonda, which is about $35,000 *more* than a 6.9.)

We aren't sure of just how much of the production sound-deadening material was in the Lagonda I drove, but it certainly seemed to be enough for me because I don't like a car that is dead quiet—and this Lagonda allowed the rumble of the V-8 to come through when I stabbed the throttle.

I already mentioned the impressive mix of ride and handling, which I had a chance to try on southern California mountain roads. All the right things seem to be there: brakes that are willing to bring the 3800-lb car to a stop without undo fuss, steering that transmits sufficient road feel without sending along all the bumps and vibrations, and an engine/transmission combination that seems as content to live with the accessories in traffic as with the climb past 100 mph on the open road. All that and you get a 2-year or 24,000-mile warranty too.

Another impressive feature of Aston Martin in the U.S. is that, in the Rolls-Royce tradition, they will send a service representative to your rescue if your Aston or Lagonda should break down. Or, as in the case of one buyer who lived some distance from the dealer, they can instruct someone nearby how to perform routine maintenance on the car.

Not only that, but when you buy an Aston Martin Lagonda you get one of the great toys made in the world today. Turn the key and the red LED display lights up like a huge, complex calculator. ("Marvelous," exclaimed the Editor, "we've got 14.2 volts.") Start the engine, it rumbles quietly, and all the numbers flicker as they rise and fall appropriately. Lightly touch a small circle on the dashboard and, beep, the lights are on. Get into gear and you're off.

No wonder a pair of young sheiks recently bought three Lagondas each and paid cash. The fact that they have that much ready cash, by the way, goes a long way toward explaining why the Lagonda, when first introduced at the Earls Court Show in 1976, was said to cost $32,000 . . . and why Doug Nye was told four months later that the price would have to be $41,500-$49,000 . . . and why when the first orders were taken in the U.S. the quoted cost would be $75,000 . . . and why the price is now $85,000.

Now to restore your faith in the American economy, we should add that there are already 29 Lagonda orders for the U.S., backed by $10,000 deposits. ◉

# Aston Martin Volante

GEORGE NAGHER

## Only 80 Americans will own this $70,000 convertible

### by William Jeanes

The new Aston Martin Volante has a top that goes down and a price that goes up, way up to $69,860. Unless, of course, you specify the 5-speed manual transmission, in which case the modest $1975 add-on extends the price to a lofty $71,835. The Volante, as you may have guessed, is an automobile aimed at the moneyed. But, unlike automotive aberrations such as the Stutz Blackhawk and others of that stripe, which are distinguished only by their ozone-layer pricetags, the Aston Martin Volante was made to please the hard-driving motorist who also happens to be rich. You may need a trunkful of Blue Chip certificates to own one, but you need only love cars to appreciate the Volante.

The 5-speed gearbox seems to be the only option available to purchasers of the Volante. You could, presumably, order the family Volante delivered with a Ford Fiesta to use as a dinghy, but by and large the car comes with just about every toy a driver could ask for. Except cruise control... and there's a reason for that, which we will get to shortly.

You may be wondering why you are being told about the Aston Martin Volante. You don't have a trunkful of AT&T stock or the 280 Krugerrands to swap for this dignified high-speed machine. Well, you are being told about this automobile because there is a principle involved, the principle of excellence. Never mind that it is Excellence At Any Cost. On the rare occasions excellence in any form makes an appearance in the automotive world, we all ought to pause and scrutinize the phenomenon. The way things are going, we will have fewer and fewer opportunities.

The Volante is British to the core, one of the last of a hand-built breed. The Volante is a *car*, not a leather-lined lockbox that is too insulated from the road. In the Volante, you are constantly reminded why you are in the driver's seat, and there is enormous pleasure to be derived from knowing that the reason is simply to enjoy the sensory excitement delivered by a genuine Grand Touring car. That you can enjoy this excitement with the top down is only added spice.

Heavy though it may be with the burden of British tradition, the exis-

tence of Aston Martin—officially Aston Martin Lagonda—is due in large part to an American named Peter Sprague. Upset at the likelihood of Aston Martin's disappearance from the automotive stage—an imminent event some years back—Sprague journeyed to London to see if he and a group of American investors might save the marque. The English press had got wind of Sprague's mission, and the young MIT graduate stepped off the plane to find lurid front pages anointing him the "Saviour of Aston Martin." Sprague, whose fortune was made with a firm called National Semiconductor, was equal to the appellation. He did indeed save Aston Martin, keeping alive its mission of building great cars that cry out to be driven.

This dedication to cars that welcome a bit of the spur is apparent at once when you slide yourself into the back-grabbing leather seat and go thrumming off into the countryside behind the long hood that covers a hand-built 5.4-liter V-8 with four cams and four twin-choke Weber carburetors. The car does what you tell it to, and if your instructions are firm, the response is rewarding and trustworthy, like that from a good horse. Both the brake pedal and the ac-

103

# Aston Martin Volante

celerator take some effort, but that is a designed-in feature according to no less a source than a member of the board of directors.

The board member in question is Henrietta, Lady Tavistock. She and her husband have been kind enough to deliver a Volante into my hands at the Rolls dealer in Palm Beach. Lady Tavistock has the brand of brunette beauty that Jackie Onassis is supposed to have but doesn't. Lord Tavistock wears horn rims, a double-breasted blue blazer, Gucci loafers and a friendly smile. The couple are in their thirties.

The Marchioness of Tavistock speaks firmly and adamantly about the purpose and personality of her favorite car. She can do this for two reasons: One, she cares deeply about the car; two, she knows what she is talking about.

"This knife-edge here on the front wing (fender) is hand formed," she says. "It's perhaps the most difficult part of the body to build. The entire body is completely hand formed from aluminum sheets hand beaten over wood forms." We are standing in front of the Norton Gallery, a jewel of Palm Beach's cultural community, and Lady Tavistock is walking around a gleaming brown-toned burgandy Volante, pointing out feature after feature. She speaks not from rote learning but from genuine interest. This knowledge and interest are the qualities that got her into the Aston Martin Lagonda boardroom to begin with. That, and a touch of circumstance.

Aston Martin's Newport Pagnell works lies near Woburn Abbey, ancestral home of the Duke of Bedford. The Duke of Bedford's son and heir to the title is Lord Tavistock. Lord Tavistock was earning a degree from Harvard as Peter Sprague studied at nearby MIT. The two friends had been close since their pre-college school days at Le Rosey in Switzerland, and the friendship was renewed when Sprague crossed the Atlantic to help make the world a better place for Grand Touring autos.

"Peter would come by to visit," says Lord Tavistock, "and we would talk about the cars. My wife had a great many opinions. Good opinions, in Peter's mind. The result was an invitation to sit on the board." Lady Tavistock accepted and immediately became a valued part of the organization. She cares about the company and, what is more, understands the positioning of its cars in the marketplace...a feat that often eludes executives of far larger auto companies.

"We build an automobile intended for people who not only want the best car available, but who also want to really *drive* the car. This car was not built for 30-mile-an-hour trips to the shops," says Lady Tavistock. "You can tell from the brakes and the accelerator," she continued. "They take a bit of effort, but they function superbly." At this point, the subject of cruise control somehow entered the conversaton. Characterizing the typical American sedan as a "perambulating drawing room," Lady Tavistock essayed the opinion that cruise control was for people who didn't truly enjoy the act of driving in the first place. She has a point. There is no denying that any responsible driver would swim in guilt if he seriously wanted a cruise control button on his Volante. Besides which, if one can afford a Volante, one can not only afford the time to drive on non-freeway roads but also the cost of an occasional citation from vigilant patrolmen.

Indeed, it is the open road that brings out the spirit of the Volante. This product of 20 weeks' work by 150 craftsmen leans into turns with the confident grace of a polo pony and the strength of a quarter horse. You *trust* the Volante. You trust it to do as it is asked and to perform in a manner acceptable in polite company. The Volante is a car for gentlemen and their women.

Much of the Volante's personality derives from the V-8 engine, a responsive brute that thunders along with nary a care for soaring gasoline prices. The engine in each Aston Martin is built by a single man. A small brass plate bears the man's name, and even though unrecognized, the appearance of a surname on a mechanical product tells you, "I built this engine and this engine will work." Not a bad shard of evidence that someone, somewhere, cares about doing something the best way they know how. The aluminum engine will power the Volante from 0-60 in a far more than respectable 7 seconds or so. If one were to ignore annoying speed limits in this country, the engine would also carry one to an honest top speed in excess of 125 mph. Whether

speeds in that realm are gentlemanly levels to attain this day and time is a question for some debate. To some people. *Not* attaining these levels might also be considered improper in some circles. This latter circle is the one to which you want to belong.

The mechanical attributes of the Volante are not unusual, unless you count the inboard disc brakes at the rear. All four discs are ventilated models by Girling. The front suspension is independent, with unequal-length wishbones, coaxial coil springs and Koni shock absorbers. The rear axle is a De Dion, with parallel trailing arms and Watt linkage, also with coil springs and Konis. The steering is requisite rack and pinion, the differential is a limited-slip, and the 5-speed gearbox drives through a 3.54:1 rearend. The entire assembly sits on a generous 102.75-inch wheelbase, and it all weighs just under 2 tons. Nothing startling there, unless you count the undoubted care with which it is all put together. Which you should.

The interior of the Volante is equally non-innovative, but in its own way is cause for celebration. There is nothing in there that is not the best, from the choice hides that provide the upholstery to the Wilton wool carpets on the floor. Well, almost nothing.

"We're a bit embarrassed about the switches," says Lady Tavistock. "It simply costs too much to have our own made, so we have to use ones from Jaguar." A forgivable act, be assured. The switches are not intrusive and will not upset your feeling of well-being as you motor along in your Volante.

From air conditioning, through a stereo tape cassette player, to the gleaming French-polished walnut burl wood found throughout the passenger compartment, the Volante's interior pleases. Astoundingly, given practice and precedent in the world of Grand Touring, the rear seat will even accommodate two adults in a condition approaching relaxation.

The Aston Martin Volante has a sphere of reality all its own. When the burgandy beauty was returned to its station at the Rolls dealer after an afternoon of motoring stylishly about Palm Beach and environs, a stately blonde woman wearing rich-person clothes walked over to the open trunk.

"Why it's just the right size for a picnic basket," she told her blazered companion. She spoke truth. The oblong luggage compartment would indeed accommodate the finest picnic basket Fortnum & Mason might assemble. Furthermore, the carpeted box was attached to the kind of car that was unashamedly intended for those who spend more on a well-filled basket of varnished wicker than many motorists spend on insurance premiums. But never mind that, for that is as it should be. And never mind that you cannot afford a Volante. After all, only 80 will be imported this year, and you can say that they ran out before you got there. Meanwhile, if you know a better way to spend a sunny spring afternoon than motoring around Palm Beach with the top of your Volante neatly stowed above a cache of *Pouilly Fuisse* and *pate de fois gras,* keep it to yourself. Any such activity would either be illegal or so shot through with debauchery that my health would be endangered.

You go your way and I'll go mine. I'll be the man with the big smile behind the wheel of an Aston Martin Volante. One that I've managed somehow to borrow. <sub>MT</sub>

## SPECIFICATIONS

### GENERAL

| | |
|---|---|
| Vehicle type | Front-engine, rear-drive, 4-pass. convertible |
| Base price | $69,860 |
| Options on test car | 5-speed manual trans. |
| Price as tested | $71,835 |

### ENGINE

| | |
|---|---|
| Type | V-8, aluminum alloy block, aluminum heads, water cooled |
| Bore & stroke | 100 x 85 mm |
| Displacement | 5340 cc |
| Compression ratio | N.A. |
| Fuel system | 4 twin-choke Weber carburetors |
| Recommended octane number | N.A. |
| Emission control | Twin catalytic converters |
| Valve gear | 4 overhead camshafts |
| Horsepower (SAE net) | N.A. |
| Torque (SAE net) | N.A. |

### DRIVETRAIN

| | |
|---|---|
| Transmission | 5-speed manual (O.D. 5th) |
| Final drive ratio | 3.54:1 (3.07:1 w/automatic) |

### DIMENSIONS

| | |
|---|---|
| Wheelbase | 102.75 in. |
| Track, F/R | 59/59 in. |
| Length | 183.75 in. |
| Width | 72 in. |
| Height | 54 in. |
| Ground clearance | 5.5 in. |
| Curb weight | 3950 lb. |

### SUSPENSION

| | |
|---|---|
| Front | Independent, unequal-length wishbones, Koni shocks, coaxial coil springs, anti-roll bar |
| Rear | De Dion axle located by parallel trailing arms, Watt linkage; coil springs, Koni shocks |

### STEERING

| | |
|---|---|
| Type | Rack and pinion, power assist |
| Turns lock-to-lock | 2.9 |
| Turning circle, curb-to-curb | 38 ft. |

### BRAKES

| | |
|---|---|
| Front | Girling ventilated discs |
| Rear | Girling ventilated discs |

### WHEELS AND TIRES

| | |
|---|---|
| Wheel size | 15 x 7 in. |
| Wheel type | Light alloy ventilated |
| Tire size | GR 235 70 HR 15 |
| Tire type | Steel-belted radials |

# A BRITISH BULLDOG

## Aston Martin go for the ultimate

**By John Miles**

*Photographs Ron Easton*

THE BULLDOG does nothing more than make a statement. It states that a firm that was near to collapse six years ago is now healthy, also that the British can still do what they do well, which is to ignore commercial sense and build a car that serves to boost an image. Such a development and styling exercise provides the outlet for Aston Martin engineers and craftsmen's skills. Such a car serves to record the state of an art. Above all, a shatteringly fast supercar like this embodies a spirit of speed and adventure, and is bound to be a talking point throughout the World.

This is no motor show mock up. No matter what its eventual fate Aston say it will be tested to its maximum. On paper it should easily win back the fastest road car of all time tag for Britain; a pointless exercise? Perhaps so with today's depressing motoring backdrop, but then Aston Martin have always wanted to build the ultimate supercar.

Aston chairman Alan Curtis's desire to build it was reason enough. Work started in early 1978 under the direction of Mike Loasby (now at De Lorean) and stylist William Towns.

The Bulldog design owes little to any other concern. The main structure is 4 in. dia. mild steel tubing. It consists of a massive tri-tube central backbone running through the cockpit section spreading and deepening at the rear into a closed four railed box which tapers slightly (in line with the outer cross-sectional dimensions of the V8 block and heads) to accommodate the engine and transaxle. This structure also provides convenient mounting places for rear suspension pick-up points.

At the front only the upper backbone tube is inclined upwards; the lower ones run forward parallel. All three blend into another massive round tube box structure attached to which

# A British Bulldog

De Dion Tube diagram labels: DE DION TUBE, GEARBOX, CHASSIS PIVOTS, BUSHED JOINTS, LINKS INTERCONNECTED WITH HARD RUBBER BUSHING TO ACCOUNT FOR LINK LENGTH CHANGE FROM CHASSIS PIVOTS, DROOP

...s a smaller 2in. diameter tube front frame for mounting the radiator and front body. Sheet steel outriggers placed vertically at the joining point carry the front suspension. There is also what might be described as a secondary structure — a perimeter frame — again consisting of 2in. dia. tubes. These form the outer edges and cross bracing in the cockpit floor which is panelled in sheet steel for additional stiffness. Further rigidity in bending and torsion is provided by a triangulated framework at the front of the engine bay. This feeds loads from the rear chassis into a tough roll-over structure, and thence forward through the roof structure and A-posts.

When special products manager Keith Martin and development engineer Steve Hallam took over the project in early 1979 they had what amounted to a box of bits; a chassis that has subsequently needed much detail alteration, various suspension parts, body panels, a dummy engine, and some drawings. Loasby's original design called for De Dion axles at both ends. Martin and Hallam immediately decided to revert to conventional unequal length wishbones using Jaguar/Lagonda type forgings at the top, and specially fabricated bottom ones. Visualising the handling inconsistencies an independent rear end might create with very wide tyres they retained the De Dion rear end and also

improved the chassis load paths from front to rear, and in bending and torsion by taking small square tubes from the main chassis top rails at the rear to each corner of the roll-over bar, also by cross bracing in the existing roof structure. The result is the stiffest chassis Aston have built so far. In discussing suspension design Hallam made the very good point that with such very wide, stiff and square shouldered tyres (the rear P7s have a 11.5 in. wide footprint) accurate control of camber change is critical to exploiting the tyre's full potential and to maintain handling consistency. A De Dion rear end assures that the tyres are always vertical to the road surface.

At the front camber change from full bump to rebound is limited to 1½ deg. A DB6-based rack gives a race-car-like 2¼ turns from lock to lock and is positioned to eliminate bump and roll steer. Anti-Ackerman steering geometry is employed.

At the rear the massive 4in. dia De Dion tube slopes upwards to a horizontal centre section in order to clear the gearbox casing. Longitudinal location is by two pairs of quite short parallel trailing arms, and here Martin and Hallam have been careful to place the pick-up points to give a degree of roll understeer, that is to say a small amount of toe-in on the laden wheel. The transaxle makes lateral location by a normal Watt's linkage physically impossible. Instead, solid-bushed lateral rods are taken from the bottom of the hub carriers to L-shaped links. These pivot at their apices on chassis mountings and are interconnected at a central point under the transaxle. The effective change in link length

when the axle moves is allowed for by hard rubber bushing (this flexes 50 thou. from full bump to rebound) at the central pivot. Coil springs and fully adjustable aluminium Koni dampers are used all round.

While traditional taper roller wheel bearings are used in the front hubs, the Bulldog employs the increasingly popular second generation SKF sealed-for-life double row angular contact ball races in the rear hubs. Large Hooke-jointed shafts transmit the drive.

Clearly a car with this sort of performance potential and kerb weight (around 34 cwt is mentioned, split 40/60 front to rear) needs the biggest possible brakes. Lockheed CanAm type four pot calipers (1¾ in. dia. front pistons, 1½ in. dia. at rear) work on 11.7 in. dia. x 1¼ in. wide slotted and vented discs. These are mounted inboard at the rear. The system is split front/rear and operates through a Girling tandem master cylinder and integral "Supervac" pedal effort booster. A separate handbrake caliper works on the right hand disc. Pad material is Ferodo 2430.

As on the racing Porsche 935s outer blading on the wheel trims is designed to promote air flow and thus assist brake cooling. These fit snugly into 15in. dia. Compomotive alloy wheels. Rim widths are 8.5 in. front and 11.0 in. at the rear, while tyres are the widest production moulded P7s available; 225/50VR front and very wide 345/35VR at the rear (as fitted to the Lamborghini Countach S). Expressed another way, the Bulldog's front wheels are shod with Porsche 3.3 Turbo-width rear tyres! As an added precaution against high speed failure the Bulldog's P7s are

buffed, balanced, and X-rayed before fitting.

The ultimate supercar? The Bulldog is certainly a big machine, measuring 75.5 x 186 in. in plan (Boxer 72.0 x 173 in.), its width being determined to a large extent by the sheer physical problem in getting a large V8 in the back plus suspension and wide wheels. Also the true mid-engined, rather than Ferrari Boxer engine-over-gearbox layout, determines a higher-than-usual track-to-wheelbase ratio of 1.76 against the Italian's 1.63; yet another good portent for handling docility.

*To get over the problem of sideways location for the de Dion tube (when there's a transaxle in the way of a Watt linkage), Aston Martin use long links from the outboard ends of the tube pivotting on bell cranks under the gearbox. The cranks are linked to each other under the centre line of the car by a flexible bush which will accommodate the 50 thou. maximum of sideways misalignment produced in the bell crank ends when the car rolls*

*Major changes have already been made to the prototype (overleaf and left) and the running car (right). The latest "cow catcher" front and vertical rear spoilers are more aesthetically appealing and a louvred rear window opening has been found necessary to ventilate the engine compartment. Door actuation is hydraulic. For easy entry their lower halves tumblehome to form the sills. Note the lip along the "inner" edge to prevent grime falling on people's heads. Wheel trims have blading to extract air and front panel lowers to reveal headlights*

BULLDOG

*Fit to fly! A shot that also emphasises the narrow cockpit area and steeply raked screen. The area behind the seats is taken up by fuel. Upholstery hides the door actuating hydraulic rams*

## A British Bulldog
*continued*

### Inside a Bulldog

Ease of entry was uppermost in William Towns' mind during the concept stage. As Vic Berris's cutaway shows, the outer chassis rails in the cockpit area hardly extend past the seats. Towns' hydraulic gull wing door design is typically adventurous, if impractical at a toll booth or in a crowded car park, when a 9ft gap is needed to swing both doors open! The lower panels are fully 5 ft. long, tumbling home at the lower edge to fill in the space normally occupied by a sill. A nice touch is the lip along their innermost edges to prevent wetted road grime dripping on occupants' heads when the doors are open. Entry *is* easy but the tall driver will have

Perspex. Both are bonded to the screen openings by a moisture curing polyurethane compound called Betaseal, manufactured by Gurit-Essex — a Swiss company. Initial surface curing takes around 20 minutes, yet full hardening, several days.

As we have said, door actuation is hydraulic. Large starter type electric motors with integral hydraulic pumps are placed either side in the front wings. Hydraulic rams stand vertically at the rear of each door opening and work the

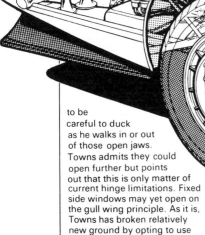

*Vic Berris*

to be careful to duck as he walks in or out of those open jaws. Towns admits they could open further but points out that this is only matter of current hinge limitations. Fixed side windows may yet open on the gull wing principle. As it is, Towns has broken relatively new ground by opting to use gas hearth drawn glass; a Triplex product that is utterly free from distortion, but curved in one direction only. To overcome the resulting styling limitations, Towns has turned the door ''upside down'' so to speak, and put character into the sides of the car by waisting the lower door panels.

The enormous, gently curving and heavily tinted screen was specially made for the Bulldog by Triplex, but for the moment the triangular quarter lights are Aston-made in

doors through twin strut linkages. Four push button switches are located in a panel beneath each quarter light. These provide opening and closing for either side and work the solenoid operated door catches. If hydraulic failure occurs, emergency handles allow the doors to be unlatched (from inside or out) whereupon they can be raised manually.

All the aluminium body panels are unstressed. Mention should also be made that Aston Martin's sheet aluminium working skills and body building experience allowed Mike Duff's full sized drawings and also ''egg box'' panel formers to be taken straight from the original third-size clay model.

Perhaps the Bulldog's most exciting aspect is a frontal one dominated by that chisel nose and dramatic screen. One is immediately impressed by the body's stark elegance; its lack of add-on bits — afterthoughts.

As ever, one of the most critical areas in a very high performance mid-engined car concerns airflow — internal and

*Four buttons under a locking panel either side operate either door. A T handle allows manual door release in the event of a power failure*

## SPECIFICATION

### ENGINE

| | |
|---|---|
| Head/block | Alloy/alloy |
| Cylinders | 8 in 90 deg V |
| Main bearings | 5 |
| Cooling | Water |
| Fan | Twin electric |
| Bore, mm (in.) | 100.0 (3.94) |
| Stroke, mm (in.) | 85.0 (3.35) |
| Capacity, cc (in³) | 5,341 (325.9) |
| Valve gear | Double ohc |
| Camshaft drive | Chain |
| Compression ratio | 7.5 to 1 |
| Ignition | Electronic |
| Fuel injection | Bosch mechanical |
| Max power | Not specified |
| Max torque | Not specified |

### TRANSMISSION

| | |
|---|---|
| Type | ZF five-speed all synchromesh type 5DS25/2 |
| Clutch | Special AP diaphragm with 10.5in. random wound centre plate |

| Gear | Ratio | mph/1000rpm |
|---|---|---|
| Top | 0.70 to 1 | 31.96 |
| 4th | 0.84 to 1 | 26.64 |
| 3rd | 1.04 to 1 | 21.51 |
| 2nd | 1.52 to 1 | 14.72 |
| 1st | 2.58 to 1 | 8.67 |

| | |
|---|---|
| Final drive gear | Spiral bevel |
| Ratio | 3.2 to 1 |

### SUSPENSION

| | |
|---|---|
| Front—location | Double wishb |
| springs | Coil |
| dampers | Telescopic |
| anti-roll bar | Yes, ¾in. di position adjustment |
| Rear—location | De Dion, parallel trailir |
| springs | Coil |
| dampers | Telescopic |
| anti-roll bar | No |

### STEERING

| | |
|---|---|
| Type | Rack and pin |
| Power assistance | No |
| Wheel diameter | 13.0in. |
| Turns lock to lock | 2¼ |

### BRAKES

| | |
|---|---|
| Circuits | 2 split front/ |
| Front | 11.67in. dia. ventilated |
| Rear | 11.67in. dia. ventilated |
| Servo | Yes |
| Handbrake | Centre lever w on separate |

### WHEELS

| | |
|---|---|
| Type | Alloy |
| Rim width | |
| —front | 8.5in. |
| —rear | 11.0in. |
| Tyres—make | Pirelli |
| type | P7 |
| size—front | 225/50VR-1 |
| —rear | 345/35VR-1 |

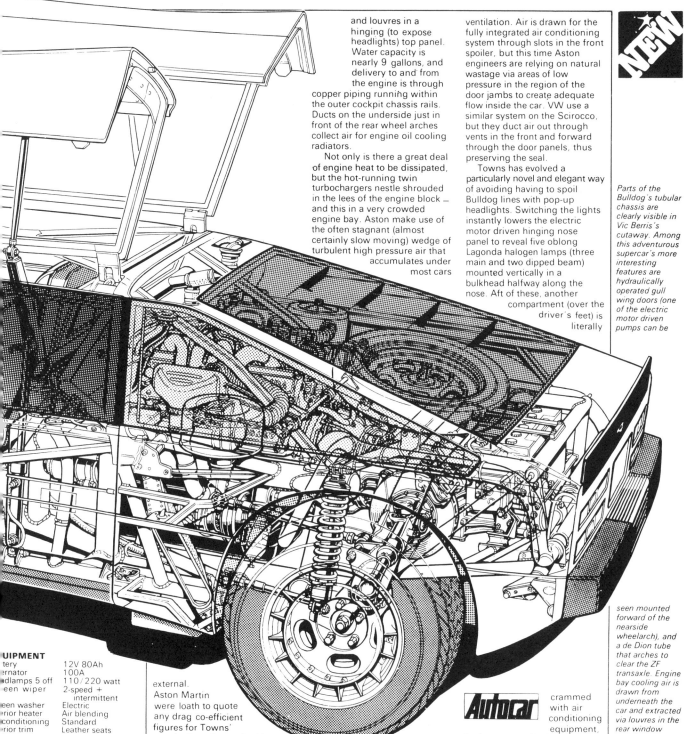

and louvres in a hinging (to expose headlights) top panel. Water capacity is nearly 9 gallons, and delivery to and from the engine is through copper piping running within the outer cockpit chassis rails. Ducts on the underside just in front of the rear wheel arches collect air for engine oil cooling radiators.

Not only is there a great deal of engine heat to be dissipated, but the hot-running twin turbochargers nestle shrouded in the lees of the engine block — and this in a very crowded engine bay. Aston make use of the often stagnant (almost certainly slow moving) wedge of turbulent high pressure air that accumulates under most cars

ventilation. Air is drawn for the fully integrated air conditioning system through slots in the front spoiler, but this time Aston engineers are relying on natural wastage via areas of low pressure in the region of the door jambs to create adequate flow inside the car. VW use a similar system on the Scirocco, but they duct air out through vents in the front and forward through the door panels, thus preserving the seal.

Towns has evolved a particularly novel and elegant way of avoiding having to spoil Bulldog lines with pop-up headlights. Switching the lights instantly lowers the electric motor driven hinging nose panel to reveal five oblong Lagonda halogen lamps (three main and two dipped beam) mounted vertically in a bulkhead halfway along the nose. Aft of these, another compartment (over the driver's feet) is literally

*Parts of the Bulldog's tubular chassis are clearly visible in Vic Berris's cutaway. Among this adventurous supercar's more interesting features are hydraulically operated gull wing doors (one of the electric motor driven pumps can be*

*seen mounted forward of the nearside wheelarch), and a de Dion tube that arches to clear the ZF transaxle. Engine bay cooling air is drawn from underneath the car and extracted via louvres in the rear window opening*

external.
Aston Martin were loath to quote any drag co-efficient figures for Towns' angular but slippery looking design. However, wind tunnel work and initial testing up to 170mph does suggest that the Bulldog's "cow catcher" front air dam and 2¾ in. high rear lip spoiler will be sufficient to maintain stability at even higher speeds.

More concern is expressed where engine and engine bay cooling are concerned. Slots in the front air dam collect air for an enormous near horizontally positioned radiator. After passing through the matrix (assisted by twin fans when necessary) the air is ducted out via grilling in the wheelarches

immediately in front of the rear wheels. This air is encouraged to flow through the engine compartment and out of tail section slats by the pronounced low pressure area that exists over the forward part of the rear window opening. Further extraction is provided through a grille covering a large exhaust pipe opening in the tail where low pressure almost always exists. An incidental advantage of this "flow path" is that air drawn from the underside helps prevent lift at high speed.

There is no direct fresh air

*Autocar* crammed with air conditioning equipment, brake master cylinder and servo, also relays, an electro-mechanical mileage recorder (battery disconnection can wipe out the electronic one) and a wiper mechanism whose inner workings are for the moment on the secret list. While the motor converts rotary into horizontal motion via a conventional arm and lever, Lucas describes the "wheelbox" that works a huge 26 in. long wiper blade through 145 deg. only as containing "a crank and six bar linkage."

Perhaps anticipating the near certainty that anybody rich enough to buy the Bulldog will

## A British Bulldog

come from foreign climes, the driver sits on the left. Inside one is confronted by a mixture of the traditional brown leather upholstery, cord and pile carpet, also veneer door and facia cappings. Everything has a wider and longer than usual aspect.

Aston are particularly proud of Bulldog instrumentation. Lagonda sensors are used, but instead of LED (light emitting diode) displays, they have changed to fast-acting liquid crystal (LCD) readouts. Six, registering speed, percentage fuel quantity, rpm, oil pressure, water temperature and battery volts, plus a row of warning lights are set in an 11 x 5 in. panel. The functions labelling is simply photographed on to Lithofilm. Being in negative form, the black artwork writing shows as transparent against black thus forming an ideal background. Each display is illuminated from behind by what Aston describe as a "luminiferous" strip which is connected by normal fibre optics to a single light source. The circuit board (produced in US by Javelina Corp as is the Lagonda one) sits neatly behind the panel. The package is a mere 3in. deep.

Fuel capacity is 25 gallons carried in two main pannier tanks and a pair of smaller wedge shaped containers immediately behind the engine/passenger bulkhead which incidentally is lined on the engine side with 10 mm thick "Vernaware" — a new material to the motor industry but well known by blast furnacemen. All four tanks are filled with Expamet "Explosafe" material. Using a fairly conventional race car technique, low pressure electric pumps draw fuel from the lowest point and deliver into a small anti surge collector where it is picked up by the Bosch high pressure pump.

*The engine compartment is crowded. Inlet air is drawn through cylindrical air cleaners mounted either side, while most of the fuel injection works are crammed into the vee. A narrow spare mounts on the chassis. The De Dion tube is visible arching over the transaxle. Note the width of the rear tyre*

## Power to spare

One thing we can be sure of is that the Bulldog will not be short of power. Aston Martin never quote outputs, but educated guesswork suggests that the hot Vantage version of their all alloy 5.3-litre V8 has at least 350-375 bhp at the flywheel. It needs this much to push the Vantage — a motor car weighing around two tons — as fast as it does. With two Garrett AiResearch T04B turbochargers Aston are claiming a massive 50-60 per cent power increase! They don't mention torque, but bear in mind that turbocharging usually increases torque more than power. Let's simply say that Keith Martin did not deny suggestions that the fuel injected twin turbo produces "nearly 600 bhp and 500 lb ft. torque" at 6,200 and 5,500 rpm respectively.

As mentioned, the turbochargers sit either side of the engine block mounted on specially fabricated stainless steel exhaust manifolds. Air is drawn through large cylindrical filters, compressed, and then delivered up to a pair of modified early V8 DBS fuel injection throttle body/plenum chambers, and, in turn, to two sets of four ram pipes wherein the injectors are sited. Boost pressure is limited to 12 psi by a wastegate connected to each exhaust manifold. These dump gas via longish pipes into the main pipes as they pass over the rear chassis tubes. One huge twin chamber silencer sits across the rear chassis. Fuel injection is DBSV8 Bosch mechanical, suitably recalibrated. The metering is mounted in the valley between the heads and is gear driven off the front of the engine.

The normal Vantage crankshaft and con rods are retained, as is wet sump lubrication, but with additional baffling in the sump to prevent oil surge. Flat topped Cosworth forged pistons (the standard

ones are slightly domed) reduced the static compression ratio to a suitable-for-supercharging 7.5 to 1. Vantage valves are used, in conjunction with specially developed camshaft profiles. The best results have been obtained by running the cam timing "advanced"; in this case with inlet valve open 100 thou. and the exhaust 30 thou. at TDC on overlap.

Total ignition advance is reduced from the normally aspirated car's 36 deg. to 28 crankshaft degrees. In addition a pressure retard system reduces this to 20 deg. at full boost. We noted that Aston favour NGK plugs on the Bulldog as do Saab on their turbos; also that all the fuel and oil lines were made in the highest quality Aeroquip hosing.

Considering the huge power and torque output it's surprising to find the drive transmitted by a single plate 10.5in. diameter AP clutch. Intriguingly, the centre plate fibres are "random wound" rather than laid concentrically, to prevent the friction material splitting radially, when under stress. The ZF 5DS 24/2 five speed transaxle (also used on Maserati Bora and de Tomaso Pantera) attaches to the back of the Aston block via an adaptor plate welded to the bellhousing.

Clearly, 200 mph is the aim. Assuming no tyre growth, fifth gives virtually 32 mph per 1,000 rpm and 198 mph at the 6,200 rpm power peak. Other maxima are 52, 88, 129 and no less than 160 mph. The Bulldog's engine is chugging away at a mere 2,200 rpm at the legal limit . . . .

So there is no denying this is a monster — an irrelevant one perhaps, yet one cannot fail to be grabbed by its stark elegance or preying looks with the doors open. Practicality is unlikely to concern the owner.

It comes as no surprise to find that after you have fitted the extra-narrow spare wheel (mounted over the gearbox) the punctured tyre has to be carried outside the car on the rear deck (a mounting has yet to be provided). Still better this than having your flaxen-haired lady friend carry it on her lap as she would have to in a Boxer or Porsche Turbo. Luggage space? for the moment there is none. Zip-up membranes (to prevent the opening doors dumping your valuables on the ground) in the doors giving space enough for a change of clothing are under consideration. Come to moment there is none. Come to think of it, the owner of this car is unlikely to dirty his hands changing wheels and will probably own a chain of outfitters with branches in every town. Of course the owner could always turn out to be a lady who likes to live life at the limit. So just what is the Bulldog like at the limit? . . . .

Docile; contained within the confines of MIRA it is a gentle giant; a big easy-going beast that in our brief motor round showed not the slightest sign of wanting to bite.

We watched the flatback arrive and unload this amazing — nobody has ever mentioned the word beautiful — but stark, assertive machine, a glimpse into the future. Spring sunlight seemed to emphasise its three subtle tones; two of metallic grey and the deeply tinted glass.

There have been teething problems earlier in the morning; the revcounter under-reads, the oil pressure gauge doesn't register at all, but a gauge check shows that there is pressure there. Keith Martin, Steve Hallam, and the other lads seem to have survived the inevitable panic to get the car ready — plus the odd all nighter. Weather apart it was like the test days I used to remember, the first one on a brand new racer. Initial shakedown driving has already resulted in a long job list, but mainly detail work.

The door operating buttons are pressed, the pumps whine. We stoop slightly, walk in, and slide legs first into the Bulldog's leather covered seats. The engine men are working to clear an airlock in the fuel injection system, the result of a faulty valve.

*Aston Martin Special Projects Manager Keith Martin briefs John Miles (below) whilst Michael Scarlett searches for more rearward passenger seat adjustment. Cockpit itself (below right) is devastingly simple for such a car, with a touch of Aston luxury trimming*

## Behind the Wheel

There is little time to collect one's thoughts. Colleague Mike Scarlett is cramped for leg room, I have barely enough, but headroom is just tolerable for a six-footer. And there is nowhere but nowhere except a minute glovebox (amusing said the Tech Ed) in which to store anything. We are sitting in the narrow corridor between broad chisel nose and the powerhouse behind; in a very simple, almost plain, leather and carpet upholstered interior broken only by the instrument binnacle containing air conditioning controls, the incredibly neat centre panel of six digital readouts and a radio to the

right. Then grouped in the centre console are rear fog light, interior light, engine cooling fan, hazard warning and door switches. And that is all.

We are gazing out of that huge tinted screen. A car like this elevates the senses. What will it really be like? Behind us mechanics are still working methodically. In front even MIRA's No. 2 circuit looks inviting. We are sitting low, unable to see any front body — the road starts where the screen ends. Peripheral vision is a bit hampered by the narrow sloping quarterlight pillar and the thicker A-post, yet they seem to obscure vision less than many a thick single pillar does.

It is time to go. After cranking over for a little time, the big V8 catches, unevenly at first, as mechanics bleed injectors while the engine is running, but it soon settles down to a typically V8 waffling tickover. Buttons are pressed again; the whining comes straight from the sound track of a sci-fi film. The doors slowly enclose us, cowl us in this projectile. From inside their hollowed panels look almost capable of carrying prone children. If these children were to lie on their backs they would see the sky, so pronounced is the tumblehome.

Earlier on, absent-minded hauling on the steering wheel while stationery had produced no movement at the wheels. On the move the steering is heavy by any standards, but that's to be expected with no power assistance, high gearing (2¼ turns) and such wide tyres. Under hard acceleration the engine note changes into a mumbling roar. First is offset, the change is precise enough, if heavy. Suspension joints chatter over the rough as we head on the track proper. Ten laps is the brief.

As the Bulldog burbles long-leggedly down the straight, first impressions are of its rock-like straight line stability, and a mildly surprising lack of neck-snapping acceleration. Even on full throttle there is no enormous clout in the back, the engine simply pulls hard — almost lazily — right through the range. One would be hard put to tell if the Bulldog is turbocharged at all. It doesn't sound as if it is pulling 6,000 rpm in the gears, or feel immediately as though there is 600 bhp at work, but then this is a heavy car and very highly geared. Such cars often feel only averagely fast until one glances at the speedometer, and this one is registering 225 kph (140 mph) on a fairly short straight. What's more, there is another 25 mph to go before changing into top gear. Aston have done 0-60 and 100 mph in 5.1 and 10.1 secs respectively, acceleration that puts the Bulldog straight into the 185 mph ball park.

As the car runs arrowlike, so braking stability is excellent. The pedal effort is less than expected, but one is still conscious of the brakes having to work hard to haul the speed back.

After five laps the instruments, a set of six constantly changing numbers (oil pressure has started to register again) are no easier to read. But how nicely the Bulldog behaves on the entry and in mid corner. Tyre howl builds up as the limit is approached. In the slower corners the front tyres can be clearly felt giving ground; understeer that can easily be neutralised with power. You can haul the car into slow and medium speed corners knowing that the rear will stay put. Traction is superb. It takes full throttle to get the rear to break away conclusively. It goes gently and progressively, with no hint of wanting to build up into a pendulous slide as a Boxer is prone to. Through the faster corners where there is insufficient driving torque to kill the understeer it feels a bit too understeer-y on the turn in, as if it might plough on if the corner is taken too fast, but then Aston already have a rear anti-roll bar made up to cure this tendency — to tighten up the rear.

The way I began to read it was this. The proper mid-engined layout keeps the centre of gravity low. De Dion rear suspension keeps the rear wheels square to the road (especially the laden one), so soft springs can be used without fear of invoking handling quirks due to camber change. A de Dion axle may be at a theoretical disadvantage on bumpy surfaces when one wheel's movement obviously effects its opposite, but then front engined Astons handle like a dream and the Bulldog promises the same. MIRA is mostly smooth. It rides the few undulations beautifully. It didn't even notice MIRA's mid-corner bump; ''Scarlett's bump''; the one he gets Morgans and MGs on to two wheels over.

We are cruising round with other MIRA traffic. Driving into the mid-afternoon sun, annoying reflections in the screen cut forward visibility seriously, making it quite difficult to judge the Bulldog's width. The Bulldog is very wide and it feels it. Its five headlights and wonderful frontal appearance are having different effects on hard working testers from Coventry. One gentleman sees the lights rather late and lurches left towards the infield; our smiles are difficult to suppress. Thereafter the Marina remains parked, while the Bulldog thunders round.

So for the moment there are niggles. Heel and toe gearchanges are awkward, legroom should be improved, and somewhere must be found for luggage — even the Stratos has door bins. I for one would have forsaken the easy entry for a more conventional cockpit. There is still some concern over engine cooling as we had to run the fans continuously, and noise levels are high.

Unfortunately an electrical fault brought our run round to a premature end, leaving us to gather our thoughts. Mine were that there are two types of shakedown test day. The one where you come away elated with the feeling of promise and hope, knowing that the chassis is good and the suspension and steering are fundamentally excellent. The engine might have been a shade off song, but will really fly on the day. At the other sort of test session, you smile just as much, but only for appearance's sake, because underneath you sense that the car is unlikely to ever deliver the goods in handling or performance.

Let's simply say the Bulldog felt most chuckable — particularly so for a heavy mid-engined car. Stiff suspension hasn't been needed to mask chassis design shortcomings. It may only be a one-off; a research and development exercise, but I came away loving the thundering beast and all it stands for, in spite of its ergonomic failings. Now I wonder how the owner of a Porsche Turbo will react when he sees that broad band of light in his mirror ☐

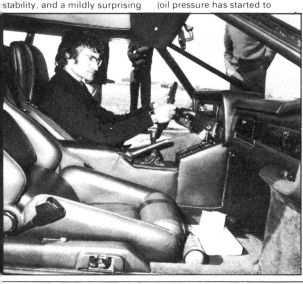

*Miles hustles the Bulldog through one of MIRA's No. 2 circuit corners — four great rubber paw pads planted square on the tarmac in a beautifully behaved mid-engined monster*

# High-Roller Ragtops

*Wherein four auto editors abscond with*
*a quarter-million dollars' worth of crème de la crème convertibles.*

• We've all heard the oft-told tales of sure-fire investment schemes gone bust, oil wells that dried up, and house-limit rolls at Vegas that came up craps. But ponder, for a moment, a far more serious calamity, the tragedy of *gaining* unexpected riches overnight. The 7-Eleven clerk who inherits a bank full of money and the securities secretary who bought Belridge Oil before merger face a tougher problem than any of us realize: how to *spend* their money. Today's gold prices are tracking 1928 Dow Jones trends point-by-point, the Susan B. Anthony dollar has no more cachet than a

quarter, and millions' worth of California real estate slides into the ocean every time it rains. Which brings us to this portfolio of three convertible assets that could safely and conveniently soak up a full quarter-million dollars of your excess cash, and simultaneously entertain you with inestimable pleasure.

Just in case you wake up filthy rich some day next week, you should be aware of the fine art of spending big money on cars. The first rule of high-roller etiquette is never, ever come right out and *ask* the price. We'll save you that trouble. The Mercedes-Benz 450SL is the bargain buy in this league at a mere $37,526. Of course, you should expect to pay a little extra for a back seat; the two-plus-two Aston Martin Volante is justifiably a bit more costly, at

$79,650. And for you really conspicuous consumers, we have the most expensive car on the face of the earth, the Rolls-Royce Corniche convertible, at a cool $140,925. Cash, check, and Manhattan office buildings are acceptable forms of payment.

The purpose of gathering these three blue-chip commodities together was not to name the one, true Smart Buy, or even the World's Best Ragtop, but rather to try and find out how much of this $258,101 mix is myth and how much is genuine coachbuilder's magic. If we had a good time in the process, well then, that's just one of the pratfalls of working at *Car and Driver*. So we started with some of our usual test procedures, carried on with several afternoons of photography in and around various high-

*Continued*

# Yeah, but What'll She Do on Rodeo Drive?

• Money talks. I've always known that, but from where I'm usually sitting, the conversation is too far away to make out the words. Then again, I'm not usually sitting in a Roller or an Aston either. When I'm trolling around in these gilt-edged convertibles, the dollar dialogue just about drowns out the stereo.

When money talks in such dulcet tones, I'm inclined to listen. And when asked to rate the status of these symbols, I'm inclined to vote along strict money lines.

Let's face it. Nobody buys one of these cars merely to make sure he gets to work every morning. Rather, they are bought to make a statement, to show that, even when you're trapped in the everyday amber of traffic, you're not just another fly. And that's why the Mercedes goes to the bottom of this exalted heap. Too many people have M-Bs already. Hell, the cleaning ladies in Bev Hills show up in them. They've discovered that the resale value holds up better than on their Cadillacs. As far as they're concerned, a Mercedes is just your basic good deal, and nothing has less status than that.

An Aston Martin will trump an M-B any day. An Aston is a gambler's car. You unroll 80 large for this convertible and you don't even know if the company is going to be in business next week to sell you spare parts. That takes guts. Drive an Aston Martin and people are going to know that the kind of trivia you worry about would be life-and-death stuff to them.

Still, 80 large is not what it used to be. Any halfway-decent welfare scam artist could pile up that much by Thanksgiving. So, for the kind of status based on pure unattainability—which is the only sort that really holds up in the cut and thrust of Rodeo Drive—it pretty well comes down to the Corniche convertible, at 141 large, or nothing. You find only the finest class of pretenders behind this wheel.

Moreover, the Rolls also happens to be a regal motorcar in every detail. It's hard to find anything lacking in a car that protects its carpets with wall-to-wall floor mats of dyed lambskin. No matter how closely I looked, there were no flaws. The inlaid veneer was magnificent. The chrome was mirror-bright. The emerald-green paint was polished to a jewel-like luster. And somehow, unexplainably, perhaps even miraculously, this car seemed to resist dirt. It was always shiny and unsullied.

Perhaps it was for this reason that finding a sprinkling of California winter gnats splattered on the gleaming grille momentarily took me aback. But then I realized that bugs, like people, probably figure a Corniche convertible is the only way to go.                          *—Patrick Bedard*

ENGINE BUILT BY BOB BUTLER
ASTON MARTIN LAGONDA (1975) LTD.

roller enclaves, and spent the remaining hours racking up miles behind the wheel. Sure, it's tough to go back to Subarus and Toyotas after Aston Martins, Sunday-afternoon soaring, and pâté de foie gras, but we manage.

Our high-rolling resulted in three editors and one photog wearing winter tans back to the Michigan office. Every belt buckle was adjusted a notch wider because of the aforementioned high-cal sojourns. And, oh yes, we did learn a thing or two about expensive cars, some of which was surprising. Money may not buy you love, but, well spent, it'll definitely buy plenty of attention. A week of stirring up a wake of twisted necks, lifted eyebrows, and more oohs than boos gave us a good feeling for the level of

respect each of these high-rollers can command.

The Rolls was far and away the winner here; it never failed to elicit the full red-carpet treatment, complete with fawning valets and gracious maître d's. The Parthenon-perfect radiator shell, sculptured mascot, and interlocked Rs that make way for the Corniche are more recognizable than the presidential seal. The Rolls-Royce that follows commands at least as much esteem. It's still the benchmark of class in cars, and quite secure in its status.

Unfortunately, California was the wrong venue for the Mercedes 450SL. This was *the* in-car a few years back, but now that upwardly mobile attorneys and physicians drive SLs in droves, its awe-

factor has fallen. In Beverly Hills, the rich folks' Disneyland, it's not at all unusual to stop for a light amid a three-car-wide silver streak, with little more than different top configurations to distinguish one SL from another: stylish ladies prefer the chic-looking soft top; men go for the steel roof no matter what the weather; while only exposure-hungry starlets seem to select topless running. Blond hair and bare shoulders will certainly turn heads, but the other two SLs invariably glide by without a nod.

Likewise, the Aston Martin Volante flew way over these blasé Californians. For most of them, 80 Gs' worth of fine British craftsmanship registers the same

*Continued*

| | acceleration, sec | | top speed, mph | braking 70–0 mph, ft | idle, dBA | interior sound level | | | EPA estimated fuel economy, mpg |
|---|---|---|---|---|---|---|---|---|---|
| | 0–60 mph | ¼-mile | | | | full-throttle acceleration, dBA | 70-mph cruising, dBA | 70-mph coasting, dBA | |
| **ASTON MARTIN VOLANTE** | 7.8 | 15.9 @ 92 mph | 128 | 225 | 59 | 81 | 75 | 75 | 10 |
| **MERCEDES-BENZ 450SL** | 11.4 | 18.1 @ 79 mph | 108 | 199 | 49 | 76 | 73 | 72 | 16 |
| **ROLLS-ROYCE CORNICHE** | 12.5 | 18.6 @ 73 mph | 106 | 205 | 52 | 76 | 72 | 72 | 10 |

impact as a nice, clean '65 Mustang. The few interested enough to search out the nameplate inevitably ask, "Say, mister, how much do those Austin Martians go for, anyway?"

That's the risk you take in flaunting this sort of wealth before the proles. Fortunately, there are compensations. You've got to limit your exposure if you want to travel about like a true high-roller. These convertibles are best savored privately, by the owner and a close circle of friends en route to the week's special event.

Both the Aston Martin and the Mercedes-Benz are drivers' cars, while the Rolls is most appropriately enjoyed in the hands of a trusty chauffeur. Even though the 450SL's chassis lacks the up-

to-the-minute refinement of Mercedes' big sedans, and in spite of a debilitating loss of power for 1980 (twenty horsepower sacrificed to tighter emissions controls), it still feels good when you're in a hurry. The stout control efforts, the open-arms way your hands lie on the steering wheel, and the rock-solid sensations that register through the bodywork, seats, and suspension settings give the SL an integrity never seriously challenged by hard running or bad roads. The best part is the unique-to-Mercedes shock damping that keeps each foot firmly planted, with just enough harshness telegraphed back to keep the driver assured that all systems are under control.

The Aston Martin takes this business-

like attitude toward motoring and adds the finest hardwoods, leather, and aluminum-bodywork artistry money can buy. The instant you fire up the four-carburetor, four-camshaft V-8, the Volante starts speaking in distinctly male tones. A basso rumble to the pipes and heavy efforts at every control leave the undeniable impression that this is a car for men of stature. Fine-limbed ladies are welcome as passengers, but they have no business worrying about driving the Volante the only way it should be driven: hard and fast. Around town, this car is sluggish and cantankerous; it's too heavy and tall-geared to launch itself from a light with authority. A Sci-

| | base price | price as tested | engine | wheelbase, in | curb weight, lbs | EPA interior-volume index passenger compartment, cu ft | trunk space, cu ft |
|---|---|---|---|---|---|---|---|
| **ASTON MARTIN VOLANTE** | $78,650 | $79,650 | DOHC V-8, 4x2-bbl carburetors | 102.8 | 4110 | 85.5 | 5.7 |
| **MERCEDES-BENZ 450SL** | 35,839 | 37,526 | SOHC V-8, mechanical fuel injection | 96.9 | 3740 | 62.8 | 6.6 |
| **ROLLS-ROYCE CORNICHE** | 140,000 | 140,925 | V-8, 2x1-bbl carburetors | 119.5 | 5180 | 81.0 | 10.0 |

rocco will beat it in maneuverability, if only because the VW has rear visibility where the Aston has a folding top. But on the road when the motor's on-cam and the bends are 80-mph or better, the direct steering, hard brake pedal, and built-in forthrightness are just right for the mission: speed with grace.

Meanwhile, the Rolls conveys just the opposite message: "Why hurry?" Toss it about like one of these sports jobs, and the 2.6-ton Corniche whips its tail like a trailer. The Rolls-Royce craftsmen have toiled diligently to achieve a "ball of silk" feel throughout, from the electrically operated shift selector to the swift-but-silent power top, and they'd

appreciate due respect. One doesn't bat a ball of silk around with a tennis racket, after all. The Corniche is overassisted and underdamped by today's standards. Unless, of course, you're ready to take life at a more leisurely pace, in which case the world that flickers and flashes back at you from the depths of the Brewster Green paint seems entirely acceptable. Set the auto-temp, crank up some Eagles on the Blaupunkt, wrap the top under its leather cover, and the Corniche will take you to all the right places. Wise owners make a point of reserving the Rolls strictly for special occasions, while striving to keep the annual odometer accumulation less than

10,000 mellifluous miles. With such a policy, the sheer envy of one's peers will appreciate this investment even more than the Corniche's devoted owner.

No doubt you'll rise above such piddling concerns as market value once you achieve full high-roller status. Which is exactly why we won't trouble you here with mundane gas-mileage, luggage-space, and operating-cost statistics. If it's necessary to pack a few things for the weekend in Vermont, just pick up the Aston's $2000 fitted luggage. Without a twinge. What could it possibly matter when you're into blue-chip convertibles? You've already learned the single most important fact of life while getting here: it's only money.

—Don Sherman

| fuel-tank capacity, gal | steering | suspension | | tires | brakes |
| --- | --- | --- | --- | --- | --- |
| | | front | rear | | |
| 25.8 | rack-and-pinion, power-assisted, 3.0 turns lock-to-lock | ind, unequal-length control arms, coil springs, anti-sway bar | de Dion, 2 trailing arms, Watt linkage, coil springs | Avon R-R Turbo Steel 70, 235/70HR-15 | all disc, power-assisted |
| 27.2 | recirculating ball, power-assisted, 3.2 turns lock-to-lock | ind, unequal-length control arms, coil springs, anti-sway bar | ind, semi-trailing arm, coil springs | Michelin XVS, 205/70HR-14 | all disc, power-assisted |
| 28.5 | rack-and-pinion, power-assisted, 3.5 turns lock-to-lock | ind, unequal-length control arms, coil springs, anti-sway bar | ind, semi-trailing arm, coil springs | Michelin Wide X Radial, HR70-15 | all disc, power-assisted |

# ASTON MARTIN LAGONDA

At last, we present the world's first full road test of Aston Martin's sensational Lagonda, fifty thousand pounds' worth of sporting luxury in a shape that draws crowds like no other saloon in the world

LONG, LOW and wide, with razor-edged styling and paintwork as black as sin, it drew crowds and turned heads like no other car in recent memory. When it was parked, passing motorists stopped their vehicles to get out and take a closer look; on the move, it stopped pedestrians dead in their tracks and other drivers swerved off course as they turned to stare. Most people loved it, some loathed it, but nobody could ignore it.

It was the Aston Martin Lagonda, ours for a week and a full road test at last, six years on from the day that the Lagonda name was temporarily revived on a short-lived four-door version of the established V8 coupé, and four years since it reappeared on the William-Towns-designed shape that was the sensation of the 1976 London Motor Show.

That the car was able to make its triumphant debut at Earls Court just eight months after the design had left the drawing board, is a tribute to the speed and flexibility with which Aston Martin's engineers can work. Yet the

fact that the prototype had not yet turned a wheel under its own power at the time of its unveiling nonetheless led some observers to suggest in the ensuing weeks that it was a one-off — an elaborate and successful publicity stunt, but never destined for serious production. And even though within a matter of weeks *Motor* had driven a working and highly promising prototype, it began to look as if the sceptics were right after all when another 18 months passed without a single car being delivered to a paying customer.

But time has proved them wrong. As we write, 50 cars have found their way into the hands of private customers since the first one was delivered in April 1978, and the Newport Pagnell factory is currently producing 3 cars a week towards meeting a waiting list that has shrunk from a peak of about 200 to its present level of about 100 firm orders.

But it is also true that the commencement of series production *was* embarrassingly delayed, by technical problems associated with the elec-

tronic digital instruments, the touch-sensitive switchgear, and the computerised this, that, and the other that had so caught the imagination of the public when the car was first announced.

In the Lagonda's final production form the electronic wizardry has been toned down; it still has the digital instrument displays, but without the complementary gas-plasma analogue displays of the major dials; and it has conventional levers in place of the previous touch-switches for the indicators, wash/wipe and gear selector functions. Gone too is the memory which could store and automatically re-select two different 'his and hers' settings of the electrically adjustable driver's seat.

In contrast, the mechanical development of the car had proceeded swiftly and with few headaches, which is perhaps not surprising since the Lagonda follows the same lines as the existing V8, Volante and Vantage models. The body is of aluminium, clothing a welded steel superstructure, and a

5.3 litre quad-cam V8 drives the rear wheels through either a 3-speed automatic or a five-speed manual transmission. Coil springs are used all round, with double wishbones at the front and a de Dion axle at the rear, and the rack and pinion steering has two-stage power assistance. The brakes employ massive ventilated discs front and rear, the latter mounted inboard either side of the final drive unit which has a limited slip differential.

At this point in a road test we would normally proceed to discuss the test car in the context of its market sector and the cars it competes against, but in the case of the Lagonda there virtually are no rivals, and for this reason we have departed from our usual practice of providing comparative data on the last pages of the test. In practice, the Lagonda, as a four-door limousine costing £49,933, the Lagonda only *has* one 'natural' rival, and that is the Rolls-Royce Silver Spirit which we have yet to test. In fact, you wouldn't be too far out if you were to view the Lagonda as a sporting alternative to the car from

## MOTOR ROAD TEST NO 40/80

 excellent   good  average  poor  bad

**Make:** Aston Martin
**Model:** Lagonda
**Maker:** Aston Martin Lagonda (1975) Limited, Tickford Street, Newport Pagnell, Buckinghamshire MK16 9AN
**Price:** £40,080.00 plus £3340.00 Car Tax plus £6513.00 VAT equals £49,933.00

Crew, particularly for confirmed Aston Martin enthusiasts whose commitments have outgrown the passenger capacity of the company's existing two door coupé models.

## PERFORMANCE

 Derived directly from the V8 and Volante models, the Lagonda's 90 degree V8 is a classic, with an alloy block topped by a pair of alloy heads, each with twin chain-driven overhead camshafts to actuate inclined valves in hemispherical combustion chambers. A battery of four twin-choke downdraught Weber carburetters feed the engine with four star fuel, and the compression ratio is now up to 9.3:1 (from 9.0:1), part of a package of recent breathing and combustion improvements that are claimed to have improved the A-M V8s fuel economy, as well as increased power. As ever, Aston Martin remain coy about their engine's precise power and torque outputs, though something in the region of 350 bhp seems a reasonable estimate, and a figure that is probably unrivalled by any other four-door saloon in the world.

Whatever the exact figure, on the evidence of the figures it is enough, even in a car tipping the scales at 39.1 cwt, to deliver a performance which, if not quite the best we have recorded on a big saloon, nonetheless comes pretty close, and is in quite another class from the Rolls-Royce. Using the transmission's manual override to hold the revs to 5,500 rpm in the gears — a figure it seemed reluctant to exceed in spite of a quoted rev limit of 6,250 rpm — our test car hauled itself away from rest to reach 60 mph in 7.9 sec, 100 mph just outside the magic 20 sec barrier in 20.2 sec, and 120 mph comfortably within a mile in 32.9 sec. The Rolls-Royce (we haven't tested the Spirit, but the figures for the Shadow II shouldn't be too far out) simply isn't in the same contest, with 0-60 and 0-100 mph times of 10.7 and 37.1 sec respectively, and among limousines it is the Jaguar XJ 5.3 (7.6, 18.4 and 30.5 sec) and the now defunct Mercedes 450 SEL 6.9 (7.9, 19.4 and 21.9 sec) that are the only cars to pip the Lagonda to the post.

In practical terms, on the road, the car's low speed sprint ability tends to be masked by the throttle's progressive action and long pedal travel, which give little clue to the acceleration that is available when you *do* floor the throttle.

In kickdown, 30-50 mph is covered in 2.9 sec and 50-70 mph in 4.2 sec, compared to 2.7/3.4 sec for the Jaguar and 2.7/4.3 sec for the Mercedes. But subjectively its the way the Lagonda keeps on accelerating in the higher 'autobahn' speed ranges which is more impressive, with a 100-120 mph time of 12.5 sec that's a match for the Merc's 12.5 and the Jag's 12.4 sec, and a maximum speed that would seem to be the equal of both of them. Unfortunately time did not allow us to take the car to Germany for an accurate check on maximum speed, but the ease with which it pulled almost 140 mph on MIRA's short straights suggest that 145 mph would be a realistic estimate. More to the point, although a high maximum is academic in itself, it does indicate that the Lagonda is capable of effortless cruising not only at the fairly modest speeds that are legal

and practical in this country, but also at the very velocities that are still possible on German autobahns; 120 mph is an entirely feasible and relaxed crusing speed.

All this has been made possible by what is essentially a high-performance sports-car engine in a luxury limousine, but the price of sports car performance is sports car type engine noise, which is out of keeping with the Lagonda's Rolls-alternative aspirations. At steady speeds engine noise is low by absolute standards but hardly in the XJ/Rolls class, while hard acceleration produces a bellow from under the bonnet which, whether you like it or not, cannot be ignored, and which has a throbby quality that subjectively detracts from the engine's high standards of mechanical smoothness.

## ECONOMY

 Obviously there is no way that a high-performance car weighing almost two tons can have anything other than a gargantuan appetite for fuel by *normal* standards. That said, the Lagonda surprised us by returning better mpg figures than we had anticipated, particularly at steady speeds when it doesn't drop below 20 mpg until it's doing almost 60 mph, and even then the fuel curve dips only gently, to 18.5 mpg at 70 mph and a very respectable 15.3 mpg at 100 mph. These figures give a cornputed touring consumption of 16.1 mpg, which compares well with the Rolls-Royce Silver Shadow IIs 12.5 mpg. With a tank capacity of 28 gallons, supplied through twin filler necks, the Lagonda should be good for well over 400 miles on each tankful if driven with reasonable restraint.

Overall we recorded 11.8 mpg, which sounds horrendous but is actually about par for the course among cars of this size and performance, and reflects, as always, a great deal of very hard driving.

## TRANSMISSION

Although a five-speed manual transmission can be specified, it seems likely that the vast majority of buyers will opt for the Chrysler Torqueflite 3-speed automatic that was fitted to our test car. This drives through a Salisbury final drive with Limited Slip Differential and a 3.07:1 final drive giving a loping top gear gait of 26.3 mph per 1000 rpm.

Except under flat-out acceleration the automatic upchanges slur through as sweetly as you'd expect them to in a luxury car, and although the 5000 rpm change-up points seem low on paper, (54 and 91 mph), in practice the gains to be made by holding the revs manually are too insignificant to be worth the bother — 0.3 sec off the 0-60 time, 1.3 sec off the 0-100 mph time.

Certainly the manual selector lever itself is no deterrent to do-it-yourself gear-changing, it has a pleasant action and sensible detents — but there's little point when the gearbox can be relied on to choose the right gear for every occasion. For overtaking, kickdown is available into 1st at up to 40-plus mph on full throttle, into second at up to 55 mph on part-throttle and to over 70 mph on full-throttle. Some caution is called for on wet roads, however, as the full-throttle change-down into 1st can be dramatically sudden, and is also unpredictable between 40 and 45 mph when the gearbox is sometimes unsure whether to select first or second.

## HANDLING

 Beneath the Lagonda's low, wide structure is a superbly developed version of Aston-Martin's familiar and well tried suspension. At the front are double wishbones, with coil springs co-axial with dampers and an anti-roll bar; and at the rear a de Dion axle located fore/aft by parallel trailing links, and laterally by a Watts linkage, with co-axial coil springs and self-levelling dampers. The specification is completed by Burman two-stage power steering (by rack and pinion) which reduces the amount of assistance at high road speeds.

The result is a limousine which can be tossed around almost like a baby sports car, once you've overcome the initial timidity inspired by the car's value. The steering is direct (1.0 turns for a 50 ft circle), crisp, and perfectly weighted to give as good an approximation to feel as it's possible to achieve with power steering. Whether hustling along country lanes or sweeping through autobahn curves at 120 mph, this two-ton car corners with little roll and a remarkable blend of both agility and stability. In a low gear you can power the tail out into progressive and easily caught oversteer, but for the most part it maintains an attitude of gentle understeer, which becomes strong near the limit but can be tamed by backing off to tighten your line without fear of a sudden switch to oversteer. As safe as it is satisfying, the Lagonda is unperturbed by mid-corner bumps and virtually its only flaw is its enormous turning circle (46.4 ft on left lock!) which can be an embarrassing nuisance in confined spaces.

## BRAKES

 It takes a potent set of brakes to repeatedly haul two tons of motor car down from 120 mph without wilting, but the Lagonda's ventilated discs front and rear are more than enough for the task; they require a firm push, but never leave any doubt about their ultimate effectiveness, as we found out when braking from 120 mph plus at the end of each acceleration run along MIRA's horizontal straights.

Our specific braking tests confirmed these and other impressions already gained on the road, of brakes that are as progressive as they are powerful, in spite of highish pedal pressures, and, on this car — untypically for an Aston — a slightly spongy feel.

With a bit of practice to avoid premature locking of the rear wheels (a flaw, but one which in this instance had little effect on the test car's braking stability), we recorded a best stop from 30 mph of 0.98 g for a pedal pressure of 90 lbs, a fine result, and a relatively even more impressive 0.88 g from 70 mph. In contrast the hand brake could manage no better than a feeble 0.14 g in an emergency stop from 30 mph, though it easily held the car in either direction on the 1-in-3 test hill.

Laden to its maximum payload, the Lagonda virtually ignored our fade test, comprising of 20 successive 0.6 g stops at 45 sec intervals from 92 mph; the required pedal pressure remained virtually constant from beginning to end. Likewise, a thorough dousing in the water splash had no effect on their efficiency.

## ACCOMMODATION

 When you've got over 17 ft to play with it would be very difficult to design a car that *wasn't* roomy, and if the Lagonda isn't a paragon of packaging efficiency (some cars undoubtedly provide more space within a smaller exterior) it is nonetheless in absolute terms a roomy car with ample room for four large adults in genuine comfort. But they wouldn't be able to take much luggage with them, for the boot is small in itself, and much of what little space it does have is robbed by the emergency lamps which are housed in large square protruberances on the underside of the bootlid.

There is no facia glove locker inside, but adequate stowage for oddments is provided by a deep lidded box between the front seats and a small tray and pockets behind the front seat backrests.

## RIDE COMFORT

 What makes the excellent handling already described an even more remarkable achievement is that it is wedded to a superb ride. Small bumps at low speeds are all but steam-rollered out of existence, bumpy country roads are hardly noticed, and you glide swiftly along motorways as if riding on air; the Lagonda achieves an almost perfect compromise — soft enough to take the sting out of any surface, yet always with sufficient underlying tautness to avoid float or wallow.

Having said all that, it seems almost churlish but should be said for the record, that the suspension does occasionally make itself heard and felt at town speeds over broken surfaces and badly laid manhole covers and occasionally we observed a trace of anti-roll bar 'waddle' at low speeds. But these are the only minor flaws to detract from an overall ride comfort that comes as close as any car's to the proverbial magic carpet class.

## AT THE WHEEL

 It terms of its ability to accommodate in considerable comfort a wide diversity of driver shapes and sizes, we'd be tempted to give the Lagonda five stars for this section. The sumptuously cushioned seats are a pleasure to sit in (though in view of the leather's slipperiness a little more side support would not go amiss), and with electric adjustment for height, reach and backrest recline all our drivers could position themselves comfortably in relation to the well spaced pedals and the small, chunky-rimmed leather bound steering wheel.

What let's it all down is the gimmicky touch-switch minor controls, which are an ergonomic disaster, though fortunately the most important minor controls for winkers, dip/flash and wash/wipe are in the form of column stalks, and those for hazards and rear fog lamps are conventional push/push buttons. The remainder are made up of touch-sensitive switches laid out on near-horizontal panels either side of the wheel and delineated by white painted circles about the diameter of a 5 pence piece. To operate them you simply touch the centre of the circle, which sounds fine in principle fails miserably in practice — because the circles are too small and too close together; because they are laid out on a horizontal surface and you have to lean forward to read the labels; and worst of all because, they have no internal illumination and so are almost impossible to find at night.

In all there are now fewer than 18 of these switches, covering everything from side, head, fog and spot lamps, through bonnet and fuel filler flap releases, to horn selection (air or electric) and cruise control. Additionally there are three circular knobs which look as if they come from a cheap hi-fi set; for the wiper delay, the instrument lighting rheostat and the air conditioning temperature control. And finally, the driver's door houses a panel of 12 more touch-switches which together look after the seat adjustment.

## INSTRUMENTS

 Here again the Lagonda's use (or misuse) of space-age technology earns a chorus of raspberries from our testers. Setting aside the fact that a vertical black slab punctuated by flickering red digits is singularly lacking in aesthetic appeal, the Lagonda's digital instruments were equally disliked for their sheer impracticality. When bright sunlight falls on the facia they become completely illegible, and at the best of time the readings (of the auxiliary gauges at least) are hard to read and digest at a glance.

There is no denying, though, that it is a comprehensive display. In the top left hand corner are the speedometer (in units of 1 mph) and tachometer (in units of 100 rpm); in the centre are the clock, voltmeter and trip mileometer

(the conventional mechanical odometer is located under the bonnet); and vertically stacked on the right are gauges for fuel level (in per cent full), oil pressure, oil temperature, water temperature, and even an ambient temperature gauge which can be selected to display either interior or exterior temperature by means of one of the touch-switches already discussed. Further such switches allow you to choose between metric or imperial speedometer readout, set the clock, and reset the trip mileometer, while yet another can be used to switch off all the instrument read-outs but the essentials — speedo, clock and fuel gauge.

## AIR CONDITIONING

 The controls of the Lagonda's air conditioning are simplicity itself — a rotary knob for temperature control, and a slide for mode and distribution, with 'economy', 'low', 'auto', 'high', 'bi-level' and 'defrost' settings.

Unfortunately the blower fan failed shortly after the car came into our tenure, which precluded a full investigation of the system's possibilities. All it is possible to say is that the system is only capable of providing an overall temperature control (you cannot have warm air to the footwells with cooled air at face-level), that it seems to work tolerably well when cooling, but is very difficult to control progressively when heating.

## VISIBILITY

 When parking the Lagonda it is advisable to take even more care than you would anyway with a car of this value, because the corners front and rear are hard to see except for very tall drivers, and the width is not easy to judge either. On

Note the fixed glass roof window over the rear seats, and individual reading lamps for the front. Headlining is beautifully formed and immaculately trimmed

Luxurious electrically adjustable seats, far left, and excellent layout of major controls, left, make for considerable comfort at the wheel, but the facia, all flat black panels, looks hideous

Rear seat passengers are also cossetted in luxury; roof window alleviates claustrophobic effect of large headrests

the move things are rather easier, though a passenger door mirror would help compensate for the blind spots caused by the rear headrests. Although set too high on our test car, the headlamps are powerful, and complemented by a comprehensive and effective wash/wipe system.

## NOISE

★★
★

If anything lets the Lagonda down as a Rolls-Royce alternative, it is noise levels, which, though low in absolute terms, are disappointing by limousine standards. The worst culprit is the throbby bellow from the engine, which is insistent · even when accelerating moderately, and simply very loud when the engine is in full cry. When cruising at steady speeds, however, the underbonnet roar ebbs away and then it is noise from other sources which dominates — rumble and thump from the tyres on indifferent surfaces, and an insistent rustle of wind noise from around the door edges. None of these are sufficient to detract from the Lagonda's splendid 100-mph-plus cruising ability,

but compared to the best from Jaguar, Rolls-Royce and Mercedes the Lagonda is not a quiet car.

## FINISH

★★
★★

Not everyone liked our Lagonda test car's all-black paint scheme, but there was no dissent about the excellent fit and finish of the exterior panels, or the sumptuousness of the traditional leather and polished walnut interior, all immaculately assembled without a screw-head in sight. And the rigidity and freedom from rattles of the body/chassis structure is a match for any car with a conventional steel monocoque construction.

More is the pity, then, that the interior is marred by the ugly, cheap-looking black facia which is a consequence of the large flat panels which house the instruments and switchgear — features which are as much an aesthetic disaster as an ergonomic failure.

Sadly to relate, our Lagonda test car also failed to live up to Aston Martin's reputation for greatly improved quality control of the past few years. The automatic centralised door locking was faulty, the lights only worked when they felt like it, the blower fan packed up half-way through our test, and eventually the car was returned to Aston Martin with the transmission stuck in second gear. In mitigation, however, it should be said that the car had endured several thousand miles of extremely hard use without attention, and we can only hope that these failures were untypical.

## EQUIPMENT

★★
★★

Everything is supplied with the Lagonda to ensure that the driver has to expend the least possible physical effort in operating his car. That automatic transmission and air conditioning are standard, goes without saying, but you also get automatic cruise control, while there are few cars in which you can adjust the

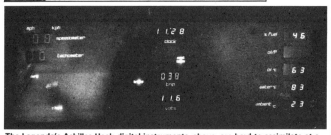

The Lagonda's Achilles Heel; digital instruments, above, are hard to assimilate at a glance, and touch switches, below, unreliable and hard to find at night

Engine bay is fully occupied by Aston's magnificent four-camshaft V8

**Boot has low sill, but is small, with space stolen by emergency lamps. Note comprehensive toolkit stored in foam-lined briefcase!**

seat, open the windows, lock or unlock all the doors, open the fuel filler flaps, release the bonnet catch, adjust the door mirror, and even find out what the air temperature is outside, all at the touch of a switch without shifting from your normal seating position. You don't even have to lock the doors when you leave the car, for the centralised door locking system does it automatically a short while after the key has been removed from the ignition.

For your £49,933 you also get variable delay wipers, a superb Pioneer radio/cassette player with automatic electric aerial, and a glass roof window over the rear seats — but no opening sunroof, and the lack of a door mirror on the passenger side does seem a bit mean.

## CONCLUSION

It would be wrong to be led by the Lagonda's startling looks and gimmicky ergonomics into dismissing it as a poseur's plaything. Beneath the gloss and the glamour the Lagonda has a superbly sorted chassis providing a ride/handling balance as good as that of any car currently available, and with effective brakes to cope with the deceptively rapid performance delivered by a potent thoroughbred engine. Admittedly it's not as refined as we had expected under acceleration, but the high speed mile-mopping ability is impressive in spite of rather intrusive wind noise. Add to that the ability to seat four large adults in lavish comfort, and it is clear that the Lagonda cannot be ignored by any potential Rolls-Royce buyer who still retains enough enthusiasm for motoring to want to drive himself rather than be conducted by a chauffeur.

Equally, for the Lagonda to succeed in such company, nothing less than total reliability will do, and on the basis of our experiences that would seem to be yet another reason for abandoning the gimmicky instruments and controls which we have already condemned on aesthetic and ergonomic grounds. As it stands, these fripperies are the Achilles Heel of an otherwise outstanding car that is a pleasure both to drive and to ride in.

## PERFORMANCE

### CONDITIONS
| | |
|---|---|
| Weather | Wind 8-18 mph |
| Temperature | 64°F |
| Barometer | 29.7 in Hg |
| Surface | Dry tarmacadam |

### MAXIMUM SPEEDS
| | mph | kph |
|---|---|---|
| Banked Circuit (see text) | 145 | 233 |
| Terminal Speeds: | | |
| at ¼ mile | 90 | 145 |
| at kilometre | 115 | 185 |
| Speed in gears (at 5500 rpm): | | |
| 1st | 59 | 95 |
| 2nd | 100 | 161 |

### ACCELERATION FROM REST
| mph | sec | kph | sec |
|---|---|---|---|
| 0-30 | 3.2 | 0-40 | 2.5 |
| 0-40 | 4.7 | 0-60 | 4.3 |
| 0-50 | 6.2 | 0-80 | 6.2 |
| 0-60 | 7.9 | 0-100 | 8.4 |
| 0-70 | 10.3 | 0-120 | 11.3 |
| 0-80 | 12.8 | 0-140 | 15.0 |
| 0-90 | 16.0 | 0-160 | 20.0 |
| 0-100 | 20.2 | 0-180 | 26.5 |
| 0-110 | 25.3 | 0-200 | — |
| 0-120 | 32.9 | | |
| Stand'g ¼ | 16.1 | Stand'g km | 29.0 |

### ACCELERATION IN K'DOWN
| mph | sec | kph | sec |
|---|---|---|---|
| 20-40 | 2.9 | 40-60 | 1.9 |
| 30-50 | 2.9 | 60-80 | 1.8 |
| 40-60 | 3.3 | 80-100 | 2.3 |
| 50-70 | 4.2 | 100-120 | 3.0 |
| 60-80 | 4.9 | 120-140 | 4.0 |
| 70-90 | 6.5 | 140-160 | 5.6 |
| 80-100 | 8.4 | 160-180 | 6.6 |
| 90-110 | 9.7 | | |
| 100-120 | 12.5 | | |

### FUEL CONSUMPTION
| | | |
|---|---|---|
| Touring* | 16.1 mpg | |
| | 17.5 litres/100 km | |

| | | |
|---|---|---|
| Overall | 11.8 mpg | |
| | 23.9 litres/100 km | |
| Govt tests | Not applicable | |
| Fuel grade | 97 octane | |
| | 4 star rating | |
| Tank capacity | 28 galls | |
| | 127 litres | |
| Max range | 451 miles | |
| | 725 km | |
| Test distance | 882 miles | |
| | 1419 km | |

*Consumption midway between 30 mph and maximum less 5 per cent for acceleration.

### BRAKES
Pedal pressure, stopping distance and average deceleration from 30 mph (48 kph).

| lb | kg | ft | m | g |
|---|---|---|---|---|
| 20 | 9.1 | 96 | 29.3 | 0.31 |

| 40 | 18.2 | 43 | 13.1 | 0.70 |
|---|---|---|---|---|
| 60 | 27.3 | 33.5 | 10.2 | 0.90 |
| 80 | 36.4 | 32.5 | 9.9 | 0.92 |
| 90 | 40.9 | 30.5 | 9.3 | 0.98 |
| Handbrake | | 214 | 65.3 | 0.14 |
| Maximum from 70 mph (113 kph) | | | | |
| 70 | 31.8 | 186 | 56.7 | 0.88 |

### FADE
Twenty 0.6g stops at 45 sec intervals from speed midway between 40 mph (64 kph) and maximum (92.5 mph, 149 kph) at gross vehicle weight.

| | lb | kg |
|---|---|---|
| Pedal force at start | 36 | 16.3 |
| Pedal force at 10th stop | 36 | 16.3 |
| Pedal force at 20th stop | 36 | 16.3 |

### STEERING
Turning circle between kerbs
| | ft | m |
|---|---|---|
| left | 46.4 | 14.2 |
| right | 43.0 | 13.1 |
| lock to lock | 2.2 turns | |
| 50ft diam. circle | 1.0 turns | |

### NOISE
| | dBA | Motor rating* |
|---|---|---|
| 30 mph | 62 | 9 |
| 50 mph | 67 | 13 |
| 70 mph | 72 | 18 |
| Max revs in 2nd | 85 | 44 |
| (1st for 3-speed auto) | | |

*A rating where 1 = 30 dBA and 100 = 96 dBA, and where double the number means double the loudness

### SPEEDOMETER (mph)
| Speedo | | | | | | | |
|---|---|---|---|---|---|---|---|
| 30 | 40 | 50 | 60 | 70 | 80 | 90 | 100 |
| True mph | | | | | | | |
| 30 | 40 | 50 | 59 | 69 | 79 | 89 | 99 |

Distance recorder: 2.6 per cent fast

## GENERAL SPECIFICATION

### ENGINE
| | |
|---|---|
| Cylinders | 8 in Vee |
| Capacity | 5340 cc (326 cu in) |
| Bore/stroke | 100/85 mm (3.94/3.5 in) |
| Cooling | Water |
| Block | Light alloy |
| Head | Light alloy |
| Valves | Dohc per bank |
| Cam drive | Chain |
| Compression | 9.3:1 |
| Carburetter | Four Weber 42 DNCF |
| Bearings | 5 main |
| Max power | Not quoted |
| Max torque | Not quoted |

### TRANSMISSION
| | |
|---|---|
| Type | Chrysler Torqueflite |
| 3-speed auto | |

Internal ratios and mph/1000 rpm
| | | |
|---|---|---|
| Top | 1.00:1 | 26.3 |
| 2nd | 1.45:1 | 18.2 |
| 1st | 2.45:1 | 10.7 |
| Rev | 2.20:1 | |
| Final drive | 3.07:1 | |

### BODY/CHASSIS
| | |
|---|---|
| Construction | Aluminium panels on steel superstructure |
| Protection | Chassis Cadulac zinc-phosphate primer; engine compartment & underside Supra PVA; Cadulac wax injection of box sections; |

Tectyl 506 — underside & running gear; Supra fibre-less Dedseal — chassis underside; Dunlop Panel-guard — high wear areas.

### SUSPENSION
| | |
|---|---|
| Front | Indendent by double wishbones, co-axial coil springs and dampers; anti-roll bar. |
| Rear | De Dion rear axle located by parallel trailing links and Watts Linkage; co-axial coil springs and self-levelling dampers |

### STEERING
| | |
|---|---|
| Type | Rack and pinion |
| Assistance | Yes |

### BRAKES
| | |
|---|---|
| Front | 11.2 in discs, ventilated |
| Rear | 10.4 in discs, inboard, ventilated |
| Park | On rear |
| Servo | Yes |
| Circuit | Split front/rear |
| Rear valve | Yes |
| Adjustment | Manual |

### WHEELS/TYRES
| | |
|---|---|
| Type | Steel, 6×15 in |
| Tyres | 235/70 VR 15 Avon Turbosteel |

| | |
|---|---|
| Pressures | 30/30 psi F/R (normal) |
| | 35/35 psi F/R (full load high speed) |

### ELECTRICAL
| | |
|---|---|
| Battery | 12V, 68 Ah |
| Earth | Negative |
| Generator | Alternator 70A |
| Fuses | 24 |
| Headlights type | Cibie, rectangular retractable |
| dip | 110 W total |
| main | 220 W total |

### GUARANTEE
Duration ..12 months, unlimited mileage
### MAINTENANCE
| | |
|---|---|
| Free service | initial |
| Schedule | every 5,000 miles |

### DO IT YOURSELF
| | |
|---|---|
| Sump | 11.3 litres |
| Gearbox | 8.5 litres |
| Rear axle | 2.0 litres |
| Steering gear pump | 2.0 litres |
| Coolant | 18.1 litres |
| Contact breaker gap | N.A., electronic |
| Spark plug gap | 0.030 in |
| Spark plug type | NGK BRs GEV |
| Tappets (hot/cold) | 0.014-0.016 in Inlet |
| | 0.016-0.018 in Exhaust |

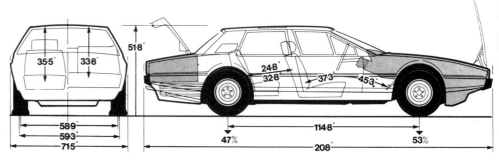

# Aston Martin
# BULLDOG

## AML's 200-mph twin-turbo boomer sets a new standard for concept cars *by Mel Nichols*

PHOTOS BY RICK McBRIDE

If you're prepared to pay upwards of $500,000, you might—just might—be able to lure the Bulldog away from Aston Martin. The Bulldog, right now, is likely to stop more traffic than anything else on the road. And when you want to leave the same traffic behind, the Bulldog will do that better than anything else, too. Beneath its incredibly low, flat body lurks AM's superb 5.3-liter V-8, boosted by two great thumping Garrett T4 turbochargers to give around 650 horsepower and a top speed between 190 and 200 mph.

The Bulldog is a spectacular car—a riveting car—to look at, to ride in, and to hear at full cry, just for the fact that it exists in a world full of 55-mph speed limits. The Bulldog embodies the spirit of the revitalized Aston Martin Lagonda Inc. (reborn in 1977 after bankruptcy). Initially, it seems too expansive and too indulgent a project for a company with such small production and which was so recently in drastic financial strife. But Aston Martin says the Bulldog was not intended as a production car, although they might build up to six replicas for people prepared to part with the kind of money required to own one. The prototype is for sale but will probably cost more than the cars to follow.

The fact is that the Bulldog is worth more than money to the people at Aston Martin. At Newport Pagnell, all who have been concerned with the project say they've learned a great deal from conceiving and building the car, most of it in the "vogue" areas of car design, where AM feels they have to remain and grow strong. The Bulldog, a mid-engined 2-seater with those twin turbochargers added to its 4-cam all-alloy V-8, has given AM new information about aerodynamics, turbocharging, sound insulation, and use of electronics and fiber optics, much of which will see service in Aston's Lagonda sedans.

As well as helping with high-speed research, the Bulldog is a first-class promotional vehicle. It will be seen at major motor shows around the world. For what it is and for what it undoubtedly will achieve for AM, the Bulldog seems to have cost surprisingly little in time and money. It took just a year for Aston's young engineers to transform it into metal from the outline-plus-chassis stage where it lay when AM's former chief engineer left to join John DeLorean in Ireland. When the car was shown to the press early this summer, it was a fully trimmed, hard-charging heart stopper.

Bulldog is a tremendously wide, squat car with a long wheelbase, a body composed entirely of clean planes, and fat, brutish wheels that protrude from its close-fitting wheel arches. There's a surprise in store when you first see the car, especially if it's on a racetrack (as when I first encountered it). On a track, most road cars—even the wildest ones—seem out of place and too tame for the surroundings. Not the Bulldog; it looks just as mean and businesslike as any

race car I've seen.

But the Bulldog really is a road-going car. Before Aston Martin let outsiders see it, they trimmed its cockpit in the finest leather; its digital controls and instrumentation had been sorted; and the electrically powered gullwing doors had been designed to suit the world's most rigorous safety standards. Up-to-the-minute safety standards run through the entire car, and it complies with all the obvious things like headlight and bumper heights, belt anchorages and cockpit visibility. Give it detox treatment and it could be sold in the US.

The body was designed by Bill Towns, an Englishman who styled all the current Aston Martins and the Lagonda sedans. The accent is entirely on flat planes, with curves or kinks only where they're absolutely needed. Towns has good reasons for doing what he has. The car has a straight, low beltline to promote maximum glass area and visibility—the bugbear of mid-engined cars. Towns used almost flat glass on all sides because one of his priorities was to have a special high-quality ripple-free glass, which can't be bent as freely or in such complex curves as the ordinary variety. So visibility from inside the car is very good and free from dis-

tortion. The curvature of the body's bottom line was to prevent a car with such a long (109-inch) wheelbase from looking like an express train, but the shape also sets up airflow characteristics that feed the car's oil coolers, located below and behind the rear door seams.

Aerodynamically, the Bulldog's sophistication shows through. The body, built initially as a quarter-scale mockup, has a drag coefficient of 0.35, which isn't fantastic (Mercedes nearly matched that with its latest production S-class sedans), but the frontal area has been kept very low. So the nose is long and low. Towns had intended to tuck under it an adjustable spoiler that didn't protrude until 50 mph, but he was beaten by time and cost.

There's an unusual chassis beneath the all-aluminum hand-shaped body. The chassis is based around a backbone of three 4-inch tubes. But instead of having strengthening sections that run along the sides of the body (over which you have to climb in low coupes), torsional strength is provided by a fully stressed roof that depends for its toughness on having two A-pillars (per side) rather than the normal one on each side.

The engine sits immediately behind the seats and drives through a 5-speed ZF transaxle—the one used in the De-Tomaso Pantera and the only one capable of handling the V-8's torque.

> ## "There's a surprise in store when you first see the car, especially if it's on a race track . . . "

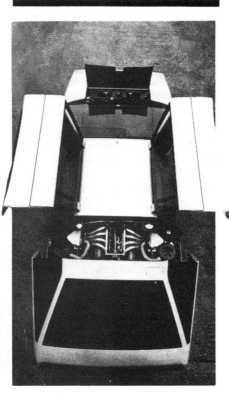

And torque the engine certainly has. Added to the light but so very potent 5.3-liter V-8 that has powered Aston Martins for years are two Garrett AiResearch T4 turbochargers working in conjunction with Bosch fuel injection rather than the Weber carburetors normally found on the V-8. With carburetors, the Aston V-8 previously was strongest in Vantage tune, where it has something over 400 horsepower. Bulldog power, Aston Martin says, is Vantage plus 60%. That means 650 horsepower, or not far from it! Traditionally, Aston Martin has not divulged their exact power figures, and they don't give the Bulldog's torque either; but you can count on well over 500 pounds-feet. What really matters is that AM has biased their turbocharging effort to give a very flat torque curve, with the accent on low-rpm oomph rather than top-end rocketry. The turbos start working hard between 2500 and 2800 rpm, but there is terrific urge well below that level. With a 3.2:1 final drive ratio, the Bulldog's very high top gear (0.7:1) gives 31.8 mph/1000 rpm, which means that the car reaches 100 mph at a leisurely 3150 rpm and would theoretically reach 200 mph at 6300 rpm.

The Bulldog's suspension is simple in principle and tough in execution. There are upper and lower wishbones at the front with coil springs and an anti-roll bar. Unassisted rack-and-pinion steering controls 15-inch alloy wheels carrying 255/50 Pirelli P7 tires. Aston Martin is dedicated to deDion rear axles, and that's what you'll find in the tail of the Bulldog, making it the first mid-engined car to use the deDion system. Aston Martin has worked out a clever way of linking it with the transmission, and it is very securely anchored. One benefit of the deDion axle is that it keeps the tires very flat on the road, an important facet when you're using ultra-low-profile modern tires like P7s.

The Bulldog's brakes are huge four-spot discs, inboard at the rear, that are direct spin-offs from Can-Am racing practice, and they are *powerful.*

The interior is luxurious, with fantastic bucket seats designed especially for the car and trimmed, like everything else in the cockpit, in fine Connolly leather. The dash is leather covered and faced with walnut. This is an *English* supercar. But it is a very modern supercar, too; all its instruments are digital (road speed, water temperature, oil pressure, voltage, and fuel level). The air conditioning and radio/tape player controls are grouped in the same main binnacle as the instruments. It spreads to either side of the 4-spoke steering wheel. Steering column stalks take care of nearly all the driving functions. Only the electric door switches and little-used controls for demisting the rear window and activating the rear foglights are located on the high, close tunnel that covers the chassis backbone.

You duck under the gullwing door and tumble down into the car, maneuvering yourself over the edge of the deep-sided seat and into it. Funny, it's a big car in length and width, but there isn't much room inside, especially down in the footwells. Anyone much over 6 feet will have trouble getting comfortable. But for me (5 feet 11), the cabin, seat, and driving position are perfect. The leather wheel nestles low on your legs, and the windscreen does provide good visibility. There's the familiar ZF gearshift with its fairly short throws fore and aft but big distances across the gate. It's not particularly heavy, but it's not a fast shift either.

Keep the switch pressed down, and the big gullwing swings down to shut you in, cutting you off from the world. Now it's just the road in front and, when you turn the key, the incredibly thunderous roar from behind your head. This time, it's real business when you press the clutch and engage 1st gear (left and back, leaving the top four gears in the main H). This time, when the clutch comes out and you squeeze on the throttle, the booming Bulldog eases forward. It doesn't leap away—although it would, no doubt, if you hit it hard enough—because it's fundamentally a very easy car to drive. It's just a very meaty, beefy sort of car, and worry though you might, there is no need to fear its tremendous power and torque or its speed. You control that power and the speed, and the car lets you know in the first few moments of motion that it gives its power and its speed very evenly and progressively.

You tread harder and the car simply accelerates harder, but somehow (perhaps because everything is so tight and well matched) it doesn't seem as though there is 650 horsepower beneath your toes and behind your head or that you're accelerating at a rate that will bring up 0-100 mph in 10 seconds flat. There is no savagery, just performance.

The engine revs easily, so that, while it does have tremendous power and flexibility at low revs and is terrifically even in its delivery of power, it is still an engine with plenty at the top as well. In fact, when I drove the car, the tachometer was reading slow, making it seem as though around 5500 rpm was the point at which the power began noticeably to tail off. The true reading, however, was in excess of 7000 rpm, so that this engine will hold together high up as well as getting there with a real willingness and spirit (the Aston people blanched somewhat, though, when they realized how far off and how dangerously low the tachometer had been).

From the outset, the Bulldog feels like a big, heavy car. You're ever conscious that there's a lot of mass as well as power behind you. And the engine noise is loud—the same awesome V-8 throb-roar that those standing and watching the car hear when it gets going. From the outside, when it acceler-

ates up through its range, it sounds so powerful and so good that it makes your scalp prickle. Then the driver lifts off, and a foot of flame comes spurting out of each exhaust pipe. So *that's* why there's a spark arrester over the exhaust pipes . . . .

Inside, the noise seems to fit with the meaty feeling of the car, so it, like the pure power, seems to lose its awesomeness. You just drive, using the same rules that apply when you drive any very powerful and very fast automobile: be precise; be accurate; don't rush; don't be rough; shift slowly; brake progressively. The Bulldog responds beautifully to that sort of treatment.

But while you don't have to fight it, you certainly have to hold it in the bends, for the steering really loads up hard when you're cornering. As I drove it, straight off the drawing board and

---

> ## "From the outside, when it accelerates up through its range, it sounds so powerful and so good that it makes your scalp prickle."

---

with very few developmental miles behind it, the Bulldog understeered and built up a lot of pressure at the steering wheel. But, while it imposes rather more effort than is desirable upon the hands and wrists, the understeer brings a welcome stability. The impression of all that weight and power behind your back can be intimidating when you're cornering well above 1 g; you don't relish the thought of the rear tires, however low and wide, letting go and all that mass taking over. You wonder whether you'd be quick enough and strong enough at the wheel to catch it. So you push harder at the wheel rim and feel reassured.

Later, when you begin to play a little more, begin to tease that weight mass and use all the power, you find that

there isn't really much question of the tail snapping out of line unless you're going incredibly fast—and I mean upwards of 150 mph for most open-road sweepers.

The car is just too unwieldy and heavy to throw about in really tight bends, and even then the pure grip is so strong that you'd have to commit yourself at an insane level to get it sliding. It seems to have perhaps even more grip than the Countach S.

No, the Bulldog is a car for very fast, fairly open roads where its prodigious power, its long legs, and its size and weight can all work fluidly together to let it eat the miles with Seven League boots. But if Aston Martin does follow the prototype with a handful of replicas (and they've already had a decent clutch of inquiries), I think they need to give the Bulldog power steering to take the hard work out of it all. Then you could just get on with it, turning into the bends without the effort that exists in the development car, secure in the knowledge that the combination of the inherent balance of the chassis, the deDion rear axle, and those wide Pirellis would still keep the tail hanging on forever and a day as you pump all that power through them. The ride is, of course, very firm, but it's comfortable and certainly communicative enough to keep a conscientious driver happy.

If, as Aston Martin claims, the Bulldog only cost them $300,000 to design and build, then it's a masterpiece. Beyond its own achievement, it shows that Aston Martin, as they push firmly into the '80s, has the people, the know-how, and the heart to build a potent and exotic car of the very first order.

Essentially, the Bulldog is a beginning; it could do with, and will certainly get, a lot of development. As it stands now, virtually straight off the drawing board, it's stunning enough. I, for one, stand in full appreciation of the marvelously balanced way in which it blends its power and its speed, cossets you with the luxury and taste of its leather interior and, at the same time, has such a hearty character. As a beginning, it's breathtaking. And who knows where it might all end? **SCg**

## NUMBER 5 **ASTON MARTIN V8 VANTAGE**

# EXCLUSIVE EXQUISITE EXHILARATING

You'd get just £1 change out of £40,000 if you bought an Aston Martin V8 Vantage. But a lucky customer can rest assured that he will own the fastest standard production car ever tested by *Motor*, as well as one of our all-time favourites

NOW THAT the dust has settled on Victor Gauntlett's takeover and absorption of Aston Martin into his Pace Petroleum empire, the future for the Newport Pagnell-based motor manufacturers looks assured. That we welcomed the news with great relief we make no secret — but not, as may be assumed, through any reasons of nostalgia, nor even the desire to retain such an essential constituent of the British motor industry's heritage. Quite simply, Aston Martin make extraordinarily good cars, machines specifically designed and engineered to maximise the pleasure of ownership and driving, machines that are lovingly and beautifully assembled as it seems only the craftsmen of Aston Martin and Rolls-Royce know how.

It is remarkable that despite all the changes of ownership of Aston in the last decade, the product continuity has been so good. We have seen, for instance, the futuristic Lagonda — notable for its stunningly good ride and handling compromise — reach production, while the stalwart of Aston pro-

duction, the V8, has been further developed into its best and most efficient form to date. The V8 is now available in automatic, as well as five-speed manual form, and in saloon or Volante (convertible) versions. It may be difficult to conceive a more sporting and even more powerful Aston Martin, but exist it does; called the Vantage, available only as a manual, and sporting low-profile tyres and a deep front spoiler, this has an up-rated engine that endows the car with simply mouthwatering performance.

We first tested a Vantage on its introduction in February 1977. Inclement weather and a variety of problems prevented our obtaining performance figures that accurately reflected the quite remarkable on-road performance. This is our first opportunity to re-examine a machine which, after our 1977 experiences, most *Motor* road testers had added to their personal shortlists of most desirable machines; after our 1981 experiences, the Vantage has gone straight to the top. Quite simply, there isn't a car made today

that combines more excitement with such an exquisitely hand-built package. Apart from the £39,999 price tag and the heavy (some might say anti-social) fuel consumption, the only major problem the Vantage presents to a prospective owner is how to keep his pulse rate under 100. Not to put too fine a point on it, the Vantage represents one of the finest means of travel yet devised.

So what is it that sets the Aston Martin Vantage apart from the more mundane devices that most of us can afford? Apart from those qualities so difficult to quantify, like exclusivity, the impression that each Aston Martin is almost honed from solid, the sheer precision of the body panel fit and the delightful bespoke interior, the Vantage is one of the very fastest cars available at any price. Only two other cars can approach the Vantage's performance — the Porsche 3.3 Turbo and the Ferrari 512 Berlinetta Boxer. Certainly the Porsche is not as fast, and while we haven't tested the Ferrari in its latest form we doubt that it matches the

Aston's pulverising performance: a maximum of 168 mph, 0-60 in 5.2 sec, 0-100 mph in 11.9 sec. It may be hard to believe, but the Aston *feels* even faster than these bare figures suggest, so punchy is the engine throughout its working range, so disdainful the ease with which it will accelerate and overtake in fifth at relatively low speeds.

Quite simply, the Aston Martin Vantage is the fastest standard production car that *Motor* has tested in its 78-year existence; it's nice to note that the British can still be best.

The V8, it will be recalled, was launched as the DBS in 1967, first being fitted with the renowned straight-six engine, then a year later with the V8 engine, the first (and still only) British engine of that configuration to have the racing-style sophistication of two overhead camshafts per bank of cylinders. Over the years, the car and the engine have been updated many times, so that the V8 of today is a long way removed from the DBS of the late '60s. The last major revision came in late 1979 when the rear body was

revised to incorporate an aerodynamic lip, the bonnet reshaped to eliminate the dummy air intake, and the interior refurbished — including a burr walnut facia.

The Vantage differs from "ordinary" V8s by having larger carburetters, and different camshafts that raise power and torque very substantially (though, as usual, Aston Martin are reluctant to quote precise figures). Enormous 255/60 VR 15 Pirelli CN12 tyres replace the normal 225/70 VR 15 Avons, while the Vantage also has uprated Koni dampers and stiffer progressive bump stops at the front — bump stops that impart a rising rate to the front springing. Externally, the Vantage can be recognised by the deep front spoiler and radiator grille shroud that incorporates two Cibié driving lights, modifications that lower the drag coefficient by about 20 per cent; again, Aston are coy about quoting an exact figure but say that the drag coefficient is in the "low 0.3s" which is significantly better than, for instance, the figure claimed by Porsche for their 3.3 turbo.

In other respects, the Vantage is the familiar Aston mixture. A steel platform chassis and superstructure is clothed in aluminium body panels. The front-mounted V8 drives the rear wheels through a five-speed ZF gearbox and limited-slip differential, while suspension is by double wishbones at the front and a de Dion axle at the back. The special Adwest rack and pinion steering is power-assisted.

At this end of the market, the number of sporting rivals is, not surprisingly, small. Nevertheless competition is very keen and the Vantage has to compete with such highly respected rivals as the Porsche 3.3 Turbo and Ferrari Boxer, both of which, at £27,950 and £36,715, are considerably cheaper. Just about the only other possible rival (apart, perhaps, from the Porsche 928S) is the much less charismatic De Tomaso Pantera GTS (£22,786). The Lamborghini Countach and BMW M1 are, alas, not imported into the UK.

Since its 1977 launch, the 5.3-litre Vantage engine has undergone some slight engine changes to improve its mid-range and low-speed torque and fuel consumption, particularly on light throttle. The adoption of a polynomial cam profile and increased duration for the inlet camshaft, as well as the adoption of a part-throttle ignition advance and revised carburetter settings, have improved the torque output from under 2,000 rpm all the way up to 5,500 rpm, without affecting the maximum power figure. Although there are no official power and torque figures available from the manufacturers, the homologation papers necessary for the car's sale in Germany quote the maximum power as being 390 bhp (DIN) at 5,800 rpm. This is very much greater than the Porsche Turbo's and Jaguar V12's 300 bhp, and even the Ferrari Boxer's 340 bhp.

Despite the Aston's obvious external size (it's six feet wide and just over 15 feet long) and bulk (at 35.1 cwt it remains a heavyweight), this is enough power to produce performance of staggering proportions. Previously straight roads become twisty, unsuspecting passengers' chins sink to their chests in incredulity. At MIRA, tyre-burning wheelspin starts produced a record-breaking set of acceleration figures: 60 mph is reached, despite an awkward dog-leg gearchange from first to second, in a mere 5.2 sec; 100 mph comes up in 11.9 sec — faster than most sporting saloons are to 60 mph; after 18.2 sec the Vantage has topped 120 mph and is showing no signs of diminishing acceleration. Within the confines of MIRA's mile-long horizontal straights we were able to better 140 mph in both directions from a standing start and still slow with relative ease for the 50 mph banking at each end.

What is so impressive about the Vantage is that this remarkable full-throttle maximum performance is achieved while retaining excellent tractability and flexibility, with little of the "cammy-ness" that can characterise such a highly-tuned power unit. True, it isn't possible to floor the throttle fully in either fourth or fifth under 2,000 rpm without the engine staggering slightly, but this is hardly noticeable on the road as part-throttle pull is clean and admirably strong. Above 40 mph in fifth the Vantage exhibits remarkably consistent pulling power throughout its speed range, particularly as the car is geared to achieve 170 mph. From 40 to 60 mph in fifth takes only 7.7 sec, for example, and all the 20 mph increments from 40 to 120 mph are faster still. A comparison of the Vantage's acceleration figures with those of the Porsche Turbo and much less flexible Lamborghini Countach of 1975 makes this mid-range performance readily obvious.

The result of this ready availability of acceleration at almost any speed in any gear makes the Aston's performance on the road seem even more remarkable. But although speeds of 150 mph or more are available on surprisingly short straights, there is no opportunity for accurately measuring the Vantage's top speed on public roads in safety. We had hoped to test the car to its maximum at VW's Ehra-Lessien proving ground in West Germany (where we tested the Porsche) but unfortunately this proved impossible within the limits of our Press schedules. However, the German magazine *Auto Motor und Sport* obtained a mean of 165.8 mph

on a private owner's Vantage in 1978, so that we have no reason to doubt Aston Martin's claim, for the current car, of 168 mph. While many may regard such a speed capability as being academic, if not downright anti-social, it endows the Vantage with a 120-130 mph cruising potential, at which speed the car feels hardly stressed.

There is no choke fitted to the Vantage and cold starting is achieved by the time-honoured Weber technique of flooring the throttle two or three times before operating the starter. The engine then starts easily and will idle more or less immediately if at all times a little lumpily. To the uninitiated, the engine would probably be considered noisy (our sound meter showed a poor 89 dB peak on full throttle acceleration), but to the car enthusiast it produces a glorious mixture of sounds: whirring cams and chains; low speed carburetter gobble; high speed exhaust howl. The note of the engine deepens noticeably at 3,000 rpm, and becomes a glorious bellow as the rev counter passes 5,000 rpm. The recommended rev limit is 6,250 rpm, to which the power unit spins with such speed and willingness that you have to watch the rev counter with great care.

That our testers all found the Vantage a delight to drive hard is reflected in the overall fuel consumption figure of 11.3 mpg. Whether or not any customer spending the best part of £40,000 on a car would be worried by such a figure is open to question, but the bald fact is that such a fuel consumption is about as bad as any. However, it should be added that it is an improvement on the original Vantage's 10.0 mpg, and that 14 mpg or more is perfectly possible while still motoring extremely quickly. *Motor's* touring mpg figure is computed from our steady-speed consumption figures and takes account of the car's maximum speed; in the Aston's case, because the top speed is so high, the touring consumption of 10.8 mpg is unduly pessimistic. We'd rate 14 mpg as being more typical.

If the driver is firm and positive in his actions, the gearchange repays him with fast, crisp gearchanges, for the lever of the ZF gearbox moves through a well-defined gate with little baulking

## ACCELERATION

| From rest | Aston Martin Vantage | Porsche 3.3 Turbo | Lamborghini Countach |
|---|---|---|---|
| mph | sec | sec | sec |
| 0-30 | 2.3 | 2.2 | 2.7 |
| 0-40 | 3.0 | 2.7 | 3.4 |
| 0-50 | 4.3 | 3.7 | 4.4 |
| 0-60 | 5.2 | 5.3 | 5.6 |
| 0-70 | 6.5 | 6.4 | 7.5 |
| 0-80 | 8.1 | 7.8 | 9.0 |
| 0-90 | 9.9 | 10.3 | 11.1 |
| 0-100 | 11.9 | 12.3 | 13.1 |
| 0-110 | 14.5 | 15.0 | 15.9 |
| 0-120 | 18.2 | 19.1 | 20.3 |
| Standing Mile | 13.4 | 13.4 | 14.1 |
| Standing Km | 24.7 | — | 25.2 |
| **In top** | | | |
| mph | sec | sec | sec |
| 20-40 | — | 9.8 | — |
| 30-50 | — | 9.6 | — |
| 40-60 | 7.7 | 9.1 | — |
| 50-70 | 6.3 | 7.2 | 12.0 |
| 60-80 | 5.9 | 6.0 | 12.6 |
| 70-90 | 6.2 | 5.7 | 10.3 |
| 80-100 | 6.4 | 6.1 | 11.0 |
| 90-110 | 6.9 | 7.3 | 11.4 |
| 100-120 | 7.5 | 8.7 | 13.7 |

except into second after a cold start. None of our drivers particularly like the dog-leg first-to-second change, but ideal cross-gate spring biasing makes the movement far easier than in most similar installations. As always, the clutch is very heavy — excessively so for busy traffic conditions — but superbly progressive and positive. Those or our testers with large feet found the pedal action awkward, however, primarily because their toes tended to foul the underside of the steering column from time to time.

For fast driving, the gear ratios are ideal, for the upper gears are close. But there is a noticeable gap between first and second and we question whether it is necessary to have fourth and fifth quite so close — though such gearing does offer the interesting possibility of passing a flat-out Audi Quattro or Lotus Esprit and then changing up . . ! In-gear maxima at 6,250 rpm are 48, 78, 114 and 139 mph, and in fifth gear the Vantage gives 26.3 mph/1,000 rpm.

There may be more modern-looking and even apparently more sophisticated cars than the Vantage, but there is no car in the world that handles better. Perhaps some that have even more enormous tyres than the Aston's (255/60 VR 15 Pirelli CN12s) are able to produce more cornering g-force, but none offer more feel, more predictability, or more control. On dry or wet roads, at high speed or low speed, the Vantage handles in such an utterly viceless way that it inspires in the driver tremendous confidence. This stems from the sheer precision and feel afforded by the steering (in our opinion, the best power-steering system in the world though it should be said that some may find the steering a little heavy at parking speeds), by the grip and progressive response of the tyres, by the excellent traction that the de Dion rear suspension allows and by the lack of bump steer or wander from the suspension. Stability, even at high speed in a cross wind, is impeccable.

Generally, the Vantage understeers gently on a light throttle, but if you start to push hard it becomes more neutral and will eventually oversteer. Of course, with about 400 bhp to play with a tail slide is available almost any time you wish — or when you *don't* wish, if you're indelicate with the throttle. But the castor action of the steering is so weighted, and the actual transition to oversteer so progressive, that such behaviour is nothing like as intimidating as it is in many very powerful cars, even on slippery, muddy surfaces; an experienced driver will find that the Aston allows him the opportunity to make the most of his skills.

It is impressive that such superb

handling has not been achieved at the expense of ride comfort. The Vantage is more stiffly sprung than the V8, but the damping is so well matched that the effect is one of firmness without discomfort. At high speed over humps there is a trace of float in the front suspension, but this is always checked very quickly and is the only significant criticism of an otherwise good ride.

On their first application from cold the brakes feel disconcertingly heavy and lifeless. Once warm, they become lighter and more progressive, and reveal themselves to be extremely powerful. Even continual heavy braking from very high speeds does not reveal any noticeable tendency to fade, though our car's brakes were prone to rumble under these conditions.

In most other respects, the Vantage is similar to the standard V8, our views on which have been well documented in these pages. By small car standards, the packaging is extravagant — plenty of space is provided for two people to travel in comfort, but the rear seat is so cramped that it is of relatively little use by adults for anything other than short journeys. The boot is of average size for the class. The air conditioning system has high output and fine control but doesn't offer a bi-level setting — the opportunity to have cold air to your face while toasting your feet. Although much of the switch-gear is incorporated into a row of push/push switches on the centre console, the important functions are controlled by two column-mounted fingertip stalks.

Vantages normally have a black interior, but our test car was fitted with the burr walnut facia of the V8 saloon (a £311.45 extra), about which, while conceding the attractiveness of such a design, we have reservations because of the stray reflections that it causes. Likewise we don't normally like leather upholstery, as it lets you slide about too much, but the Vantage's seats are so well shaped that this isn't a valid criticism.

We've already mentioned the rather noisy, but delightful sounding, engine. For the class of car, the Aston is not unduly noisy, though a little worse than average. The tyres keep up a constant, if distant, pitter-patter over any broken surfaces and wind noise at speed is noticeable though never intrusive.

Lastly, everyone who saw the car was absolutely captivated by the delightful craftsmanship that had so obviously been put into the machine. Finished in metallic blue, our test car's body had a near-perfect fit of body panels, while the interior is covered by so much exquisitely trimmed leather that one wonders if Aston have to use a herd of cattle for each car.

Far left: exquisitely trimmed interior offers lots of space for two front seat passengers, but rear seats (left) are cramped for adults

Below: Vantages normally have a matt black interior but our test car had the V8 saloon's wooden facia

Left: traditional English treatment for the instruments, including the shiny walnut. Flanking the speedometer and rev counter are four other minor gauges (not shown)

The magnificent 5.3-litre four-cam V8 is all muscle

# MOTOR ROAD TEST NO 21/81 ●
# ASTON MARTIN V8 VANTAGE

## PERFORMANCE

### CONDITIONS
| | |
|---|---|
| Weather | Wind 10-18 mph |
| Temperature | 52°F |
| Barometer | 29.3 in Hg |
| Surface | Dry tarmacadam |

### MAXIMUM SPEEDS
| | mph | kph |
|---|---|---|
| Mean (estimated) | 168 | 270 |

Terminal Speeds:
| | mph | kph |
|---|---|---|
| at ¼ mile | 106.5 | 171 |
| at kilometre | 131 | 210 |

Speed in gears (at 6250 rpm):
| | | |
|---|---|---|
| 1st | 48 | 77 |
| 2nd | 78 | 125 |
| 3rd | 114 | 183 |
| 4th | 139 | 223 |

### ACCELERATION FROM REST
| mph | sec | kph | sec |
|---|---|---|---|
| 0-30 | 2.3 | 0-40 | 1.9 |
| 0-40 | 3.0 | 0-60 | 2.9 |
| 0-50 | 4.3 | 0-80 | 4.3 |
| 0-60 | 5.2 | 0-100 | 5.5 |
| 0-70 | 6.5 | 0-120 | 7.3 |
| 0-80 | 8.1 | 0-140 | 9.3 |
| 0-90 | 9.9 | 0-160 | 11.8 |
| 0-100 | 11.9 | 0-180 | 15.1 |
| 0-110 | 14.5 | 0-200 | 20.5 |
| 0-120 | 18.2 | | |
| Stand'g ¼ | 13.4 | Stand'g km | 24.7 |

### ACCELERATION IN TOP
| mph | sec | kph | sec |
|---|---|---|---|
| 20-40 | —* | 40-60 | —* |
| 30-50 | —* | 60-80 | —* |
| 40-60 | 7.7 | 80-100 | 4.4 |
| 50-70 | 6.3 | 100-120 | 3.2 |
| 60-80 | 5.9 | 120-140 | 3.9 |
| 70-90 | 6.2 | 140-160 | 3.9 |
| 80-100 | 6.4 | 160-180 | 4.5 |
| 90-110 | 6.9 | 180-200 | 4.3 |
| 100-120 | 7.5 | | |

*Would not pull full throttle below 40 mph

### ACCELERATION IN 4TH
| mph | sec | kph | sec |
|---|---|---|---|
| 30-50 | 7.2 | 60-80 | 4.7 |
| 40-60 | 6.2 | 80-100 | 3.4 |
| 50-70 | 5.1 | 100-120 | 3.0 |
| 60-80 | 5.1 | 120-140 | 3.1 |
| 70-90 | 5.2 | 140-160 | 3.3 |
| 80-100 | 5.2 | 160-180 | 3.3 |
| 90-110 | 5.5 | 180-200 | 4.3 |
| 100-120 | 6.5 | | |

### FUEL CONSUMPTION
| | |
|---|---|
| Touring*† | 10.8 mpg |
| | 26.2 litres/100 km |
| Overall | 11.3 mpg |
| | 25.0 litres/100 km |

| | |
|---|---|
| Fuel grade | 97 octane |
| | 4 star rating |
| Tank capacity | 23.0 galls |
| | 104.3 litres |
| Max range† | 320 miles |
| | 518 km |
| Test distance | 1,543 miles |
| | 2,483 km |

*Consumption midway between 30 mph and maximum less an allowance of 5 per cent for acceleration.
†See text

### NOISE
| | dBA | Motor rating* |
|---|---|---|
| 30mph | 65 | 11 |
| 50 mph | 70 | 16 |
| 70 mph | 75 | 23 |
| Max revs in 2nd | 89 | 60 |

(1st for 3-speed auto)
*A rating where 1 = 30 dBA, and 100 = 96 dBA, and where double the number means double the loudness.

### SPEEDOMETER (mph)
| Speedo | 30 | 40 | 50 | 60 | 70 | 80 | 90 | 100 |
|---|---|---|---|---|---|---|---|---|
| True mph | 27 | 36 | 44 | 53 | 62 | 71 | 79.5 | 88 |

Distance recorder: 7.8 per cent fast

### WEIGHT
| | cwt | kg |
|---|---|---|
| Unladen weight* | 35.1 | 1783 |
| Weight as tested | 38.8 | 1971 |

*with fuel for approx 50 miles

Performance tests carried out by Motor's staff at the Motor Industry Research Association proving ground, Lindley.

Test Data: World Copyright reserved; no unauthorised reproduction in whole or part.

## GENERAL SPECIFICATION

### ENGINE
| | |
|---|---|
| Cylinders | V8 |
| Capacity | 5340 cc (326 cu in) |
| Bore/stroke | 100/85 mm |
| | (3.93/3.34 in) |
| Cooling | Water |
| Block | Aluminium alloy |
| Head | Aluminium alloy |
| Valves | Dohc per bank |
| Cam drive | Chain |
| Compression | 9.3:1 |
| Carburetter | 4 × Weber 48 IDF/3 |
| Bearings | 5 main |
| Max power | Not disclosed |
| Max torque | Not disclosed |

### TRANSMISSION
| | |
|---|---|
| Type | 5-speed manual |
| Clutch dia | 10.5 in. |
| Actuation | Hydraulic |

Internal ratios and mph/1000 rpm
| | | |
|---|---|---|
| Top | 0.845:1 | 26.3 |
| 4th | 1.000:1 | 22.2 |
| 3rd | 1.220:1 | 18.2 |
| 2nd | 1.780:1 | 12.5 |
| 1st | 2.900:1 | 7.7 |
| Rev | 2.630:1 | |
| Final drive | 3.54:1 | |

### BODY/CHASSIS
| | |
|---|---|
| Construction | Tubular steel chassis with steel superstructure and aluminium panels |

### SUSPENSION
| | |
|---|---|
| Front | Independent by unequal length wishbones, co-axial coil springs and telescopic dampers. Anti-roll bar |
| Rear | De Dion axle located by parallel trailing arms and transverse Watts linkage. Coil springs and telescopic dampers |

### STEERING
| | |
|---|---|
| Type | Rack and pinion |
| Assistance | Yes |

### BRAKES
| | |
|---|---|
| Front | Ventilated disc, 10.75 in dia |
| Rear | Ventilated disc, 10.38 in dia |
| Park | On rear |
| Servo | Yes |
| Circuit | Dual, split front/rear |
| Rear valve | Yes |
| Adjustment | Automatic |

### WHEELS/TYRES
| | |
|---|---|
| Type | Alloy 7 in × 15 |
| Tyres | Pirelli CN12 255/60 VR 15 |
| Pressures | 30 psi F/R (normal) |
| | 35 psi F/R (full load/high speed) |

### ELECTRICAL
| | |
|---|---|
| Battery | 12V, 68 Ah |
| Earth | Negative |
| Generator | Alternator 75 amp. |
| Fuses | 12 |
| Headlights type | Cibie Z180 halogen |
| dip | 220 W total (inc auxiliaries) |
| main | 240 W total (inc auxiliaries) |

**Make:** Aston Martin
**Model:** V8 Vantage
**Maker:** Aston Martin Lagonda Ltd, Tickford St, Newport Pagnell, Buckinghamshire MK16 9AN
**Price:** £32,106 plus £2,675.50 car tax and £5,217.22 VAT equals total of £39,998.72. Extras fitted to test car: wooden interior, £311.145; electric passenger door mirror, £149.50; detachable headrests, £119.60 each. Total as tested £40,696.87.

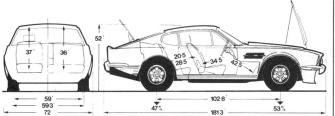

# The Best of
# British

**Dated, even doomed — but what magnificent anachronisms!**
**Roger Bell** drives the Aston Martin Vantage and the latest lean-burn Jaguar XJS, two of the world's fastest cars. Tighten your belts

A WORD of advice. Never argue the case for a £40,000 car that will barely carry four people, do nearly 170mph and consume as much petrol as five frugally driven mini Metros. You'll lose. I had such a session recently with a couple of motoring mavericks and failed even to convince myself that it was a very rational act. Why, for £40,000 you could have an Audi Quattro — arguably the most complete, uncompromising supercar yet made — as well as a luxury boat or a light aircraft for the price of an Aston Martin Vantage. According to Porsche's new chief, Peter Schutz, boats and planes and other extravagant toys are more of a threat to bespoke behemoths like the 928, Jaguar XJS and Aston Vantage than other cars are. So the rationale is not without authoritative foundation. That said, long may there be sufficient land-loving enthusiasts around, rich and nutty enough to fork out forty grand to keep Aston's anachronistic masterpiece alive.

Make no mistake, Victor Gauntlet, Pace Petroleum's chief who recently became the latest owner of Aston Martin, has inherited a masterful anachronism in the Vantage. It was a bit dated over a decade ago as the DBS, launched in 1967 with a straight-six engine that was supplanted a year later by the big quad-cam V8. Many detail changes for the better have been made since then, not least the replacement (in 1971) of the troublesome Bosch mechanical fuel injection by good old Weber carbs. But essentially the car remains as it was — a heavyweight Hercules that belongs to a past age of supercars which the Quattro dated but hopefully didn't kill overnight.

Herculean is the word. The 5340cc all-alloy V8, a massive hunk of muscle, powers a steel-tube chassis carrying an aluminium-clad superstructure of equally megalithic proportions in which the efficient utilisation of space came a long way down the list of design priorities. Accommodation is outrageously poor for a 15 footer, six feet across.

Whatever the faults of the first DBSV8, lack of performance wasn't one of them, as our group test of uppercrust bargains (page 65) underlines. Performance tests by our weekly IPC companions, *Autocar* and *Motor*, indicate that the latest Vantage is not that much quicker than the original DBSV8. That said, against a stopwatch it is still arguably the fastest production car made anywhere in the world (only the Porsche 3.3 Turbo and Ferrari Boxer are likely seriously to rival it), and unquestionably one of the most exciting to drive, with a 0-100mph time of 12 seconds, even though it tips the scales at over 35 cwt.

To propel so much car so vigorously demands colossal power. Aston Martin, like Rolls-Royce, don't reveal exactly how much, but each hand-built Vantage engine, carrying the name of the craftsman who assembled it (what a lovely touch!), is alleged to give around 400bhp, give or take 5bhp or so, which is considerably more than Porsche's 3.3 Turbo. In sound (loud) the ferocity (vicious) it certainly *feels* that potent, even

though it's a very tractable engine, pulling cleanly from 2000rpm, but not violently until 3000rpm, by which time there's a deep, gutteral intake roar — music to some ears, tiresome to others — and an exhaust howl from the car we tried which was not fitted with rear silencers and generated more decibels than seemed to me desirable on a long cross-country journey.

Despite the huge 255/60 Pirelli tyres fitted to the Vantage, brutal starts will spin the wheels in the dry and deposit expensive black lines as long as a cricket pitch on the road. It takes no more than a provocative prod on the long-travel throttle in the wet to dislodge the tail, though power slides are rewardingly easy to check and hold against opposite lock. In this respect, the car's handling — aided by a splendid de Dion rear end which keeps the wheels upright and unsprung weight down — is impeccable. Yet for all that the Vantage is by no means the easiest of cars to handle, which is not quite the same thing. Despite power assistance, the Adwest rack and pinion steering, marvellously sharp and accurate, is quite heavy (it's better weighted on the lesser cars which don't have so much front rubber to swivel), and the clutch requires a thigh-building heave which is exacerbated by the awkward arc of the floor-pivotted pedal. The change of the ZF five-speed box, making up in strength what it lacks in refinement, needs a firm hand to, though the action of the short-throw lever is precise enough, apart from the tricky first-to-second dog-leg. Maxima in the intermediates at 6250rpm — the recommended limit though there's no red line on the tacho to say so — are in round figures 50, 80, 115 and 140mph. At a loping cruising gait of 120mph in the long-striding fifth (giving 26.3mph/1000rpm), the engine is ambling at under 4600rpm, and at the legal limit of 70mph it's doing less than 2700rpm. This tall gearing in part accounts for the high top speed of around 168mph, but it also gives the impression of relatively leisurely lugging, though the engine will in fact slog vigorously from 2000rpm, which is just as well in town when your clutch foot is beginning to feel the strain. The brakes, massive ventilated discs all round, need a firm push too, especially when they're cold, but their performance is otherwise beyond reproach. I made the 0-100mph-0 time less than 18 seconds.

You're fairly well anchored in leather-bound armchairs, though there are certainly more supportive seats around for countering the sort of g forces the Vantage can generate. Ride quality, normally good, is marred on my scoresheet by excessive vertical heaving on long-wavelength undulations, especially at speed. In other respects, creature comforts are of the highest order and the burr walnut and leather decor of the test car, kindly lent to us by Victor Gauntlet himself, quite stunning. The initial impression is of a very fine finish, but there's no disputing the detail flaws, which would never have escaped Rolls-Royce checks, observed with some glee by my maverick friends.

The classic be-spoilered Vantage, like its less muscle-bound but more elegant predecessors, still figures on my short list of great cars; it's a memorable driving machine if you're in the right mood. That it belongs to a dying breed, not far from extinction now that the Quattro has rewritten the book of standards (and OPEC the laws of locomotion) makes it all the more desirable. But for all its great qualities, I found the Vantage a rather tiring — and in some respects rather tiresome — machine that after long stints at the wheels started to sap my enthusiasm, suggesting that it's a car to savour in relatively small doses, not live with all the time. Who has a daily helping of caviar for breakfast? At least my enthusiasm was never drained quite so fast as my wallet; whether you can afford it or not, a car that does 11-14mpg is not a car for the Eighties.

With such low-volume production, Aston could get away with such anti-social extravagance. Jaguar couldn't. Following MG's demise, Triumph (who have lost their sports cars) and Rover (moved to lesser quarters following lagging sales) are not the only specialist branches of BL in trouble. Jaguar are in deep water too — or at least they have been, with a range of gas gobblers of questionable build quality for which demand has savagely dwindled, superb cars though they are. Yet Jaguar's Browns Lane stalwarts forward a convincing plan for survival by fighting the recession on three fronts.

The first priority was to improve quality, which the company's new highly respected, straight-talking chief executive, John Egan, concedes was poor when he arrived in April, 1980. There's tangible evidence to support his claim that, following a ruthless reappraisal of their own and suppliers' standards, the build quality and reliability of a Jaguar is now every bit as good as that of a Mercedes. Cutting costs (over a third of the workforce has been shed recently) and locking in to delivery dates for foreign markets, none of which Jaguar intend to abandon, least of all those in Germany and the States, were key elements in the recovery programme too. The fourth relied on what Jaguar have always done best: advanced engineering.

There was only one significant way to improve Jaguar's 5.3 litre sohc V12, incontestably the world's finest production engine, and that was to make it less thirsty. And economy on top of quality is what Jaguar desperately now need. In percentage terms, quite staggering gains have been made with the V12 using new cylinder heads employing 'Fireball' combustion chambers originated by the Swiss engineer Michael May. May's objective first demonstrated on a VW Passat some years ago, was to derive stratified charge levels of efficiency without the complexity of auxiliary fuelling, pre-chambers and elaborate control. In consultation with May, Jaguar started work on the new head in 1976 under Harry Mundy, one of the four engineers originally responsible for the V12 in the first place (Walter Hassan, William Heynes and Claude Bailey were the others). The combustion chambers are of split level, with the exhaust valves set lower than the inlets which operate in bath-tub combustion chambers. A swirl-inducing ramped channel connects the two. New taper-seat plugs (requiring very low tightening torque) ignite the exceptionally lean mixture in a low-turbulence area from a novel twin-coil set-up developed by Lucas in which the secondary coil, mounted ahead of the radiator to keep it cool, acts as a large inductor. High axial swirl in the chamber, for good flame initiation, propagation and complete burning, allows the use of an exceptionally high 12.5:1 compression ratio — the key to the engine's high efficiency — using normal 97 octane petrol.

Mixture is fed to the chambers by Lucas digital electronic injection, as before (the V12 started life with a quad-carb induction which was replaced in 1975 by Lucas-Bosch fuel injection that cuts off

# THE BEST OF BRITISH

the fuel supply on the over-run — a ploy used by Jaguar long before BMW started making a big splash about doing the same thing in the interests of economy). Much of the development work was carried out first on an experimental single, later on a slant-six — literally one half of a V12 — pointing the way ahead to future developments, perhaps. Jaguar certainly acknowledge that May-head principles will be used on their next generation of engines which, like the XK six and V12, are likely to represent a quantum leap forward in engine technology.

Make no mistake, the new XJS HE (for High Efficiency) is still a pretty thirsty car, and Jaguar's claim that 'economy is comparable with that of many mundane family saloons' (they don't say which) is hard to swallow. Use *all* the performance of what is allegedly the world's fastest production automatic and you won't do much better than 15mpg, though 20mpg is certainly within reach of tender-foot drivers, as the official steady-speed figures underline. Compare them with those of the fractionally slower superseded car (in brackets): 56mph 27.1mpg (21.9), 75mph 22.5mpg (18.6), urban cylcle 15.6mpg (12.7). These remarkable gains have been achieved, what's more, at very modest expense: tooling for the new heads cost a puny £½ million, most of which was accounted for by new transfer machinery for the revised spark plug location. Applying the May head to an existing ohc vertical valve setup is, in production terms, a relatively easy opertation, it seems.

Dated it may be, even doomed as an anachronism hardly in line with modern trends, but the XJS HE is still a magnificent car. As someone once said, it's difficult accurately to describe the sensuous smoothness of its V12 engine without recourse to erotic, even pornographic prose. The party trick with early manuals in order to demonstrate the uncanny flexibility was to stop, switch off, engage top and twist the starter key. The car

would take off like a turbine. You can't do that now, which is perhaps just as well, as all HEs have GM 400 automatic boxes controlled by a T-handle selector that is certainly not in the Mercedes class (what else is?) when it comes to nimble manual shifting, though the transmission normally changes gear imperceptibly left to its own devices. At low engine speeds (quite likely high road ones) so smooth and quiet is the engine that only a sway of the rev counter needle betrays that a change has occurred. At first, the car doesn't feel as viciously quick as the makers claim, perhaps because it lacks that sudden thrust which we've become accustomed to from so many turbo tearaways. The effortlessness of the thing must have something to do with it too. The impression is deceptive, for the smoothness and peace of the engine masks the vigour of its delivery, which Jaguar claims to be one horsepower under 300bhp. Acceleration is similar to that of the superseded 285bhp car (0-60mph in 7 seconds, 0-100mph in 16), and the top speed marginally higher at 155mph. It would have been quicker still had the increase in power and torque not permitted an even higher axle ratio (2.88:1 instead of 3.07) in the interests of even greater economy. Top now gives 27mph/1000rpm so at 100 mph, the engine, red-lined at 6500rpm, is little more than ambling at 3700rpm.

Larger 215/70VR15 tyres (formerly 205/70), specially developed for Jaguar and Rolls-Royce by Dunlop, also help lift the gearing as well as provide more grip. Despite the car's girth and weight, both of them excessive, the HE is a remarkably nimble car. Assisted steering gives quite sharp response and is nothing like so lifeless as that used on the saloons. If there's any quirks in the handling, I failed to discover them in 170 road miles. There are no overt signs of front-end plough, wayward oversteer or throttle sensitivity mid bend: the car simply goes where you aim it without fuss, and there's certainly nothing so rude as S-bend lurch or excessive roll to discourage spirited cornering, or unruly wheelspin (prevented by a limited slip diff) when

gunning away on the turn. Straight line and fas sweep stability is also impeccable — far bette than that of the big coupe Mercedes which surprisingly, are a mite twitchy on the Auto bahnen where they ought to excel. Jaguar' fabled ride/handling balance has few equals an no peers, except perhaps for the Audi Quattr again — and even that remarkable car doesn' ride so serenely as the XJS.

For so large a car, weighing 3900lb, accommo dation in the back is outrageously poor (as in th Aston) of what is little more than a two-plus-two Stopping the hulk hard from over two miles minute, you sense that the all-disc anchors ar being subjected to horrific thermal loads, yet th brakes are never less than reassuring, and a lesser speeds they're fantastic. I wouldn't wan to travel very far in the back but up front it's great way to travel in a cabin that's been refur bished with leather and elm burr timber in response to American demand for traditiona English decor.

Dial-a-temperature air conditioning, which works very well, and an advanced micro computer controlled stereo/radio/cassette, wit electronic memory system, are among the man swanky items of standard equipment. There are several cosmetic changes as well — five-spoke alloy wheels, new bumpers that reduce weigh and length (at least on British spec cars), and double coachlines down the side. None of these or numerous other detail improvements funda mentally change the car, though. It's the lean burn head that's given the XJS a new lease of life that the coming convertible will undoubtedly extend. Whether the HE and the latest range o improved saloons (the V12s also have May headed engines) will see Jaguar through to 198 when the all-new XJ40 arrives remains to be seen.

Jaguar or Aston? Ignoring the difference in price (the new XJS HE costs £18,950, £21,05C less than the Vantage), the brutal performance banshee wail and extrovert driving style that the Aston encourages makes it by far the mos exciting of the two to hustle hard. The Jaguar's strong suits, other than its still formidable oomph superb manners and impressive economy, are its uncanny smoothness, comfort and refinement. In all honesty, they are not close rivals so you really need one of each to suit your mood.

The use of leather and elm burr timber has improved the XJS HE interior, above, although the Aston cabin, below, still looks the more luxurious and impressive.

## Vantage v XJS HE

| Specification | Aston | Jaguar |
|---|---|---|
| Cylinders | V8 | V12 |
| Capacity | 5340cc (326cu in) | 5345 (326cu in) |
| Bore/stroke | 100/85mm | 90/70mm |
| Block | Aluminium alloy | Aluminium alloy |
| Head | Aluminium alloy | Aluminium alloy |
| Valves | dohc per bank | sohc per bank |
| Compression | 9:3:1 | 12:5:1 |
| Induction | Four Webers | Lucas digital injection |
| Max power | approx 400bhp | 299bhp |
| Transmission | 5-speed ZF manual | GM400 3-speed auto |
| mph/100pm top | 26.3 | 27 |
| Chassis | Tubular steel with aluminium-clad superstructure | Unitary steel body/chassis |
| Front Suspen. | wishbones, coils anti-roll bar | wishbones, coils anti-roll bar |
| Rear suspen. | de Dion axle, trailing arms, Watts linkage, coils | ind. by lower wishbones, upper driveshafts, radius arms, twin coils |
| Steering | ass. rack and pinion | ass. rack and pinion |
| Brakes | ventilated discs | discs, ventilated at front |
| Wheels | alloy 7in x 15 | alloy 6½in x 15 |
| Tyres | 255/60 VR15 | 215/7015 |
| **Performance** | | |
| Max speed | 168mph | 155mph |
| 0-60mph | 5.5 sec | 7.5 sec |
| mpg range | 11-14 | 15-20 |

# ASTON MARTIN VOLANTE

*GT motoring on the grand scale: one of the last of a breed*

PHOTOS BY RON WAKEFIELD

ALTHOUGH ASTON MARTIN has been building cars for 60 years, the company had only produced a grand total of 9600 up until the middle of 1981. All of them have been in the sports and Grand Touring category, and only four models have had a production run of more than 1000 cars: the DB4, DB5, DB6 and the current V-8.

Obviously, the production of luxury cars on such a small scale is a high-risk occupation and, in consequence, Aston Martin has had its fair share of financial troubles over the years. However, it was completely reorganized five years ago by a consortium headed up by American Peter Sprague and Englishman Alan Curtis. The intention of this pair was to get the company back on its feet and then act as caretakers until new owners could be found. Almost by accident, they found Victor Gauntlett, whose main claim to fame is that he started Pace Petroleum on virtually no capital and turned it into the biggest independent chain in Britain with some 400 gasoline stations in southern England. At

38, Gauntlett is a ball of fire—and a great car enthusiast with sufficient resources and determination to mold Aston Martin the way he wants it.

We last tested an Aston Martin in 1977; a lot has come to pass in the automotive world in the last four years. The major change is that cars in general have become very much smaller and lighter; therefore, because Aston Martin has not been in any financial position to bring out an entirely new model, the current Volante (along with its coupe companion, now called simply the V-8) is very big and heavy in comparison with its peers. It is in many ways sad to see cars of this type gradually disappearing, but economic forces have dictated that eventually they will be things of the past; and anyway, car designers are rapidly finding ways of achieving the same results with far greater economy.

The current Volante model dates back to 1970, when Aston Martin introduced the DBS V-8 as a coupe only. The engine goes back even further and there was even a racing version of it in the

135

early days. This was in keeping with Aston's long history of participation in racing, which dates back to the company's first appearance at Le Mans in 1921.

Our 1977 test car was a coupe and now we have the convertible Volante model, which was added in 1979 and is built on the same platform chassis but suitably braced for additional strength. In fact, starting with the 1980 models, the convertible's rigidity has been further improved by the use of a big X-brace connecting the central floor pan with the underbody behind the rear suspension. Another X-brace crisscrosses underneath the floor of the trunk; the result is a convertible that can't be criticized for lack of rigidity.

The Volante convertible top works well. A nicely made cover hides it when it is folded; the snaps holding it are a bit stiff, but once the cover is removed, operation of the power-raised or -lowered top is simple. As a safety precaution, though, it is necessary to engage the emergency brake before the top will move. At speed with the top down, there is surprisingly little buffeting; whether the windows are up or down doesn't seem to make much difference.

The interior is finished in the best tradition of British luxury cars, with seats upholstered in Connolly hides and beautiful burl walnut that has exactly matching veneers on both doors and on either side of the instruments. In good British tradition, the steering column is adjustable for reach, rather than being of the tilt variety more common today; with the wheel all the way toward the driver, the directional-signals and washer/wipers stalks are a bit far from the wheel. There are a number of nice convenience touches, such as twin fuel fillers (opened by a switch in the glovebox) that, both feeding into the same tank, mean that you don't have to drag the filler hose over all that aluminum and paintwork.

From the exterior the car could be described as large, imposing and thoroughly traditional when compared to such cars as the

Ferrari Boxer or Lamborghini Countach. However, this also means that the Aston is easy to get into and out of and that you can see where you are going when you are in it. It is somewhat heavy in appearance, particularly in the rear and, as with most convertibles, it is neither as handsome as the closed version nor at its best with the top up. However, such detractions are normal sacrifices for the joys of convertible driving, which for a while we thought were gone forever through government edict.

From the driver's seat, the first thing you notice is a huge hump in the hood, there to accommodate four Weber carburetors and a box around them for evaporative emission control. The carburetors have a manual choke for starting, which in cold weather needs to be set carefully and then adjusted gradually as the engine warms up to avoid an over-rich mixture. Perhaps as a

## AT A GLANCE

|  | Aston Martin Volante | Maserati Quattroporte |
| --- | --- | --- |
| Curb weight, lb | 4330 | 4750 |
| Engine | V-8 | V-8 |
| Transmission | 5-sp M | 3-sp A |
| 0–60 mph, sec | 8.9 | 9.3 |
| Standing ¼ mi, sec | 16.8 | 17.1 |
| Speed at end of ¼ mi, mph | 84.5 | 85.0 |
| Stopping distance from 60 mph, ft | 165 | 182 |
| Interior noise at 50 mph, dBA | 70 | 68 |
| Lateral acceleration, g | 0.667 | 0.742 |
| Slalom speed, mph | na | 55.2 |
| Fuel economy, mpg | 13.0 | 9.0 |

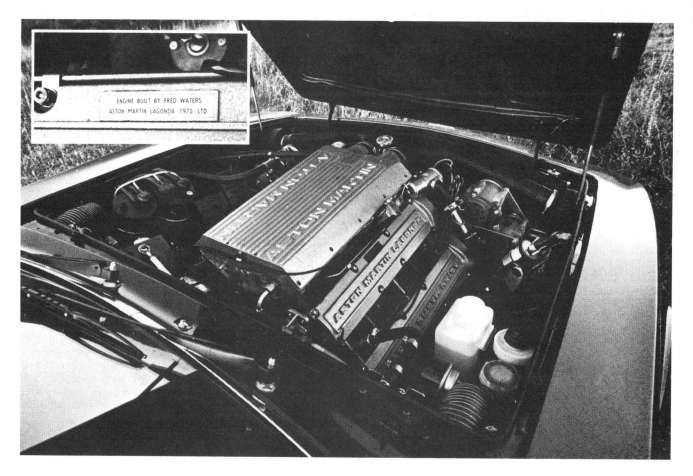

# ROAD TEST
# ASTON MARTIN VOLANTE

SCALE: 10 in. (254 mm) DIVISIONS

## PRICE

| | |
|---|---|
| List price, east coast | $115,000 |
| Price as tested | $115,000 |

Price as tested includes std equip (air cond, AM/FM stereo/cassette, elect. window lifts, leather interior, etc)

## IMPORTER

Aston Martin Lagonda Inc, 14 Weyman Ave, New Rochelle, N.Y. 10805

## GENERAL

| | | |
|---|---|---|
| Curb weight, lb/kg | 4330 | 1964 |
| Test weight | 4435 | 2011 |
| Weight dist (with driver), f/r, % | 50/50 | |
| Wheelbase, in./mm | 102.8 | 2611 |
| Track, front/rear | 59.0/59.0 | 1499/1499 |
| Length | 189.5 | 4813 |
| Width | 72.0 | 1829 |
| Height | 54.0 | 1372 |
| Ground clearance | 5.5 | 140 |
| Overhang, f/r | 39.4/47.3 | 1001/1201 |
| Trunk space, cu ft/liters | 6.4 | 181 |
| Fuel capacity, U.S. gal./liters | 27.5 | 104 |

## MAINTENANCE

Service intervals, mi:

| | |
|---|---|
| Oil/filter change | 5000/5000 |
| Chassis lube | 5000 |
| Tuneup | 30,000 |
| Warranty, mo/mi | 24/24,000 |

## ENGINE

| | | |
|---|---|---|
| Type | | dohc V-8 |
| Bore x stroke, in./mm | 3.94 x 3.35 | 100.0 x 85.0 |
| Displacement, cu in./cc | 326 | 5340 |
| Compression ratio | | 8.0:1 |
| Bhp @ rpm, SAE net/kW | est 300/224 @ 5600 | |
| Equivalent mph / km/h | 144 / 232 | |
| Torque @ rpm, lb-ft/Nm | est 350/474 @ 4500 | |
| Equivalent mph / km/h | 117 / 188 | |
| Carburetion | | four Weber (2V) |
| Fuel requirement | | unleaded, 91-oct |

Exhaust-emission control equipment: four catalytic converters, two air pumps

## DRIVETRAIN

| | |
|---|---|
| Transmission | 5-sp manual |

Gear ratios: 5th (0.84) .......... 2.97:1

| | |
|---|---|
| 4th (1.00) | 3.54:1 |
| 3rd (1.22) | 4.32:1 |
| 2nd (1.78) | 6.30:1 |
| 1st (2.90) | 10.27:1 |
| Final drive ratio | 3.54:1 |

## CALCULATED DATA

| | |
|---|---|
| Lb/bhp (test weight) | 14.8 |
| Mph/1000 rpm (5th gear) | 26.5 |
| Engine revs/mi (60 mph) | 2260 |
| Piston travel, ft/mi | 1260 |
| R&T steering index | 1.10 |
| Brake swept area, sq in./ton | 211 |

## CHASSIS & BODY

| | |
|---|---|
| Layout | front engine/rear drive |

Body/frame ....steel platform frame & body superstructure, aluminum panels

Brake system......10.8-in. (274-mm) vented discs front, 10.4-in. (264-mm) vented discs rear; vacuum asst

| | | |
|---|---|---|
| Swept area, sq in./sq cm | 468 | 3019 |
| Wheels | | cast alloy, 15 x 7 |
| Tires | | Avon Turbo Steel 70, 235/70HR-15 |
| Steering type | | rack & pinion, power assisted |
| Turns, lock-to-lock | | 2.9 |
| Turning circle, ft/m | 38.0 | 11.6 |

Front suspension: unequal-length A-arms, coil springs, tube shocks, anti-roll bar

Rear suspension: De Dion axle on trailing arms & Watt linkage, coil springs, tube shocks

## INSTRUMENTATION

Instruments: 85-mph speedo, 7000-rpm tach, 99,999 odo, 999.9 trip odo, oil press., oil temp, coolant temp, ammeter, fuel level, clock

Warning lights: oil press., brake sys, ignition, low fuel, choke on, catalyst overheat, rear-window heat, seatbelts, hazard, high beam, directionals

## ACCOMMODATION

| | | |
|---|---|---|
| Seating capacity, persons | | 4 |
| Head room, f/r, in./mm | 38.0/36.0 | 965/914 |
| Seat width, f/r | .2 x 21.5/2 x 18.5 | .2 x 546/2 x 470 |
| Seatback adjustment, deg | | 75 |

# ROAD TEST RESULTS

## ACCELERATION

Time to distance, sec:

| | |
|---|---|
| 0-100 ft | 3.6 |
| 0-500 ft | 9.2 |
| 0-1320 ft (¼ mi) | 16.8 |
| Speed at end of ¼ mi, mph | 84.5 |

Time to speed, sec:

| | |
|---|---|
| 0-30 mph | 3.1 |
| 0-50 mph | 6.9 |
| 0-60 mph | 8.9 |
| 0-70 mph | 11.4 |
| 0-80 mph | 15.0 |
| 0-100 mph | 25.5 |

## SPEEDS IN GEARS

| | |
|---|---|
| 5th gear (5500 rpm) | est 142 |
| 4th (6000) | 131 |
| 3rd (6000) | 109 |
| 2nd (6000) | 76 |
| 1st (6000) | 47 |

## FUEL ECONOMY

| | |
|---|---|
| Normal driving, mpg | 13.0 |
| Cruising range, mi (1-gal. res) | 344 |

## HANDLING

| | |
|---|---|
| Lateral accel, 100-ft radius, g | 0.667 |

## BRAKES

Minimum stopping distances, ft:

| | |
|---|---|
| From 60 mph | 165 |
| From 80 mph | 291 |
| Control in panic stop | good |
| Pedal effort for 0.5g stop, lb | 35 |

Fade: percent increase in pedal effort to maintain 0.5g deceleration in 6 stops from 60 mph ....nil

| | |
|---|---|
| Overall brake rating | good |

## INTERIOR NOISE

| | |
|---|---|
| Idle in neutral, dBA (top up) | 58 |
| Maximum, 1st gear | 84 |
| Constant 30 mph | 66 |
| 50 mph | 70 |
| 70 mph | 76 |
| 90 mph | 82 |

## SPEEDOMETER ERROR

| | |
|---|---|
| 30 mph indicated is actually | 27.5 |
| 60 mph | 57.0 |

## ACCELERATION

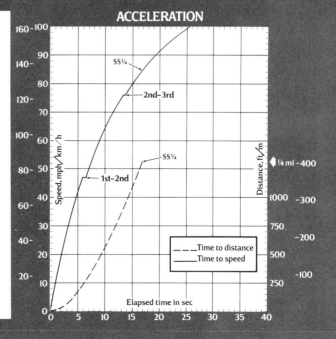

byproduct of the somewhat old-fashioned induction equipment, the engine now has four catalytic converters and two air pumps to meet current emission standards.

Each Aston Martin engine is individually assembled and bears a plaque with the assembler's name inscribed on it. The 4-camshaft engine is exceedingly handsome and the engine compartment in general is surprisingly uncluttered for such a complicated car; those items that require regular servicing are relatively accessible. What we have here is the long-familiar Aston Martin V-8 of 5340 cc, driving through a ZF 5-speed transmission in our test car although a Chrysler TorqueFlite automatic is available as an option and more commonly installed in production. Aston Martin gives no power figures for the engine, but it must be very substantial because the car weighs well over two tons and can accelerate to 60 mph in less than 9 seconds. In that last test (see the 1979 *Guide*) the 0–60 time was 1.5 sec quicker, however, and though this car weighed 200 lb more, that wouldn't fully account for the loss in performance. We therefore estimate the engine's output at about 300 bhp, down from our earlier estimate of 340—substantial output indeed in these days of anemic engines. It would be a pleasure to try a European version without the fetters of all those emission-control devices.

The engine is mechanically quiet, its major sounds coming from the cooling fan and the exhaust's throaty burble. Everything went well with the test car's engine until we went to the track for our performance tests. After a few runs it started to lose power, which was eventually traced to a catalytic converter that had started to collapse internally. After repairs, we got the performance figures shown in the data panel. Generally, when driven hard the engine exhibited no traces of over-carburetion, nor of being excessively leaned out or retarded, as is sometimes the case with high-performance carbureted engines that have been modified to meet emission-control regulations. But even after a thorough going-over, our test car's engine—one of the first 1981s in the U.S.—never would run quite cleanly at high revs. Instead, somewhere above 4500 rpm, it would always falter momentarily before going on toward its useful limit of 6000 rpm.

To stop all the momentum generated by the (estimated) 300 bhp and 4200-plus lb, Aston Martin fits ventilated disc brakes with vacuum assistance; for directional control rack-and-pinion steering is used with power assistance. Though the Volante's front suspension is garden variety, at the rear there is unusual chassis engineering with a De Dion tube on trailing arms and a Watt linkage, sprung by coils.

With previous versions of the car, we were critical of a harsh ride at low speeds and the excessive brake-pedal effort required to stop the car. The harshness at low speeds has been much reduced by the use of different shock absorbers and tires. The latter are Avon Turbo Steel 235/70HR-15, Avon being a relatively small tire company in England to which Aston Martin has been faithful for a long time, particularly during the racing years. The

Avons of our test car, of a rather soft mix to complement the convertible's nature and structure, tended to squeal considerably in low-speed cornering and the car did not have very impressive cornering power on the skidpad, although it remained essentially neutral throughout. Unfortunately, the excessive brake-pedal effort remains although the brakes do haul the car down fairly well from speeds far beyond the legal limit.

The 5-speed ZF transmission works well and precisely but requires considerable effort to shift. Its shift pattern is unusual in that 1st is to the left and toward you with reverse opposite. The movement from 4th to 5th is not quite a straight line, which means that until you get used to it you have to be conscious of what you are doing when shifting from 4th to 5th to avoid ending up in 3rd.

However, once out on the open road, the car is responsive enough, endowed as it is with nearly 5.5 liters of exotic engine. Of course, one pays a price for this type of performance, and the price is a fuel consumption rate of 13.0 mpg. However, it can be assumed that the owner of a car such as the Aston Martin Volante, which carries a price tag of $115,000, is much more interested in the availability of gasoline than the price.

Actually, the Volante is a relic of the grand days of grand touring when you could drive as fast as you liked, gasoline was something you merely shelled out a few bucks for and the peasants just kept out of your way. Unfortunately, or fortunately, those days are long gone, and Aston's new boss Victor Gauntlett is well aware of the economic and social changes that have taken place in recent years. Rumors are that a new and much smaller model, to be produced fairly soon, will be of about BMW 530i size and be priced at about $30,000 in today's dollars.

There is a wealth of talent at Aston Martin and a loyal labor force that takes pride in its skills, but until now it has not been possible to make full use of these assets because of a lack of working capital. It is the intention of Gauntlett to change the situation and we can expect to see some interesting developments from Aston Martin in the mid-Eighties.

# Aston Martin's Lagonda

## Simply superb

IF your only experience of the fabulous Lagonda was through city traffic you could be forgiven for thinking of it as just another very comfortable, even sumptuous, slightly noisy, fuel-guzzling giant of a car. You would be right about the sumptuous comfort, the size and the fact that it uses fuel in large quantities. It is certainly noisier at low speeds than many relatively mundane cars, but you would be very wrong about the "just another", for in the Lagonda is a unique blend of the best in luxury car comfort with sports-car road manners and performance.

That drive through city traffic would have left you in no doubt about the status the Lagonda imparts to those lucky enough to ride in it, for all heads turn, realising instantly that this is no motor car for ordinary mortals. Its sleek and elegant lines attract stares like no Ferrari or Rolls-Royce, and despite the fact that "Lagonda" appears in letters only a quarter of an inch high on each wheel trim and in the centre of the dummy radiator grille, an astonishing number of pedestrians can be seen mouthing the name: to run a Lagonda is to belong to a very exclusive and privileged group, for only some 160 have been built so far, and many of those have been exported.

When the prototype, William Towns designed, Aston Martin Lagonda first appeared at the London Motor Show in 1976, it caused a sensation and was undoubtedly the star of the show. Its immense length and wedge-shaped styling drew the crowds as much as did the novel electronically controlled instruments and the panels of touch switches — "practical futurism with sophisticated style and splendid luxury" was how we described it at the time. In the intervening years, the design has undergone the transition from prototype to production and there have been one or two changes to detail as Aston Martin's policy of continuous development has borne fruit. However, the major specification is just the same as that prototype, and it is a credit to the design team at Aston Martin that they should have achieved such excellent results from the word go with such limited resources for development and testing.

The quality of craftsmanship which goes into any Aston Martin product is a throw-back to an age when only the best was good enough: any doubts about the loving care which goes into the production of these cars is soon dispelled by a visit to the Newport Pagnell factory (see MOTOR SPORT for October 1980) and the Lagonda we had for an all too brief test was a shining example of this devotion to quality. With 11,000 miles, many of them no doubt very hard, showing on its under-bonnet odometer, the only signs that it was not a new car were slight wear on the pedal rubbers, two small chips in the silver paint where a careless petrol pump attendant had allowed the nozzle to catch the paintwork, a slight rattle from the perspex instrument display cover, a smaller, very occasional tick from the passenger door and wear on the tyres.

A steel monocoque forms the basis of the load bearing structure and this is clad with aluminium panels: linen tape is trapped between the two, preventing any electrolytically induced corrosion. The body is carefully inhibited at each stage of its construction, heavily undersealed and is given innumerable coats of paint, carefully rubbed down, before final assembly.

Front suspension is by coil springs located by unequal length wishbones and damped with co-axial telescopic shock absorbers; the king pins are ball-jointed. At the rear is an up-rated version of the De Dion arrangement used for the sports cars which is located by trailing parallel arms and a Watts linkage; coil springs are used and damping is by self-levelling telescopic shock-absorbers. The 15″ steel wheels are shod with 235 / 70 HR Avon Turbosteel tyres.

The engine is, of course, the familiar, all alloy 90°, V8 unit, with four camshafts, which has been in production for many years now. In Lagonda guise, it has a 9.5:1 compression ratio and is equipped with four Weber 42 DNCF carburetters and Lucas electronic ignition. Power outputs are not quoted, and the maximum engine speed permissible (intermittently) is 6,250 r.p.m. Drive to the rear wheels is taken through a Chrysler Torqueflite three-speed automatic gear box (there is no manual option) and a limited slip differential. The final drive assembly is rubber mounted, and the overall ratio is 3.07:1 which Aston Martin quote as giving 24 m.p.h. per 1,000 r.p.m. in top.

Inside, the Lagonda is staggeringly opulent. The test car had pale blue Connolly leather upholstery, with dark blue piping along the seams at the seat edges. The same dark blue leather was used for trimming the edges of the matching
*Continued*

## LAGONDA — continued

Wilton carpeting and for the facing of the rear parcel shelf. The top of the dash was of black leather and the head-lining was a pale grey felt. Walnut veneer trims for the doors and dash complete the furnishings.

The front seats are adjustable over a wide range, using six of the press buttons fitted in a control panel in each door. With their loose leather facings, these seats are a joy to sit in for hours on end, and provide excellent location, although one passenger complained that the squab was too short for the long-legged. High head-rests are fitted, but may be removed to give the rear-seat passengers a chance to see where they are going. The rear seats are fixed, but are equally comfortable. Inertia reel seat belts are fitted front and rear, those at the back disappearing into slots high on the seat shoulder. The central armrest separating the two rear seats can be folded away to provide room for an occasional fourth passenger. Legroom at the back is good, but not as much as one might expect from the tremendous overall length of the car, since the

*THE quality of the upholstery and interior trim is of the very best. Faced with Connolly hide, the seats are extremely comfortable and there is plenty of room for four, or occasionally five, to travel in opulent comfort, although rear-seat passengers will find their forward view restricted by the large headrests on the backs of the front seats.*

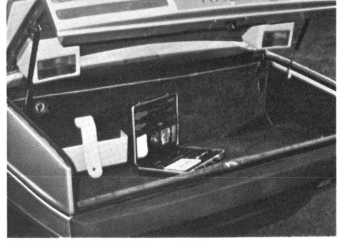

*DAUNTING at first sight, the unique instrumentation and switching of the Lagonda are easy to learn and simple to use.*

*LUGGAGE capacity is not as large as might be expected being reduced by the secondary rear-lamp clusters and the brief-case full of tools.*

mechanism required for the electrical adjustment of the front seats means that it is impossible for the rear passengers to slide their feet under the front seats.

The transmission tunnel is a substantial hump, surmounted by a leather trimmed centre console which extends back to between the front seats, containing ashtrays and cigar lighters, front and rear, the excellent Pioneer stereo radio and cassette player, an oddments tray alongside the gear selector, and a lockable bin as well as a neatly covered fuse-box. Surprisingly, there is no glove box above the passenger's knees — the space being entirely taken up with the air-conditioning plant. Map pockets are let into the backs of the front seats and the speakers for the stereo system are concealed behind perforated leather facings in the front doors and the rear parcel shelf.

Visibility from the driver's seat is generally excellent, although with the long, low nose and the high rear it is difficult to judge length when manoeuvring, and the broad base to the windscreen pillar creates something of a blind spot at certain road junctions, as well as partially

obscuring the optional extra near side rear-view mirror. A fixed tinted glass panel in the roof over the rear seat passengers' legs ensures that plenty of light reaches the interior of the car, although we can imagine the air-conditioning plant having to work overtime on a bright summer's day. Surprisingly, the windows in the rear doors are not openable — the controls for the front windows being in the door switch panels, as well as the seat controls and joy-sticks for external mirror adjustments. Neat sun-visors are covered with the same material as used for the head lining, but it is surprising to note that Aston Martin have not fitted a vanity mirror.

Settling in to the driver's seat for the first time is something of a daunting experience, for the controls are like no other car. Flanking the small diameter, leather rimmed, single spoke steering wheel are two panels containing no less than seventeen touch switches, three rotating rheostat switches and a slide lever. Above these panels is a large blank, black fascia behind a perspex screen, and in front of that, the bonnet disappearing into the distance. In the door is another panel

containing fourteen more switches — the passenger is let off with only ten in the nearside door panel. A twist of the ignition key, and the blank space starts to come alive as the digital display instruments record the state of the various functions.

Turning the key further activates the starter motor, and with the throttle just open by a hair's breadth, the engine will fire and settle down to a 700 r.p.m. tick over, if it is warm. If not, a couple of vigorous pumps on the throttle pedal are required, followed by a half minute warm up period with the engine running at some 2,500 r.p.m. before it will settle down. Engine r.p.m. is displayed in large red figures at the top left of the instrument display, directly below the speedometer. Moving the gear selector back from park, through reverse and neutral to drive requires gentle pressure on the selector lever knob to overcome the safety detents, which prevent inadvertent selection of bottom or neutral while on the move, and causes a flurry of activity on the display as the illuminated monitor records the

*Continued*

*EACH front door has a switch panel — that on the driver's side controlling seat adjustment, the central locking, window opening and mirror adjustments.*

*DOMINATED by the air intake for the four Weber carburetters, the under-bonnet view of the Lagonda is an example of purposeful planning, with every available space being used. The red air horns ("country horns") are by Maserati and are backed up by mellow sounding "town horns".*

position of the selector lever.

The hand brake, acting on the rear discs through independent calipers, holds the car against the natural drag of the transmission but once released (by raising the lever to the right of the driver's seat, depressing the button and lowering the lever again) the car edges forward at a fast walking pace with the engine still at tickover. With gentle pressure on the accelerator, the car glides away with a gentle wuffle from the exhausts, and is soon in top gear, the torque converter smoothing out the changes. Heavier pressure, and the Lagonda leaps forward, accompanied by a strong exhaust note as the revs rise quickly between changes.

Our first few tentative miles were through the thick of a London rush hour as we made our way across town from our City offices to the M4. Insulated from the outside world by the luxury of the interior, and with the radio for company, the stop-go traffic was rather less frustrating than usual, in fact it was almost a pleasure to be traffic-bound, but we were very conscious of the size of the Lagonda (longer by an inch than a Silver Spirit, but slightly narrower and seven inches lower) and rather disappointed at first with the level of noise coming through to the passenger compartment from the exhaust, especially during brief bursts of moderate acceleration. Significant road noise was also apparent, especially over poor surfaces.

Moving the large car through traffic proved to be no problem — the rapid response to the accelerator, excellent brakes and good all round visibility enabling us to join in the cut and thrust of Hyde Park corner with confidence. Once through the West End and on the approach to the M4, the controls, switches and digital instruments were all becoming familiar, the column of five red digital figures on the right for percentage of fuel remaining, oil pressure, oil temperature, coolant temperature and ambient temperature (either internal or external, to choice) balanced the two larger figures on the left, and the time, trip-mileage and battery voltage were all displayed centrally, together with the information that the side lights were on, and the gear selector was in drive.

As the flow of traffic speeded up passing Windsor and Slough, so it became apparent that the Lagonda is in fact a very quiet car; not so silky-silent as a V12 Jaguar, or so refined as a Rolls-Royce, but cruising at a steady 60 m.p.h., there is slight rumble from the tyres, no noticeable exhaust noise and only the occasional thump from the suspension as the car runs over some of the worse repairs to the road surface.

Beyond Maidenhead, and out of the sodium lights, we began to feel that the digital display was overbright for comfortable night driving: no problem. On the right panel is a rheostat switch which enables the driver to reduce the intensity of the display, while above the left knee is another rheostat to dim or extinguish the lamp which illuminates the display and switches from above; rather surprisingly, the switches were not illuminated from behind. A further reduction in interference from the controls can be achieved by pressing the "eso" (essential services only) switch, which extinguishes all figures but the speedometer, clock and fuel gauge. If any of the other functions reach danger level, the eso facility is over-ridden and the relevant display flashes.

With clear road in front, at last, driver effort was further reduced by making use of the cruise control. Easily set by pressing the "engage" switch when cruising at the desired speed, the control will maintain that speed far more accurately than the most diligent driver until it is either over-ridden by use of the accelerator — for instance when overtaking — or cancelled by touching the brakes. In the first instance, the cruising speed will automatically be resumed once the accelerator is released while, in the latter, normal control is maintained until the "resume" switch is operated.

As our plans involved an early start the following day, we called at a filling station to replenish the 28-gallon tank. There are fillers in each rear-quarter, covered with flaps which are opened by pressing the appropriate switch in the right-hand panel. Unlike so many cars equipped with twin fillers, the Lagonda fills easily and quickly without having to release the second cap. Nineteen gallons sloshed merrily in and the fuel gauge, which had been reading 5% (indicating 1.4 gallons remaining, in addition to the five gallon reserve) rose to read 82%, despite the fact that there was no possibility of encouraging any more fuel into the tank. This reduced our faith in the accuracy of the gauge, although, of course, it was no more inaccurate than the gauge in many an expensive car which reads empty when there are still five gallons left, and never reads completely full . . . it's just that putting a numerical value to the contents of the fuel tank implies a greater degree of accuracy!

Removing the ignition key activates the automatic central locking system, and requires some care. At the end of our first journey, after parking the car, we felt it appropriate to make some notes. But what more natural than to turn the engine off and remove the key before doing understeer significantly, particularly in the damp conditions, but it didn't, having the neutral handling of a small sporting saloon.

Once properly acquainted with the car's characteristics, it was easy to maintain our rapid speed along this windy road, keeping the car taut and providing a comfortable ride. XJ-S passengers would have felt reasonably happy keeping up, but anyone foolish enough to have told the chauffeur to try in a Rolls would not have been at all well.

We found the automatic down change rather too sensitive for a car with such massive torque available at quite modest engine r.p.m.; when applying gentle pressure to the accelerator to increase speed when coming out of, say, a fifty mile an hour corner, the gearbox would, as likely as not, change down only to change up a few yards later. With experience, it was easy to prevent this happening and so maintain the smoothest possible ride, but it did mean that there was not much between a gentle gaining of momentum and a burst of rapid acceleration in second. However, we had many miles to go, and were quite content with the latter.

From rest, like most automatics, the Lagonda seems to take time to gather its skirts before running, even on full throttle. Our best time to 60 m.p.h. on the digital speedometer (which was accurate at that speed) was a shade over nine seconds, which is not particularly impressive, even taking into account the two tons kerb weight. Most of that nine seconds is taken getting to 30 m.p.h., by which time the engine is revving freely, and the power being produced. In drive, on full throttle, up changes take place at just over 50 m.p.h. and 80 m.p.h., but using the manual over-ride these speeds can be extended to nearly 70 m.p.h. and well over 100 m.p.h. at the 6,250 r.p.m. limit. Using the over-ride, the magic "ton" comes up in just on 20 seconds, and 120 m.p.h. in half a minute — impressive by any standards.

Equally impressive is the fade free stopping power of the huge ventilated-disc brakes which inspired confidence and were able to stop the massive car very quickly.

With this kind of performance on tap, our progress through the Welsh countryside was hardly hindered by slow moving vehicles. The Lagonda, now feeling much smaller and more compact as we were fully accustomed to it, being able to take advantage of the smallest section of clear road for safe overtaking, when, of course, the sensitive automatic down-change is useful, although we would still rather use the manual over-ride and choose when the change in ratio is to be made.

By now, deep in rural Wales, the roads were absolutely filthy, and we had to stop to clear the door windows of splashed mud to restore safe side vision. The Lagonda was plastered. Despite the deep spoiler across the back of the car, the swirl of air behind us must have created a real whirl of mud-laden moisture in our wake for the AML 1 number plate was quite unreadable, and the car had been clean only 150 miles previously. In these conditions extra caution was necessary, for the Avon tyres, designed primarily for carrying a heavy car in smooth comfort and hush, were giving hints of not coping quite as well as we had expected from our experience on damp roads earlier in the day, and we did not feel inclined to try sliding the Lagonda around!

Heading back, after our journey through Powys, to Hereford and Gloucester during the early afternoon the occasional drizzle, with which the adjustable delay wipe mechanism had coped admirably, gave way to gentle rain and then to heavy rain as we approached Cirencester. Surprisingly, we found we had to reduce speed to maintain visibility, since even on fast speed the wipers would not cope with the heavy down-pour.

By the time we finished the day's motoring, having been up to London for the Aston Martin Owners Club annual prize-giving (appropriately enough), the Lagonda had covered 550 miles of very varied motoring and this driver, having driven for over 500 of them, was feeling no more tired than if he had sat in an armchair all day.

The remainder of our 800 mile stint with the car was spent on short journeys, for which it proved just as comfortable and useful as it had for the longer trip. Parking such a large car in a busy high street is obviously difficult, since large enough gaps do not appear very often, but with reflections on shop windows to assist in judging length, it is easy enough to manoeuvre. The boot, which may be opened either with the key or by pressing a button in the central cubby box, is not as large as anyone brought up on a diet of Rolls-Royces might expect, and care has to be taken when loading it to ensure that room is left for the duplicate rear-lamp cluster fitted to the underside of the boot-lid — necessary because the main tail lights are arranged along the edge of the boot.

Fuel consumption over the 800 miles worked out at an average of 13.5 m.p.g., but in view of the poor conditions and press-on style of driving, an owner could expect better than 15 m.p.g. The oil level on the dipstick (no electronically controlled gauge for this) had hardly decreased.

If the test car was our own, we would request attention to the erratically reading fuel gauge, a faster fast wipe, and a less sensitive down-change when taking it for its next service. Other than these quibbles, which are very minor, it is very difficult to fault this glorious car.

How much? Rather like having your shoes made by Lobb, your jewellery cleaned at Asprey, or your saddlery prepared by Swaine, Adeney Brigg & Sons, if you have to ask, you can't afford it. Priced to give only pennies change from £53,500, it is one of the most expensive cars on the market — it feels like it to drive it and to ride in it. Quality is hardly ever cheap.

P.H.J.W

CONTINUED FROM PAGE 50

ment and quite solid knocks traversing expansion joints.

You won't find a machine more bored with the 55-mph speed limit. Loafing along just about doesn't warm its oil. You need 80 on the dial before things start happening the way they should.

In the twisty sections, the shifter should stay in third to keep revs over four grand where the cam profiles can do some good. You grip the big steering wheel firmly and feed in the orders with broad, decisive sweeps of your wrists. The on-center steering vagueness that haunts low-speed tracking vanishes, and the tire tread feels like it's at your fingertips. Ride harshness fades as the speed goes up and the V-8 hits stride.

Rushing deep into switchbacks is a breeze because the brakes quickly burn off all the speed the engine can muster on the short straights. The hard Avon rubber is silent in its work until one tire scratches at the limit of adhesion. A front wheel is the first to slide, both in braking and cornering, so the tail of the car always stays politely in line.

As the road unwinds, the Aston Martin's natural gait shifts upward. The top limit is 135 mph, so you have essentially a land-bound Learjet at your disposal. This may seem narrowly applicable to grounded double-zero agents, but law-abiding citizens seem to enjoy the V-8 as well. It is best suited to wide open plains and long day journeys, but good outward visibility helps diminish the usual anxiety over driving such exotica in congested cities. And a forwarding party isn't necessary for the luggage, since the spare is under the floor and the fuel tank is situated over the rear axle.

The interior carries four in a highly functional level of luxury. The wraparound of the back seats is a bit confining, but the walls are spaced wide enough and the ceiling high enough that no one should feel encapsulated. Top priority of course goes to front occupants with such considerations as an adjustable footrest, eight vent registers and the mystical Blaupunkt Berlin stereo radio stalk. The leather seats are more in the tough-hide, 50-year vein than the kid-glove Italian school.

Driving is treated as serious business in the Aston Martin, and the sweep of dials and controls tell you there are things you must know and do to stay on top of the situation. The speedometer will clock you to 200 mph if necessary. The handbrake is also fairly unique among the world's cars. Pushing the top button locks the lever in a braking position rather than releasing it. This fly-off design is made to order for hillclimb starts and bootleg turns.

The driver is also asked to tolerate a few British eccentricities like the centigrade scale for oil and water temperature plus a few strange markings like "Demist" and "Flick-wipe." This is much less an imposition than the slightly awkward seating position. The foot pedals are too close to the seat for the steering wheel's position. The gear lever is also too far back so it takes a tight kink through the elbow to shift. The last irritation is the ignition-switch location, which is right where a tall person's right knee would prefer it not to be.

On the whole, none of these complaints could dent the repute of such an aristocratic automobile. The Aston Martin V-8 is one of those dearly satisfying concoctions from the past that we are lucky to experience today. And craftsmanship like this should never be allowed to fade quietly into the history books. ●

# The Nimrod Aston Martin

The All-British entry prepared for Le Mans

# Aston's return

*This month sees the 50th 24-hour race at Le Mans ... and the return of Aston Martin.*
*MICHAEL BOWLER charts the background to the Nimrod project*

CHASSIS NUMBERS of ERAs, Maserati 250Fs and famous registration numbers can slip off the tongue with all the familiarity of a childhood nursery rhyme. Aston Martins too have their share of numerical mystique. To the pre-war enthusiast it is the works LM series that have the cachet; post-war and registration numbers like VMFs and EMUs hold sway with the DB2 and DB3S, while the limited edition DBR1 is now recalled by chassis number. Then there came a mere handful of four that were called by their design number; as the Mini was once ADO 15, so Aston Martin used DP, or Design Project.

In hindsight, other Astons have been called by their project number and the 1959 DP199 was the prototype DB4GT, but the three prototype designs for GT cars in 1962 and 1963 were familiarly called Project 212, 214 (two cars) and 215 at the time. Project 212 has hardly stopped racing since and has been owned since 1964 by Viscount Downe, who raced it at that time under the Dawnay Racing banner, and we will return to him later. Only one of the 214s survives and that is being rebuilt at present, while 215 has been recreated to more or less original form after a major road accident.

To all but the factory, the project numbers stopped there but the DP book has continued and twenty years on some 1,000 designs have been added, mostly on development of Aston Martin and Lagonda passenger cars, although latterly other Tickford work has been included, such as the Frazer Tickford Metro, the Lancia Hi-Fi and the Toyota Sunchaser. A glance at a couple of recent entries will show that the factory were engaged upon producing 520 and 560 bhp versions of their familiar all-aluminium production V-8; the 520bhp version with carburettors is DP1231, while the fuel injected version giving around 560bhp was started earlier and is covered under DP1229, a vital part of the Nimrod project.

So what is Nimrod? Despite the fact that Aston Martin Lagonda is moving in the right financial direction, it will be many years, if ever, before the factory that gave Britain its only World Sports Car Championship could contemplate a return to racing. There are, however, plenty of people who want to put the name of Aston Martin back on the modern tracks — mostly the same people who keep the flag flying by racing the historic Astons. One such long-standing Aston supporter — as well as dealer and restorer — is Robin Hamilton, whose premises near Burton-on-Trent have long resounded to the song of Aston racing engines, both six cylindered and eight-cylindered.

To sports car enthusiasts Le Mans is Mecca; Robin had been to Le Mans twice in the seventies with a highly developed version of a standard Aston Martin V-8, once in normally aspirated form when the car lasted the full 24-hours but finished outside its allowed average speed, and once with twin turbo-chargers but the now lowered car failed to last the distance. To return to the great French circuit with the right tools for the job became Robin's ambition, however long it was to take.

In fact the opportunity was to come fairly soon. People were becoming tired of the nominal sports cars that had contested the world's championships since the days of the Porsche 917 — its replacements were merely two-seater GP cars detuned to last longer and with little road-going justification. The Americans had seen this first and had introduced GT Prototypes with a 1000kg minimum weight and a production connection for the engine according to its size. Finally the world ruling body, the FISA, announced back in 1979 that they too were going to adopt this principle for the 1982 season; unfortunately it has taken most of the intervening two and a half years to finalise the rules and they were still changing them in January 1982!

In essence they learnt from the American GTP rules, but decided to cut the minimum weight limit to 800kg and establish a production connection by the simple expedient of saying that the engine has to come from a manufacturer who has a car homologated in the new Groups A or B (i.e. 5000 or 200 cars a year); it doesn't have to come from one of those cars, just one of those car-makers who can build any form of racing or prototype engine, and, since that applies to all the current Grand Prix engines bar the Hart we haven't actually made the desired progress — Ford hurriedly reacquired the Cosworth which keeps most of the established race-car constructors happy, like Lola, March, Rondeau to name but half a field, leaving Porsche to look at one of the many shelves in their research department while Aston Martin, who produce the ideal engine for a stock-block formula could only keep developing what was fundamentally a fifteen year old design, albeit considerably strengthened over the years. Hopefully the new formula — Group C — will continue further down the path of sanity and ask for production-derived engines.

However there is a sting in the tail for the engine rules as the FISA have brought in a minimum fuel consumption requirement which stipulates the maximum amount of fuel to be carried at 100 litres and the number of fuel stops at roughly one per hour — for a high speed race like Le Mans this is equivalent to 6½ mpg, but for the shorter six-hour 'sprints' it works out at nearer 4.8 mpg, but the emphasis is placed firmly on fuel efficient engines and low drag shapes; these are dictated only in minimum height, a requirement for two decent-sized equal seats and a flat floor section between the wheels to reduce the unnatural ground effect that GP cars can obtain.

Initially then, Robin Hamilton decided to embark on the production of a GTP to American rules and approached Lola designer Eric Broadley to create and build a suitable chassis; this Broadley did and Hamilton was able to start building his car with his own body, wind-tunnel-developed at MIRA, in mid-1980 as and when time and funds allowed, with the start of the 1982 season as the goal and Le Mans 1982 in particular. Since then rules have decreed that Le Mans can't be your first race in a season but, more importantly, that whoever builds the chassis the engine maker comes first — i.e. Ford-Lola not vice versa.

At this stage in the story Robin Hamilton still had a part-completed car in January 1981

when Aston Martin Lagonda underwent one of its periodic changes of ownership. Custodians for the previous six years had been the American Peter Sprague and Alan Curtis; during 1980 their board, which also included Denis Flather and Peter Cadbury had been joined by Tim Hearley of CH Industrials (formerly Coventry Hood and Sidescreen) and Victor Gauntlett of Pace Petroleum. Come 1981 and Sprague and Curtis felt they had done their stuff and were ready to hand over to someone, which left Hearley and Gauntlett with little option but to rule the roost themselves as joint Chairmen with the Pace Chairman taking the Executive role. Newsmen, knowing of Victor's love of old cars and racing, soon asked when Aston would return to the racing field; the answer could only be that, much though Victor would love the chance, Aston Martin as then constituted would be unlikely ever to have the money or chance, although the possibility was one of the early studies undertaken by the engineering department.

Robin Hamilton needed little more encouragement and rapidly invited the Aston executive to visit the Fauld workshops where Le Mans car building was making only steady progress. It didn't take too long for the two to reach an amicable agreement and for Victor to introduce a third party, Peter Livanos from

Aston Martin's American subsidiary — sadly rule changes, which made American and European rules ultimately so different, divorced the American, leaving Hamilton and Gauntlett to found Nimrod Racing Automobiles after almost more discussion on the name than on the articles of association. Nimrod was to build up no fewer than five chassis, three for the team and two as spares or for sale to other teams; the existing first chassis was to continue although by then it was becoming obvious that it was essentially an American-spec IMSA car, but it was to be a useful development mule. Part of the Nimrod deal was that Aston Martin Tickford would produce the engines for the cars hence the DP numbers. Work started on the fuel-injected version straight away as it was felt that this had to be the most efficient way to go for the right combination of power and consumption, but that the factory would also produce less powerful carburettor engines for preliminary chassis/car development.

With the added impetus of fresh capital injection work proceeded quite rapidly and the Goodwood launch part date was met with no all-nighters on November 19th. In fact shakedown runs had already started at a private test-track near the Hamilton works. That Goodwood day was a highly successful launch; Stirling Moss, Jack Fairman and Eric

Thompson represented the old guard of Aston racing, James Hunt, Derek Bell and Nigel Mansell were relatively modern while the future possibles included Bob Evans, Tiff Needell and Chris Craft. With superb weather and a lunch in Goodwood House it was memorable stuff.

With the bally-hoo successfully over for the time being, work continued in testing of car and suitable drivers. The intention had always been to get good British drivers who weren't still wanting to prove their F1 potential in Nimrod's cars; of the three possibles at Goodwood, Chris Craft stayed with the Japanese Dome but Evans and Needell joined the team with the 1981 F2 champion Geoff Lees having the added virtue of living in Atherstone, not too far from Hamilton. Ray Mallock also did much useful test mileage as the car gradually took its final form in a fairly normal series of test-days based on Silverstone; the times started to come down and the car was comfortably under 1m.30s., which had been Derek Bell's fastest time in the Porsche 917 at the Silverstone British GP meeting that year, by the close of the season, which, for Nimrod, included a December trip to the Dubai GP meeting to help wave the Aston flag in the United Arab Emirates, in fact Derek Bell drove the car at Dubai and did much of the early testing, which was characteristically generous of the two times Le Mans winner already contracted to Porsche for this year.

There was deliberately nothing innovative about the Nimrod; endurance racing calls for reliability and driveability more then sheer speed — integrity of design and construction is more likely to last 24 hours than breathtaking ingenuity. The chassis follows established monocoque practice but it has been lightened and strengthened since the first car; engine and transmission are carried on a tubular framework cantilevered from the rear bulkhead which has the advantage of retaining accessibility, but also means that the car can be easily adapted to carry other units — like Ford or Chevrolet for other teams. Rear suspension loads are thus fed into that bulkhead too which is the stiffest part of the car. Suspension design follows Lola practice in that it is fully adjustable over a variety of roll centres — in fact there has been little new in racing car suspension design while the Grand Prix brigade pursue their blind alley of ground effect and zero suspension travel. Ground effect under the car has been ruled out with the Group C cars, although a limited effect can be achieved at the rear from underbody tunnels, on Nimrod as well, so the bulk of downforce has to come from body-shape and rear wing.

Nimrod has been developed in the MIRA windtunnel to provide a very slippery shape with good downforce front and rear in both a straight line and in yaw (either in cornering or side winds); a recent 200mph test at Elvington showed that stability was as good as predicted. It is surprising what apparently minor changes can do to lift coefficients; just a fore-and-aft movement of that 'splitter' on the front can change lift from positive to negative lift, and,

whatever it feels like to the driver, it is reassuring for the team manager to know where he is starting.

There was a certain amount of criticism about the way that the car appeared to go at Dubai, but it was running on hard slave tyres which don't work too well on sandy ball-bearings and the wing was wooden and temporary. With a winter of refinement behind it the car started the 1982 testing well and was soon under the 1m.25s. level at Silverstone, which is quick but there was no-one with whom to compare as last year's times were all for lighter ground effect Group 6 cars, and no other Group C car was as ready as Nimrod. At that stage a halt was called on further testing of the first car while the new lighter chassis was completed with minor adaptation required for the fuel injected engine with its extra ancillaries.

Shakedown testing took place at Donington this time and it was immediately apparent that all the settings established for the first car were in fact directly transferable to the new one — practice supporting theory for once — and there was a new crispness about the handling behaviour from the more responsive injection engine. I once coined the short-lived phrase 'drive-line rigidity' after testing a Formula 3 Alexis with Daf transmission — there wasn't that solid coupling between right foot and contact patch that makes a car power responsive and controllable; an engine with a hole in the power curve just where you want it is much the same.

It was somewhat of a relief for the team that the first round at Brands Hatch was postponed till the end of the season — Nimrod was no more ready than anyone else and hadn't been tested on the humps and hollows of the

Kentish circuit. They hadn't planned to be at Monza as they didn't want the first race so far from home, so the debut will be at Silverstone for, appropriately, the Pace Six Hours. And for that there will be three Nimrods available with two of them going on to Le Mans.

The works team has been joined by none other than the owner of Aston Martin DP212, Viscount Downe, who has thus now added a DP1229 plus body and chassis to a stable that also includes DBR1/1; that is the kind of enthusiasm that Aston Martin engenders. Simon Phillips, Aston owner, who has regularly competed at Le Mans (with a Ferrari Boxer last year) with Aston specialist Richard Williams running his team, will be overall coordinator for Silverstone and Le Mans as well as probable driver. Mike Salmon, DP212's regular and Le Mans almost veteran driver, Ray Mallock (Nimrod tester and works Aston V-8 driver) and American Stephen Earle (he runs the Laguna Seca historic event) are the four from which three will be chosen for Le mans. Joining the Nimrod supporters isn't just a simple question of buying a racing car, it's more like joining a modern extension of the Aston Martin Owners Club.

Nimrod may not have been built at Aston Martin but it has certainly been produced with the blessing and goodwill of anyone who has ever had anything to do with one of Britain's most famous marques, including the two coachloads of Aston employees who are paying their way to watch and listen to their engine at Le Mans. Let's hope DP1229 will one day become as famous as DP 212, but famous in its day by winning at Le Mans.

*Photo by Peter McFadyen shows the works Aston powered Nimrod at its recent public debut at Silverstone.*

# Hard-charging
## English-style

*Gavin Green, ignoring comments about Valiant Chargers, takes to the Pom countryside with $150,000 worth of made-to-measure muscle car — Aston Martin's 240 kmlh V8 Saloon*

"GEES, IT looks like a Charger," said my Australian friend as I showed him my new road test car. The remark peeved me. I told him the body panels were aluminium and were hand-beaten into shape, that it could do a genuine 240 km/h and that the upholstery was hand-stitched leather with a burr walnut veneer dash. I told him it was worth $149,750 in Australia and that it took 20 weeks to build. But he still thought it looked like a Charger.

Over the next three days and 1600 km

I came to understand what that Philistine-like friend of mine meant. In character, the Aston Martin V8 Saloon is not unlike the Charger V8/Falcon GT/Monaro GTS350-type Aussie supercar of a bygone era, nor for that matter unlike a rorty-engined Mustang or Camaro. It is a big car, dominated by its eight-cylinder engine breathing through four twin-choke Weber carburettors. It is fast simply because it has a lot of kilowatts being pumped through its Torqueflite automatic

transmission (although a less popular ZF manual is also available). Aerodynamics? Go to Italy if you want a sports car with that. Fuel consumption? That is something seldom worried about by Aston owners. This car, you see, is plainly a muscle car, just like its now-deceased Australian brethren. The difference, though, is that the muscle of the Aston is refined and is clothed in the finest of three-piece English suits, not a pair of Stubbies and a T-shirt.

The Aston Martin V8 Saloon (actually a four-seater coupe) is the least expensive model in the four-tier range from Newport Pagnell, which has recently gone on sale in Australia following a seven-year Aston Martin drought, broken when Bob Jane became the company's importer last year. At $64,000 in England (or a whopping $149,750 in Oz), it fits in beneath the more musclebound but otherwise identical Vantage and the droptop Volante, and well beneath the $90,000 in England ($229,500 in Australia) rakish, super-luxury Lagonda.

The engine is a known quantity to Australians, dating from 1967. A monstrous-looking thing of masculine beauty, it features an aluminium alloy block and heads, four overhead camshafts and benefits from being balanced and dyno-tuned. The 5.34 litres produce 254 kW, although Aston Martin, like similarly secretive Rolls-Royce, won't tell you so. Torque is estimated at just below 550 Nm. The power is put to the ground via GKN Kent Alloy wheels wearing Avon 225VR15 tyres.

In typical Aston Martin fashion, the aluminium body is rivetted over a steel chassis, the whole package weighing 1750 kg. Front suspension is via unequal length wishbones, coil springs and an anti-roll bar while at the rear there's a de Dion axle with Watts linkage and coil springs. The rack and pinion steering is power assisted, with 2.9 turns lock to lock and a poor turning circle of 11.6 metres. Four Girling ventilated discs do the stopping.

Charger-like or not, there's no doubt this old British warhorse is a classy-looking car. The metallic blue paint of the road test machine (hand sprayed, naturally) glistened in the sun like a newly-cut diamond, the finish being mirror smooth. Inside, the white hand-stitched leather upholstery, with thin black piping, clung to the seats and dashboard like it was its natural skin. The burr walnut facia was impeccable; the thin leather three-spoked steering wheel entirely appropriate on a car of this kind.

Aston Martin's assembly standards have wallowed over the past 20 years, but there's no doubt the Newport Pagnell factory is currently turning out its best-ever product in terms of quality control. No car is better made. Perhaps as proof of this my test car, wearing its much-admired AMV8 registration plate, had not a rattle nor squeak — despite more than 32,000 km under its wheels. As a testimony to the hardness and quality of the paint, there was not a stone chip to be found, amazing for a car which must have enjoyed so much of its life on motorways at well over the legal speed limit. Only the odd creases in the leather-upholstered seats betrayed its age. Mind you, there are some complaints when it comes to inside appearance.

The air-conditioning control panel on the facia, supplied by Coolaire (which makes the air-conditioning unit) is a cheap and nasty-looking plastic affair which would look more at home on the dash of an old Chevy Impala. It's the standard after-market Coolaire fitment. Aston Martin says getting its own control panel made would be too expensive for the tiny volume of cars produced. Equally, and for the same reason, the automatic transmission selector panel is shabby.

But, these irritations aside, the dashboard is very tasteful in appearance. There is a plethora of instruments, as you'd expect of an Aston Martin. However, in typical British sports car-style they are scattered on the main console with little consideration for a driver's line of sight. With hands on the wheel only the central three gauges — tachometer, oil pressure and speedometer — are visible. The other white-on-black gauges (ammeter and fuel level to the left, water and oil temperature to the right) are blocked by the driver's hands.

A quick tug on the fly-off handbrake to the left of the driver's legs, and you're away. You quickly notice that the auto gearbox is a fairly lazy affair: give the throttle a tickle and the super powerful engine seems barely disturbed — like a sleeping bear being prodded into life by a nervous trainer. But give the engine a harder jab and it unleashes its muscle.

From rest you'll see 100 km/h in 7.3 seconds. And out on the open road, 160 km/h comes so effortlessly that it is hardly a feat at all. On to 200 and the car is still jumping forward. So you give it its reins and watch it move on to 220, the engine breathing so easily that you know more is in reserve. But you back off. The car has proved its point: the big engine will move the two-tonne brick very quickly indeed. Naturally, there is wind noise to accompany fast motoring in such a blunt-nosed car. And naturally there is some degree of high-speed wander — more than I remember from my last drive in a Porsche or Ferrari.

Through tight country lanes the Aston is surprisingly agile. It can be hustled along with real supercar-like handling and roadholding, but you're always aware it's a big car, without the sharpness of response of a Ferrari. You're still satisfied. This Aston Martin is very much a man's car: from its musclebound powertrain to the incredibly heavy (albeit power-assisted) brake pedal which many women would find physically impossible to depress. Sadly, you're aware that most people who buy this car won't give a damn about hustling along tight country lanes. Most owners are not enthusiasts.

In line with this new generation of "soft" owners, things are very comfortable and plush inside. The seats hold the occupants very well, be it in high-speed cornering or high society posing. I had not the slightest ache after 1600 rapid kilometres. The ride is also comfortable, although don't expect the suspension refinement of a Jaguar XJ. There's more mechanical noise evident with the Aston as well. Similarly, don't think that a 4667 mm long body (only 39 mm less than a VH Commodore) means plenty of room for four; it doesn't. Adults cannot fit in the back seat in comfort — there's insufficient head and leg room. And the luggage capacity is poor in relation to many similarly-sized but cheaper coupes. Nonetheless, when it comes to carrying people or goods, the Aston easily outscores most other exotics, particularly the mid-engined variety.

And, for its engine's flexibility and ease of driving, it also outscores most of its Latin competition. That engine has *so* much torque that the big car gallops up hills without a flicker of protest and without an automatic transmission changedown being necessary. Indeed, once on the move you need only one gear — top. Similarly, the car's overtaking potential is phenomenal. Following some proletarian means of transport you simply give the throttle a firm jab and conquer.

Naturally, however, the proles get their own back when it comes to refuelling time. The sight of the Aston pulling up next to the bowsers is guaranteed to please your local garage proprietor. I scored 5.1 km/l (14.5 mpg), which is better than I had anticipated.

The fuel consumption is not the only thing that makes this car somewhat of an anachronism. In most other ways, from its blunt nose to its heavyweight mass, this is a sports car from another era, arrogantly snubbing the trends which most other exotic-car makers are following. However, don't interpret that as a criticism. Rather, the Aston Martin V8 helps preserve the big-engined muscle car syndrome — and it does it in a most elegant and refined way. Personally, I'd rather have a Ferrari or a Porsche, and keep the change. But if you'd rather the hand-craftsmanship and that beautiful, effortless engine, and you have a spare $150,000, then you'll be unlikely to regret your choice. Unless, of course, someone likens it to a Valiant Charger . . .   □

# AutoTEST

# Aston Martin V8
## automatic
### *Mesomorph*

**Aston Martin V8**

June 1980 saw the introduction of mechanically revamped Aston Martin V8. Engine modifications include larger inlet valves, "Vantage" type pistons (giving 9.3 instead of 9.1 to 1 compression ratio) new "quieter" camshaft profiles and revised ignition system. Peak power (still officially unquoted) now comes at 5,000-5,500 instead of 6,000 rpm, but the torque curve is significantly flatter.

Overall efficiency is also improved via Chrysler's recently introduced TorqueFlite transmission with automatically engaging top gear lock-up.

**PRODUCED BY:**
*Aston Martin Lagonda (1975) Ltd.,*
*Tickford Street,*
*Newport Pagnell,*
*Bucks, MK16 9AN.*

**SOLD IN THE UK BY:**
*Aston Martin (Sales) Ltd.,*
*33 Sloane Street,*
*London,*
*SW1X 9NR.*

OVER THE past few years there have been times when Aston Martin looked all but extinct. They were a company caught in severe economic times, making large, powerful and thirsty cars, plus in their case, a car that is desperately expensive to produce thanks to the great proportion of pure hand crafting involved.

New backers with a more businesslike approach appeared. The product has improved, and within the last two years prices have risen dramatically. The big Aston V8 has also been made as frugal as possible.

The modifications introduced in mid-1980 were mainly aimed at improving the efficiency of Aston's 100 x 85 mm dohc 5.3 litre V8 and the associated Chrysler TorqueFlite three speed automatic transmission, which now has an automatically operating drum type clutch within the torque converter. It operates in top gear only and locks the fluid coupling at road speeds between 45 and 80 mph (dependent on throttle opening). As far as the engine is concerned the changes were aimed at further improving bottom end response and torque. Larger "Vantage" type inlet valves were fitted. The associated pistons provide a slightly higher compression ratio (9.3 instead of 9.1 to 1). Camshaft profiles have a shorter opening period, and less lift. The Lucas Opus breakerless ignition system now has a combined vacuum/air pump driven advance and retard mechanism.

Aston Martin still do not quote power outputs in this country, but in Germany they are obliged to. This huge — by current standards — all-aluminium motor produces 306 bhp (DIN) at 5,000-5,500 rpm and a massive 318 lb ft torque at 4,000 rpm. Aston say peak power is unchanged, but produced 1,000 rpm lower down than before, but more to the point the torque curve is flat from 2,000-4,000 rpm.

Minor changes include the incorporation of the boot catch into the central locking system, electrically released fuel filler covers, a lamp failure warning light, and gas struts to assist bonnet opening.

As before, the Aston V8 tipped MIRA's scales at 35.4 cwt (distributed a slightly nose heavy 53/47 front to rear). By any standards it is a heavy car, yet not the heavest in the class; Ferrari quote their 400i at no less than 38 cwt unladen.

## Performance
*Urge a-plenty*

Gently — or viciously — opening the throttle brings a train of eight throttles into action. The effect is immediate. Muffled induction pulses build to a bellow and the car surges forward. The response is simply delicious and most overtaking manoeuvres require little movement of the throttle — a gentle squeeze. Conditions permitting 100 mph is a ludicrously easy cruising gait.

The abiding impression is of always having enormous reserves of power and torque available — of simply having to caress the throttle for the car to bound forward.

As before we found it best not to "stall" the torque converter during standing start tests, but to apply a little throttle against the brakes, then release them as the throttle was pushed firmly down. On dry roads there is just a momentary squeal of protest from the tyres. The nose pitches up slightly and the headlong rush starts.

Recent experience of powerful automatic cars has shown that there is usually very little to be gained by shifting gear manually. The Aston was an exception to this rule. While full throttle shifts from 1 to 2 occurred close to peak power at 5,000 rpm, the 2 to 3 change would happen at a surprisingly low point (around 4,400 rpm or 80 mph) leaving the engine running momentarily at around 3,000 rpm. Changing manually and using 6,000 rpm as the change-up point in both gears, the car was quicker; by 0.3 sec to 60 mph, 1.6 sec to 100 mph and 2.0 sec to 130 mph (the faster times are published). But even using the extra 1,600 rpm the difference in acceleration times is not great, and gives some idea of the huge spread of torque. At the recommended 6,250 rpm "intermittent" rev limit gear maxima are 65 and 108 mph. Left in Drive we were very impressed with the smooth unobtrusive way in which upchanges occur — and the gentle manner in which "lock up" takes place on light throttle openings at around 45 mph. A

good indication of the degree of slip that would otherwise be present is given as lock up takes place at moderate speeds and throttle openings. In this situation the engine loses as much as 300 rpm. At higher speeds and throttle openings, the change into top gear and lock up occur simultaneously so nothing but a normal upchange is felt. On the test car kickdown from 2 to 1 and 3 to 2 was available below 37 and 66 mph respectively. The latter point is considerably lower than the 85 mph on the last V8 tested, but this allowed top gear acceleration figures to be taken from as low as 70 mph (against 90 mph before). A particularly good point is Aston Martin's continued use of the correct selector gating with detents to prevent inadvertent selection of 1st and neutral, leaving free movement only between Drive and 2nd.

Although the engine does not feel the least bit flat at the top end Aston say the fatter torque curve has been paid for with a power curve that drops fairly sharply above 5,500 rpm, so at first we were slightly surprised to find the car giving a marginally faster maximum than before. Closer inspection reveals that there is now a much closer match between peak power and the top speed, the car pulling quickly and without fuss up to a mean maximum of 146 mph at 5,550 rpm.

A vertically moving lever on the facia in front of the driver's left knee works the choke. During a warm test period this control could usually be left alone. A couple of prods on the accelerator were all the enrichment required for the engine to fire immediately and run cleanly after a moment's coaxing. Getting the engine to fire when hot took

more time (especially if the car had been left standing). No matter what throttle position chosen, its rather hesitant eventual pick up suggested some fuel vapourisation had been taking place.

## Economy
*Still thirsty*

For a number of reasons the test period included rather more testing, town running, and short journeys than we would have liked, and this certainly had some effect on the overall figure. Final calculations showed the Aston had returned 14 mpg (after adjustment for a 4.5 per cent over-reading mileometer) compared with 13.0 mpg before. Measurements taken at constant speeds up to 100 mph showed significant improvements from 40 mph onwards (when the transmission has locked up); better than 20 mpg at a constant 60 mph (against 17.5 mpg for the older model) and at 100 mph the new car was doing 14.6 instead of 11.3 mpg, so once motorway speeds have been reached the new car uses around 20 per cent less fuel.

However the gains in everyday driving seemed rather less than this, and were barely evident at all if anything like the full performance potential was used. The best brim to brim figure seen was 17.5 mpg but only with that delicious response used sparingly, speeds kept down to 80 mph, and not too much town running. The fuel tank holds 25 gallons, giving the new V8 a reasonable range of around 300 miles before the fuel warning light starts to flash, which it does with around three gallons in reserve. Opening the glovebox lid reveals two push buttons, one of which releases both fuel filler covers via electromagnetic catches. With the Jaguar-type filler caps leading via short pipes directly to the tank, there are no time-wasting delays when brimming — though when taking the fuel to the filler neck, it pays to open both fillers in order to let the tank breathe more easily. Care must also be taken not to open the boot while refuelling since the filler covers are fouled by the boot front edge. It came as no surprise to find this large V8 using some oil, but at 500 miles per ½ litre its thirst was rather less than before.

## Noise
### Road induced — mainly

Little change here. At low speeds the car ambles along with the muffled noise of individual combustion pulses coming from under the bonnet. Open the throttle wide and these grow into the deep throated bellow produced by intake and exhaust systems; a noise that totally befits the Aston's slightly brutish image.

Mechanical refinement improves as the speed increases, the lusty note heard on hard acceleration dying away to a murmur on the very light throttle opening required to maintain three figure cruising speeds. As in many cars of this type this is replaced mainly by road generated noise. Tyre roar is present on all surfaces and is particularly evident on coarse concrete. After some time spent at speed one also notices a low frequency boom period in the car and that the tyres, 235/70VR-15 Avon Turbosteels generate significant rumble and thump over cats' eyes, road joints and poor surfaces. The suspension seems to

have difficulty in accepting sharp inputs such as potholes or drains, either of which can produce a quite violent bang (see later comments on road behaviour). The tyres squeal rather more than expected when cornered hard.

As we have noted before the Aston's rather angular but purposeful shape belies quite low

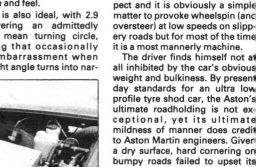

levels of wind noise. There is some subdued buffeting evident from around 80 mph, but this never develops to the point where it become obtrusive. The overall result is an acceptably refined grand touring car — one that does not tire the occupants after a long journey — but certainly one with interior noise levels more in line with or even above those found in the Porsche 928S or Maserati Kyalami.

## Road behaviour
### Good

Praise is again due for the unobtrusive way the Aston's power steering eases the driver's work.

At parking speeds steering efforts are heavier than most, but we would judge its weighting as just about perfect, especially for a car of this type and feel.

Gearing is also ideal, with 2.9 turns covering an admittedly poor 41ft mean turning circle, something that occasionally causes embarrassment when making right angle turns into narrow streets. Cornering roll is very well controlled, and for such a heavy car, response to small steering inputs is good. At normal cornering speeds the car simply goes where it is pointed and for this reason one also feels less than usually inhibited at threading such a big (and valuable) car through small gaps in the traffic.

On straight roads, there was a certain "looseness" around the straight ahead on the 36,000 mile test car; not we felt a steering malady, but perhaps something caused more by the Aston's damping characteristics (see later text).

The "primary" stability is ex-

cellent, and that Aston handling inspires a great deal of confidence. Any car with this much torque and power deserves respect and it is obviously a simple matter to provoke wheelspin (and oversteer) at low speeds on slippery roads but for most of the time it is a most mannerly machine.

The driver finds himself not at all inhibited by the car's obvious weight and bulkiness. By present day standards for an ultra low profile tyre shod car, the Aston's ultimate roadholding is not exceptional, yet its ultimate mildness of manner does credit to Aston Martin engineers. Given a dry surface, hard cornering on bumpy roads failed to upset its clearly very well tied down de Dion rear axle. If pushed to its limit it is the front end that loses adhesion first. The driver clearly feels steering loads increase through "caster effect" and tyre deflection, then a progressive build up of understeer. Although test track treatment suggested that a more neutral state of balance would have got us round bends a fraction faster, such a degree of ultimate understeer leaves the Aston with almost no adverse reaction when backing off in mid slide. More to the point, it has a very stable feel in fast corners on the road and, as we have already implied, excellent straight line stability — virtually unaffected by blustery conditions.

Ride quality is rather an odd mixture. At low speeds on all but the sharper surface changes, wheel movements feel un-inhibited and supple, but even at these slow speeds one is conscious that at the same time the suspension finds difficulty in accepting the sharper input. Thus the apparent ride comfort is interrupted by potholes and badly broken surfaces, which can cause a shock and noise input plus some kickback through the steering wheel. At higher road speeds (when the inputs are obviously fast) one again feels the front suspension particularly less able to absorb minor ripples and other "high frequency" surface imperfections. On straightforward bumpy B roads, when wheel movements are larger but slower, the car rides rather better taking bumps and road camber in a firm but comfortable manner, though in this case the really hard driver may experience the front suspension running to the limits of its travel, and thus the car getting bumped off line. A car of this weight and performance clearly needs very powerful brakes, and when it comes to stopping the Aston excels. Pedal efforts for check braking are slightly higher than the norm but utterly in keeping with the character of this muscle car. A minor criticism is that the gentlest braking takes a little practice to achieve with smoothness because of what seems initially like rather jerky servo action, but thereafter the response rises nicely in line with pedal effort, an 80 lb load

sending the fluid in our U-tube decelerometer plunging below 1.0g. This performance is made just that bit more commendable by the fact that the front brakes did not finally lock until a 100 lb load was applied and even then the g-meter was showing a deceleration rate of better than 1g, a response pattern which should inhibit brake locking particularly on wet roads.

The impression of a car with immense reserves of stopping power was confirmed during our speed related fade test (10 consecutive 0.5g stops from 98 mph in this case) which the Aston cast off with barely any change in pedal pressures, though there was a little brake judder during the final three runs.

The hand brake is of the fly-off type where the button is pressed to lock rather than release the lever. With a firm pull it held the car quite satisfactorily facing either way on MIRA's 1 in 3 test slop (being automatic the car could always be parked on the transmission lock of course). The combination of the engine's torque and a torque converter allowed the restart to take place with comptemptuous ease.

## Behind the wheel
### Traditional Aston

The sheer quality of the Aston's interior is impressive; the appearance of fine quality hand-stitched leather upholstery – and headlining – Wilton carpet, plus heavily laquered walnut dashboard, gear selector surround, and door cappings.

Wide doors allow easy entry to the front seats which have plenty of fore and aft adjustment and a conventional turn-wheel for the back rake movement. Normally they are comfortable and supportive, but by virtue of their comparatively generous width and lack of side shaping they do not provide particularly

good sideways location, especially for drivers of thinner build. The hard driver might prefer the optional cloth upholstery. With the steering column adjustable for reach, long or short armed pilots are well catered for though it would be far better if the stalk controls could be arranged to move as well. A full set of Smiths instruments is provided, the ancillary ones monitoring oil and water temperatures, battery volts, fuel contents, and oil pressure; the latter dead centre mounted and flanked by the rev-counter, and 170 mph speedometer (3 mph fast at 100) which incorporates a touch-to-reset trip distance recorder. Though clearly marked, the main dials remain rather small and from some driving positions the wheel rim masks the tops of the dials. Wipe/wash plus flick wipe switching is via the left hand stalk, leaving the variable intermittent operation (2-10 sec) controlled by a separate switch/rheostat on the centre console. Indicators, dip/main beam and horn operation are on the right hand stalk. A straightforward "twisting knob" main lights switch is placed on the right hand facia. Jaguar-type push button switches in the centre console look after ancillary functions. Both door mirrors are electrically adjustable (via controls on the driver's door).

In spite of the bulbous hump which dominates the over-the-bonnet view, sharp wing edges allow the car's width to be accurately judged. Tolerably thin screen and side glass pillaring also permit the driver a reasonable wide angle view, but as before rear visibility is very restricted because of the thick C pillaring and shallow rear glass.

Another area where the Aston rates no better than a supercar average is in its heating and ventilation. There is no fresh air ram flow whatsoever, and all air entering the car (whether heated or

not) runs through the air conditioning system which is turn is engaged via the fan switch. On the first two (of four) speeds the fan is quiet and there is a good flow of cool air through the facia vents, but the system could not be adjusted to provide much flow to the footwells (or to the outer side window demist vents) and like most systems with a water valve heat control, variations in temperature take time to occur and are difficult to stabilise.

## Living with the Aston V8

Needless to say creature comforts abound. Central locking is standard. The electric windows work promptly and the forgetful will like the way they can be operated with the ignition switched off. Opening the glovebox lid (a vanity mirror is mounted on the reverse side) reveals two buttons; one to release the fuel filler covers, and the other the boot. The glovebox itself is wide but shallow and with only a small centre arm rest locker (this contains a map reading light) and pockets in the front seat backs, oddments space is not a strong point. Small niggles are that no less than three keys are required to operate the various locks and ignition switch, and the seat backs tip via rather awkward to operate catches. Once installed, rear seat passengers have a quite tolerable time of it unless they are tall. There is a fold-down centre arm-rest, and the seats have nicely shaped shoulder supports, while the front seat passenger has a wide and substantial foot rest. The interior light has a fade switch.

The bonnet release is a sturdy vertical action lever in the kicker panel adjacent to the driver's right knee. The forward hinging bonnet props via the gas struts that also assist in its opening, to

reveal the dramatic-looking all aluminium double overhead camshaft engine. Items requiring daily attention are easy to check, and although service attention is required every 5,000 miles, it looks a relatively simple and straightforward (if not cheap) car in its class to maintain.

The fuses are instantly accessible behind a leather trimmed panel in the facia at knee height to the passenger. A car-sized spare wheel, jack and tools are accommodated in a large well beneath boot floor level. The fuel tank sits between the rear seat passengers and boot thus takes up a lot of space. Its presence also limits the size of the boot opening. Luggage space is nevertheless sufficient for most purposes and can be made better use of with the optional Aston Martin fitted luggage kit.

## The Aston Martin Lagonda range

The "basic" V8 tested here and the mechanically identical Volante convertible can be had with manual or automatic transmission for £39,999 and £47,500 respectively. The blisteringly fast Vantage comes only in manual form at £42,499. Finally there is the William Towns styled Lagonda at £56,500.

# HOW THE ASTON MARTIN V8 PERFORMS

Figures taken at 32,936 miles by our own staff at the Motor Industry Research Association proving ground at Nuneaton.

All Autocar test results are subject to world copyright and may not be reproduced in whole or part without the Editor's written permission.

## TEST CONDITIONS:
Wind: 0-5 mph
Temperature: 13 deg C (55 deg F)
Barometer: 29.9in. Hg (1015 mbar)
Humidity: 70 per cent
Surface: dry asphalt and concrete
Test distance: 1,041 miles

## MAXIMUM SPEEDS

| Gear | mph | kph | rpm |
|---|---|---|---|
| Top (mean) | 146 | 235 | 5,500 |
| (best) | 148 | 238 | 5,600 |
| 2nd | 108 | 177 | 6,250 |
| 1st | 65 | 105 | 6,250 |

## ACCELERATION

**FROM REST**

| True mph | Time (sec) | Speedo mph |
|---|---|---|
| 30 | 2.8 | 30 |
| 40 | 3.9 | 41 |
| 50 | 5.1 | 51 |
| 60 | 6.6 | 61 |
| 70 | 8.3 | 71 |
| 80 | 10.6 | 82 |
| 90 | 13.1 | 93 |
| 100 | 16.0 | 103 |
| 110 | 20.1 | 113 |
| 120 | 25.2 | 125 |
| 130 | 30.8 | 135 |

Standing ¼-mile: 14.8 sec, 98 mph
Standing km: 26.9 sec, 123 mph

**IN EACH GEAR**

| mph | Top | 2nd | 1st |
|---|---|---|---|
| 0-20 | – | – | 1.7 |
| 10-30 | – | – | 2.2 |
| 20-40 | – | – | 2.3 |
| 30-50 | – | – | 2.4 |
| 40-60 | – | 3.5 | 2.6 |
| 50-70 | – | 3.6 | – |
| 60-80 | – | 4.1 | – |
| 70-90 | 6.1 | 4.7 | – |
| 80-100 | 5.9 | 5.5 | – |
| 90-110 | 7.2 | – | – |
| 100-120 | 9.0 | – | – |
| 110-130 | 11.0 | – | – |

## FUEL CONSUMPTION

**Overall mpg:**
14 (20.18 litres/100km)
3.2 mpl

**Constant speed**

| mph | mpg | mpl | mph | mpg | mpl |
|---|---|---|---|---|---|
| 30 | 22.0 | 4.8 | 70 | 19.1 | 4.2 |
| 40 | 21.3 | 4.7 | 80 | 17.7 | 3.9 |
| 50 | 21.0 | 4.6 | 90 | 16.7 | 3.7 |
| 60 | 20.5 | 4.5 | 100 | 14.6 | *3.2 |

| Autocar formula: | Hard | 12.6 mpg |
|---|---|---|
| Driving | Average | 15.4 mpg |
| and conditions | Gentle | 18.2 mpg |

Grade of fuel: Premium, 4-star (98 RM)
Fuel tank: 25 Imp. galls (114 litres)
Mileage recorder reads: 4.5 per cent long

**Official fuel consumption figures**
(ECE laboratory test conditions; not necessarily related to Autocar figures)

Not applicable to small volume manufacturers

## OIL CONSUMPTION

(SAE 20/50) 500 miles/½ litre

## BRAKING

**Fade** (from 98 mph in neutral)
**Pedal load for 0.5g stops in lb**

| | start/end | | start/end |
|---|---|---|---|
| 1 | 42/38 | 6 | 40/48 |
| 2 | 42/44 | 7 | 40/48 |
| 3 | 40/46 | 8 | 40/48 |
| 4 | 38/46 | 9 | 40/48 |
| 5 | 40/46 | 10 | 40/48 |

**Response** (from 30 mph in neutral)

| Load | g | Distance |
|---|---|---|
| 20 lb | 0.20 | 150 ft |
| 40 lb | 0.45 | 67 ft |
| 60 lb | 0.78 | 39 ft |
| 80 lb | 1.05 | 29 ft |
| Handbrake | 0.25 | 120 ft |

Max. gradient: 1 in 3

## CLUTCH

## WEIGHT
Kerb, 35.4 cwt/3,969 lb/1,802 kg
(Distribution F/R, 53.3/46.7)
Test, 38.9 cwt/4,353 lb/1,977 kg
Max. payload, 1,180 lb/536 kg

## DIMENSIONS

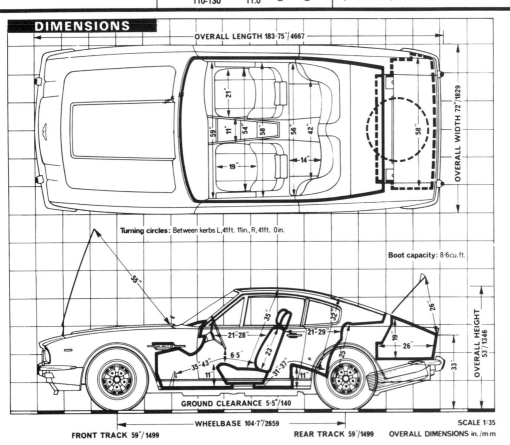

OVERALL LENGTH 183·75"/4667

OVERALL WIDTH 72"/1829

Turning circles: Between kerbs L, 41ft. 11in., R, 41ft. 0in.

Boot capacity: 8·6cu. ft.

OVERALL HEIGHT 53"/1346

GROUND CLEARANCE 5·5"/140

WHEELBASE 104·7"/2659

SCALE 1:35

FRONT TRACK 59"/1499    REAR TRACK 59"/1499    OVERALL DIMENSIONS in./m m

## PRICES

| | |
|---|---|
| Basic | £32,1 |
| Special Car Tax | £2,675. |
| VAT | £5,217. |
| **Total (in GB)** | **£39,998.** |
| Seat Belts | Standa |
| Licence | £80. |
| Delivery charge (London) | |
| Number plates | £15. |
| **Total on the Road** | **£40,093.** |
| (exc. insurance) | |

**EXTRAS** (inc. VAT)
*Two auxiliary driving lights £299.
Rear seat belts £119.
*Passenger's side electric door mirror £149.
Headlamp wash/wipe £255.
*Detachable headrests (ea) £119.
Cruise control £398.
* Fitted to test car

**TOTAL AS TESTED ON THE ROAD** £40,661.

Insurance    Group 8 (on applicatio

## SERVICE & PARTS

| Change | Interval 5,000 | 10,000 | 20,00 |
|---|---|---|---|
| Engine oil | Yes | Yes | Yes |
| Oil filter | Yes | Yes | Yes |
| Gearbox oil | No | No | Yes |
| Spark plugs | No | Yes | Yes |
| Air cleaner | No | Yes | Yes |

**Total cost** £170.42 £272.01 £281.
(Assuming labour at £14.50/hour inc. VAT)

**PARTS COST** (including VAT)

| | |
|---|---|
| Brake pads (2 wheels)—front | £55. |
| Brake shoes (2 wheels)—rear | £13. |
| Exhaust complete | £506. |
| Tyre—each (typical) | £159. |
| Windscreen (laminated) | £469. |
| Headlamp unit | £22. |
| Front wing | £1,023. |
| Rear bumper | £323. |

## WARRANTY
12 months' unlimited mileage

## SPECIFICATION

**ENGINE**
| | |
|---|---|
| | Front; rear-drive |
| Head/block | Al. alloy/al. alloy |
| Cylinders | 8 in 90-deg V/wet liners |
| Main bearings | 5 |
| Cooling | Water |
| Fan | Viscous |
| Bore, mm (in.) | 100 (3.94) |
| Stroke, mm (in.) | 85 (3.35) |
| Capacity, cc (in.³) | 5,340 (326) |
| Valve gear | Dohc |
| Camshaft drive | Chain |
| Compression ratio | 9.3-to-1 |
| Ignition | Breakerless |
| Carburettor | 4 × Weber 42 DCNF |
| Max power | Not quoted (see text) |
| Max torque | Not quoted (see text) |

## TRANSMISSION
| Type | Chrysler Torque Flite 3 speed automatic with top gear lock up |
|---|---|

| Gear | Ratio | mph/1000rpm |
|---|---|---|
| Top | 1.00 | 26.4 |
| 2nd | 1.45 | 18.2 |
| 1st | 2.45 | 10.8 |
| Final drive | Hyphoid bevel, limited slip | |
| Ratio | 3.06 | |

## SUSPENSION
| Front—location | Independent, double wishbones |
|---|---|
| —springs | Coil |
| —dampers | Telescopic |
| —anti-roll bar | Yes |
| Rear—location | De Dion tube, four trailing links + Watt linkage |
| —springs | Coil |
| —dampers | Telescopic |
| —anti-roll bar | No |

## STEERING
| Type | Rack and pinion |
|---|---|
| Power assistance | Yes |
| Wheel diameter | 15.0 in. |
| Turns lock to lock | 2.9 |

## BRAKES
| Circuits | Two, split front/rear |
|---|---|
| Front | 10.75 in. dia ventilated disc |
| Rear | 10.38 in. dia. ventilated disc |
| Servo | Twin vacuum |
| Handbrake | Centre lever working on rear discs |

## WHEELS
| Type | Cast alloy |
|---|---|
| Rim width | 7 in. |
| Tyres—make | Avon |
| —type | Radial ply |
| —size | GR70 VR15 |
| —pressures | F 30, R 30 psi (normal driving) |

## EQUIPMENT
| | |
|---|---|
| Battery | 12V 68Ah |
| Alternator | 75A |
| Headlamps | 110/120W |
| Reversing lamp | Standard |
| Electric fuses | 15 |
| Screen wipers | 2-speed plus intermittent flick wipe |
| Screen washer | Electric |
| Interior heater | Water valve |
| Air conditioning | Standard |
| Interior trim | Leather seats, leather headlinin |
| Floor covering | Carpet |
| Jack | Screw pillar |
| Jacking points | Two each side under sills |
| Windscreen | Laminated |
| Underbody protection | Zinc primer and pvc; wax in box sections |

## Aston Martin V8 £39,999

Front engine,
rear drive

Capacity
5,340 c.c.

Power
Not quoted (see text)

Weight
3,969 lb/1,802 kg

Autotest
24 July 1982

## BMW 635 CSi £22,950

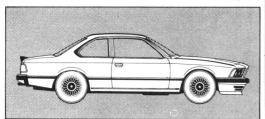

Front engine,
rear drive

Capacity
3,430 c.c.

Power
218 bhp (DIN)
at 5,200 rpm

Weight
3,175 lb/1,442 kg

Autotest
To be published

## Jaguar XJ-S HE £19,708

Front engine,
rear drive

Capacity
5,343 c.c.

Power
299 bhp (DIN)
at 5,500 rpm

Weight
3,824 lb/1,735 kg

Autotest
24 April 1982

## Maserati Kyalami £25,998

Front engine,
rear drive

Capacity
4,136 c.c.

Power
265 bhp (DIN)
at 5,500 rpm

Weight
3,640 lb/740 kg

Autotest
July 1978

## Mercedes 500 SEC £28,700

Rear engine,
front drive

Capacity
4,973 c.c.

Power
231 bhp (DIN)
at 4,750 rpm

Weight
3,545 lb/1,610 kg

Autotest
None so far

## Porsche 928 £21,827

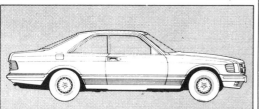

Front engine,
rear drive

Capacity
4,474 c.c.

Power
240 bhp (DIN)
at 5,250 rpm

Weight
3,342 lb/1,518 kg

Autotest
3 April 1981

## MPH & MPG

### Maximum speed (mph)

| | |
|---|---|
| Jaguar XJ-S HE* | 153 |
| Maserati Kyalami* | 147 |
| *Aston Martin V8* | 146 |
| Mercedes 500 SEC† | 145 |
| Porsche 928 (A) | 140 |
| BMW 635 CSi* | 139 |

### Acceleration 0-60 (sec)

| | |
|---|---|
| *Aston Martin V8* | 6.5 |
| Jaguar XJ-S HE | 6.5 |
| Porsche 928 (A) | 7.2 |
| BMW 635 CSi* | 7.3 |
| Mercedes 500 SEC† | 7.5 |
| Maserati Kyalami* | 7.6 |

### Overall mpg

| | |
|---|---|
| BMW 635 CSi* | 21.8 |
| Jaguar XJ-S HE | 16.0 |
| Porsche 928 (A) | 15.9 |
| Maserati Kyalami* | 15.3 |
| Mercedes 500 SEC† | 15.2 |
| *Aston Martin V8* | 13.3 |

†Figures for 500 SEL pre "energy concept"
*Figure for manual version

Other competitors in this most refined of classes must be the Ferrari 400i (£35,300), the Kyalami-like but Ford powered De Tomaso Longchamp (£21,827), Porsche 928S (£25,950) or even Porsche 3.3 Turbo (£27,950). Note should be made that an automatic Kyalami is only available in 4.9 litre form (£29,900) for which we have no data. If we were to judge from preliminary results on one of the latest "Energy Concept" 500SELs Mercedes have dramatically improved fuel consumption, which would leave the SEC standing much higher overall. Of the rest, the Jaguar still provides the most remarkable blend of smooth performance and quite tolerable economy. But if you require the best possible blend of performance and economy it has to be the BMW. Of the V8s, it is the Mercedes and Porsche that have the edge on mechanical refinement, but the Aston has the sheer attention grabbing mid-range acceleration. Such performance still has to be paid for — in terms of fuel consumption.

## ON THE ROAD

In spite of the recent harshening of 12 cylinder Jaguar ride with the adoption of Dunlop's D7 tyre, this car still has the most outstanding blend of ride refinement, handling and grip. In most respects the new Mercedes comes close — some may even prefer its higher geared and more immediately responsive steering, but even this car cannot match the Porsche handling response — its ability to change direction fast. In balanced throttle cornering — on dry roads — all three develop moderate understeer, whereas even the latest BMW Coupés (even though they incorporate suspension modifications first seen on the 528i) will still oversteer quite readily at all times. Still, the new 635CSi is unquestionably more mannerly than its predecessor, sharing much in the way of balance with the Maserati.

None rides badly. A P7 shod Porsche probably suffers most from road induced row with the Aston also near the bottom in this respect. It is nevertheless a likeable and totally predictable machine, perhaps without the Porsche's grip or response, and more prone to understeer than the rest, but a car with enormous animal "muscle car" appeal, and brakes as effective as any in the group.

There are no serious complaints on heating and ventilation, but rather crude control systems on the Aston and Maserati leave them least likeable, while Jaguar and Mercedes rate the best in this important respect.

## SIZE & SPACE

### Legroom front/rear (in.)

*(seats fully back)*

| | |
|---|---|
| *Aston Martin V8* | 43/36 |
| Maserati Kyalami | 43/35 |
| Mercedes 500 SEC† | 44/31 |
| BMW 635 CSi | 45/32 |
| Jaguar XJ-S HE | 42/30 |
| Porsche 928 (A) | 42/27 |

†Figures for 380 SEC

With front seats adjusted a little forward, the Aston and Maserati provide quite reasonable space for four, and the Italian compares well with the Jaguar, BMW or Mercedes where luggage carrying capacity is concerned. Meanwhile in spite of its apparent bulk, the Porsche is strictly a 2 + 2. The other grand tourers *can* carry normal sized spare wheels, but if stricken by a puncture, the Porsche owner will either have to drive illegally on his extra narrow crossply Goodrich "spacesaver" spare, or get the car trailered to the nearest tyre fitting depot. On the plus side the Porsche does have rather more load carrying versatility than the others thanks to its opening rear hatch window.

## VERDICT

Irrespective of price, the Jaguar still stands out as the most remarkably refined, effortless and mannerly form of transport. In dynamic respects Mercedes have closed the gap and recent "Energy Concept" modifications have made these beautifully built big engined cars much more efficient, but if it is the real tops in efficiency you are after only the BMW can provide that. The Maserati, Aston and Porsche? The latter is possibly the best made car here (besides the Mercedes). It handles well — if not perfectly — and has enormous dry road grip, but like the Maserati it lacks the mechanical and road noise suppression of the XJS and SEC. The Italian is also rather sporting in character, and certainly has exclusivity on its side, which leaves us with the Aston. It has virtually doubled in price in four years. Its carburettored 5.3-litre V8 still needs a lot of fuel in spite of some improvement in efficiency, but it does have enormous mid range performance, a traditional muscle car character, predictable handling and braking that matches up, plus a very imposing appearance. The problem is that a top quality hand build product has to be paid for — dearly.

# Men only

**Deftly clipping on his chest toupee and clutching a copy of The Right Stuff, Mark Hales belts himself into a *real* Aston Martin**

There is always a supposition that putting the engine behind the driver spells racing car; anywhere else is a bit of a compromise, and as such best left to the saloon car men.

Not necessarily true. Arthur Mallock and Sons have been happily disproving this theory for years, producing front engined sports racers which can lap almost as fast as Formula Three cars.

Sure the Mallock is small and light and doesn't really bear much relation to a road car, but no matter, even when the concept is scaled up it can still be made to work, and work well.

As a road car however, the big engined sports/GT is sadly a dying breed. Fuel costs and speed limits have taken an inevitable toll on their production, and there is definite lack of practicality in their every day use. Such machines are usually kept as a second car, used to blow the blues away on fine days and those fortunate enough to own one will resort to the BMW for everyday hacking, or more likely nowadays, a Golf GTi.

The Italians, notably Ferrari, still produce true Grand Tourers, but joy of joys, so do the British. Aston Martin is alive and well, and in the V8 Vantage there exists a Grand Tourer in the purest tradition, capable of seating two plus two in reasonable comfort and gobbling miles with the sort of ease and style you

thought had disappeared with the advent of emission control.

Motive power is an Aston designed light alloy four-cam V8, rather than the lump of Detroit iron found lurking in an Iso or De Tomaso. Not that there's anything wrong with American V8s, they're just not Grand in the Touring sense.

The Aston engine is also situated at the front thereby leaving room for seats behind the driver.

Clothed in a body made of traditional aluminium and luxuriously appointed inside, this is a stylish machine of vast performance.

But the price of style is high; a new V8 Vantage will set you back £44,999 and secondhand ones are expensive in proportion. Small production runs also mean expensive spares, and Aston engines, although reliable when treated well, are notoriously expensive to repair and rebuild.

Thus it might follow that racing the marque is the privilege of a well-heeled few and, rightly or wrongly, those who do have acquired the cachet of a clique.

David Ellis does not fit the stereotype of an Aston racer, nor would he want to: a broad-shouldered, soft-spoken Lancastrian, he runs his plant sales business from the family farm just north of Wigan. As an individual he is down to earth and practical, and the engineering skills reflected in his car are

completely self-taught. As he says "If I don't understand something I'll read the right books until I do".

The story of this man's Aston began after David had watched a friend hillclimbing a Vintage Ulster at Wiscombe. Interested, he took his automatic V8 road car back to Wiscombe and promptly won his class. Suitably fired with enthusiasm, David decided to buy a car which could double as roadburner and race car.

Looking at the beast now (known affectionately to David as his Chariot) it is difficult to imagine the car sitting in a London showroom, but that is exactly where David bought it in 1977. Six months old to be precise, resplendent in the same yellow as now, and sporting a manual gearbox, naturally.

On arrival from London the car was quickly checked over and taken to Silverstone where David scored a ninth from 30 starters, and at Brands Hatch a third place, after a battle with

shed some 5.5cwt, and the addition of Dunlop slicks to the standard wheels brought Silverstone lap times down to 63 seconds (91mph) and began the start of an intense but usually friendly rivalry with the Hyde Vale car driven by Ray Taft.

The aforementioned mods helped towards wins at St. John Horsfall (a yearly Silverstone pilgrimage), a third consecutive year's win at Wiscombe hillclimb, and sprint success at Curborough, but the increased speed revealed some severe shortcomings in the braking department and David decided to give 1980 a miss while he engineered the final stage in the evolution of his definitive Vantage racer.

It was during this winter gestation period that the car first acquired its dramatic low-rider appearance, achieved by lowering the body on the chassis and losing some four inches of frontal area, a useful way of reducing drag. The body and paintwork are the sole responsibility of John Iball who works for David and has been involved with the project right from the beginning.

### . . . it is difficult to imagine the car sitting in a London showroom, but that is exactly where David bought it in 1977

The basic chassis remains but there is a semi-spaceframe to help support the body and to carry the transaxle, of which more later.

The body is not in fact as low as it first appears, but the effect is exaggerated by huge 19 inch diameter Speedline wheels, purchased from rival Preece, and originating from the defunct Leyland Jaguar XJ Coupé project.

Rubber has always been Dunlop and is currently very low profile 300 x 650 front and 330 x 700 rear on 12 inch and 14 rims.

The major advantage of using such large diameter rollers is that most of the rim width can be inset without clashing with calipers and wishbones. This moves the actual steering point nearer the centre of the tyres and makes the steering light enough to remove all power assistance. The latter has actually been machined from the standard rack which, having been designed for power, is a reasonably quick ratio. The disadvantage of inset wheels is a lack of brake cooling, hence the scoops on the

outside of the rims. However the brakes have given no trouble since the standard front items were replaced with enormous 12.5 inch ventilated AP items and 4-pot alloy calipers.

Looking at the discs, it isn't the diameter which strikes you so much as the thickness, nearly two inches in this case, and a major factor in heat dissipation.

Being front engined, a greater forward weight transfer under braking leaves the rear brakes with an easier job, and the standard Aston 10-inchers are retained with 4-pot calipers. Master cylinders are separate front and rear, and operated by an adjustable bias balance bar.

### . . . as so often happens in motorsport, eligibility hangs on the semantics of a single word

The wishbones connecting this lot are all longer than standard, Aston-factory manufactured, and rose jointed. Uprights are standard Vantage, and springs are 400lbs on Koni spring damper units; surprisingly soft for such a big car. In general, the suspension is not that far removed from standard, using most of the production mounting points, rose joints replacing rubber wherever possible.

The rear suspension is de Dion, a large tube uniting the hubs, curving up and over the differential unit which is firmly mounted in the centre. Large double-jointed shafts transmit power from diff to hubs, and fore and aft location of these hubs is provided by one top and one bottom link, facing forward on either side.

The Bilstein combined coil/shock absorber units are vertically mounted from the hubs and carry 200lb springs, again somewhat less than I would have expected.

Central to the new rear suspension setup was a 5-speed ZF transaxle. Now everybody knows the Vantage does not normally have such a fitment, but AMOC racing rules stated that any production Aston component could be used; the experimental Bulldog had already been announced and David presumed that he could use a ZF transaxle as was fitted to the Bulldog, and incidentally the De Tomaso Pantera.

This unit contains both differential and gearbox and he mounted it at the rear along with the clutch and starter; drive from the engine being supplied via an XJ6 propshaft. It's an arrangement similar to that now

Win Percy and Robin Hamilton, having led for nine laps. He then followed up this result with a win at a Curborough sprint meeting.

Encouraged, naturally, David fitted Piper cams and Konis and with an all-up weight of 33cwt and still on road wheels, trim and tyres he found himself able to lap Silverstone Club Circuit in around 67 seconds, an average of 85mph. That speed was comparable with the best production sports times of the day.

Stiffer lower springs were added but still the Ellismobile was short of power compared with the 'works' Vantage driven by Ray Mallock. "He pulled away from me like I had a slipping clutch" recalls David.

By now there was no turning back and it had become a burning ambition to beat not only the works car but also the two men then consistently doing the winning, Mike Salmon in Aston's Project 212 and Dave Preece in a modified DB4. Furthermore he wanted to do it with a road class Aston, but a race at Mallory Park towards the end of 1978 convinced David that he would have to lighten his car and move into the modified class to do it.

Thus, for 1979, the removal of all that lovely leather trim and the air conditioning (!) helped

employed in the Porsche 924 and Alfa GTV, which helps to shift weight towards the rear of the car.

The de Dion tube had to be cut and moved up to clear the ZF unit which is taller than the standard Salisbury differential.

There were development problems of course; upon starting the engine for the first time the vibration nearly shook the car to pieces, but a centre bearing in the prop soon took care of that, and the 1981 racing season was already beckoning with the added attraction of the ASCAR series which was to be extended to include British Astons as a challenge to the American muscle cars.

Last but not least, the engine came in for the Ellis treatment. The Vantage engine is already in a comparatively high state of tune; around 400bhp is (unofficially) claimed by the factory for the production item, so vast horsepower gains could not be expected. David modified the heads himself, retaining the standard valves which are already as big as it's possible to go without the exhaust valves clashing with the inlets when both are open.

Cams are factory Nimrod specification driven by chains, and pistons are Cosworth items made to Ellis specification.

Vantage crank and rods are good quality steel anyway and these were balanced and fitted with a lightened flywheel which transmits an estimated 500bhp through the ubiquitous AP triple plate F1-type clutch.

Topping the whole unit is an F5000 injection system, bored out and fitted with bigger butterflies and a row of vertical stacks which necessitate the hump in the bonnet which has been rudely dubbed "dromedary" by the opposition.

### Upon starting the engine for the first time, the vibration nearly shook the car to pieces

Finally David designed his own dry sump system round a Pace belt driven pump and an Ellis designed, fabricated alloy sump pan, all fed by a large alloy tank just under the rear window filled with 40 Grade Castrol R.

So did it all work? After a few inevitable teething problems and the odd oil fire it was time for the yearly Silverstone Horsfall visit, where David stormed to win from the back of the grid including a 10-second penalty, and then won a second race later in the day, setting a best lap of 57.7 seconds, comfortably over the 100mph barrier. He also defeated former F1 driver and fellow beardie, Mike Wilds, guesting in arch-rival Taft's Hyde Vale car at Mallory, before going to the Blackpool sprint where the Aston crossed the finish line at 148.79mph, the same time as recorded by F1 cars on the same day!

The potential of the car was obvious; perhaps it was a little too quick, for sadly, the AMOC then wrote to David telling him his car was ineligible in that form. The Bulldog, in the eyes of the AMOC, was not a "production" car, and as so often happens in motorsport, eligibility hangs on the semantics of a single word.

Now David could have been forgiven for throwing in the towel there and then, but he is made of sterner stuff than that, and he simply returned to the workshop to undo a proportion of his winter's work.

It is recent history that the car is just as quick now with its "standard" ZF 5-speed gearbox and Salisbury Powr-Lok dif – ironically it weighs only 20lbs more.

Fortunately, Oulton's picturesque twists and turns were dry and the sun was shining when John arrived with the Aston sitting incongruously on Ellis Plant Sales' flat back Leyland truck, complete with its crane!

I had always wondered how the car surrendered its lofty perch, but all became obvious as the whole back of the truck tilts on hydraulic rams and the car rolls gently back on short ramps.

Nothing like making the best use of existing equipment!

Meanwhile David had arrived in his Lagonda, and with the booster battery connected, the racer's engine crackled into life with a delicious whiff of Castrol R. Once warm and having been pronounced fit by its owner, I prepared to try the car.

Sitting fairly high, visibility is good, always a confidence-inspiring factor in a strange car. Interior impressions are dominated by the vast transmission tunnel, another consequence of the lowered body, with its stumpy gearlever almost at shoulder level.

The gearbox is a brutal affair with a notchy change, apparently typical of the ZF, and needing accurate matching of the revs to ensure a clean downshift. Upchanges were fine and easily accomplished, only the bottom four ratios being employed round the tight confines of Oulton.

The brakes are powerful and reassuring, slowing around a ton of car easily but needing a hefty prod, which I prefer. Smaller master cylinders would reduce effort but increase pedal travel – you take your choice.

The steering, while extremely heavy at low speeds, lightens once the car is on the move, although at touring speeds the scuttle shakes and the whole car feels vague and imprecise. Press-on harder and the machine becomes progressively tauter, turning-in with an agility which is remarkable for its size.

Even when travelling at racing speeds the car totally belies its aggressive appearance, gentle understeer being the primary handling characteristic. Of course, with 500bhp available it's possible to poke the car sideways on slow corners, but the suspension transmits the power remarkably effectively to the tarmac at all times, and the car never feels as if it's waiting to bite the unwary. It is nevertheless a very physical machine to drive – you can't lay back and twirl the wheel, Stirling Moss-style –

bent arms and hunched shoulders are the order of the day.

It is also decidedly hot, and with 2.25inch primary pipes feeding silencers in the sills right next to you, cabin temperature easily soars to that of a turkish bath.

As tested, the Ellismobile was sporting a G5-type rear wing which is not used for ASCAR events, and the extra downforce at the rear perhaps gave rise to a little more understeer than would be normal.

When the time came for the final three flying laps I found that an easy balance of throttle-against-understeer was achievable, particularly round the tricky double apex corner leading on to the comparatively short main straight.

From there, a quick blast through third and fourth gears, accompanied by a one-bank bellow from the exhaust exiting by my right elbow, I reached some 130mph incredibly quickly before treading hard on the brakes and carefully slipping down through the gears to second and Lodge corner. A nasty corner this, tightening to the right and falling away into adverse camber – a feature which is waiting to trap the unwary.

A late apex and the Aston powers through with just a touch of easily controlled oversteer, then into the dip and up the hill, over the hump which causes the revs to rise as the rear wheels part company with the track, into third

### It's a very physical machine to drive – you can't lay back and twirl the wheel, Stirling Moss style – bent arms and hunched shoulders are the order of the day

past the pits and briefly fourth before Old Hall, which is reached at around 110mph. Brake, down to third, round without drama, follow the curve right and we're into the long downhill lefthand sweep at Cascades – another tricky one – but the Aston is as good as gold, mildly understeering in fourth at around 110mph, taking care to get back over to the left and hard on the brakes for Foster's, the tightest corner at Oulton.

Getting stopped and down to second gear requires determination, but again the car exhibits no vices. It was important however to remember the car's size and to keep the wheels off the inside kerbing, which is high enough to pitch you out of control.

A short blast follows, then into third and now a glorious drift round Knickerbrook, snatching fourth up the hill, the car getting light over the crest, and then left down to Druids' double apex once again.

I used 7000rpm as a limit, some 3/400rpm short of the angry ultimate, and was pleased to note that I had lapped the tortuous 1.65 mile circuit at over 91mph, a remarkable tribute to the track manners of this big, powerful car.

The Aston has now helped David to over 80 trophies and holds lap records at every circuit he has visited.

More commendable perhaps is that David Ellis, assisted only by John Iball, has built his car without recourse to major professional help. It has cost money of course, but the overall bill was substantially less than some of the opposition, and David had the satisfaction of knowing he is beholden to no-one.

I was flattered to be the first person to drive the car besides its owner, and thoroughly enjoyed the experience. CCC's breathless thanks to all concerned. ∎

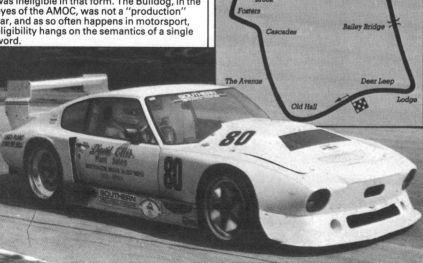

Map labels: Druids, Clay Hill, Knicker Brook, Fosters, Cascades, Bailey Bridge, The Avenue, Deer Leep, Old Hall, Lodge

## A day at the wheel of an ultimate statement

**DRIVING IMPRESSION**

Is $150,000 too high a price for a car, no matter how nice? Is Aston Martin's 4-door Lagonda really a *car*? Might Paul Simon have had an Aston customer in mind when he said, in "A Simple Desultory Phillipic": "He's not the same as you and me"?

We pondered these questions during a day with Aston Martin's new offering. Morris Hallowell IV, president of AM's U.S. operation, lent us one of these supreme tributes to the handcrafter's art, for a long lap around Southern California's varied roadscape. Besides having a memorable drive, we realized a Truth. Whatever the Lagonda may or may not be (it *is* a car, by the way, and an excellent one), the only real considerations behind such a purchase are simple questions: Do you want one? and, Can you afford it? Answer those queries and the whole matter is decided.

**I.** *Sunset Boulevard. It dips and winds*

*through Bel Air and Beverly Hills. New money, created by a still-young entertainment industry, has raised Tudor and Spanish and French Regency architecture. Thus the richest of the rich choose to spend their money, buying that which pleases them and letting their purchases speak well for their taste and station. Sunset must be one of the few streets in America where one could set out in a Lagonda, planning to nod cheerily at all the drivers of Quattroportes and Silver Spirits.*

Aston Martin is like no other company; Aston Martins are unlike other cars; and Aston Martin buyers are unlike other car purchasers. Since Lionel Martin, in 1913, engine-swapped his way to victory in the Aston Clinton hillclimbs—establishing the badge for his creations—quality has always been the overriding priority in the shops of Newport Pagnell. Martin's stated intent at

### by Kevin Smith

PHOTOGRAPHY BY WILLIAM CLAXTON

the outset was to build "a quality car of good performance and appearance, a car for the discerning owner/driver with fast touring in mind." Aston Martin has forever remained true to that ideal, creating as a result many delightful automobiles—and nearly as many financial crises. Wrote T.C. Browne in his history of Aston Martin *(Sports Car Graphic,* Spring 1981), "The vehicles have always been built up to a quality standard and never down to a price, which may explain why it is so difficult to find anyone who ever made any money building Aston Martin cars."

While other manufacturers progressed into mass production and automation, AM continued to rely solely on skilled craftsmen with torch or wrench or hammer in hand. And it does so to this day.

Over 1800 worker hours go into making a Lagonda, and the team finishes two of the touring sedans a week. Modern economics have made constructing automobiles in this manner and at this pace brutally expensive. Aston prices pushed into six

# Aston Martin Lagonda

figures a couple years ago, and with the Lagonda—AM's first new design since 1967—the ante has been upped a substantial amount.

Appearing in 1974 as a show car, the Lagonda was conceived to demonstrate the seriousness and technical expertise of the company, which was in dire straits—yet again—at the time. Peter Sprague was then the latest in a long line of AM financier/saviors, and he wanted something to make a splash. Aston Martin took the Lagonda from the drafting table to an Earls Court show debut in just seven months, a feat made possible only by the staff's familiarity with prototype construction techniques. They use these techniques for every car they make.

High technology met higher tradition in the original show car. Its complex, all-digital instrument panel nestled in a warm leather and walnut fascia, and the time-honored 4-cam V-8 hid under angular, modernistic body work. Extensive development and problem-solving have filled the intervening years, but as it goes into production, the finally-for-sale Lagonda matches its ground-breaking show-car parent in concept.

Perhaps buyers who are slightly different from Aston's historic clientele will respond to the Lagonda, which adds elements of the avant-garde to the existing AM formula of luxury, comfort, performance, and hand-built quality. But in at least one key respect, the new customers will fit the old mold: They will still be people with vast sums of money to indulge their tastes.

Morris Hallowell tells of a time he visited a West Coast dealership as a call came in from a local fellow interested in owning an Aston Martin. Hallowell chatted with the gentleman for five minutes, drew up the paperwork, and drove a car to the given address. The caller ushered Hallowell into his private office, drew the blinds, opened a desk drawer, and took out $120,000 in currency. Hallowell reports that sum failed to dent the supply in the drawer.

**II.** *Interstate 405, the San Diego Freeway. Nowhere is our car dependency more clear than on this major commute artery, spanning the Los Angeles basin from top to bottom, roughly paralleling the edge of the Pacific Ocean. Cars of every description share its lanes around the clock, doing what cars are meant to do: transporting people. Waiting at home may be a climate-controlled garage (or a lucky space at the curb) and a water-repellant cover (or another night of salt-sea air). But here, now, it's fender-to-fender in the frenetic parade of mobile America. A unique automobile may or may not be noticed. What's expected is that it will perform its duty, hold up, and keep moving with the masses. Tools, after all, must not fail or complain.*

An Aston is a heavy car, especially by current weight-conscious standards. It is built with great solidity and strength, and is intended, given proper maintenance, to last the rest of its buyer's life. A story (perhaps improved in the telling) recalls an Aston Martin driver in England who crested

a blind hill at night, doing in excess of 100 mph . . . and broadsided a fair-sized camper trailer crossing the roadway. The driver politely stopped his Aston, turned around, and went back to see what all the commotion had been.

"Handmade" truly describes the sturdy grand touring cars from Aston Martin. Everyone knows about the engine builders (four of them), each of whom takes a week to assemble a 5.3-liter alloy V-8, affixing his hallmark to his handiwork. Few people, however, know that the chaps who butt-weld the aluminum body sheets (without filler rod), leaving absolutely untraceable welds, have served *14-year* apprenticeships to attain their skills.

Raw steel in sheets and tubing enters the Aston Martin workshop to become the basis of another Lagonda. Workers cut and jig-weld this material into a complex boxed platform chassis with tubing superstructure. The remarkable aluminum body work is then built up over this, with linen sheets separating the steel and aluminum to avoid long-term electrolysis problems. In the spray booth, 17 coats of lacquer (in any color a customer may think of) are applied by hand, each one allowed to dry, then hand-rubbed.

Meanwhile, cuts from 11 hides are being selected (one woman does this) to create this Lagonda's interior. The leather, together with insulation, trim, and wiring, joins the body on the closest thing to an assembly line Aston Martin has.

Following five hours of dyno time and any necessary adjustments, a V-8 engine is "signed" by its builder and installed along with the rest of the driveline and the suspension. At this point, the car is assembled but far from finished. An inspection and a test drive of 150 miles locates details that need further attention. When finally no more tools will be wielded around it, the

young Lagonda returns to the paint booth for its final six coats. A cleaning lady goes over the entire car inside and out, and this Lagonda is ready for its owner.

Such painstaking work produces a stunning piece of automotive art and a stoically dependable mechanism. Workmanship is excellent, though these techniques do not yield the same consistency of finish that buyers may look for in mass-produced cars. Seams actually hand-sewn in leather never have the cold accuracy of that imitation stitching a machine molds in plastic.

Structural integrity of the 4500-lb Lagonda feels reassuringly high, and no less an authority than the federal government supplied a dynamic evaluation of strength. Word is, after NHTSA crashed a Lagonda into a cement wall at 30 mph (can you imagine?) for certification purposes, the doors still opened and closed faithfully.

**III.** *Shoreline Drive, Long Beach. The lanes are open to traffic now, as they are 361 other days of the year. But concrete barriers line the route and grandstands rise on both sides. The Grand Prix circus is in town. In 48 hours, the most sophisticated single-purpose wheeled vehicles in creation will rip and scream over this very pavement. Today, there is no sound. The sunlight has that soft, silvery quality common near Pacific waters. Still, the promise of impending drama radiates from the race-day trimmings. Cars with more horsepower than most private airplanes, yet weighing little more than two big motorcycles, will hurtle through these same now-innocent bends, exploring the limits of automotive performance.*

Aston Martin's treatment of horsepower ratings has long been to substitute "Unquoted" for an advertised number. Unofficial estimates commonly run around 300, and that seems about right. The beautiful DOHC alloy engine, with a neat regiment of Weber 42 DCNF carbs to feed its 5340 cc, moves the big car from rest to 60 mph in under 9 secs, and to a top speed that's close to 140.

Of course, the flat-out performance specs of this car are not particularly relevant to its purpose, other than to confirm its status as a high-performance motor car. The engine ticks over silently but with a gentle lope, the red numeral 9 of the digital tachometer indicating 900 rpm. A light touch on the throttle pedal brings the power on line instantly, and the V-8 pulls with authority from 2000 rpm right through 6000. It has a duality of character completely appropriate to the car's mission: At moderate speeds and under light acceleration, it works as unobtrusively as a well-trained butler. But let it know you feel like a bit of a go and it rolls up its sleeves with

a hearty rumble.

A small-diameter, low-mounted, single-spoke steering wheel links the driver with a power rack-and-pinion system that responds accurately and keeps effort reasonable, though the action is heavy enough to feel like it really is controlling something. The Lagonda arcs through turns in fine fashion, feeling dead predictable and showing its mass only in a trace of ponderousness when first turning in to a hard corner or in a fast right-left-right combination.

Conventional wishbones and coil springs control the front wheels. The rear suspension uses the nearly extinct de Dion rigid axle tube with chassis-mounted differential and U-jointed halfshafts, plus automatic load-leveling. The ride is plenty comfortable, yet true to the motoring spirit, it is firm, taut, and very well controlled. The tall Avon tires set no records for cornering force capabilities, underscoring the Lagonda's forte of high-speed touring rather than high-g scratching.

A Lagonda driver feeds orders into the chassis from a comfortable—if somewhat unusual—command position in the cockpit. Control relationships are basically fine, aided by the 6-way power front seats, but that brute of an engine forces feet toward the outside of the car. The throttle pedal lies directly under the steering column, requiring the driver to adopt a slightly side-saddle position. Pressure-sensitive "switches" (actually just circles drawn on the control panel) are not identifiable by feel, and demand more attention than conventional controls. And in bright light the

clear pane over the digital readout complex picks up a reflection that interferes with the otherwise readable LEDs. However, none of these items poses anything like a serious problem; and anyway, to dwell on how this car compares with other pieces of transportation is to utterly miss the point. The Lagonda is a precious possession, and how it makes its owner feel when he looks at it and rides in it is the beginning and the end of its rationale.

**IV.** *Pacific Coast Highway. The southern stretches of this famous road do not offer quite the tortuous driving nor the rugged scenery of the northerly Morro Bay-to-Monterey run, but it's interesting nonetheless. Below Newport Beach, the 2-lane highway sweeps across open rolling hills that break in bluffs down to the surf. Riders exercise their horses on the slopes above the sea. The road twirls and dives suddenly, runs along the sand, and rises again to lead into the tourist/artist settlement of Laguna Beach. Here, magnificent glass and wood mega-homes cling to the ocean cliffs, while simple bungalows lie scattered up the canyon draws. Small wonder people of comfortable means and creative ways choose this quietly lovely niche in the coastline to let their spirits breathe.*

If sheer pleasure is what the Lagonda is supposed to deliver, it appears well equipped for success. Aston Martin designers and craftsmen have taken great pains to ensure the comfort and contentment of Lagonda passengers. Every deep-padded seat has armrests available. Exquisite aromas emanate from the supple leather that trims almost every visible surface, and the walnut veneer is thin-sliced and butterflied to coordinate the pattern in the woodgrain. Each occupant has a reading light, and those in back benefit further from the smoked-glass roof panel added expressly to make the rear compartment more bright and airy. Music for any mood floats (or leaps) out of an absolutely leading-edge Blaupunkt 8001 stereo.

Augmenting this sitting-room comfort is
**CONTINUED ON PAGE 187**

*Vantage is beautifully trimmed in leather and walnut; air conditioning is a standard feature. Oddly British touches include fly-off handbrake and old-fashioned Smiths dials. Front air dam gives distinct looks*

The Aston Martin Vantage is a daunting prospect. If the awesome power of its near 400 horsepower V8 is not enough to set the nerve ends tingling; if the fact that our test car is the personal property of Aston's chairman, Victor Gauntlett, does not occasion a moment's hestitation; if the £47,499 price tag does not induce caution into even the most blasé of motoring writers, then the sheer size of the beast is enough to take the breath away.

It's massive in every way; right up from the nearly 11 inch wide tyres that plant a footprint on the ground which would obliterate the prints of two family saloon tyres. It's six feet wide and 15 feet long, scaling in at a heavyweight 35 cwt – the weight of two Ford Escorts – and from the driving seat it feels every inch and every ounce of its size, as it curves away out of sight in every direction,

though it has been steadily developed ever since.

The V8 uses a pair of chain driven overhead camshafts for each cylinder bank and four huge double-choke Weber carburettors, shrouded by a massive air filter, squat in the central vee of the engine to supply fuel. The Vantage engine differs from the standard in having bigger carburettors and differently profiled camshafts to change valve timings. Aston Martin don't quote power outputs for any of their engines: a peculiarly British deference shared with Rolls-Royce, but in Germany, where facts and figures rule, 390 bhp at 5800 rpm is listed on the car's official homologation papers – a figure that only the Lamborghini Countach's claimed 375 bhp comes near.

To put that power even more in perspective, a Jaguar V12 produces 295 bhp, a Ferrari Boxer 340 bhp, an

and try a little harder; discover that this engine goes on and on revving; that the Vantage simply goes on accelerating. Discover that as the revs climb through 5000 this relaxed V8 gathers pace; its muted rumble becoming more and more the roar of a race engine given its head as it howls past 6000 and shows its hidden reserves of breathtaking power.

What it all means is that the Vantage starts accelerating where most other cars stop: there isn't any need (and not a lot of pleasure) in hustling it through full revs, flat out gear shifts to get the last tenths of acceleration performance to 60 or 70 mph.

But cruise in fifth gear along an autobahn at 100 mph, floor the throttle and feel it surge forwards almost as if it were starting from rest. 100 to 120 mph takes just eight seconds. With the speedometer needle reading 150 mph it is still accelerating: not

# Heavy metal

## Is it a dinosaur or simply a beautiful monster? We assess one of the last of the British supercars

the massive bonnet bulge a constant reminder of that fearsome power.

It's been called a legend and a dinosaur – arguably with some truth to each – but it is certinly the most powerful car in Britain and, debatably, the fastest car in the world. To try to understand some of the magic that has kept the tiny Newport Pagnell company alive through years of business turmoils, we have been driving the Vantage; the high performance version of the V8 coupe that has been Aston Martin's mainstay for so many years.

The Vantage's long pedigree defines its classical mechanical layout. In an era of mid-engines, turbocharging, and even four-wheel-drive in exotic cars, it's almost refreshingly simple: a huge 5340 cc V8 with twin overhead camshafts for each cylinder bank, driving through a five-speed ZF gearbox to a de Dion rear axle, located by trailing arms and a Watts linkage, an arrangement renowned for its theoretical purity of operation.

The body construction dates back to a time when most cars were built as the Aston still is – by hand – and uses a tubular steel chassis frame with a steel substructure. Hand-formed aluminium panels clothe the exterior, where the smooth. curves and simple angles of hand finishing create a flowing elegance in the huge machine.

The V8 engine of the Vantage – in fact it powers all the AM and Lagonda models – goes back some 16 years,

Audi Quattro 200 bhp, and an F1 racing car about 600 bhp.

Other mechanical changes on the Vantage include those enormous wheels – for the '84 model we've driven they are even bigger than before, with Pirelli P7 tyres on eight-inch BBS alloy wheels replacing the former seven-inch rims.

## PERFORMANCE

### VANTAGE ●●●●●

However deservedly one can praise a highly-tuned small engine or turbocharging as a way of boosting performance, in the end there really isn't anything to compare with the outrageous ease with which a big capacity power unit delivers the goods when required.

At first acquaintance the Vantage doesn't perhaps seem the world beater its facts and figures suggest: there isn't the snap away from a standstill of, say, a sporty BMW or the urgent revviness of a Porsche.

The big V8 just does everything with an effortless grace; drifts the car off from a standstill, smooths it up to three figure speeds. Everything is cultured, unflustered, relaxed and relatively quiet: let the revs drop down to 2000 or even less and it will still respond smoothly and easily when needed again.

And then…and then you begin to realise that you have only been using half revs and usually little more than half throttle. You find a longer straight

picking up the odd mile an hour as breeze or incline permits but accelerating positively towards its still distant goal, a maximum speed of near 170 mph.

Certainly there are but a handful of places left in the world where a Vantage driver can travel legally, let alone sensibly, at that speed, but all that power and performance doesn't just translate into mind-boggling top speeds, it means contemptuously easy acceleration at almost any speed in any gear. Who need worry about gear shifting when 80-100 mph in fifth gear takes only a second longer (6.7 secs) than in fourth (5.7); only a couple of seconds more than in third (4.2 secs)?

Paradoxically, it also makes the Vantage a very safe car in all but the most demented of hands. The sheer momentum built up when that mass is accelerated hard is awesome and, faultless though the massive all-round ventilated discs are at stopping the beast, one is always aware that this is no lightweight racer to be buzzed casually around the lanes.

## HANDLING AND RIDE

### VANTAGE ●●●●

This is no car to be driven straight armed and Gucci shod; it's a blood and guts machine which will scare off poseurs with its bulk and its weight. It has to be driven like the old fashioned sports-racer it is, firmly and authoritatively into corners with a firm pressure on the throttle and a tight grasp on the leather steering wheel.

The power and size of the Vantage make exploration of its handling on public roads laughably inadequate. It can consume the sort of curving country roads that are a challenge to smaller fry with consumate ease.

But on any road it is the beauty of the steering that makes the first and lasting impression. It's power assisted: the machine would surely be impossible to move without such help but power assistance and a sensible 2.8 turns between extremes of lock have simply served to create steering which is firm and positive in character, with nothing lost in accuracy.

Latest Vantages with their Pirelli P7 tyres on those wider wheels put a usefully larger area of rubber down on the road, which makes the handling much nearer neutral in its ba-

lance. The power oversteer that could be induced in earlier models is now near impossible in the dry, such is the grip of the massive rear end, and it is only in greasy conditions that real care is needed (as it is with any high performer) but here, too, the latest Vantage feels a considerable improvement on the sometimes untidy earlier car.

The Koni dampers of the suspension have been uprated to help.

Even with such big tyres the ride is generally surprisingly good, though the car does joggle and jar over some poor surfaces. It's softer sprung than many of its peers, the de Dion rear axle which keeps the wheels vertical allowing the designers more freedom on their choice of springing, and this not only improves the ride quality but gives the Vantage the handling predictability that comes with a bit of body movement through corners.

It's easy to be daunted by it all: the calf-straining 60 lb pressure needed on the clutch pedal; the heavy brakes; the slow, awkwardly gated gear change and, above all, the Vantage's bulk; most of it, like an

iceberg, dangerously out of sight and making the judgment of width, particularly at night on busy London roads a heartstopping business at times.

## LIVING WITH THE CAR
### VANTAGE ●●●

The controls are heavy and the clutch, in particular, genuinely tiring in traffic but once accustomed to its quirks the Vantage is a straightforward machine to live with by exotic car standards.

The gearchange is one of those quirks. The ZF 'box's five-speed pattern puts first gear out on a dog-leg, away and back from the driver, and the change both into and out of it is ponderous. Selecting reverse is a knack in itself, too, for first must be engaged before slipping straight across into reverse; try to slot straight into reverse from neutral and you will

have nothing but crunching gear teeth caused by the internal friction of the 'box. The change through the rest of the 'box is reasonably quick but, again, needs some practice to learn the curious springing of the gate.

The dashboard of the Vantage has a traditional and very British simplicity about its walnut veneer and straightforward Smiths dials. As always, though, in such cars one recognises switchgear and minor details from cheaper, mass produced cars. Any small manufacturer's car is an amalgam of bought-in components from larger companies but, somehow, they still strike a jarring note in an interior so expensively and elegantly finished in wood and leather.

There's a full in-car-entertainment system, too, and you can hear it, for the Vantage is decently quiet when cruising along. The engine is a distant rumble and only wind and tyre roar interfere. Accelerate hard or travel at steady speeds over 120 mph and it does become noisy though.

Despite its external bulk, it's not a big car inside. The leather front seats are a generous size and shaped for

comfort on a long run rather than any rally-style body hugging, which can leave the driver clinging to the wheel for side support sometimes during very quick cornering. Headroom is not over-generous but most sized drivers fitted in, the changing seat position keeping head clearance constant. There's more back seat space than a Porsche or Lotus Esprit can offer but is still cramped, coupe style, and suitable only for occasional adult use. The boot isn't particularly large, either; especially with the bulky spare wheel creating a sizeable hump in the floor, but as this is primarily a car for two, there's probably room enough.

## COSTS
### VANTAGE ●

If you have to ask the price, you can't afford the goods. Will anyone who can pay the £47,499 price tag of the Vantage seriously worry about its fuel thirst or its running costs?

If they do, they'd better look elsewhere. Fuel consumption of 11-13 mpg was evidence of our enthusiasm for the car but, in all honesty, it isn't likely to get a lot better on longer acquaintance.

Insurance will be the most expensive imaginable, save a handful of rarer and still more costly to repair exotics, and don't expect servicing – every 5000 miles – to be a cheap affair either, though the straightforwardness of its construction argues in its favour against more sophisticated exotica from foreign parts. But, just as an afterthought, think of the tyres: those massive Pirellis cost the best part of £250 each and a car like the Vantage could gobble a set in a year's motoring without a care.

## VERDICT
### VANTAGE ●●●●

Rationality cries out what a foolish car this is: too big, too thirsty, too fast for modern roads. It doesn't have the precision and agility of a modern-day supercar like the Lotus Espirit Turbo, but where the Lotus has a clear pedigree to the racing cars of today – slippery, turbocharged, mid-engined, ultra efficient – so the Aston Martin harks back to racers of the past – bigger, heavier, less sophisticated, more forgiving but no less fast.

And that is, perhaps, the secret of the Vantage's attraction: it's a timeless classic, it will be as much pleasure to drive in ten years' time as it is now, for it appeals to the red-blooded enthusiast who will relish its magnificent performance and revel in the straightforward pleasure of its viceless handling. It's the ultimate expression of a classical motoring theme – the big capacity, front engined, supercar – and while other cars may be better all-rounders none can offer what the Vantage does: the ultimate in every respect.

| CAR | Aston Martin Vantage |
| --- | --- |
| **PRICE** | **£47,499** |
| Other models Price span | coupe, conv £42,498-£52,498 |

## PERFORMANCE

| | |
| --- | --- |
| Max Speed (mph) | 168 |
| Max in 4th (mph) | 140 |
| Max in 3rd (mph) | 115 |
| Max in 2nd (mph) | 80 |
| Max in 1st (mph) | 50 |
| 0-30 (sec) | 2.4 |
| 0-40 (sec) | 3.0 |
| 0-50 (sec) | 4.1 |
| 0-60 (sec) | 5.9 |
| 0-70 (sec) | 7.4 |
| 0-80 (sec) | 9.1 |
| 0-90 (sec) | 11.5 |
| 0-100 (sec) | 13.6 |
| 0-400 metres (sec) | 14.5 |
| Terminal speed (mph) | 103 |
| 30-50 in 3rd/4th/5th (sec) | 5.0/6.7/- |
| 40-60 in 3rd/4th/5th (sec) | 4.6/6.1/- |
| 50-70 in 3rd/4th/5th (sec) | 4.3/5.5/8.8 |
| 60-80 in 3rd/4th/5th (sec) | 4.3/5.5/7.3 |
| 80-100 in 3rd/4th/5th (sec) | 4.1/5.7/7.7 |
| 100-120 in 3rd/4th/5th (sec) | -/6.3/8.4 |

## SPECIFICATIONS

| | |
| --- | --- |
| Cylinders/capacity (cc) | V8/5340 |
| Bore x stroke (mm) | 100 x 85 |
| Valve gear | 2 x dohc |
| Induction | 4 Weber 2 choke |
| Compression ratio | 9.3:1 |
| Power/rpm (bhp) | 390/5800 |
| Max torque/rpm (lbs/ft) | not quoted |
| Steering | PA/rack pin |
| Turns lock to lock | 2.8 |
| Turning circle (ft) | 40 |
| Brakes | S/Di(V)Di(V) |
| Suspension front | I/WiC |
| rear | deD/TA/W/C |

## COSTS

| | |
| --- | --- |
| Test mpg | 11-13 |
| Govt mpg | not listed |
| Tank galls (grade) | 25(4) |
| Major service miles (hours) | 5000(14.0) |
| **Parts costs** | |
| Front wing | £979 |
| Front bumper | £353 |
| Headlamp unit | £20 |
| Rear light lens | £10 |
| Front brake pads | £48 |
| Shock absorber | £164 |
| Windscreen | £449 |
| Exhaust system | £754 |
| Clutch unit | £401 |
| Alternator | £185 |
| Insurance group | 9 |
| Warranty | 24/50,000 |

## EQUIPMENT

| | |
| --- | --- |
| Alloy wheels | yes |
| Air conditioning | yes |
| Central locking | yes |
| Electric windows | yes |
| Leather trim | yes |
| Sunroof (electric) | option |
| Headlamp wash/wipe | no |
| Stereo radio/cassette | yes |
| Remote boot/fuel filler open | yes |

## DIMENSIONS

| | |
| --- | --- |
| Front headroom (ins) | 37 |
| Front legroom (ins) | 34-42 |
| Steering-wheel-seat (ins) | 14-22 |
| Rear headroom (ins) | 36 |
| Rear kneeroom (ins) | 20-28 |
| Length (ins) | 183 |
| Wheelbase (ins) | 103 |
| Height (ins) | 53 |
| Width (ins) | 72 |
| Track (F/R) (ins) | 59 |
| Int. width (ins) | 56 |
| Weight (cwt) | 33.9 |
| Payload (lbs) | — |
| Boot capacity (cu. ft) | 9 |

**KEY. Valve gear:** dohc, double overhead camshaft. **Steering:** PA, power assistance; rack pin, rack and pinion. **Suspension:** I, independent; Wi, wishbones; C, coil springs; deD, de Dion axle; TA, trailing arms; W, Watts linkage. **Brakes:** S, servo; Di(V), ventilated discs.

# Viva Volante!

*"The rarest of all modern-day Aston's is the open Volante, even rarer is a Volante with the super-car performance of a Vantage engine. The factory prefer to deny that such rare beasts exist, but we have watched one being made."*
*Philip Young pays tribute to a truly Great car . . .*
*with Graham Murrell photography*

THE golden wings on the front of Aston Martin's curved snout have always symbolised something very special in motoring. The name evokes deep emotions, traditions the Newport Pagnell craftsmen understand very well.

Today, Aston Martin production has been overtaken in demand by the more modern, razor-edged styled and less overtly sporting Lagonda. But all of the products of Newport Pagnell are the results of bespoke tailoring, and each car is only laid down for its three-month-long manufacture to the individual orders of each customer. So the Aston Martin models of today are very much an enigma, and even more special.

The basic design has been around for a long time now, and the mighty all-alloy V8 of 5,340cc could be said to have been redundant long ago.

But it goes on as a rare and beautifully made reminder of the times when an executive's express could combine the virtues of large-engined sportscar performance and traditional handling, with excellent feel, cloaked in comforts of the highest quality. Aston are widely rumoured to be working on an entirely new generation of Aston sportscar, for unveiling in a couple of year's time. When that happens, the enormous degrees of workmanship and macho performance of the current Aston range will be hailed as classics. Aston Martin have never made a car which did not go down at the end hailed as a classic. Already the factory is getting plenty of requests to keep the current *concept* alive.

The soft-top Volante version is Newport Pagnell's rarest of all. At present production is split with Lagonda's outnumbering Astons by three to one. And for every five Astons made, only one is the convertible. The Middle East is Newport Pagnell's biggest customer, closely followed by America – the demands from the regularly hot climes are for an excellent air

*The performance of the automatic version is nothing short of sensational, 30 to 50mph is better than any rival at 2.4 seconds, it hits 100mph in 17.3 seconds, and 120mph in 28 seconds, a Porsche 928 can not live with such searing power delivery, even with manual transmission – in full flight an Aston takes some catching. And it can outbrake a good many rivals too.*

conditioning system above the joys of wind-in-hair motoring.

So the Volante is already the rarest of all the modern-day Astons. Even rarer is a car the factory do not particularly want to openly talk of . . . a Volante combining the fearsome 400-plus bhp of the "superfast supercar", the Aston Vantage. All Volante's get the standard-spec engine, said to be worth 100 bhp less than the Vantage (the factory do not speak of power outputs, and as the makers of one of the World's fastest accelerating cars, they have good reason to rest their case that 'performance is sufficient'.

However, persuasive customers have been known to ask for some extraordinary favours to be incorporated in their cars, and at the end of the day, its the aim of the factory to please paying customers. And so one or two Volante's have escaped with the ultimate engine spec under the bonnet – carrying off the hand-made engine with the Vantage performance.

But such examples are known to be certainly less than can be counted on one hand – we know such cars exist because we have seen one being made. It must stand as the fastest open-top car in the World, and certainly one of the most desirable of convertibles.

Power from the Vantage is searing and relentless, the mighty thrust that lifts this great 4,000 lbs of British craftsmanship can blast past 60 mph in 5.3 seconds. Goodness knows what it's like with the top down . . . which is why Newport Pagnell have never been keen on making such a beast. In coupé form with a decent fixed roof, ah, that's another matter . . . a form of motoring Aston have always been rather good at producing.

The Aston we photographed before it was whisked away for its journey to the Middle East showed plenty of extrovert examples of a customer combing the parts-bin to make his Volante even rarer than the 'normal'. This Volante sat on the bigger BBS wheels and fat Pirelli

P7 tyres normally reserved for the Vantage. However, under the bonnet we were assured was the "right and proper" engine. It was still capable of impressive but smoothly unruffled rapid flight, when it came to making repeated runs for the benefit of Graham Murrell's camera.

Who needs Vantage power, when the attractions and enjoyments from this open car are deeper, more subtle? In a lonely lane twisting and turning across traditional English countryside, the Volante was in its element. With the top down and a low sun flicking through the trees, this very grand Grand Tourer brought home just what a unique car it is.

Despite the age of its design, the ride and handling is still extraordinarily good. It is firmly damped, but well sprung. Inevitably there is a trace of scuttle shake, but that is only really noticeable at low speeds, at a pothole or bump when the low-profile high-performance Pirellis are not giving their best. Were it ours, we would opt for the much softer side-wall of the British Avon, super in the wet, if not as ultimately sharp as the P7s.

We needed little reminding of just how good the Newport Pagnell power steering has become . . . a similar AdWest rack as found in Jaguars but with far superior weighting. It is said that Aston have merely re-geared a cog and the conversion is simplicity in itself. On the road, the Aston Martin power-steering is among the World's finest — no argument.

The penalty for soft-top motoring is that the power-drive for the hood takes up most of the boot space, what is left is good enough for a single large suitcase, but the factory make the best use of available space with a bespoke set of travelling cases. The hood is

'double skinned' and simply terrific, giving excellent resistance to drumming.

It means that when the need arises to change the car's personality from swish tourer to purposeful performance car, it can whisk to 60 mph in 6.5 seconds, and hit 150 mph with the hood drum-tight.

It has a lot going for it: The Aston has imposing appearance, beautifully made craftsmanship — Aston's are probably better-made now than for many a year, with very tough quality control — coupled with that enormous mid-range bite. And predictable handling to cope.

It is a big car to drive fast, but rewards the good driver with a "togetherness" of purpose to be expected from a thoroughbred.

But that three-months-of-making-everything-by-hand carries its cost. You would be having to bargain hard to persuade an Aston Martin salesman to give you much change out of £45,000.

While there are a few high-performance supercars to compete for your cheque-book, there is nothing so thoroughly British and quite so sporting as the Aston. And *nothing* that offers the combination of performance with traditional open air delights of the Volante.

Exclusivity, alas, never comes cheap.

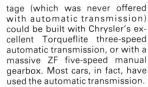

IN MANY ways, we think, the Aston Martin V8 is the Last of the Dinosaurs — massive, heavy, powerful, and impressive. Like the dinosaurs, it has really outlived its original age and purpose, and has not adapted to new conditions. Can extinction be far way by now?

The V8, in fact, is a Supercar, the ultimate indulgence any driver can be granted. It is not a machine for efficient transport, not for convenience, not for versatility, and not for operating economy — but merely for pleasure, performance and perhaps for posing as well.

Because production has always been limited (little more than 3,500 V8s and derivatives have been built since 1969) this makes the car a very exclusive *Buying Secondhand* prospect, not the type of car which can be found in many dealers' showrooms. It meant that, when assembling this feature, we had to search hard to find representative examples, and their values. Anyone determined to find a V8 will already have turned away from the obvious competition from Ferrari, Maserati and Lamborghini. The only feasible British competitor is the Jaguar XJ-S, which can be found more easily, and at much cheaper prices.

Although the original car was called DBS V8, and introduced in 1969, we have limited this survey to the later development, called simply V8, which was introduced in the spring of 1972, and is still available from Newport Pagnell.

## Defining the pedigree

The origins of this car are rooted in the DBS of 1967, a new fastback close-coupled four-seater car, fitted with the long-established 4.0-litre twin cam six-cylinder Aston Martin engine. The V8, complete with its all-new four-cam 90-degree V8 5.4-litre engine, was added to the range in the autumn of 1969, while the original six was built until 1973.

All cars in this family are built on the same pressed and fabricated steel platform chassis, to which the steel and light alloy body shell is added. All have coil spring independent front suspension, power-assisted rack-and-pinion steering, and de Dion rear suspension by coil springs. Naturally for cars of this performance, four-wheel ventilated disc brakes are standard, the tyres are

Note: The numbers of Aston Martins sold in the UK is very limited, and the secondhand market is very "thin" indeed, so these values can only be a rough guide. The Vantage coupé in particular is extremely rare, and each individual sale is a matter of individual negotiation from buyer to seller. The fitment of manual or automatic transmission has a negligible effect on the value of the cars — the manual, in fact, being very rare indeed.

VR-rated radials on 7.0in. rims of 15in. diameter, and a great deal of hand-crafting is featured in the construction. In some respects — such as the use of the Salisbury final drive — proprietary components are bought in, but much of the V8's running gear is unique.

Most cars have been built with Chrysler Torqueflite automatic transmission, though some have the alternative ZF five-speed manual gearbox.

## V8 Evolution

The original cars, built from 1969 to the spring of 1972, were called DBS-V8, and were distinguished by the use of four headlamps. Following a change of company ownership, however, the car was revised, with different nose styling and two (larger) headlamps. At the same time it was christened Aston Martin V8, and is the car which forms the basis of this survey. At this stage, the engine featured Bosch mechanical fuel injection.

From the summer of 1973 the specification was changed again, the most important difference being that the Bosch injection, which had given many problems, was abandoned in favour of four downdraught twin-choke Weber carburettors. Although there were other specification improvements, the basic styling was not changed, as indeed it has not been changed throughout the life of the car.

Since then changes have been confined to progressive updating

of the car's equipment, two upratings of the (unspecified) engine output, and the addition of the Vantage version, and the Volante convertible, all detailed below.

In addition, of course, the Aston Martin Lagonda saloon of 1974-75 was a seven-off four-door version of the V8, while the current Aston Martin Lagonda uses basically the same floorpan, but lengthened, the same running gear and same suspension.

## Engine

All engines so far built have been versions of the 5,340 c.c. Aston Martin V8, featuring a light alloy block/crankcase, and light alloy cylinder heads, with four overhead camshafts, part-spherical combustion chambers, and massive power output which has never been revealed. Differences between types have really been confined to carburation, breathing arrangements, and camshaft profiles.

Aston Martin never admitted to any power figures for these engines, but it was once estimated that the original Bosch-injected cars must have produced at least 330 bhp, and the carburetted derivative slightly less.

From the spring of 1977, the Vantage tune was produced, with up to 450 bhp, no doubt a prodigious thirst, and a really phenomenal performance. This tune has never officially been made available on normal V8s.

In mid-1977, too, the normal V8 engine was given 15 per cent more power, according to the company (370 bhp, perhaps?), with different camshaft profiles and the Vantage's exhaust system, while from summer 1980 further changes included the use of new heads incorporating smaller ports, larger valves and yet another camshaft profile.

In spite of all this, as *Autocar's* road tests confirm, the car's performance seemed to change very little.

## Transmissions

This is a short and simple section, for all cars *except* the Van-

tage (which was never offered with automatic transmission) could be built with Chrysler's excellent Torqueflite three-speed automatic transmission, or with a massive ZF five-speed manual gearbox. Most cars, in fact, have used the automatic transmission.

The Torqueflite has been used on many cars outside the Chrysler Corporation (not only when matched to a Chrysler engine as in Jensens and Bristols), as for instance in the Maserati Kyalami/Quattroporte family.

## Body choice

The majority of all cars built have been the four-seater coupés which are, in fact, rather more roomy in the rear than expected, and comfortably wide (the car itself is 6ft 0in. wide). These ride on a 8ft 9in. wheelbase, with an overall length of 15ft 3in.

From June 1978, however, Aston Martin also offered the alternative of the Volante convertible, with the same basic "chassis", and body except for substantial under-floor stiffening, and the use of a power-operated foldaway hood whose only disadvantage was that it reduced boot stowage from 8.6 cu. ft. to 5.1 cu. ft.

## ENGINE AND BODY AVAILABILITY

| Engine | V8 Base Engine | V8 with 15% extra power | V8 in Vantage tune |
|---|---|---|---|
| DIN bhp | —not quoted in any instance— | | |
| V8 Coupé 2-door | 1972-77 | 1977-date | 1977-date |
| V8 Volante Convertible 2-door | | 1978-date | |

Note: No peak power figures have evr been quoted by AML. All we can say is that the original power output was "sufficient", the 1977 version was "sufficient plus 15 per cent", and the Vantage tune "sufficient plus 40 per cent."

## SPARES PRICES

| | V8 | Vantage |
|---|---|---|
| Engine assembly-bare (exchange) | £11,385.00 | £11,960.00 |
| Gearbox assembly (exchange) | £3,413.95 | £3,413.95 |
| Clutch pressure plate (new) | £70.97 | £70.97 |
| Clutch driven plate (new) | £30.37 | £30.37 |
| Automatic gearbox with convertor (exchange) | £798.77 | n.a. |
| Final drive assembly (exchange) | £1,066.91 | £1,066.91 |
| Brake pads – front (set/new) | £55.63 | £55.63 |
| Brake shoes – rear (set/new) | £15.54 | £15.54 |
| Suspension struts – front (pair) | £303.90 | £376.86 |
| Suspension dampers – rear (pair) | £113.28 | £113.28 |
| Radiator assembly (exchange) | £345.60 | £345.78 |
| Alternator (exchange) | £159.51 | £159.51 |
| Starter motor (new) | £108.68 | £108.68 |
| Front wing panel | £1,125.36 | £1,125.36 |
| Bumper, front (exchange) | £304.23 | £304.23 |
| Bumper, rear (exchange) | £251.22 | £251.22 |
| Windscreen, laminated | £516.33 | £516.33 |
| Exhaust system complete | £867.24 | £867.24 |

All the above prices include VAT at 15 per cent.

*Opposite page: The V8 is nothing if not distinctive. This is a later model with blanked off bonnet scoop. Main visible difference on the Vantage muscle car (far left) is the big air dam beneath the front bumper. The Volante convertible (left and above left) features a power-operated foldaway hood*

Naturally it was sold at a considerable price premium (£7,000 more in 1979, £10,000 more today), and secondhand values are higher, accordingly.

When the Weber carburetted engine was adopted in 1973, this meant a deeper bonnet bulge, there were improved seats and ventilation, and electric door locking, with revised switchgear.

The Vantage had unique features including a blanked-off grille and bonnet scoop (apparently these were not very effi-

Volante is not a very usable body style in the British climate, and the Vantage is really far too fast, costly, and specialized, to be truly practical in the UK. Choose the latest V8 that you can afford (your insurance company, in any case, will be horrified), and be sure that the amazing cost of service is not going to bankrupt you in a very short time. A normal 10,000 mile service, incidentally, costs more than £300, even if nothing untoward has to be tackled.

Rather you than us!

*Right: Facia on the earlier cars looks decidedly dated now. Rocker switches on either side of the clock control electric windows, with heating/air conditioning controls below, and ahead of the ashtray six push-push controls for hazard warning lamps, heated rear window and so on*

*Above: Fuel tank limits space and dictates rather narrow opening*

*Right: A handbuilt underbonnetful; huge air box dominates and covers the four twin-choke Weber carburettors*

cient in any case!), a deep front spoiler, extra driving lamps, and a rear spoiler.

There were revised instruments for all models in 1977-78, and from the autumn of 1978 the facia of the export-type Volante was adopted on all other V8-based bodies, while at the same time a much smoother bonnet bump (without a scoop on any derivative), and an integral rear spoiler were standardized.

## Availability and choice

In the UK, or in most countries, for that matter, this section is best summarized: limited availability, so not much choice, unless you are very rich, and prepared to spend months looking around. Perhaps only 30 or 40 V8s a year have been sold in the UK in the past 10 years (and *very* few Vantages or Volantes) in any case. In addition, there are only 21 Aston Martin dealers in the UK, few of which ever have more than one V8 in stock, and ready for sale.

Our choice would certainly be made among the automatic transmission V8 coupés, for the

## CHASSIS IDENTIFICATION

**2-door 4 seat coupé**

| | Chassis No. |
|---|---|
| **September 1969:** Aston Martin DBS V8 introduced. | |
| **April 1972:** Aston Martin V8 introduced, replacing DBS V8. Differences mainly visual, with two headlamps instead of four headlamps. | 10501 |
| **Summer 1973:** Original variety of V8, with fuel injection, discontinued, at: | 10789 |
| Supplanted by new version of V8, with four downdraught Weber carburettors, deeper bonnet air scoop, and other improved details. From: | 11002 |
| **December 1974:** Production suspended, due to financial difficulties, at: | 11390 |
| **June 1975:** Production re-started at: | 11391 |
| **April 1977:** Normal V8 Coupé now joined by much more powerful (40 per cent more) Vantage version, externally distinguished by a blanked off front grille, plus front and rear spoilers. First Vantage: | 11686 |
| **August 1978:** Normal V8 revised, with 15 per cent more power, smaller bonnet hump, and many decorative improvements, from: | 12032 |
| **June 1980:** Normal V8 engine revised with new cylinder head, different porting, higher compression ratio, torque converter lock-up, and other details from; | — |
| **2-dr 4-seater convertible** | |
| **June 1978:** Volante convertible version of V8, with normal-tune, *not* Vantage, engine always fitted. | 15001 |
| All later changes to accord with normal V8 improvements. | |

## What to look for

Without doubt, the most important feature to look for on an Aston Martin before anything else, is the car's service record (1). This hand-built, robust performance machine only really deteriorates if it is not regularly looked after. Prevention rather than cure is the most sensible course of action, especially as in the case of an Aston some "cures" come very expensive.

### Mechanical

The all-aluminium V8 engine will last almost for ever; certainly there should be no need for a bottom end overhaul until at least 120,000/130,000 miles (2). Early 1975-76 power units do suffer from tappet noise. If this is the case, then the answer will be to replace the camshafts and do a top-end overhaul. This in itself is expensive and will probably cost around £3,000. One model to avoid at all counts because of engine problems are the early versions with their Bosch mechanical fuel injection systems. These temperamental systems are always in need of fine adjustment and although it is possible to convert the engine, the age of the vehicle in relation to the cost usually makes such work prohibitive.

The transmission, however, should create no problem whatsoever. As the majority of models were fitted with the Chrysler Torqueflite automatic gearbox, the few manual versions that exist have become much sought after (3). Early model exhaust systems (4) were

*Left: Leather, Wilton carpet and walnut give the Aston a quality interior, with comfortable seats especially suited to large frames. Above: Tolerable legroom and adequate headroom for rear passengers. Soft head-restraint pad on front seat was an extra*

## SPECIFICATION AND PERFORMANCE

| | V8 Coupé 2-dr Auto | V8 Coupé 2-dr Manual | V8 Coupé 2-dr Auto | V8 Coupé 2-dr Auto | V8 Vantage Coupé Manual |
|---|---|---|---|---|---|
| Tested in *Autocar* of: | 6-9-73 | 18-10-75 | 14-10-78 | 24-7-82 | 9-4-77 |
| **Specification:** | | | | | |
| Engine size (c.c.) | 5,340 | 5,340 | 5,340 | 5,340 | 5,340 |
| Engine power (DIN bhp) | | | Not quoted | | |
| Car length | | | 15ft 3in. | | |
| width | | | 6ft 0in. | | |
| height | | | 4ft 2.2in. | | |
| Boot capacity (cu.ft.) | 8.6 | 8.6 | 8.6 | 8.6 | 8.6 |
| Turning circle (kerbs) | | | 41ft 0in approx | | |
| Unladen weight (lb) | 3,930 | 3,990 | 3,970 | 3,969 | 4,001 |
| Max. payload (lb) | 750 | 750 | 1,180 | 1,180 | 1,180 |
| **Performance:** | | | | | |
| Mean maximum speed (mph) | 146 | 145 | 146 | 146 | 170* |
| **Acceleration (sec):** | | | | | |
| 0-30 mph | 2.6 | 2.5 | 3.4 | 2.8 | 2.2 |
| 0-40 mph | 3.7 | 3.6 | 4.5 | 3.9 | 2.8 |
| 0-50 mph | 4.8 | 5.9 | 5.7 | 5.1 | 3.8 |
| 0-60 mph | 6.2 | 7.5 | 7.2 | 6.6 | 5.4 |
| 0-70 mph | 8.2 | 9.3 | 8.9 | 8.3 | 6.9 |
| 0-80 mph | 10.2 | 12.5 | 11.0 | 10.6 | 8.5 |
| 0-90 mph | 12.7 | 15.2 | 13.2 | 13.1 | 10.8 |
| 0-100 mph | 15.7 | 18.4 | 15.8 | 16.0 | 13.0 |
| 0-110 mph | 19.8 | 23.7 | 19.8 | 20.1 | 15.8 |
| 0-120 mph | 25.0 | 29.3 | 24.2 | 25.2 | 20.7 |
| 0-130 mph | – | | 29.8 | 30.8 | 26.0 |
| Standing ¼-mile | 14.7 | 15.2 | 15.3 | 14.8 | 13.7 |
| **Consumption:** | | | | | |
| Overall mpg | 12.4 | 11.7 | 13.0 | 14.0 | 13.5 |
| Typical mpg | | | | | |
| – easy driving | 16 | 15 | 17 | 18 | 18 |
| – average | 14 | 13 | 14 | 15 | 15 |
| – hard driving | 11 | 10 | 12 | 13 | 12 |
| Mpg at steady 70 mph | 15.9 | 17.5 | 15.9 | 19.1 | 18.8 |
| Fuel grade | 4-star | 4-star | 4-star | 4-star | 4-star |
| Oil consumption (mpp) | Nil | 800. | 250 | 500 | 600 |

*Estimated maximum speed.

made from steel and so are very prone to corrosion. Most Aston specialists replace these with complete stainless steel versions, so this is worth checking.

Any test drive should highlight the two major problems that do occur with neglected Astons. A car regularly driven hard can destroy the balance of the prop shaft (5). It is a bonded prop shaft, with one section going into the other with a rubber bonding in between, so any feeling of excessive vibration probably means that it is running eccentrically. The steering can also be a problem (6). The steering column couplings are two universal joints and these do tend to wear with age, which can lead to erratic steering and a lot of knock being felt through the wheel. Repairing this does not use many new parts, but it is very labour-intensive. Cars around the 50/60,000 mile mark should also be checked

for leaks from the steering column.

Attention should be given to the front suspension (7), because with some models it may be necessary to replace the king pins. This may be expensive, but failure to do so could be dangerous as it can lead to suspension collapse. If the bottom king pins have been neglected, what tends to happen is that they seize on to the cones inside and this can lead to the holding down nut becoming unwound.

The same is true for the rear subframe (8), which with neglect can crack. The rear subframe carrier holds the diff unit in position. The large amount of power that goes through this unit can mean that the securing bolts become loose and if this happens the whole lot will be able to move about and can cause cracking.

## Body and trim

Check if the car has been involved in an accident, and if so whether the repair has been completed to the necessary standard. The Aston Martin's light alloy body (9) is made up of separate panels so minor knocks can be repaired by replacing the panels. Check the matching of the acrylic paintwork. Stone chips on the bodywork can also be a problem, especially to the V8 Vantage with its huge front air-dam. A second stone-chip area is just behind the rear wheels (10) as the combination of large fat tyres and no rear mudguards can lead to some unsightly markings.

Rubber seals perish with age, even on an Aston Martin. The most serious area on this model is the bottom of the rear screen (11). The angle of the screen means that water collects at the bottom edge, and when the rub-

ber perishes, finds its way into the boot. This is a very common fault, some seven out of 10 models will suffer from this; the answer of course is a new rubber screen surround.

Corrosion does not tend to be a major problem as the body is made from aluminium but one area where water, mud and road salt does collect is behind the front wheelarch splash-guards on the inside of the rear of the front wings (12). This corrosion trap needs to be cleaned out regularly.

Inside, the all-leather trim should wear well. The seats in the V8 are a lot better than the predecessors in the DB range and should not sag at all, although it is possible for the securing bolts to loosen.

The air-conditioning system can cause problems (13), and a pointer to this is whether the car has had a radio fitted by a non-Aston Martin specialist. To fit a radio the facia must be pulled down, and as soon as you do this all the pipes from the air conditioning unit come unplugged. This is a major problem for any non-Aston dealer, for if they are put back in the wrong order, the result can be very expensive. The heater valve (14) is also prone to leaking which will often mean a new control valve being fitted.

The underlying point with such a car is that it needs regular attention. This was stressed to us by Aston Martin specialists Richard Williams Ltd, of Padfield Road, Brixton, London SE5 who kindly helped us in the compilation of this article. Regular attention at the model's 10,000 miles service intervals should prevent a lot of the problems mentioned here.

# GETTING ON FAST!

IT'S NOT always good news when the voice at the other end of the phone is calling to offer a car to test. It could be the PR man from Boremobile Motors suggesting that we might like to test the '84 model now that it's got a new range of interior trim colours. Or it could be some obscure Comecon import so awful that we'd be doing the man a favour *not* to publish a test on it. But when the car is an Aston — well, you've got to show willing, haven't you? Even if the car has done 77,000 miles.

"A road test with a difference", is how it was put to us by the man from Aston, obviously confident in the condition of the Press Department's well used demonstrator which he was now offering to us for a last-fling appraisal before its honourable retirement. Well, why not? Given the awful condition of some supercars even when they're brand new, this could be interesting — and besides, the last time we'd sampled the regular V8 Automatic Saloon had been in 1978, since when the factory had improved economy by a claimed 15 to 20 per cent. That would be worth checking out in itself, even if there wasn't much prospect of getting meaningful performance figures from such a high-miler. So we made a date.

I don't know if Aston planned it that way, but the latest car to carry the famous AM V8 registration

plate was delivered to *Motor* 1,000 days, to the day, after it had first gone into service with the Aston Martin Press Department. Since then, it had clocked up 77,000 miles in the hands of nearly 200 different journalists. Say Aston, "Although it has been well looked after and regularly serviced, it has not received special treatment nor been wrapped in cotton wool — with that sort of mileage in such a short space of time, we have hardly seen it here at Newport Pagnell!" Apart from regular servicing every 5,000 miles, we are told, repairs

and replacements have been confined to a new steering rack at 32,500 miles, a replacement cylinder head (due to a water leak) at 40,000 miles, a radiator repair at 45,000 miles, a new gearbox and torque converter at 50,000 miles and a complete set of brake discs at 60,000 miles. In addition the leather had been "re-Connollised" at 65,000 miles.

The original idea, then, was presumably for us to write a "what amazing condition this car is in for its age" story — but that didn't really work. Apart from a few more

suspension bonks and rattles, we couldn't really tell it apart from a new Aston — in their notes, our testers gave it five star ratings for finish. End of story. But that's not really enough to fill three pages, so in the end we treated it like any other test car which has had a specification change since we had last tested one.

In this instance the important changes have been to the power train, notably the 5340 cc V8 engine which, for 1980, got revised

Still going strong after 80,000 miles, Aston Martin's V8 press demonstrator showed Jeremy Sinek a surprising turn of speed before it was put out to pasture

"polynomial" cam profiles (claimed to be quieter than of old, as well as altering the power and torque characteristics), modified carburetter and ignition settings, quieter Vantage-type pistons, and a small compression increase from 9.0 to 9.3:1. It doesn't seem much, but in combination with the latest Chrysler Torqueflite automatic transmission, which now has torque converter lock-up on top gear, the

result was a claimed economy gain of between 15 and 20 per cent.

In the end we did take AM V8 to the test track, and were glad we did. Forget about the high mileage — this car's performance is right up to scratch, and that means *quick*. Despite grotty testing weather the figures we got are every bit a match for the 1978 car's and, in one important respect, significantly better, for the maddening flat spot that once made it impossible to launch this massive machine cleanly off the line has been all but eliminated. This gives the current car an initial head start that slashes almost a full second off the 0-30 mph time — down from 3.6 to just 2.7 seconds — and brings the 0-60 mph time down from 7.5 seconds (which never really did the old car justice) to a much more realistic 6.6 seconds. At higher speed the difference diminishes (perhaps reflecting the current engine's less free-revving nature at the top end) but with 100 mph coming up in 16.7 sec and 120 mph in 25.6 sec the Aston is right in the same ball park with the Porsche 928S (6.5 sec to 60 mph, 16.3 to 100 and 24.3 to 120) which currently ranks as the fastest-sprinting automatic that we've tested. Flat out, neither car is a match for the Jaguar XJ-S's 152.4 mph but, given the poor testing conditions, the 143.0 mph lap we recorded after a short run-up round Millbrook suggests that on a good day the Aston should easily equal the 145 mph we've always estimated for it in the past. Economy? We saw 13.5 mpg overall, which makes it still a thirsty brute even for this type of car: but it's a 26 per cent improvement over 1978's abysmal 10.7 mpg . . .

A decent modern four-speed

*Sumptuous leather and polished wood trim in the style only the British know how. Even with fixed wheel and no seat tilt, driving position is superb. Below: magnificent engine looks immaculate - and it is!*

auto would no doubt benefit both performance and economy, but the present three-speed is pretty fair: it shifts supremely smoothly in moderate driving (if less so under hard acceleration) and there are sensible detents for the selector lever. Roadholding isn't P7-grippy, but fine basic poise and stability from the chassis continue to combine with what's arguably still the best power steering in the business — meatily weighted and wonderfully communicative. When you first try a gentle low-speed stop on cold brakes you realise why the pedal is so massive — so there's room to press with both feet — but when you really need them they warm to the task magnificently. The ride is deceptive, with plenty of suspension sound-effects to give an initial impression of harshness, until you realise that very little actual movement gets through to the cabin. Small bumps and ripples are virtually steam-rollered out of existence, though you do *hear* them. Refinement generally is no threat to Jaguar, with plenty of tyre rumble — and wind noise, too, if it's a blowy day — to underlie the awe-inspiring bellow of the engine when it's working hard. Some things don't change.

What started as an assessment of a somewhat elderly individual car is starting to masquerade as a straight road test update, so let's end it here. The rest of the story reads as before. That this individual car has worn superbly is a credit to the craftsmen who fashioned it — but it's an as-new example of a design that is old. In the nicest possible way, the Aston Martin V8 is a very old-fashioned motor car. By rights they really ought not to make them like this any more, but thank goodness they do . . .

**Lagonda Limousine: Conversion by Tickford involves adding a ten-inch section behind the B-pillar — but the price is very high**

# £110,000 LAGONDA

THERE ARE times when even a £65,999 Aston Martin Lagonda is simply not large enough, especially when it comes to a matter of rear seat legroom. This does not imply that the car is at all cramped in the rear, but it does not really qualify as a limousine, where dignified entries and exits can be made on all occasions.

To overcome this problem, and to extend even further the Lagonda's sales appeal in its major markets, the United States and Middle East, Aston Martin's specialist coachbuilding division, Tickford, has produced for the Motor Show a long wheelbase version which has a title almost as impressive as the car's appearance — Lagonda Limousine by Tickford. For the sake of brevity, the name does not appear on the car itself.

The construction of the Lagonda makes it a relatively simple job to extend the car's length, but great care has been taken to

**The result: Limousine style leg-room for the first time**

ensure that the limousine does not look simply like a long wheelbase, standard, Lagonda. The car's construction follows the same pattern as that of the rest of the Aston Martin range. The car is built round a very strong fabricated steel chassis, which is then clad with aluminium bodywork. For the Lagonda Limousine, the cut across the chassis is made just behind the B-pillar, where an additional ten inches is grafted in. This puts the car's wheelbase up from 114.8 to 124.8in, with the extra length being entirely in the legroom area. The rear seats remain in the same relationship to the rear bulkhead as on the standard wheelbase Lagonda.

Doors are expensive things to make or convert. The limousine gets a pair of new and much wider rear doors. The glass is divided vertically more or less equally, with the rear section fixed and the front section winding electrically.

The limousine's entirely new roof panel increases the car's overall height towards the rear to just over 53in. The front and rear screens from the original car are retained, and the roof panel is trimmed in vinyl.

The ten-inch extension adds only a little to the 4,550lb weight, so little has been needed on the mechanical side, apart from providing a longer rear section of the propeller shaft, a heavier-duty centre bearing and a new, extended exhaust system. The tyres remain 235/70VR15 Avon Turbosteels.

There are separate air-conditioning systems front and rear, a rear window blind and a comprehensive in-car audio system. All that is included in the price of £100,000 or, should you want one in Britain, £110,000.

As for such additional luxuries as TV, video, on-board computer, radio telephones or cocktail cabinets, then Tickford will be delighted to fit them — at a price. For the British market, you first have to buy and register a standard Lagonda prior to its conversion; this is done to avoid the various Type Approval traps.

# Of dreams and dollars

*It's the most expensive car on the Aussie market, a show-stopping
235 km/h luxo-cruiser measuring nearly twice the length of a
Daihatsu Charade Turbo — and costing 25 times as much.*

By Peter McKay

IT'S BIG and bold and slung low. And it's guaranteed to bring the populace to a halt, first entrapped by the exaggerated styling, then captivated by the luxury and performance and, finally, staggered or bemused by the price.

The Aston Martin Lagonda is not to be ignored. An extravagant automotive package that has bathed in controversy since an exhibition prototype first saw the light of day at the 1976 London Motor Show.

Behind the scenes, plenty happened between then and the delivery of the first production Lagonda in April 1978.

There were lengthy holdups linked to problems with the electronic digital instruments, touch-sensitive switchgear and all the rest of the computerised Buck Rogers stuff that had the Earls Court show crowd agog (Remember, this was eight years ago – a long time in technology terms).

Mechanically, there have been few headaches. The aluminium body cloaks a welded steel superstructure, and a 5.3-litre quad-cam engine — the same that propels other vehicles in the Aston Martin line-up — drives the rear wheels through the mandatory three-speed

Chrysler Torqueflite transmission.

Coils are employed at each corner, with double wishbones up front and a de Dion axle at the rear.

With a kerb weight of 2024 kg — equivalent to two Honda Accord sedans — and a speed potential of 235 km/h, the Lagonda needs, and gets massive ventilated discs all round, the rears mounted inboard adjacent to a limited slip differential.

The rack-and-pinion steering scores two-stage power assistance and, with 2.3 turns from lock to lock, is certainly direct enough. But the Lagonda has the turning circle of the Flying Scotsman — 14.2 metres between kerbs. And between walls the figure is a lot higher.

The Lagonda's nearest local marketplace rivals, by virtue of price and exclusivity, are the Rolls-Royce Silver Spirit and Camargue. On the road though it's a case of the tortoise and the hare. The Lagonda outperforms the Rollers in every department. It really is the sporting alternative to the Silver Lady.

Australians haven't exactly been forming a queue on the right to own a new Aston Martin Lagonda. Not at $235,000 a pop they haven't.

Now that the prices of Rollers have taken a tumble — the top-of-the-line Camargue toppling from $245,000 to $225,000 — the Lagonda is the priciest new hunk of metal, plastic and rubber on four wheels in this country. Just 15 grand away from a round quarter of a million bucks. Costing as much as a handy-sized mansion, it's definitely one for the big noters; a plaything for the princely. Bob Jane is the local concessionaire for Aston Martin if you're got your cheque book ready.

The Lagonda is the hottest local seller in the AM range although Australian sales of seven (including one up for grabs in an art union lottery) hardly suggests an overworked showroom floor. Biggest market, not surprisingly, is the Middle East where the demand could comfortably account for every Lagonda that trickles (about three a week) off the Newport Pagnell (Buckinghamshire) line. Plainly, petrol and parking spaces are not hard to find in Sheiksville — nor money.

In Oz, road test Lagondas *are* hard to find. Mr Jane and his merry salesmen have been in no hurry to make one available for local motoring writers. That's understandable, considering the value of the merchandise. Ours for this story came courtesy of Brents, in Melbourne. We spied (only those with a white cane and Labrador could have missed it) the big, brown beast lurking in the yard. And sure, said Brents' boss Maurie Duchini, it's yours for half a day. First shock was the price. A 1982 model Brents executive car, it was anyone's for just $145,000, or 90 grand under today's going rate for a newie. A suggestion, perhaps, of hefty depreciation the instant a new car transaction is concluded.

First impressions were the rakish lines — long and squat, but slung low. It's just 1.3 metres tall. Most un-British, with styling that might have come from Motown-by-the-lake. Fat Avon doughnuts filled the wheel arches. Frontal treatment has an Oriental squint with peekaboo headlights and a grille no larger than a regular number plate. Luggage space is pathetic. Lavish interior of beige Connolly hide and polished

walnut is spoiled by a hideous black leather instrument binnacle that looks like an afterthought.

Move in closer. Front doors open wide for easy entry; that's good. Head and leg room in the rear is lousy; that's bad. Strange too that the rear-door glass is fixed (the current model now has rear windows that open). The glass moon roof located above the rear seats is likewise a fixture. Thank heavens for the standard air conditioning. Yet another idiosyncrasy; there's no glovebox, but instead designer William Towns has decreed the Lagonda will have a small lockable compartment between the front buckets. The seating is electrically adjustable — a group of switches on each front door governs tilt, recline and fore-aft movement. Front leg room is generous and achieving a comfortable position is child's play though ultimate comfort is restricted by the seat shape which isn't as good as it looks. The occupant sits on, rather than in.

Blue chip technology is one of the Lagonda's big conversation pieces, but for the wrong reasons. The finger-sensitive "keyboard" barely lifts itself out of

the gimmick category. The touch controls are delineated by white painted circles the diameter of a one-cent piece. Problem; the circles are too small and too bunched, and because they have no internal illumination, impossible to read after dark. A knob or a control that the fingers can actually feel would be an improvement.

The controls are for a whole bunch of items — lights, bonnet, horn (select either a muted in-town or more strident country mode). As well, the driver can dial-up the air temperature (inside or outside) and take his pick of a speedo indicating in either mph or km/h.

Instrumentation is comprehensive but probably no more informative than that of a well-equipped Japanese family car. And it must be said: our Oriental friends do it better. The display is often difficult — make that impossible — to decipher in harsh sunlight.

And then there's the self-locking system. The object is to automatically secure the car to prevent unauthorised entry. About 20 or so seconds after the driver removes the key from the ignition — thwump — the doors lock without further

prompting. Great in theory but potentially embarrassing should the locking mechanism activate while the key remains in the ignition and the occupants are all on the outside. But that would never happen, you say. Oh yeah. Tell it to Lagonda owners who've had to send home for the spare set of keys.

How this big cruiser negotiates the twists and turns of narrow London streets tests the imagination. The tale of a search for a parking spot in the West End could not have a happy ending. Idling through city traffic isn't the Lagonda's forte. Noise intrudes; there's a steady V8 exhaust beat and the ride is impaired by suspension thump.

However, give the Lagonda a long stretch of highway, and it comes into its element. Noise levels subside. The exhaust note is wafted away by the breeze, and modest wind noise suggests aerodynamic efficiency. Still, under hard acceleration the sporty V8 throbs in a way that points the bone at the effectiveness of the car's sound deadening.

The Lagonda is a luxury limousine powered by what is plainly a high-performance sports car engine. Undoubtedly it is a fast motor car. Certainly, it will cruise at lock-you-up-and-throw-away-the-key speeds. When pushed it'll run all the way up to 235 km/h. But it isn't a

machine that revels in some on-the-limit tear-arsing on a switchback mountain road. Sure, it's agile and sure-footed for its size. But it's too bloody big to be a load of fun on a narrow, snaky stretch.

Like R-R, Aston Martin believes it's non-U to reveal power and torque figures — 250/260 kilowatts is our guess. The proof's in the pudding anyway, and this car must be among the fastest four-door limos around.

Acceleration times for the big heavyweight are not all that startling, at least until it hits its stride; moving all that bulk from rest is no easy task even for an efficient V8. Zero to 100 km/h takes close to nine seconds. The 160 km/h mark goes by in under 21 seconds and it'll handle the standing one-kilometre blast in under 22 seconds.

Aston Martin has made concessions to sporting motoring in the auto transmission selection gate configuration — it has free movement between Drive and Second, which is where it's most needed. Movement between other gears is protected by detents.

Only the crass would ask about fuel economy in a vehicle of this price. We're crass; we asked. Actually it isn't all that hard on gas ... around 21 litres/100 km or 13.5 mpg. Capacity of the dual tank system is 127 litres which at least gives

the Lagonda a sensible touring range.

In the rarified atmosphere of six-figure price tags (and then some), the Aston Martin Lagonda stands as one of the more outstanding examples. It is not a car for all tastes. But it has that undeniable mystic of exclusivity, a car that for all but a very few can be nothing more than a dream.

## Stayin' alive

IT WASN'T enough for Uncle Sam to pinch London Bridge — and the Queen Mary. Shock. Horror. Bloody 'ell. The Yanks have got Aston Martin. That most aristocratic of English car makers is now owned lock, stock and barrel by those bombastic types from the other side of the Big Pond.

The Poms might suggest that being snaffled up by the Americans is preferable — but only just — to the alternative of a slow death. Dying was perhaps the lone option. Certainly, a few years ago Aston Martin was terminally ill and looked destined to follow to the knackery some other prominent if not always fondly-remembered Brit marques. On tombstones in the great automobile graveyard are names like Armstrong Siddeley, Jensen, Frazer-Nash, Hillman, Riley, Sunbeam, Wolseley, Singer, Humber ...

The trans-Atlantic salvage operation was concluded when the US distributors of Aston Martin, Automotive Investments Incorporated, recently bought the remaining 45 percent of the company to take its holding to 100 percent.

English-born Victor Gauntlett, kept on by the saviours as executive chairman, was delighted with the move. And so he should be with unemployment — even among the old-school-tie bunch — running rampant in the Old Dart.

The Yanks have managed to do what the English failed to manage in recent times and that's give Aston Martin sales a fillip to the tune of 60 percent, in both the US and Britain.

Aston's history has been a chequered one. And with some black phases. Founded in 1913 as Bamford and Martin, it has never strayed far from its early sporting heritage. Even after tractor millionaire David Brown took over the company in 1947 (starting the famous DB series), Aston remained unswervingly committed to performance motoring (with luxury also taking a high profile). But like many other British auto firms, red was the dominant colour in the balance sheets. The company went into voluntary liquidation in 1975, when it was taken over by a consortium with the unimaginative name of Aston Martin (1975) Ltd. The instability didn't end then, however, and five years later ownership changed to CH Industrials/Pace Petroleum, under joint chairmen Mr T. Hearley and the aforementioned Mr Gauntlett.

These days the accountants have ceased blowing out their brains; production efficiency has been improved and the company sells in advance every car it makes. There are four models in the range: Aston Martin V8, Vantage, Volante convertible and the Lagonda. All powered by a 5.3-litre twin OHC alloy bent eight topped with four Webers.

Fortunes can only improve with the Lagonda model set for a Stateside introduction. If ever a car looks right for the American tastes, then it has to be the Lagonda, with its bulk and different styling.

Australia takes three of the Aston models; the Volante, the sporty five-speed manual Vantage, and the Lagonda.

Lagonda is, of course, an even older British automotive institution although today the name survives only as a model badge on an Aston Martin.

Lagonda's colourful history dates back to 1906, but it is best remembered for its succession of fine sports and touring cars in the 1930s. The legendary WO Bentley went to Lagonda in 1935 after his own company was absorbed by Rolls-Royce. Bentley handled the design work for the late-1930s cars, through to the post-war period. His last Lagonda appeared in 1948, under David Brown.

Prince Philip, among others, was a Lagonda sports car aficionado in the 1950s. Phil the Greek was — perhaps still is — something of a rev head. He managed to wean himself off Lagondas when the marque ceased in 1964. The current wedge-shaped Aston four-door saloon, designed by William Towns, is the only model carrying the Lagonda tag. Prince Philip has yet to buy one. □

*The touch panel on either side of the steering wheel controls myriad functions. Creature comforts abound but there's not much boot space.*

# ASTON MARTIN
# VOLANTE

## *Traditional, tasteful & terrific*

BY THOS L. BRYANT
PHOTOS BY JOHN LAMM

THE ROMANCE OF open-air motoring may be best exemplified by the Aston Martin Volante. This is a powerful, luxurious and slightly old-fashioned car that commands respect from passers-by and engenders love from driver and passengers alike. Once you've driven this marvelous convertible, you will never forget it.

The Volante is a product of Aston Martin Lagonda Limited of Newport Pagnell, Buckinghamshire, England. Aston Martin was founded by Lionel Martin just before World War I. Martin wrote some years later about how the name came into being: "After reviewing all the flowers, beasts, birds and fishes that we knew, we got to place names, and as my Singer had recently scored a point or two at the Aston Clinton Hill Climb, the first part of that name was adopted with acclamation and my humble cognomen appended to it."

By 1947, Aston Martin was in financial difficulty and was offered for sale. David Brown, known to his friends as DB, was an engineering industrialist and car lover, and he was thrilled to have the opportunity to purchase one of

# ''..mechanical excellence...
# unsurpassed luxury.''

England's most famous marques. Later that year, he also purchased the Lagonda company. Curiously, its name came from America: Lagonda Creek in Springfield, Ohio. That was the early home of Lagonda founder Wilbur Gunn, who later emigrated to England and built his first car in 1898.

Throughout their individual histories, Aston Martin and Lagonda were companies that believed in racing to improve the breed, and successes were garnered at Le Mans and most every other major European track in the Twenties and Thirties. This heritage was continued by David Brown into the Fifties, culminating in Aston Martin's 1959 triumph at Le Mans and capture of the World Sports Car Championship. This racing background is evident in today's cars from Newport Pagnell, which boast exhilarating performance characteristics other super-luxury cars simply can't match.

Tracing its heritage back through the various Aston Martin DB models of the Fifties and Sixties, the V-8 Volante is grand touring at its finest. I recall a warm day in southern California when it was my assignment to spend hours driving a Volante along winding mountain roads for a television production. Tough duty, eh? As the miles rolled by, this magnificent open car transported me halfway across the world and I was driving through the south of France and along the Riviera, soaking up the warm Mediterranean sun.

That is the sort of feeling this spectacular car promotes. To quote the factory's brochure: "In an age when romance has all but been sacrificed to the cold pursuit of efficiency, the Aston Martin V-8 Volante not only stands proudly apart from the crowd, but its 5.3-liter engine gives it the ability to leave the crowd a long way behind."

That V-8 engine produces a more than ample amount of horsepower and torque; Aston Martin has a policy of not revealing such figures, but best estimates place the bhp total at 300 at 5600 rpm, while torque amounts to some 350 lb-ft at 4500. Four Weber carburetors rest atop the intake manifold, giving the Aston engine a rather old-fashioned aspect perfectly in keeping with the car's styling. There is beauty to be found in things mechanical, and a look under the hood of the Volante will confirm that—it is a gorgeous powerplant. The block and cylinder heads are cast in aluminum alloy. And, as you may know, each engine is hand assembled by a craftsman who affixes a plate with his name on it to the outside—if the engine returns for service or repair, there's no doubt about who has responsibility for making it perfect again.

Outside the U.S., the Volante convertible can be ordered with either a 3-speed automatic transmission or a 5-speed manual; in this country, only the automatic is available because it's the only gearbox used for meeting U.S. emissions. Also available to driving enthusiasts in other parts of the world is the "Vantage" engine version of the coupe. Though this engine doesn't come in the convertible, it is worth noting. In *Road & Track*'s test of the "World's

Fastest Cars" (September 1984), an Aston Martin Vantage turned in a phenomenal 175-mph top speed! But fans of the Volante will not be embarrassed when it comes to performance. This convertible will do a claimed 139 mph before running out of speed, and that should be sufficiently fast for anyone.

In addition to its mechanical excellence, the Volante boasts interior appointments of unsurpassed luxury. The carpeting is deep-pile Wilton, the upholstery is Connolly leather, the dashboard is lacquered walnut, and the top is the finest money can buy. The windows glide up and down electrically, the AM/FM stereo-cassette provides marvelous sounds and the climate control system can keep you comfortable no matter the weather outside. Add to all that the suite of fitted leather luggage also available, and you come to the realization that Aston Martin owners are pampered, indeed.

Few of us have the wherewithal (read money—$120,000) to own a new Aston Martin Volante. I'm sure I never will. But just to have the chance to drive one for a day is a wonderful adventure. The big V-8 turns over quickly and easily with a flick of the ignition key, and then rumbles sedately as you move off from rest. Mountain driving with the top down is better than any amusement park ride. The sun floods the passenger compartment with warmth while the wind is directed over and around the occupants. The V-8 handles the uphill climb effortlessly, with the automatic dropping down a gear whenever necessary.

You won't be setting any records for covering the winding road ahead—the Volante is simply too big and too heavy to

## "...Aston Martin owners are pampered, indeed."

be considered nimble, but there is no doubt Aston Martin designers have racing experience and history. The independent front suspension and De Dion rear axle located by trailing arms and Watts linkage provide thoroughly acceptable handling and marvelous ride characteristics. The Volante hugs the road through the Avon steel-belted radial tires, while the power assisted rack-and-pinion steering gives the driver excellent feedback. Aston Martin believes that high performance cars should have exceptional braking ability, so the Volante has vented discs, front and rear.

The Volante is not a car for everyone—they don't build that many. But for the man or woman who appreciates the finest, prizes exclusivity and is perhaps something of an Anglophile, there is nothing to compare.

## U.S. SPECIFICATIONS

### GENERAL

| | | |
|---|---|---|
| Curb weight, lb/kg | 4010 | 1818 |
| Wheelbase, in./mm | 102.8 | 2611 |
| Track, front/rear | 59.0/59.0 | 1499/1499 |
| Length | 184.0 | 4670 |
| Width | 72.0 | 1830 |
| Height | 54.0 | 1370 |
| Fuel capacity, U.S. gal./liters | 25.8 | 97.5 |

### ENGINE

| | | |
|---|---|---|
| Type | | dohc V-8 |
| Bore x stroke, in./mm | 3.94 x 3.35 | 100.0 x 85.0 |
| Displacement, cu in./cc | 326 | 5340 |
| Compression ratio | | 8.0:1 |
| Bhp @ rpm, SAE net/kW | | est 300/224 @ 5600 |
| Torque @ rpm, lb-ft/Nm | | est 350/474 @ 4500 |
| Carburetion | | four Weber (2V) |

### DRIVETRAIN

| | |
|---|---|
| Transmission | 5-sp manual |
| Gear ratios: 5th (0.84) | 2.97:1 |
| 4th (1.00) | 3.54:1 |
| 3rd (1.22) | 4.32:1 |
| 2nd (1.78) | 6.30:1 |
| 1st (2.90) | 10.27:1 |
| Final drive ratio | 3.54:1 |

### CHASSIS & BODY

| | |
|---|---|
| Layout | front engine/rear drive |
| Brake system | 10.8-in. (274-mm) vented discs front, 10.4-in. (264-mm) vented discs rear; vacuum assisted |
| Wheels | cast alloy, 15 x 7 |
| Tires | Avon Textile, 225/70VR-15 |
| Steering type | rack & pinion, power assisted |
| Turns, lock-to-lock | 2.9 |
| Suspension, front/rear: | unequal-length A-arms, coil springs, tube shocks, anti-roll bar/De Dion axle on trailing arms & Watt linkage, coil springs, tube shocks |

# Aston Martin Vantage Road Test

CONTINUED FROM PAGE 71

characteristic chattering when the engine is ticking over (at a steady 900 r.p.m.) in neutral and, if beefy, is delightfully positive and quick so long as the driver is equally positive in his actions. The toe of my 8½ clutch foot occasionally grazed a protruding piece of metal when depressing the pedal.

A furious, throaty roar from the Webers and twin exhausts greets modest pressure of the right foot, rising to an ecstatic howl when the power starts to come in above 2,000 r.p.m. By no stretch of the imagination could this be called a quiet car, yet the nature of the noise and its level is not painful to the ears – to the enthusiasts who are likely to buy the Vantage it will be joyous music, as it was to me.

Its performance is simply stupendous and relentless. While Boxers, Countachs and Porsches habitually eat their clutches if full-power standing starts are attempted, this Aston simply lays a trail of rubber as the big clutch bites positively, and then takes off like a scalded tiger, the tachometer needle hurtling round the clock so fast that there is hardly time to ram the lever forwards into second. Recommended maximum revs are 6,250 r.p.m. but Aston's Director of Engineering, Mike Loasby, tells me that the engine is safe for 7,000 r.p.m. The performance is such, the torque so massive, that few will be brave enough, or find the necessity to use high revs. After all, the advisory 6,250 r.p.m. limit offers speeds of 45 m.p.h., 73 m.p.h., 107 m.p.h. and 130 m.p.h. in the gears. This powerful engine never runs out of breath – or at least the driver runs out of road or bravery first! – and the continuing surge of power as the speedometer needle soars past 120 m.p.h. in fifth is a rare experience in a road car. I had that needle as far as 150 m.p.h. and even then there was no sign of the acceleration tailing off, which suggests that a Turbo would be hard-pushed to hang on to a Vantage. Mention of the Porsche Turbo reminds me that with the Aston's beautifully crisp, normally aspirated engine there is no question of a "step" in the acceleration, as there is when the Porsche's turbocharger cuts in and out with the rise and fall of engine revolutions through the gears: the Vantage power is consistent. Traction and

*What other 170-180 m.p.h. super-car has four seats and "proper" luggage space to boot?*

acceleration out of corners (the combination of De Dion, limited-slip and massive tyre footprint really works), its overtaking performance in any gear is simply incredible.

Those Vantage spoilers have far more than a cosmetic effect. Loasby was loathe to divulge their influence on penetration and drag, but conceded that the results were impressive, the figures as low as any he knows, and a big improvement

on the standard bodywork. Their effect on high speed stability is unmistakeable to the driver. The last V8 I drove, in 1975, started to become light on the front end and to wander slightly as soon as three figures were reached; this Vantage showed absolute stability up to my 150 m.p.h. maximum, making it a very reassuring and comfortable high-speed cruiser.

So this Aston sounds like a racing car on the road? In outright performance yes. Yet this is matched by remarkably fuss-free, flexible low speed behaviour in town, the engine happy to run down to below 1,000 r.p.m. Part of the secret lies in harnessing the immense power with a very progressive, smooth throttle action. Too much throttle with too few revs will cause the occasional hiccup. A healthy crackle from the air box and exhausts accompanies over-run from high revs, although I suspect this might have been exaggerated on the test car by a loose silencer baffle. The idea of blanking off the radiator grille seems strange; in practice, more than enough air passes through the radiator to keep the water temperature at a steady 95 degrees in or out of town, which Loasby says is about right (the handbook recommends 85 degrees for the earlier, standard V8 – apparently the latest type of Smiths instrument, as fitted to the Vantage, has varied the reading).

Not only in performance does this Aston prove that the mid-engined exotica are not the be all and end all. This 35 cwt. projectile has leech-like roadholding (almost 0.9 g. cornering power, says Mike Loasby), which suffers little on wet roads, although I would suspect the fat tyres might be prone to aquaplaning in really heavy rain, a common super-car drawback. When it does start to slide it does it gently, predictably, with none of the mid-engined viciousness. Excellent handling and positive steering which shows hardly a trace of assistance shrink this big car into a joyful plaything, a driver's delight. It rolls somewhat if pushed very hard, though this doesn't seem to upset the equilibrium of its handling. Such speed and weight has enforced very hard pads for the 10.75 in. front, 10.38 in. rear vented and grooved disc brakes, so that hard pressure is needed to stop from slow speeds on cold pads. In fact the twin-servoed brakes need a hefty touch at all times, but they reward with marvellous stopping power, capable of 1.2 g.

The stiff Konis have tautened the far from velvety ride. It has to be firm to give this 35 cwt. car the sports car handling it possesses and the owner capable of appreciating the fine qualities of this Aston's performance and handling is unlikely to be upset by the occasional jolt on his backside.

Looking back at what I have written, and prompted by a similar observation by our MD, who happened to look over my shoulder, I wondered whether I might have been over-enthusiastic about this bulky, yet astonishingly agile Newport Pagnell product. On second thoughts I think not: it excited me, enthralled me, I enjoyed every moment of driving it and that is, surely, what a car built purely for the fast-driving enthusiast is all about. Here is a car with the performance and handling of a racing car and the luxurious appointments of a limousine, with none of the accommodation or visibility drawbacks of mid-engined super cars. The Vantage may look old-fashioned in some eyes, but traditional style and hand-built quality has a lot to recommend it. Fortunately there are sufficient wealthy connoisseurs around to make it viable. Long may it survive! – C.R.

---

# Aston Martin Lagonda

CONTINUED FROM PAGE 165

the electronic dazzlement of the driver information systems. A Dallas firm developed and supplies the hardware that produces a light show of red, amber, and green readouts. Large digits report road speed (in either miles or kilometers per hour) and engine revs, while an array of smaller displays monitors oil pressure and temperature, water temperature, volts, fuel level (in percentage of supply remaining), time of day, trip and overall mileage, and ambient air temperature (inside or outside) at the touch of a spot. Other indicators inform the driver which lights are on (side, main, or fog) and which horn mode is operating (low-intensity town or high-blast country). Should all this flashing and glowing ever become too much, a button kills all displays except for speed and fuel level (though the system will flash on any reading it considers critical).

The elegant, tantalizing interior of a Lagonda comes wrapped in lean, angular body work that is modern without being overstated. The crisp edges defining gentle curves are the work of William Towns, an independent designer who formerly worked for Aston Martin, so the Lagonda shape was created in-family, if not exactly in-house.

At more than 17 ft (208 in.) overall, the Lagonda spans as much distance as a Corniche or Silver Spirit. Yet it stands lower than a 911 at the roofline. The dart-like silhouette moves through the air with a sibilant whisper, and through traffic with unrivaled aplomb.

No identification appears on the exterior of the Lagonda save tiny badges on the grille and wheel centers. On a busy street it can pass largely unrecognized. But those who do take note, whether they have actually identified it or only realized it's something unique, are usually spellbound. They know intuitively this is a rare and valued piece of work, and they stare as they might if they came upon an unexpected Rodin bronze decorating a public place. Yes, it looks roughly like something they are familiar with—it is, after all, a car. But it is clearly so much more. It requires time in contemplation to absorb the meaning and magic, the essential absurdity and boundless delight of a hand-fashioned automobile that only 100 people a year in the entire world can have. A Lagonda truly is rolling sculpture, a celebration of uniqueness in a threateningly uniform world.

Is Aston Martin's Lagonda "worth" five XJ6s or a pair of Quattroportes? To anyone who has to think like that, no, of course it isn't. But to seriously ask what this car is worth or how it compares to others is to miss the real issue.

Do you want a Lagonda? Can you afford a Lagonda? End of discussion. ⓂⓉ

BROOKLANDS
BOOKS

# Rolls Royce & Bentley

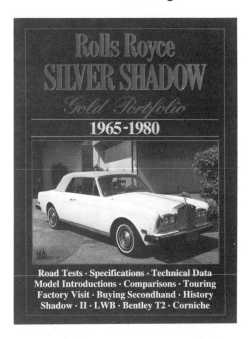

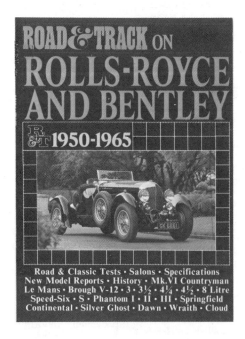

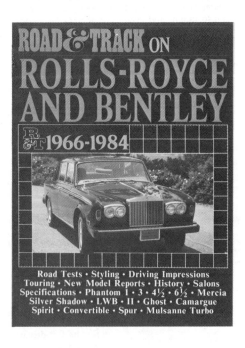